Building Client/Server Applications with VB .NET: An Example-Driven Approach

JEFF LEVINSON

Building Client/Server Applications with VB .NET: An Example-Driven Approach
Copyright © 2003 by Jeff Levinson

ISBN (pbk): 1-59059-070-8

Printed and bound in the United States of America 12345678910

Trademarked names may appear in this book. Rather than use a trademark symbol with every occurrence of a trademarked name, we use the names only in an editorial fashion and to the benefit of the trademark owner, with no intention of infringement of the trademark.

Technical Reviewers: Mary Romero Sweeney, Eric Mashlan

Editorial Directors: Dan Appleman, Gary Cornell, Jason Gilmore, Simon Hayes, Karen Watterson, John Zukowski

Managing Editor: Grace Wong

Project Manager: Tracy Brown Collins

Project Editor: Janet Vail

Copy Editor: Kim Wimpsett

Compositor: Susan Glinert

Artist and Cover Designer: Kurt Krames

Indexer: Kevin Broccoli

Production Manager: Kari Brooks

Manufacturing Manager: Tom Debolski

Distributed to the book trade in the United States by Springer-Verlag New York, Inc., 175 Fifth Avenue, New York, NY, 10010 and outside the United States by Springer-Verlag GmbH & Co. KG, Tiergartenstr. 17, 69112 Heidelberg, Germany.

In the United States, phone 1-800-SPRINGER, email orders@springer-ny.com, or visit http://www.springer-ny.com.

Outside the United States, fax +49 6221 345229, email orders@springer.de, or visit http://www.springer.de.

For information on translations, please contact Apress directly at 2560 9th Street, Suite 219, Berkeley, CA 94710. Phone 510-549-5930, fax: 510-549-5939, email info@apress.com, or visit http://www.apress.com.

The source code for this book is available to readers at http://www.apress.com in the Downloads section.

For my grandparents Bobbie and Harry without whom I would never have made it this far.
Also, for Ric and Sandi Royce, my parents in every way that counts. Thank you both for everything.
—Jeff Levinson

Contents at a Glance

Contents

Foreword

YOU ARE PROBABLY THINKING, "This is just another .NET book." That was what I thought at first, when I was asked to read a couple of draft chapters by Jeff. Well, I have to admit that this is not just another .NET book. Jeff has really done a fine job in this book; he describes the logical process and notes the considerations you must take into account to create excellent code. He uses examples of code and personal experience to effectively illustrate his points. Furthermore, Jeff has captured some keen insights in this book that have come from the projects he has worked on in the recent past. The reader will definitely benefit from these shared insights. I first met Jeff at a meeting with mutual customers over a year ago. Jeff was tasked with architecting, prototyping, and then leading a team of developers to create an application for this customer using the new Microsoft .NET Framework technology that was actually in beta at the time. I worked with Jeff on several of the challenges he faced. I was impressed by his professional skills and deep technical acumen. He uncovered some issues and really put me to task in assisting him in gathering answers because when Jeff asked for help, I came to expect that it was not a trivial issue.

The Microsoft .NET Framework technology and the Microsoft Visual Studio .NET developer product have created a lot of buzz and excitement with developers who have taken the time to try it. The enthusiasm being shared reminds me of the Visual Basic (VB) 1.0 days more than 10 years ago. For with VB 1.0, Microsoft Windows development became more commonplace and accessible to all. Visual Studio .NET has truly created a similar market phenomenon. The following are much more accessible to everyone: the power of object-oriented programming, services such as transactions and threading, reflections (which Jeff really does a fine job of explaining), and cross-language debugging (with more than 24 languages from which to choose). Moreover, the innovations in ASP.NET—such as the code behind, the core Extensible Markup Language (XML) and Web Services support available in the .NET Framework, or the new dataset object in ADO.NET—all combine to open new possibilities for developers to solve complex problems quickly.

It is probably that last point that typifies most developer experiences and is the most notable. Visual Studio .NET simply delivers on the promise of Rapid Application Development (RAD). That means there is more time to really do due diligence around the process and functional modeling that most developers forego. There are real possibilities of leveraging others' code using the object-oriented capabilities of the .NET Framework, and it is true that you simply write less code because of the rich class libraries in the .NET Framework. Powerful debugging delivers compressed time frames for testing, and server-side deployment for Windows Applications (WinForms) and Web Applications (WebForms) yields the lowest total cost of ownership in the industry. Jeff's book lays this all out for you in a logical and progressive fashion using plenty of examples and tips.

Now let me tell you a little about who I am: I graduated from Pacific Lutheran University in 1979 with a bachelor's degree in engineering/physics and a bachelor's degree in music (I play violin and classical guitar). I then earned my master's degree in electrical engineering (MSEE) from the University of Washington in 1983. I started work as a systems programmer for a Seattle-based engineering firm. I later worked for Hewlett-Packard and then was hired on at Microsoft in 1990 where I currently work as a .NET solutions architect.

I started my programming journey some 25 years ago when I was asked to automate a college physics lab using a Wyse programmable calculator that was the size of a small table. Wow, was that a blast! I then moved on to programming the following: a Univac 1170; an IBM 1130 using Hollerith cards and an IBM 029 card punch; an HP1000 RTE system using paper tape and a TTY terminal; an HP3000 using Fortran, Cobol, and RPG; a DEC VAX 11/780 using C; 8085 PIO boards using assembly; Microsoft Windows using C, C++, and Visual Basic. And now I am using C# in conjunction with the .NET Framework.

I must say that when I look back at the productivity gains and technology strides in this industry, it really is amazing. For those of you who are just starting your programming experience today, Visual Studio .NET is a great place to start. I dare say that you will be looking back some 25 years from now and see just as much progress. Who knows, computers will probably program themselves by then!

—Steven J. Houglum
.NET Solutions Architect
Microsoft Corporation

About the Author

Jeff Levinson grew up in Southern California and attended San Diego State University. He subsequently went on to a career in the film and TV industry as a 1st Assistant Cameraman and a 2nd Assistant Director. After six years he decided to change careers to what had been simply a lifelong hobby—programming. He has done contract work for many large companies (EDS, U.S. Borax, Motorola, and Boeing) and several smaller companies. He currently works for Excell Data Corporation and has been contracted to Boeing Commercial Airplanes, Information Systems for more than two years

as a senior developer/technical architect. He holds the following Microsoft certifications: MCP, MCSD, MCDBA, and MCAD. In his spare time he likes to play RPG games and spend as much time playing golf (more accurately, looking for his ball in the rough) as possible.

About the Technical Reviewers

Mary Romero Sweeney is the author of *Visual Basic for Testers* (Apress, 2001). She has been programming and testing software for many years and is a frequent speaker at Software Test conferences. Mary is a college professor and provides training and consultation on software development and test topics through Exceed Technical Training (http://www.ExceedTraining.com). Visual Basic, of course, is her favorite programming language, but when she is not programming and testing in Visual Basic, she spends time with her two kids, Ryan and Keilan. She has a bachelor's degree in mathematics and computer science from Seattle University.

Eric Mashlan has a degree in philosophy with a minor in theology. He started programming soon after cofounding 49 West Coffeehouse in Annapolis, Maryland. Eric sold his share in the restaurant, moved to Hawaii with his now-wife Angela, and got his first job developing mortgage software in Access. Ever syncretistic, he soon discovered the importance of the existential component of software design. He is often overheard mumbling questions such as, "Who wrote this? Was there an architect? Why is it here? What is its purpose?"

Eric currently works for Fujitsu Consulting in Seattle, Washington, and has spent the past three years designing and developing finance and contract software for Boeing Commercial Airlines. Eric specializes in Visual Basic 6 and has been working with VB .NET since the Beta 1 release.

Acknowledgments

I AM NOT going to list anyone in order of importance, except the first person on this list. This book would not be in your hands without the efforts of Mary Sweeny. She introduced me to my editor at Apress and worked tirelessly to technically edit this book. In addition, she provided excellent suggestions along the way. I truly believe this book would not be half of the work that it is without her. From clarifying my explanations to helping organize my thoughts, she helped with it all. Thanks for everything, Mary!

From Apress I would like to thank Karen Watterson, my editor. I thank her not only for providing much-needed encouragement but also for suggesting some additional content that I had not planned to include in this book. And I thank her for knowing almost everything going on in development circles, from major initiatives to little-known Web sites. I would also like to thank my project manager, Tracy Brown Collins, without whom I would never have gotten this book finished. She kept getting me back on track and pushed me when I needed it. If this book comes across as readable, it is entirely through the dedication of Kim Wimpsett, my copy editor. Being a typical developer, it seems that I needed some additional work on my grammar and organization…. And thanks to Janet Vail, my production editor, for catching all the last-minute mistakes and making life easy on me.

I would also like to offer a special thanks to Dan Appleman and Gary Cornell. I spent my early programming career reading everything that they wrote. To have this book published by their company is a huge honor for me.

Eric Mashlan, who also worked as a technical editor on this book, was a tremendous help. He not only helped find and correct mistakes, but he also offered helpful suggestions for the reader.

I owe a great deal of thanks to all of my coworkers at Boeing Commercial Airplanes, Information Systems. They have all been extremely supportive through a busy year, and the encouragement was much appreciated. I feel the need to point out two individuals in particular: David Nelson is an associate technical fellow within Boeing, and he offered a great deal of support and ideas, several of which are in this book. I appreciate all of the support you gave me, David—thanks! The other person I would like to thank is my project manager, Jeremy Winn. No other person over the course of the previous year has had a greater impact on my professional career than Jeremy. When a person reaches the level of being a technical architect and designing applications, they are assumed to have a certain level of knowledge. What Jeremy gave me was the ability to understand, deal with, and lead a team of developers in a professional manner. He showed me that the job of an architect is to be able to deal with everyone on an equal footing and from a position of knowledge and understanding. It is a gift I cannot even begin to repay, but I hope this will do for a start. Thank you, Jeremy.

Further, I would like to thank special individuals from Excell Data Corporation: Elaine Anderson and Brian Romas. As my resource managers they were both, in their unique ways, very supportive of this project and of my career in general. Of course, it might have been that they were being this way as part of their jobs… just kidding.

Last by definitely not least, I would like to thank all of the members of my family for their support over a tumultuous year and all of the years before now. In particular, my best friend, Adam Royce, has constantly been supportive of me in everything I have done in both my personal and professional life. Again, it is another debt I cannot repay. Thanks for everything, Adam!

Introduction

As a teacher I have had the opportunity to walk students through examples in order to teach them. I have had the opportunity to hear their feedback on the texts used in the development classes. And I have always heard the same thing—if they did not have a teacher to teach them, the book alone would have been useless. And that sums up why I decided to write this book. Too many books, for whatever reason, show you how to use a piece of functionality, but they do not show you where to use the functionality, when to use it, or why to use it. This book is for all those developers who want to be able to read a book and know how to implement the contents in a real-world application. This book takes all of the pieces of the application and puts them in relationship to each other. It is not an advanced book, but it does allow an intermediate developer to step into the realm of n-tier applications. This book makes that step almost painless.

What This Book Covers

This book walks you through building an n-tier application. It takes you through a lot of the intricacies of building a distributed application including remote communication and business rules. Specifically, the book covers the following:

Chapter 1: This chapter briefly introduces the different types of architectures currently in use in business. It discusses the pros and cons of each of the different architectures, and it examines where and how the Microsoft .NET Framework fits into the architectural models.

Chapter 2: This chapter begins your development of the application that you will create throughout the book. You will start to gain an understanding of cross-process communications, and you will set up Internet Information Server (IIS) to host the middle-tier components you will create. In addition, you will learn about the use of the web.config file and set up the initial project structure in Visual Studio .NET.

Chapter 3: In this chapter you will examine the different decisions you need to make when designing an n-tier application and the impact those design decisions will have on your project. This chapter examines the concepts of object modeling, remoting, interfaces, and visual inheritance. Once you have an understanding of these concepts, you will begin building the application. At the end of this chapter you will see just how much time and effort the .NET Framework can save.

Chapter 4: In this chapter you will learn about error handling. You will examine the differences between error handling in Visual Basic 6 and Visual Basic .NET. In addition to understanding how to handle errors, you will learn how to implement a robust error handling scheme that can be used throughout an organization. Additionally, you will learn how to write errors to a database and, in the event the database is not available, how to redirect those errors to the Windows Event Log.

Chapter 5: This chapter shows you how to handle the heart of any application, the business rules. You will examine techniques for coding business rules and informing the user that they have violated a business rule. You will learn how to create your own application errors and incorporate them into your project. You will also create a class that keeps track of an object's state (whether it has been edited or contains any rules that have been broken). Finally, you will learn how to display a list of your object's business rules to the user so that they have a complete list of rules.

Chapter 6: In this chapter you will step back and work on creating a usable Multiple Document Interface (MDI) form that can serve as a host for all of the other forms in your application. You will learn how to recursively load menus, display key status (indicate the state of keys such as the Caps Lock and Num Lock keys) on the status bar, and implement a series of interfaces in your forms with which the MDI form can interface.

Chapter 7: This chapter takes a slightly more in-depth look at business rules as you move on to creating a second set of working objects. You will explore some advanced considerations when building relationships between objects.

Chapter 8: Consolidating code is the focus of this chapter. You will begin by creating a reusable base class that will serve as the base for all of the business objects in the application. And you will use this base class to streamline your application development. The second half of this chapter delves into creating an enterprise template project. Using the methods demonstrated in this chapter, you will be able to create a basic n-tier application template.

Chapter 9: This chapter examines advanced business rule concepts. During the course of this chapter you will create a complex business object and learn how to handle the differences between server-side and client-side business rules. Additionally, you will learn how to handle more complex object interaction and image data in SQL Server.

Chapter 10: This chapter introduces you to an advanced .NET topic: reflection. You will learn how to create attribute classes that contain metadata to describe your objects. You will learn one technique to reduce any application by thousands of lines of code. In addition, you will build generic methods that can consume objects based on their attribute tags and that are completely independent of the object itself. You will also learn to examine all attributes of a class through code to accomplish these tasks.

Chapter 11: This chapter switches to the development of a Web service based on the code that you have previously written. You will learn how to create a Web service, consume a Web service, and publish a Web service with Microsoft's UDDI Server. After that you will learn how to programmatically enumerate through an entire UDDI Server.

Chapter 12: Here you will create an ASP.NET application using the components you have already created. You will put a Web application frontend onto, first, the Web service and, second, the components that back the Web service. You will learn best practices for storing usernames and passwords to connect to a database, and you will learn how to store a user's username and password in the database. Finally, you will learn how to display business rule violations to the user on your Web form and how to use Microsoft's validation controls to do this.

Chapter 13: If you ever wanted to know how to get your application ready for a global audience, then this is the chapter for you. It introduces how to globalize and localize your application. You will localize both your Web application and your Windows application so that it is useable in English, French, and Spanish. And you will learn some techniques that can save you work if you decide to localize an application later.

Appendix A: In this appendix you will create a small utility so that you can incorporate Unicode characters in your application in a method similar to that used in Microsoft Word.

Appendix B: This appendix includes a list of valuable reference books that contain supplemental information.

Who This Book Is For

This book is for developers with a moderate level of skill who are looking to create n-tier applications. Maybe you have been developing in Visual Basic 6 and your company wants to move to distributed applications using Visual Basic .NET, but you do not know where to begin. You do not even need to be developing n-tier applications—maybe you just need a good introduction to business rules and how to handle them. Perhaps you need to convert an existing application so that it is available as a Web service. If you are in any of these situations, then this book is for you. You will find a wealth of information to help you with any of these goals, and in the process you will build a working n-tier application.

Before reading this book, you should have a working knowledge of Visual Basic .NET and the .NET Framework in general. However, you do not need to have an advanced understanding of objects, n-tier application design, or application architecture. If you do, so much the better, but if you do not, you will learn the concepts you need by reading this book.

Downloading the Application Code

All of the code for this book is available for download from the Downloads section of the Apress Web site (http://www.apress.com). It is broken up into chapters, and each chapter contains a readme.txt file with specific instructions on installing the code for that chapter. You will have to work through Chapter 2, "Building an N-Tier Application," to set up IIS because you cannot preconfigure it. Even if you do not enter the code yourself, you should spend the time to read through all of the code and explanations because reading about an n-tier application is no substitute for writing an n-tier application.

I hope that you get a great deal of usefulness out of this book and that it serves as a solid introduction to the building of n-tier, enterprise-wide, quality applications.

—Jeff Levinson
January 2003

CHAPTER 1

Understanding Application Architecture: An Overview

THIS CHAPTER PROVIDES a broad overview of the different types of application architecture, including the advantages and disadvantages of each. It examines single-tier, two-tier, three-tier, and n-tier applications and describes how they fit into a modern enterprise. Then this chapter covers these architectures from a traditional point of view and showcases these application architectures with an emphasis on distributed applications. This includes a discussion of each of the application layers (presentation, business, and data) and how they interact with each other across network boundaries. Finally, the chapter throws the Microsoft .NET Framework into the mix and displays the power that this new development framework provides developers. This serves as an introduction to the application architecture you will be creating throughout the rest of the book.

 NOTE   For those developers who are already comfortable with these concepts, you can skim this chapter and move on to Chapter 2, "Building an N-Tier Application," where you will create the infrastructure of the application used throughout this book.

An *architecture* is the overall design of an application; it directly impacts how an application is coded. The different architecture types serve different purposes. Some architectures are for single users, and others are for a number of users in a shared environment. Not all applications need to use an n-tier architecture just because it is the buzzword of the day. There are ample reasons to use a two-tier architecture, which is a perfectly acceptable solution. What follows is a brief explanation of each tier, when to use them, and why to be cautious when making this decision.

Introducing Single-Tier Architecture

A *single-tier* architecture is an architecture in which the entire application resides on the user's machine. Before networking became so easy and cheap, this was frequently the design of choice. Nowadays you will find this architecture used rarely and almost never in conjunction with enterprise data. The obvious drawback to single-tier architecture is that the data lives on a local machine, and no one else can access it. In a fast-moving enterprise where information is everything, this is not a good situation.

The advantage to this architecture, from a developer's standpoint, is that it is relatively simple to code. The developer does not have to worry about security, concurrent access, network connectivity, or any of a hundred other issues that plague multitier applications.

For the purposes of the modern enterprise, single-tier architecture no longer exists. Most of my experience with this architecture has been relegated to upgrading small applications developed using Microsoft Access. Frequently users will create spur-of-the-moment applications using a wizard to accomplish repetitive needs that are only applicable to them. This type of application is often a candidate for being upgraded to a two-tier application.

Introducing Two-Tier Architecture

The two-tier architecture is the most predominate architecture in corporate America. Although the Internet is slowly changing this model, do not be fooled into thinking an Internet application is not also a two-tier architecture—it depends on how it is written. Simply put, a two-tier architecture is one where the application runs on the user's machine and the data is stored in a central location on a network (refer to Figure 1-1).

By its very nature, a two-tier application is not scalable beyond a certain point. There are several reasons for this. One reason is the number of connections a database can maintain concurrently. Imagine that one million users try to access the database at the same time...need I say more? There is no way to effectively manage the connections to the database when the connections are being created on the user's machine (as opposed to being able to pool database connections). Another reason why a two-tier application is not scalable beyond a certain point is application functionality in relationship to the business process that the application supports. Take a situation where a business process changes and the program has to be altered. The company may have to roll the upgraded application out to 30,000 users, which is usually too cost prohibitive to do. Scalability does not have to just reflect whether an application can support a growing number of users but also how expensive it is to support them.

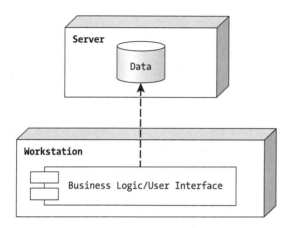

Figure 1-1. A two-tier application architecture

Then there is the concurrency issue; that is, what happens when two or more users try to access the same record in the same database at the same time to make changes to it? Usually one or more users are blocked from making changes, which can cause the application to temporarily hang. In a two-tier application, this can be both a positive and a negative aspect of the application. The positive aspect is that one user cannot alter a record that another user is modifying. The negative aspect is that it can cause the second user's query to wait if there is a lock on the record they want to read. If the application is programmed correctly, the lock should not last for more than a few milliseconds, but on some database platforms, if the user who placed the lock is prematurely disconnected from the database, the result is a lock that cannot be removed except by the database administrator or by the database after a certain period of time. This has the potential to cause numerous problems. This particular issue is never a problem with a three-tier application, but other, more complicated issues appear with regard to this aspect of the database (see the sidebar "Database Concurrency Issues").

Database Concurrency Issues

When multiple users try to update a single record at the same time, you will have concurrency issues. In a single-tier application, this is never an issue because there is only one user accessing data. In a two-tier system, you as the developer have the option of implementing either pessimistic or optimistic locking—however, this depends on the Relational Database Management System (RDBMS) because not all databases support optimistic locking. In most two-tier applications, you are always connected to the database when you are reading and writing data. If you set up pessimistic concurrency, when one user is trying to update a record, no other user can update the record at the same time (they will receive an error message explaining that the record is locked). If you implement optimistic concurrency, you will have to write code to handle the occurrence of one user updating a record that is not current. In a three-tier application, the developer must always handle database updates because no connection is maintained with the database. In most cases, this applies to a well-written two-tier application as well.

Microsoft's new database access technology, ADO.NET, can help to make many of these issues easier to solve—but even ADO.NET will only throw an exception saying that someone else has updated the record. It is still up to the developer to handle this situation, and it is rarely solved the same way on any two applications. How you handle this situation depends mostly on what the users want.

So, with all of these issues, when is a two-tier architecture a good solution? Usually it is when there are only going to be a small number of users who will ever use the application. When I say *small number*, I mean about 100 or fewer users. Another time to use two-tier architecture is when other applications will not need to access the functionality provided by the two-tier application. Take for instance an application that performs some function that is only needed in this one instance—you probably will not need to worry about incorporating this functionality into other applications. Because the functionality does not need to be reused, there is no point in creating a reusable component.

So, what is the major drawback to a two-tier system? Every time I have written a two-tier application for a small number of users, someone has come up to me and said, "That is a great program, can we use it also?" And from there it snowballs. All of a sudden, this little application I wrote for five users is suddenly being used by 15 people, and then 40 people, and then so on and so forth. Eventually someone comes to me with some serious performance problems of the application. My typical answer comes across as something like, "No, you're kidding?" At a certain point, sarcasm became a way of life for me....

However, there are things you, as a developer, can do to mitigate this risk. There is a right way and a wrong way to write a two-tier application, and typically—you guessed it—the developer chooses the wrong way. The wrong way takes less forethought when designing the application, which means the developer can show results almost immediately. In the long term, though, development will slow because it is done on a "think up things as you go" approach. The wrong way also causes an immense amount of work to be re-done when upgrading the application from two to three tiers. And this happens more often than developers would like to believe. Figure 1-1 showed a two-tier application that is not scalable beyond a certain point. However, Figure 1-2 shows a better way to build a two-tier application.

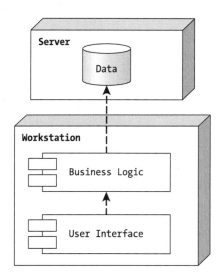

Figure 1-2. Correct architecture for a two-tier application

The right way to build a two-tier application is to treat it as a three-tier application and just install all the components on the user's local machine. This approach will cause development to initially be slower because more thought needs to go into the application in the initial stages. But, after you develop this initial strategy, the coding will go much faster and smoother, and many of the surprises that would normally catch you along the way are handled before they become issues. By building the application this way, when performance problems start cropping up, it is a small step to move the business logic and data access code off of the local machine and onto an application server. Problem solved. The only issue you will really have to deal with is where to put the business rules. (We talk a little more about object modeling and business rules in Chapter 3, "Creating the Application Infrastructure.")

Introducing N-Tier Architecture

A *three-tier* (or *n-tier*, I explain the difference shortly) application is when the application components are spread out over three or more computers and there is a high degree of separation between the user interface, business logic and data access, and the data components. If there is no degree of separation, you are bound to have a failed application when it is time to perform maintenance. This separation is referred to as a *loosely coupled* design. We discuss these concepts later in the "Exploring the Benefits of N-Tier Architecture" section. From a logical perspective, this separation typically looks like Figure 1-3.

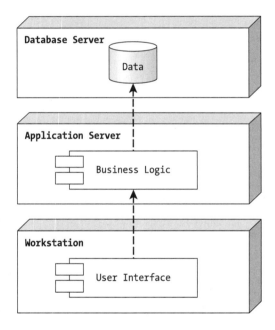

Figure 1-3. A typical three-tier application design

Notice in Figure 1-3 that the center node is called the *Application Server* and that it hosts, in the logical design, only the business logic components. In any application, the application is the part of the system that controls the application's logic. The database is just a place to store the data and the user interface is just the means to get that data there, but the business logic contains all of the functionality for dealing with data. As you start writing this application, you will see that the business logic is the most important component of any application.

Understanding Application Layers

A *multitier* application consists of three layers: the presentation layer, or user interface; the business logic layer that can be broken up into two parts, the user-centric part and the data-centric part; and the data layer, which is generally the database. Any application that physically separates these layers into different components can be considered a multitier application, regardless of where the components are deployed. You saw these layers in Figure 1-3—except the business logic layer separation. Figure 1-4 shows the business logic layer, which is discussed in the "Introducing the Business Logic Layer" section.

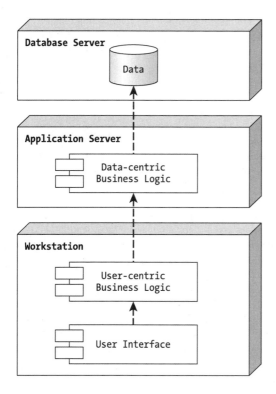

Figure 1-4. A three-tier design with data-centric and user-centric components

Introducing the Presentation Layer

The *presentation layer* presents data to the users. It does not have any other purpose. There should not be any business logic in the presentation layer. I say *should not be* because typically this is where most applications start running into trouble. They start putting business logic into the presentation layer, and then maintenance problems start popping up. The presentation layer will also catch unexpected application errors and gracefully handle them and display them to the user. I say *gracefully* because that application should not do what many applications do, which is to display an error and then promptly shut down, causing the user to lose all of their work up to that point. That is not exactly the right way to handle application errors! The presentation layer is linked to the business logic layer by referencing one or more business logic components.

Introducing the Business Logic Layer

The business logic layer contains all of the application's logic. That is, the business layer validates all of the data entered into the system. There are many different opinions as to where logic should be placed and how it should be broken up. Many people advocate putting it in the database, many people advocate putting some of it in the presentation layer so that the user can have immediate feedback, and some people advocate putting it into the logic layer. So, now it is time to give it my take….

You should put all of the logic into the logic layer. You should also place a subset of that into the database. And some of the logic errors that a user can cause should be reported immediately, but you should also place that logic in the business logic layer—the user-centric part of that layer. In doing this, though, you need to examine some issues. If the logic changes, it must be changed in several places. Obviously, for the purposes of maintainability, this is a bad idea. But for the purposes of data integrity, it is a great idea. The immediate feedback to the user is questionable, but it all depends on your particular tastes or, more importantly, the user's particular needs.

I advocate putting some of the data validation into the database because I have frequently discovered that someone will go into the database to edit data, thereby bypassing the application logic. Although this is the least desirable situation, it does happen and the application needs to be prepared to handle it. Also, if another application is going directly into the database (again, not the best situation), some aspects of the data should be checked because the application is bypassing a majority of the business logic. You should put these checks into the database as check constraints, referential integrity checks, triggers, and default values. I do not advocate putting business logic into stored procedures. You should tie the logic directly to the tables in which the data is going to be inserted.

User-Centric Business Logic

The user-centric business logic should, in a perfect world, check for only one thing: that the data falls within the limits of the database constraints. These types of checks would generally be to validate the maximum length of a string or that a value cannot be null. If there is a column defined in the database as varchar(20) and the user enters a value that is 26 characters in length, this would violate the database constraint. The reason for these checks being performed in the user-centric logic is mostly for performance reasons. Why should the application make a call to the remote components if there is absolutely no possibility of the data being right? It simply wastes processing power on the server and network bandwidth. Another reason is to give immediate feedback to users on mistakes they have made. When I talk with users about how they want errors reported to them, they mostly say they want to know when they have an error immediately after they make it. In most cases, this just is not practical in a distributed application, but the user-centric logic helps you move toward the user's needs.

Data-Centric Business Logic

The data-centric business logic contains all of the application's logic. It contains both database constraint validation and true business logic validation. This is the component placed on the application server. All of the rules that are checked in the user-centric component must also be checked again, and all of the rules stored in the database should be checked here as well. The real power of the data-centric business logic is its ability to get information from the database in a fast manner to validate the data stored in the object.

Take, for instance, an example in which an employee can get no more than a 5-percent raise each year. Let's assume this percentage is stored in a table in the database so that it can be easily changed. When the user enters the pay raise amount and saves the record, the business rule may require that the pay raise entered is checked against the value in this table. So, the data-centric object will retrieve this value from the database to validate the data it has been given. This is a much faster solution than making a call to the application server and from there to the database from the user's workstation. In some circumstances, you may have to validate the data between systems that the user interface knows nothing about. In that case, the only option is to perform the validation in the data-centric objects.

Introducing the Data Layer

Finally, we come to the data layer, which in this case is the database. The database consists of tables of data, stored procedures, views, and various mechanisms to constrain the data entered into the tables. The only business logic contained in the database should be the logic associated with the table columns, as mentioned previously. One important thing to consider when designing the database is how tightly the data layer is tied to the data-centric objects. When designing an application, you must take into account the likeliness of moving to a different RDBMS in the future and what the capabilities of that database might be.

For example, SQL Server can return multiple result sets from a single stored procedure, but Oracle cannot. So if you use stored procedures for data retrieval, think about the amount of work that might be necessary if you have to change the database you are using. Another issue to consider when using stored procedures to access data is the amount of dependency your objects will have on the format of those stored procedures. SQL Server allows you to pass parameters to a stored procedure out of order, but Oracle does not. If you have to change databases, you may end up having to rewrite a large majority of the code in the data-centric objects. You can—and should—plan for situations such as these.

If you look at the difference between Figure 1-3 and Figure 1-5, you will see that moving from a three-tier application to an n-tier application is a matter of how the components are hosted.

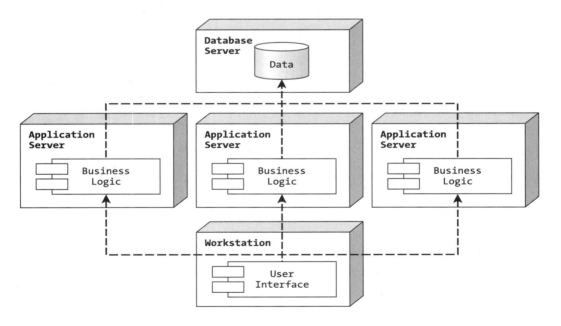

Figure 1-5. An n-tier application design

The physical difference is that you can have as many computers as you need to host the business logic, and the application will be load balanced (see the sidebar "Communicating across Process Boundaries"). The one major advantage of an n-tier architecture over a standard three-tier architecture is that an n-tier application is highly available. In other words, if you have three application servers and two of them go down, you can still run the application. In a three-tier architecture, if the application server goes down, so does the application. This is not a pretty thought in a modern business environment.

Communicating across Process Boundaries

Currently, you accomplish cross-process communication (now referred to as *process boundaries*) by one of three means. The first is via the Distributed Component Object Model (DCOM). All of the developers who have used DCOM will attest to the amount of work, hardships, and frustrations they have gone through to make it work correctly. When it does work, it works great. It makes the component location transparent to the calling code and allows you to call methods on it without doing a whole lot of work. It is the configuration part that is difficult.

The next means of cross-process communication is Microsoft Transaction Server (MTS). This provides even more functionality (especially for a large number of concurrent database accesses) than DCOM and is easy to configure. There are a number of steps involved to make the configuration work, but it is no longer a mystical type of process. MTS allows the application server to be involved in transactions with the database. On top of the database making sure a transaction commits the right way, there is the additional backup of MTS. It also allows several transactions to be called at once but treats them as one atomic transaction. This does not come without a small price, though: The code placed into MTS needs to be modified to tell MTS whether there is an error. Granted, the code is simple, but it is still extra work. MTS also gives rise to what Microsoft now calls *code-access security*. With MTS you have the ability to invoke the CallerIsInRole method to determine how the user logged onto MTS (which could be Windows authentication) and allow code to make decisions based on their security level.

Finally, there is COM+. COM+ simplifies the MTS model a little and adds some more features and ease of use, but it is basically built on the same technology as MTS.

For more information on these technologies, go to the Microsoft Knowledge Base Web site (http://support.microsoft.com/default.aspx?scid=fh;[ln];kbhowto).

Exploring the Benefits of N-Tier Architecture

The three-tier, or n-tier, architecture provides several advantages over a two-tier client/server architecture.

Loosely Coupled

N-tier applications are *loosely coupled*, which means that the different parts of the application (presentation, business logic, and data) are basically independent of each other. For example, the data sits in a database on the server, and any application that wants to use it can. The business logic processes data and for the most part does not care in which type of database the data is stored or through which type of interface the user enters the data. The presentation layer displays data. It does not care about the data itself or the application logic because it does not process or manipulate the data.

Even though the three layers are loosely coupled, you still need to take into account some coupling. These couplings mostly depend on the particular circumstances of the application and the changes you may need to make in the future.

Encapsulated

All of the functionality of each layer is *encapsulated* in one location within the application. If you wanted to change the business logic layer, instead of replacing several parts of the application (as you would have to do with a two-tier implementation), you only need to replace one small section that does not affect the presentation or data layer. The same goes for replacing or altering parts of the data or presentation layers. Although there are some changes that you may need to make when altering the data layer, these are mostly minor and deal with column names or connection settings. If the business logic or data layer needs to change, the entire application does not need to be redistributed, and it can continue to be used without interruption.

Scalable

Scalability is really what makes an application an n-tier application. All of the other benefits are applicable to both three-tier and n-tier applications. *Scalability* is the ability of an application to grow and handle more load than it was originally developed for. This is an important point because an enterprise application is rarely built to be used by 500,000 people in the beginning. Usually, the number of users ramps up gradually as the business realizes how valuable the application can be to other parts of the business. You should design all three-tier applications to move to n-tier applications. To make an application scalable, it must be able to have its business logic spread out over many machines and have this location be transparent to the user interface and the database. If you design the application correctly using .NET, you do not need to do additional work to move the application from three tiers to n tiers. The "Exploring How .NET Scales Applications" section explains how .NET implements this scalability.

Extensible

An n-tier application can be *extended* transparently. That is, you can add additional functionality without breaking the existing functionality. In part, you can achieve this using an object-oriented design when building any size application, but even this does not keep you from having to rework large parts of the code in a two-tier application to add functionality. With the three-tier design, you can add functionality with less work because of the separation of functionality.

Maintainable

Most people tend to overlook whether an application is *maintainable,* and this often causes the greatest amount of difficulty later. I have not been involved in a business that has not changed its business processes on a daily, monthly, or yearly basis (depending on the type of business). An application that cannot be maintained is a useless application. Even though it may work at the time that it is built, in most cases you will find that by the time you are done building the application some part of the business has already changed! If your application cannot handle the changes, then it is broken before it ever gets used. I have heard developers lament too many times that the application they wrote does what it was supposed to do. Only, they seem to have forgotten that what it is supposed to do is support the business, which changes over time. Rarely is this a good or acceptable excuse in today's fast-moving business environment. I cannot stress this enough: For an application to be considered successful, it must be able to be changed easily and inexpensively.

So, how does having three tiers make an application more maintainable? It helps in speed of change and cost. If a business rule changes, the business logic layer can change easily enough—you do not need to re-deploy the application. What if the business decides to move to a Web-based system? If everything is coded in the forms, the task is impossible, and it is better to rewrite the application. If the presentation layer is separate from everything else, then you only have to code up the navigation and forms, but the bulk of the application is intact. What if another application wants to use the business logic you built into your application? Simple. Let them have access to your components or, with .NET, build a Web service (you will write and consume your own Web service in Chapter 11, "Web Services and the UDDI"). In a two-tier application you would have to provide the other application with the logic that you use and then they would have to incorporate it in their application. This sounds like a simple prospect because you do not have to do any work. But what happens when the business logic changes? Then, not only do you have to change your code, but so does the other application. Trying to keep these changes in sync is impossible in a large enterprise (or even a small enterprise).

Planning Application Deployment

Application deployment is the location of the physical components that make up the application and the computers on which those components reside. It helps to map out the communication that needs to take place between the components as well as the references between components. Figure 1-4 depicts a Unified Modeling Language (UML) diagram that is both a deployment and component diagram. This was created with Visio for Enterprise Architects, which ships with the enterprise version of Visual Studio .NET. It is not a strict UML diagram in the sense that there is a database object represented on the diagram. This object does not exist in the UML language, but I have chosen to use it to represent the database here. The nodes (square boxes) represent the deployment part of the diagram and each node represents a computer. The components are displayed inside the nodes to depict where the components will reside physically. This diagram gives you an overall understanding of not only where everything will live, but also of the process boundaries that exist.

The layout of the physical architecture is important to complete before the application development has begun. A change in the component layout may force changes in references, how objects are instantiated, and how they are called. Typically, if a components location must change late in the development cycle, then the change could cause a great deal of rework. Having a deployment diagram finalized before coding begins is always the best idea.

I recommend you create a diagram like this for every project so you understand where your code will go in the final application. Note the diagram in Figure 1-6, which corresponds with Figure 1-4 except that it is a high-level overview of the application structure. Notice that Figure 1-6 is almost identical to Figure 1-4 except that the components are named in Figure 1-4 and the relationship between the components, and not the computers, are illustrated. Figure 1-6 would be something that is shown to a business user, and Figure 1-3 is how a developer should see it. Each diagram is a valid design and deployment diagram that can help everyone understand the overall design of the application.

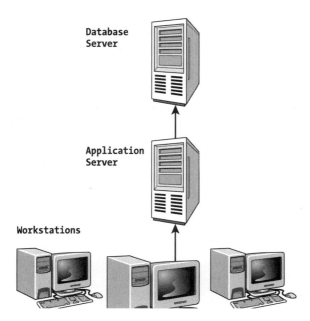

Figure 1-6. High-level architecture diagram

Developing Enterprise Applications with .NET

Microsoft has taken all of the right steps forward with the .NET Framework. DCOM is gone, and so are all of the inherent headaches that went with it. You no longer need to use COM+ to create scalable applications, although you can certainly use it if needed for the situation. Security is a lot easier to implement and a lot more robust in the .NET Framework—especially when working in an enterprise. There are several ways to go about building an enterprise application with .NET, including with ASP.NET, with Windows Forms, and with Web services. You will briefly look at the different techniques to create an enterprise application in the following sections.

Using ASP.NET (Web Forms)

With all the talk of the Internet simplifying everyone's life, it is natural that ASP.NET and Web forms are getting a lot of press. In my opinion, they get too much press, but I talk about that further on (see the "Using Windows Forms with a Distinctly .NET Twist" section). Prior to ASP.NET, I did not care for building Web applications because of the lack of power of the interface and the need to use a scripting language to control all of the programmatic access to the interface, but Microsoft hit a home run with this implementation. ASP.NET takes all the best parts of Visual Basic (or C# or whatever other .NET language you choose to use) and all the best parts of ASP, and combines them to make a rock-solid, easy-to-use, powerful Web development platform.

The structure of Web forms is a little different from before. Now, there is a visual interface (the Web page) and the markup language that generates the Web page (HTML, XML, VBScript, JavaScript, and so on). This is just as in Visual InterDev, but Microsoft added the code behind the Web form. It is the code behind the Web form that contains most of the power (referred to as the *code-behind* file). This layer contains code in a .NET Framework language (such as C# or Visual Basic .NET) that is linked to the Web page. This allows developers to respond to events using a structured, object-oriented language with which they are familiar. It also allows the average developer to program a Web site without having to learn a new language such as ASP. In most cases, the code you write in the code-behind module will be automatically translated into HTML by the Integrated Development Environment (IDE). In addition, the developer still has the full power of ASP.NET to use as they want. The controls that Microsoft has created make building an interface using Web forms almost as easy as building an interface with Windows forms, with a couple of differences.

Because a Web interface is still fairly limited, all of the power of the regular .NET Framework controls are not available to the Web versions. For example, you can fill the listbox control in the Windows.Forms namespace just by adding objects, but you must use the standard string entry for the listbox provided by the Web.UI namespace. There are many differences such as these that take a little getting used to but are beyond the scope of this book to cover in detail.

In the enterprise, this type of implementation has many advantages. The first advantage is that you can update the application without having to redistribute it to the users. In many corporate environments, the users do not have permission to install applications on their machines. In these cases, an additional mechanism is needed to perform the installation. In many cases it requires a group administrator to go around to all the machines, log on, and perform the installation. This is not only expensive, but it is time consuming. While one group of users has the new application, another group is still using the old application. This makes upgrades extremely difficult. Another advantage to using ASP.NET is that the application does not need to be installed on the user's machine at all! An additional advantage is security. Using Internet Information Server (IIS), you can authenticate users when they first go to an ASP.NET Web site using one of several forms of authentication (discussed in more detail in Chapter 2, "Building an N-Tier Application"). It provides a double layer of protection—on the Web site and at the database level.

Web forms, however, usually lead to a two-tier architecture, not a three-tier architecture. Most of the applications I have seen that are Web forms based contain much of the logic in the .aspx.vb file (which is the code behind the form module). This means the business logic is tightly coupled with the presentation layer. You must remove the logic from the code-behind page and move it into separate classes and a separate assembly if you desire to decouple these layers.

Using Classic Windows Forms

This method is *classic* because of the large shift in development to Web interfaces and because many people believe that Windows applications will no longer be used as enterprises gradually make the shift to Internet and intranet-based technologies. This is far from the truth, however, especially with the advent of .NET, as I explain in the next section. Windows forms are standard windows built into an application that needs to be installed onto the user's machine. With .NET, the installation can be as simple as copying files onto the user's machine, or it can be more involved and actually need a setup program to be run. If the application only needs to be installed using XCOPY, it helps mitigate some of the expense of upgrading the application. You can simply place the new files on a server and instruct the user to download them to the local machine in the correct directory. If the application requires an installation, the drawbacks mentioned in the previous section apply here.

There is also one other difficulty in this type of application. The users need to have the .NET Framework installed on their machines. Although the .NET Framework redistributable file is fairly small (only 20MB), it still requires someone logged on with the privileges to install an application. And if the users have this privilege, then there is still the matter of the users having to go out and get the package to install. Alternatively, you can include this package in a setup program—although this only has to occur once, it does need to occur.

Using Windows Forms with a Distinctly .NET Twist

The .NET Framework is really a marvel of programming. It is the best thing to hit the programming world since Visual Basic first hit the market. The power of an application to be able to read information about itself during runtime is incredible. In .NET parlance, this is called *reflection*.

NOTE Reflection has been available in Java since its inception. However, .NET takes reflection and builds on it to make it more powerful through the introduction of custom attributes. Chapter 10, "Using Reflection," covers this in more detail.

You can deploy Windows forms, with reflection, using a method called *auto-deployment*, which can be an effective alternative to the downsides of Web application development. So, what exactly is auto-deployment, and why do I suggest it? Auto-deployment uses what is known as a *stub* architecture. That is, one small executable file is copied to the user's machine. This stub has almost no functionality and is very small (I suggest using a splash screen, which typically turns out to be a whopping 15KB in size). The only function it has is to load the main part of the application from an IIS server. As long as the assemblies are not too large, the amount of time necessary to download the actual application is fairly short. The application downloads in a trickle fashion. Let's say, for example, that the application is 10MB and the presentation part of the application is about 7MB. The presentation part is broken up into 14 assemblies that are only 500KB in size. The splash screen would load up the first form, which would presumably be the main form, and all of the other forms contained within that assembly. The application would not start downloading 7MB worth of data; it would only download 500KB of data. Even over a dial-up connection (yes, people still have those), this is not such a large delay.

The great news about using this technique is that the download only needs to occur once. The next time the user runs the application, the first thing that it will do is check the version number (this is where reflection comes in) of the assembly located on the local machine against the version number of the assembly on the remote machine. If they are the same, the application uses the locally cached version. Otherwise, it downloads the updated version. But the great trick about all of this is that the code to achieve this lives only in the stub. The rest of the forms can instantiate other forms in the normal manner. The reason for this is that the assembly knows to go back and look in the same place as it was originally loaded from for the next piece of code. This makes development of this type of application incredibly easy because you can develop the application entirely on your machine and then at the last minute convert to the stub architecture by the addition of the stub. That's all there is to it.

 CAUTION There is one issue with this type of stub deployment at the time of this writing. Through tests I conducted for a project, I found a bug with this type of deployment. It works great for a two-tier application but not for a three-tier application. The error occurs because the needed assemblies are being searched for in the wrong directories. Microsoft has confirmed this is a bug and is in the process of correcting it.

It makes installation of the application easy because you can place a link to an EXE file on a Web page and the user can save it to their machine and run it.

Although this does present the problem of needing to have .NET on the local machine, it makes updates very cheap and easy. No one has to stop using the application; they will just get the new version next time they log on.

NOTE The .NET Framework, in conjunction with IIS, uses what is called a *shadow copy* mechanism. That is when the actual component that is deployed is not the component that is accessed. The component that is accessed is actually an in-memory representation of the component. Therefore, if an application needs to be updated, the new components can just be copied on top of the old, and the next time a call to the components are made, the new versions will be used. When the last connection to the old version is released, that version will be removed from memory and the new version will be used.

In the future this may be a preferred method of application development, but it still requires the .NET Framework on the local machine. I hope in the future Microsoft will create a mechanism like the one used by Java to prompt the user to download the .NET Framework the first time they try to run an application such as this, but that may be a long way off.

Using Web Services

Everyone has been jumping on the Web services bandwagon lately. I have seen so much press and heard so many people give their opinion of this "new" technology that it has just become too much. What are Web services? Well, it turns out that Web services are just Remote Procedure Calls (RPCs). This is not new technology. It has been around for a long time. So what makes Web services special then? Well, that is the real trick—being different from the crowd. And .NET's Web services are special indeed. What makes this implementation of a RPC different is that the data is sent as a self-describing Simple Object Access Protocol (SOAP) message. This means that it is not only platform independent but that you cannot embed viruses in a call to a Web service (nor can you return a virus from a call to a Web service).

In terms of .NET, creating a Web service is simplicity itself. You stick the <WebMethod()> tag in front of a function (or subroutine, but you will not see that often because probably you are trying to get some data from the service). That is all there is to it. .NET takes care of the rest for you. It takes care of deserializing the SOAP request that is sent to it and serializing the data into the SOAP format for return to the caller. It works absolutely transparently. And you can call Web services from Visual Basic 6 and other languages as long as they can parse a SOAP string.

Java also has Web services, but its implementation is new and not a core part of the language (as of this writing); in other words, it is an add-on at this point.

A key part of consuming Web services involves being able to find available Web services. You locate these services by searching a Universal Description, Discovery, and Integration (UDDI) directory. Currently there are two major public UDDIs, put out by Microsoft and IBM. (These are actually just one UDDI that is replicated between Microsoft and IBM.) For a business to be able to use and consume its own Web services, the business must eventually set up its own UDDI directory. You will learn about setting up an enterprise UDDI and making it usable by the enterprise in Chapter 11, "Web Services and the UDDI." Later on in the book you will also create your own Web service, and you will learn how to register the Web service with a UDDI. Microsoft and IBM also maintain test UDDI directories for people to practice registering and searching for Web services.

Exploring How .NET Scales Applications

There are several ways in which .NET can scale an application, but there is one easy way to do this: IIS. If the components are hosted in IIS, then it is a simple matter of moving them from a single box to a Web farm. A *Web farm* is just a group of IIS servers that have traffic sent to them by a load balancing router. Microsoft also provides a server called *Application Center Server*, which is designed to act as a load balancing server in place of a router designed for this purpose. As a developer there is only one thing you need to plan for to achieve this scalability: Your components must be stateless. *Stateless* components are those that do not maintain any information between calls. Assume that you have an object called *objPerson* that contains information about a person. The following lines of code indicate an object that is *stateful*, or maintains state between calls:

```
objPerson.FirstName = "John"
objPerson.LastName = "Smith"
objPerson.Save
```

As you can see, three calls are made on the person object, and it can be assumed that when you call the Save method of the person object, you are saving the first and last name of the person. The next example shows a stateless object:

```
Public Structure structperson
     Public FirstName as string
     Public LastName as string
End Structure

Private Sub Save()
     Dim sPerson as structPerson
     Dim objPerson as Person

     sPerson.FirstName = "John"
     sPerson.LastName = "Smith"

     objPerson = new Person
     objPerson.Save(sPerson)
     objPerson = nothing
End Sub
```

As you can see in this example, there is only one call made on the person object, and it is passed all of the data it needs in the one call. After the call is made, the information will either be saved or it will not be saved, but the object will not maintain that information. It does not need to because the calling code maintains the necessary information.

The difference between the first example and the second example is important. There are two different types of calls that you can make to remote objects: SingleCall and Singleton. *SingleCall* is when a new object is created for every call made to the remote object by a different client. *Singleton* is when one object is created on the server and every connection to the server uses this one instance of the object. In terms of scalability, if you are using the SingleCall method and 500,000 users hit the server at the same time, 500,000 copies of your object will be created. You would find yourself quickly running out of memory! Using the Singleton method, you can have as many connections as you want, but only one object is ever created. The key to this is that the objects must be stateless, as in the second example; otherwise the different processes would interfere with each other.

Summary

This chapter has given a broad overview and introduction into architecture design and its advantages and disadvantages. You have seen how .NET implements different technologies for achieving enterprise applications and different ways in which you can leverage .NET in an enterprise environment. The next chapter introduces you to the application that you will create throughout this book as well as how to set up the application infrastructure. It will employ a number of techniques discussed in this chapter. You will find as you read this book that it is far from theoretical; specifically, you will put into practice all of the techniques needed to create an enterprise-level application by building a working n-tier application.

CHAPTER 2

Building an N-Tier Application

CHAPTER 1, "Understanding Application Architecture: An Overview," covered the basic structure and the pros and cons of different types of application architectures. You will spend the rest of this book building an n-tier application with a Windows, Web, and Web service interface that is accessible by virtually any device in one way or another. By the time you are done building this application, you will have an in-depth understanding of the process involved in building n-tier applications, including the ability to build them quickly and efficiently and the tradeoffs you need make.

NOTE   This application uses the Northwind database that ships with SQL Server. Microsoft Access also supplies this database, but because of the way this application is being written, you cannot substitute Access for SQL Server. You can download the 120-day trial version of SQL Server at http://www.microsoft.com/sql.

Making Design Choices

The application you will build is flexible yet easy to maintain and extend. To that end, you have some choices to make early on to really understand how your objects are going to communicate and the tradeoffs you need to make.

Understanding Cross-Process Communication: Remoting Channels

The first decision to make is always which technologies the components will use to communicate remotely. This choice will have a wide-ranging impact on your application, both for the present and for the future. The .NET Framework provides several methods for communication that include COM+ and a new technology called *remoting*. Remoting is the .NET term for cross-process communication and is the preferred method for communication in .NET. There are many different aspects to remoting that would fill a book or two, so I will not cover all of the details here.

NOTE An excellent book that explains a great deal more about remoting and all of its permutations is *Advanced .NET Remoting* by Ingo Rammer (Apress, 2002). This book contains an in-depth explanation of all of the remoting techniques and options.

When using remoting, you create a *channel* to the remote objects, and you pass data over this channel. You can create two types of channels to communicate between objects: a Transmission Control Protocol (TCP) channel or a Hypertext Transfer Protocol (HTTP) channel. This choice is an important one that will influence everything from transmission speed to extensibility to security. In this chapter, you will use an HTTP channel because the objects will be hosted in Internet Information Server (IIS). This gives you the ability to use Windows Integrated Authentication, which provides a more secure environment. It also allows you to upgrade to a Secure Sockets Layer (SSL) connection with no changes to the code if you choose to do this.

TIP The ability to upgrade to an SSL connection is indeed great. You can create a highly secure application without having any real knowledge about how to encrypt and secure data. However, you must also measure the impact of this to your application. An SSL connection means the channel will be encrypted, but an encrypted channel will be slower and will degrade the performance of an application.

Using IIS to host your remote components also gives you the ability to load balance your application by placing it into a Web farm; again, this requires no additional effort on your part.

Understanding Cross-Process Communication: Data Serialization

The data that is passed over the remoting channel is serialized. You use two built-in data formats when serializing data over a remoting channel: binary and Simple

Object Access Protocol (SOAP). Picking the right format is just as important as picking the right type of channel. Binary data is just that—it is binary data, and as such it is a compact stream of data. Data that is serialized into the SOAP format is not very compact and will always create a larger "payload" to deliver across the channel.

NOTE   If you are not familiar with SOAP, it is a type of Extensible Markup Language (XML) format in that it is a self-describing text format. You do not need to know anything about it when serializing the data, but because there are so many things you can do with a SOAP message, you should become familiar with it. You can find out more about SOAP at http://msdn.microsoft.com.

One advantage that the SOAP format has is that it is nonexecutable code and is therefore "safe." That is, it can pass through firewalls where binary data cannot. However, because this is a book about enterprise development, let's assume that all communication will occur within the firewall. Because you want the fastest possible communication speed, you will use the binary format.

CAUTION   This choice does indeed have far-flung consequences. If you are creating a Web site that is hosted externally of your enterprise, using binary format will not work. If you envision the application expanding beyond the firewall, then you must use the SOAP format. However, .NET gives you the ability to change the type of serialization with almost no effort if you decide to make a change later.

Now that you have made these crucial choices, it is time to set up IIS to host your middle-tier components.

Setting Up IIS

Let's jump in and get IIS set up for use with your application. On the taskbar, go to Start ➤ Programs ➤ Administrative Tools ➤ Internet Information Services (if Administrative Tools is not available on the Programs menu, you can access it through the Control Panel or by editing the properties of the taskbar and selecting Show Administrative Tools). This brings up the IIS console, as shown in Figure 2-1.

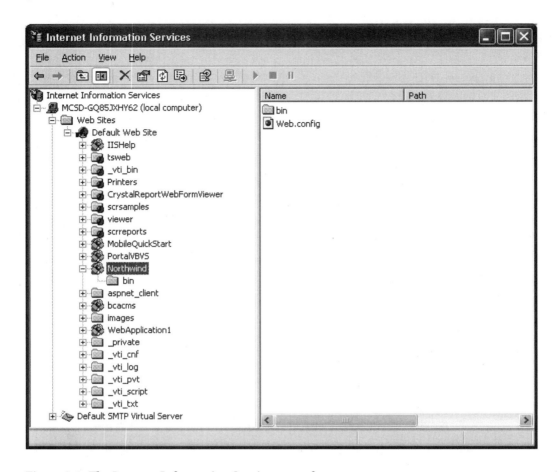

Figure 2-1. The Internet Information Services console

First you will create your own virtual directory. To do this, follow these steps:

1. Right-click the Default Web Site node located under the Web Sites folder. Select New ➤ Virtual Directory. Click past the first screen, enter the name *Northwind* as the alias for your virtual directory, and then click Next.

2. On this screen, you will select the physical directory to which the virtual directory points. Select Browse, browse to the C:\inetpub\wwwroot folder (if you used the default installation with IIS; otherwise, browse to wherever your wwwroot folder is located), click the Make New Folder button, and enter the name *Northwind*. Click OK, then Next, Next, and then Finish.

3. Back on the IIS console, you should now have a Northwind node under the Default Web Site node. If you click the node, you will notice that nothing is in the folder right now.

Next you will create the web.config file, which will contain your server application settings and remoting listeners.

 NOTE Listeners "listen" for a request to be made on a certain channel and then route the request to the correct object for processing.

Creating the web.config File

The web.config file contains application-specific configuration information. An application can have multiple web.config files, which is common in ASP.NET applications (although an application can only have one web.config file per directory). This application will require only one web.config file. You have two ways to create a web.config file: manually or by creating an ASP.NET application within the IDE and letting Visual Studio .NET (VS .NET) create a template web.config file for you. Listing 2-1 shows the default web.config file that is created with a new ASP.NET application.

Listing 2-1. The Default web.config File

```
<?xml version="1.0" encoding="utf-8" ?>
<configuration>
  <system.web>
    <compilation defaultLanguage="vb" debug="true" />
    <customErrors mode="RemoteOnly" />
    <authentication mode="Windows" />
    <authorization>
        <allow users="*" />
    </authorization>
    <trace enabled="false" requestLimit="10" pageOutput="false"
          traceMode="SortByTime" localOnly="true" />
    <sessionState
            mode="InProc"
            stateConnectionString="tcpip=127.0.0.1:42424"
            sqlConnectionString="data source=127.0.0.1;user id=sa;password="
            cookieless="false"
            timeout="20"
    />
    <globalization requestEncoding="utf-8" responseEncoding="utf-8" />
  </system.web>
</configuration>
```

NOTE When .NET creates this file, it is fully commented with helpful tips on how to use each section. I have removed the comments for brevity, but you can view them by generating this file from a template.

See the sidebar "Using a Compilation Tag" for information on an undocumented issue with ASP.NET.

Using a Compilation Tag

When you are building an application on your own computer, there are almost never any problems. But when you move into a team development environment and eventually into production, things get a little more difficult. I was working on a team a few months ago and we were using a development server to host our middle-tier components. It happened to be that the server was under my control, so it was running under my credentials. When other members of my team deployed the components to the IIS server, they kept getting an error message when they tried to run the application. The message they got was the following: "Access Denied to CommonDC." (CommonDC was the name of our data-centric component.)

After working with Microsoft for a few days, we determined that the cause of this error was a lack of permissions on the shadow folder. ASP.NET uses a shadow copy mechanism to hold a component in memory. This shadow copy lives in the folder C:\WINDOWS\Microsoft.NET\Framework\v1.0.3705\Temporary ASP.NET Files\[application name]. None of the other developers had permissions to this folder, but the permissions were granted to the ASP.NET worker process on the server. This works fine until you start using impersonation. When you are using impersonation (see the "Setting Up Authentication and Authorization" section), the process runs under the user account of the user logged on to the application. None of them had permissions to this folder, so they always got this error. I had to run the application first and then everything was fine.

To work around this, we had to give read/write access to this folder to all of the groups authorized to run this application. The compilation tag allows you to change the location where the shadow copies are created—but the user logging in still needs read/write permissions to this folder on the server. This may be considered a security issue, but I do not see it as much of one because they have to be authorized to get to the application anyway. This is never a problem when you are not using Windows authentication.

To create the web.config file manually, do the following:

1. Navigate to the Northwind folder you just created (this should be in C:\Inetpub\wwwroot\Northwind).

2. Add a new text document and rename it to *web.config*.

3. Enter the information in Listing 2-1 into this file.

To create the web.config file using VS .NET, do the following:

1. Start VS .NET.

2. Select File ➤ New Project.

3. In the Visual Basic Projects node, select the ASP.NET Web Application and click OK.

4. Note the folder that the project was created in (by default, if you do not change the application name, it will be in C:\Inetpub\wwwroot\WebApplication1), close VS .NET, and copy the web.config file from the ASP.NET application to the Northwind folder.

Now that you have a web.config file, you can examine and customize it for your needs. Let's start with the security settings in the configuration file.

Setting Up Authentication and Authorization

Before explaining the security settings in the web.config file, you need to understand two commonly misused words: authentication and authorization. *Authentication* is determining *who* has access to something, and *authorization* is determining what they have access to. You need to understand this important distinction when designing the security of your application.

Consider the following lines of code within the web.config file you just created:

```
<authentication mode="Windows" />
<authorization>
    <allow users="*" />
</authorization>
```

As you can see, the authentication mode is Windows by default.

TIP Microsoft has made a major change with the .NET Framework. Whenever the Framework is setting the default for a property that has to do with security, it will always set it to the most restrictive setting possible. This is a good practice for developers in general.

There are three other possible authentication modes for an application: Forms, Passport, and None. Because this is an enterprise application, you will be using the Windows authentication option. In an enterprise, all users of your application will probably be authenticated against the same domain, so this is a viable choice. However, this is one of those choices you must make carefully. By choosing Windows authentication, external users will not be able to use the application unless all connections are made via a general domain account that the ASP.NET process can run under. Finally, you should consult a security professional because there are many more implications to this decision than can be discussed here.

Web applications use Forms authentication that can present a user interface to collect login information from a user. Because you are calling your objects over a remoting channel with no interface, this is not an option. You can use Passport authentication either within the enterprise or externally of the enterprise, so it is a good balanced choice. It does require that users have a Passport account, and the service cannot be incorporated for free.

NOTE For more information on using Passport authentication in your application, go to the following Web page: http://www.microsoft.com/netservices/passport/. You can also download the Passport Software Development Kit (SDK) at http://msdn.microsoft.com/downloads/default.asp?url=/downloads/sample.asp?url=/msdn-files/027/001/885/msdncompositedoc.xml&frame=true.

The authorization mode is set to an asterisk (*) by default. An asterisk, in conjunction with Windows authentication, means that any user who can be authenticated against the domain will be granted access to the application. For the purpose of building this application, this is OK; however, when building a real application, this is a bad idea. When you are developing an application, you should always develop it with the lowest level of authorization possible. How many times have you, as a developer, written an application that worked fine on your development systems but after you installed it you received a bunch of errors? A lot of this is because the users do not have Admin access on their systems, and therefore you should not have Admin access on yours. You should modify this because there are certain things you must have Admin access to do, but if you do develop under an Admin logon, you absolutely must be rigorous during testing to ensure that the testers do not test under an Admin account.

You can also use the authorization tag to allow Windows groups (or *roles,* as they are referred to in this file) and to deny both users and groups.

CAUTION   When you deny users or groups, you must place the deny tags before the allow tags. This is because .NET will stop checking for valid authentication the first time it hits an allow tag that permits the user access. Likewise, .NET will also stop checking for valid authentication the first time it hits a deny tag that rejects the user.

Add the following line below the closing authorization tag:

```
<identity impersonate="true" />
```

This line allows IIS to use the connected user's Windows information when connecting to other resources on the network.

CAUTION   If you do this in a tightly controlled environment, such as in a secure environment at work, you need to be cautious of one thing. If you deploy SQL Server on another machine, you must make sure the machine that hosts IIS is authorized for trusted delegation. If you do not, when you try to log on to SQL Server, you will receive an error that says "DOMAIN\ANONYMOUS_USER denied." There is a good reason for this. It can be a security problem if trusted delegation is on. You can find more information about this on the Microsoft Web site in the Knowledge Base Article Q325894.

Using the appSettings Section

Many times there are specific settings that you would like to keep in a configuration file so that you always have access to them and so that you can easily change them. The appSettings section of the web.config is precisely for this purpose. The appSettings section can hold any values you want it to hold. This application will store only one setting in this file—the database connection string. The reason you want to store the connection string here is so that when your database location changes, as it does when moving from development to testing to production environments, you do not have to recompile your application.

Add the following tag below the opening configuration tag but above the opening system.web tag:

```
<appSettings>
    <add key="Northwind_DSN"
     value="Trusted_Connection=yes;server=localhost;Initial Catalog=Northwind" />
</appSettings>
```

This connection string assumes you are using the same machine that is hosting IIS to host SQL Server. If this is not the case, replace localhost with the correct server name. Because you are using Windows authentication in SQL Server, you do not need to include any user IDs or passwords in this string, so it is OK to place it in this file. However, if you plan to include this information because you cannot use Windows authentication, it is best practice to encrypt this information before you place it into this file.

Understanding Remoting Configuration Information

The system.runtime.remoting section shown in Listing 2-2 controls whether IIS will be able to find the remote object when your client code comes looking for it. System.Runtime.Remoting is the .NET namespace where the remoting classes are located. The channels tag says that you are going to use the HttpChannel as opposed to the TcpChannel.

NOTE   Note that you have not specified which type of formatter you will be using (binary or SOAP). This is because .NET will use whichever formatter it detects when the connection is made.

The service section describes all of the components whose services are being made available through IIS. The wellknown tag registers the object with IIS so it knows what to do when a request is made. In other words, IIS listens for calls made to these specific Uniform Resource Indicators (URIs). The mode can be either Singleton or SingleCall. The difference is that with a Singleton object, only one object is ever created; with SingleCall, one object is created for every client that makes calls to an object. Using SingleCall could spell disaster for a large application where scalability is the key to success. However, when using Singleton, you must make sure the object does not maintain state.

TIP There is one area where you would want to have a Singleton object maintain state. Take, for instance, an application where three users are logged onto the application and one user makes a change to a database that the other users need to know about. With a Singleton object, you can call a delegate on the client (if that client is set up to receive a delegate), or you can have the clients routinely poll the remote object for changes. This is an excellent way to keep all clients up-to-date on the current state of the application.

The type tag contains the fully qualified object that you will be calling. In this case, the object is called *Regions,* and it is located in the NorthwindTraders.NorthwindDC namespace. The object type following the comma lists the assembly in which the class is located—in this case, NorthwindDC.

CAUTION Do not include the assembly extension or you will receive an error when you try to call the remote object.

The final tag, objectUri, contains the value you will use to connect to this object. This will become clearer when you start building your local objects.

TIP You have used the extension .rem for your objects' URI. This is a naming convention more than anything. When a remote object will be serialized as a SOAP message, the extension is .soap.

This wellknown tag is the one you will duplicate and change as you progress through building the application. Add the remoting section (shown in Listing 2-2) to the web.config just above the closing configuration tag.

Listing 2-2. The Remoting Configuration Information

```
<system.runtime.remoting>
    <application>
      <channels>
        <channel ref="http"/>
      </channels>
      <service>
        <wellknown mode="Singleton"
            type="NorthwindTraders.NorthwindDC.RegionDC, NorthwindDC"
            objectUri="RegionDC.rem"/>
      </service>
    </application>
  </system.runtime.remoting>
```

Next, navigate to the C:\inetpub\wwwroot\northwind folder (or wherever you created the folder), and create a new folder called *bin*. Lastly, in the IIS console, right-click the Northwind node. Select Properties and then click the Directory Security tab. Click the Edit button located under the Anonymous Access Authentication and Control section. This brings up the dialog box shown in Figure 2-2. Clear the check box next to Anonymous Access, and make sure that only the Integrated Windows Authentication box is checked.

Figure 2-2. IIS Authentication Methods dialog box

Click OK and close all the open property windows. You are now done configuring IIS.

Setting Up the Microsoft .NET IDE

Finally, you get to the VS .NET Integrated Development Environment (IDE). To begin, load VS .NET. Once it loads, follow these steps:

1. Select File ➤ New ➤ Blank Solution. Name the solution *Northwind*. This creates an empty solution with no files, and the IDE will be empty.

2. Now you need to add the individual projects to the solution. Select File ➤ Add Project ➤ New Project. Select the Class Library project type, as shown in Figure 2-3. Enter the project name as *NorthwindDC*.

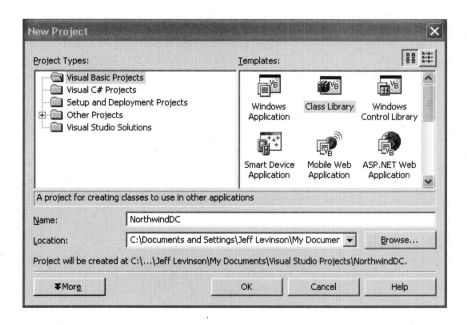

Figure 2-3. VS .NET New Project dialog box

3. Repeat the previous steps to add two more class library projects, one called *NorthwindUC* and another one called *NorthwindShared*.

4. Now, add a Windows Application project called *NorthwindTraders.* Later on you will learn how to put a Web frontend and Web services frontend onto your application.

5. Next, right-click the solution (at the top of the Project Explorer window), select Add ➤ Add Existing Item, and browse to the Northwind directory that contains the web.config file. Select web.config and click Open. VS should now look like Figure 2-4.

6. Right-click NorthwindTraders and select Set as Startup Project. This causes this project to launch every time you run the application from within the IDE. Once you are done with this step, the NorthwindTraders project will be bold in the Solution Explorer.

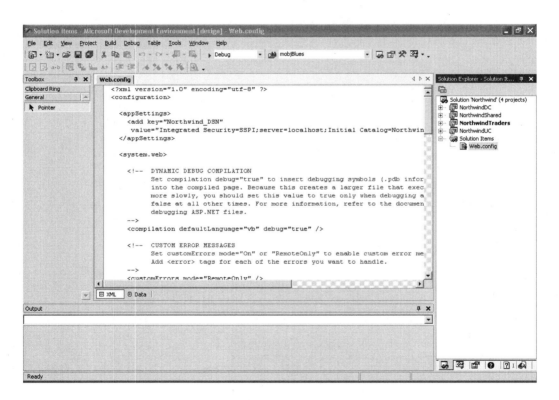

Figure 2-4. Visual Studio, Northwind solution

Now you need to set up the application namespaces. *Namespaces* are a feature of .NET that allows the developer to control where classes are referenced from within code—regardless of where the class actually resides. For example, if there are two separate blocks of code that exist to handle errors, and these blocks of code are in different assemblies, you can make that fact transparent to yourself and other developers through the use of namespaces. It is also a great way to group functionality within your application, exactly as Microsoft did with the .NET Framework base classes. For example, everything related to input and output is located in the System.IO namespace, even though the code may be located in many different assemblies. There are two different places to enter namespace information, and they are generally used in conjunction with one another. Right-click the NorthwindDC project and select Properties. Figure 2-5 shows the properties for the NorthwindDC project. Make sure that Common Properties, General is selected from the tree view, and you will see a textbox for RootNamespace, which currently reads NorthwindDC. Change this to NorthwindTraders.NorthwindDC and then click OK.

TIP   Break up your code into logical units of functionality using namespaces. It makes it easier for developers working in teams to find specific blocks of code. Create your namespaces using a common naming convention such as the following: Company.Division.ApplicationName. This will ensure that even in large organizations namespaces will never cross over each other. This will cause fewer problems when developers start reusing code from other applications.

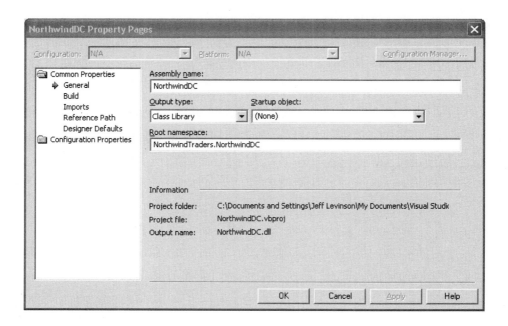

Figure 2-5. NorthwindDC general property page

Repeat these steps for the NorthwindUC and NorthwindShared projects so that the namespaces read NorthwindTraders.NorthwindUC and NorthwindTraders.NorthwindShared. You do not need to change the namespace of the NorthwindTraders application because its root namespace is already NorthwindTraders. The second place to change namespaces is in a code module, as shown in this block of code:

```
Namespace Errors
    Public Class ValueTooLongException
        Inherits System.ApplicationException

        Public Sub New()
        End Sub
    End Class
End Namespace
```

If you added this namespace declaration in the NorthwindShared project, you would reference this code throughout the rest of the project by using the following line of code:

```
NorthwindTraders.NorthwindShared.Errors.ValueTooLongException
```

Because that would be a lot of typing to do every time you wanted to use the ValueTooLongException class, you can use the Imports keyword at the head of each code module to import the namespace, just as you would with any of the .NET Framework's namespaces. For now, you will not be adding any namespaces, but you will as you progress into the application.

The last step is to add all of the references you will need to create between your assemblies and to add two additional assemblies from the Global Application Cache (GAC). Expand the References node of the NorthwindDC project and you will see that the only references are System, System.Data, and System.XML. Right-click the References node and select Add Reference. This brings up the Add Reference dialog box, as shown in Figure 2-6.

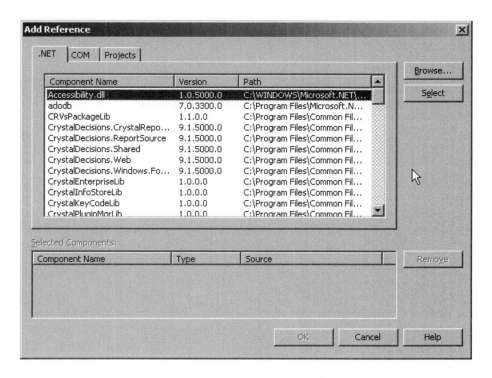

Figure 2-6. Add Reference dialog box

From the .NET tab, select the System.Runtime.Remoting assembly by double-clicking it. Then, switch to the Projects tab, as shown in Figure 2-7.

From the Projects tab, select the NorthwindShared project by double-clicking it. Both of these components will appear in the dialog box's Selected Components list. Then click OK. This adds two more entries under the References node in the NorthwindDC project. You are not going to add any references for the NorthwindShared project, but you will need to add some references for the NorthwindTraders project. Right-click References in the NorthwindTraders project and select Add Reference. Then select System.Runtime.Remoting from the .NET tab, and from the Projects tab, select the NorthwindShared and NorthwindUC projects and click OK. And finally, in the NorthwindUC project, add a reference to the NorthwindShared project.

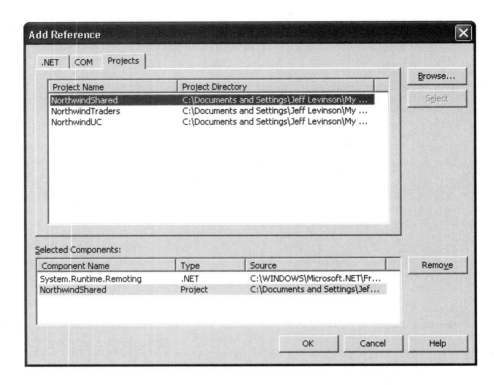

Figure 2-7. The Projects tab of the Add Reference dialog box

This completes the solution setup for the NorthwindTraders application. The resulting application architecture looks like Figure 2-8.

NOTE If you have Visual Studio for Enterprise Architects, you also have Visio for Enterprise Architects. You can reverse engineer the solution to Visio by first selecting the solution in the Project Explorer and then, from the main menu, selecting Projects ➤ Visio UML ➤ Reverse Engineer. This will reverse engineer the solution into a UML diagram from which this static structure diagram was created. It will also add the Visio file to your solution under the Solution Items folder.

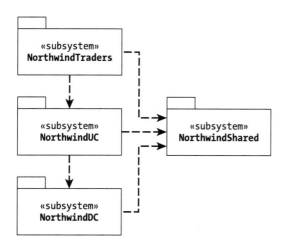

Figure 2-8. Northwind application architecture

This is the logical view of the application; it does not address the physical distribution of the application because that will be somewhat different from what is seen here. Chapter 3, "Creating the Application Infrastructure," examines the physical object model for the application and moves right in to coding the application (after all, that is why you are reading this book, right?).

Sticking to Naming Conventions

Every application should have a naming convention, which should be fully documented in the project's technical standards document. It does not even matter if this is different from project to project, but it must be consistent within the project.

The projects you have just created are named the way they are for specific reasons. The letters *DC* at the end of the NorthwindDC project mean that this component contains data-centric objects. The *UC* at the end of the NorthwindUC project mean that this component contains user-centric objects (both of these object types were discussed in Chapter 1, "Understanding Application Architecture: An Overview"). The NorthwindShared project contains objects that will be used (shared) by other components.

As you can see, the naming convention is straightforward. Too many applications use a cryptic naming convention, and it becomes difficult to understand the interactions or the purpose of the objects. Chapter 3, "Creating the Application Infrastructure," delves into how the applications components are used in conjunction with one another.

Summary

This chapter introduced you to the application you will be building throughout this book. You should have an understanding of some of the tradeoffs you have when making your initial design decisions. Also, you gained some insight into basic security with IIS and the .NET Framework. You have also gained an understanding of your objects, where they reside, and how they will communicate. In Chapter 3, "Creating the Application Infrastructure," you will build a robust and reusable set of base classes that you will be able to inherit from when creating the user interface throughout the rest of the application. You will also create a basic set of working business objects that will allow you to retrieve data from SQL Server and display it to the user.

CHAPTER 3

Creating the Application Infrastructure

THERE ARE MANY ASPECTS of an application's infrastructure, including overall application conventions, coding patterns, and basic sets of reusable functionality. In this chapter you will not only examine the application architecture and the structure of the remoting calls, but you will also start developing working code for your application. This involves creating the stored procedures, shared objects, data-centric and user-centric classes, and a basic Windows interface.

You will see the difference between the application's logical model and the physical implementation of that model. In doing this, you will learn some of the additional choices you need to make and the consequences of those choices.

The business objects created in this chapter will provide the basic structure for all of your business objects and will eventually give you the ability to reduce and consolidate your code.

The user interface consists of base classes that implement a number of the application's features and that you will inherit from for almost all of the other forms in the application. Once you have a small part of the application working, you will enhance the user experience by implementing finding and sorting capabilities and a custom print routine that you will write once but reuse everywhere.

Designing the Physical Application Architecture

Designing the physical application architecture is a very different process than designing the application logically. The logical design process is a more high-level type of design, and the physical design process says, "OK, I have this map for building the application, now how do I actually get from point A to point B?" Although this is not an in-depth book on application architecture, it gives you an overview of how you convert a logical model to a physical model.

Before you begin writing an application designed for an enterprise, it is important to understand the big picture—not only in your own application but also in the enterprise for which you are building it. Although this book does not show an enterprise's overall architecture, you can examine an application's architecture from both a high and low level. This is critical to writing a solid application.

The Importance of Application Analysis and Design

A little more than two years ago I was working on a large enterprise application, which was billed as the latest-and-greatest financial tool for the company's financial division. The total time for development was supposed to be around three years. I came onto the application a year and a half into development, and at last word it was expected to last another five years.

Although this in itself is enough to raise eyebrows, it might surprise you even more that in the entire time that I was there, I never saw an architectural model. The application was written in Visual Basic (VB) 6. In July 2002, the number of lines of code (excluding comments) was around 45,000.

That is not such a large amount of code, but maybe this will put it into perspective: There were no DLLs in the application, and there were fewer than 40 classes. All of the coding was in the forms, and there was no object-oriented design or methodology applied. A rough guess by some of the developers put the line count of duplicated code at around 10,000. As such, different methods that had the same routines had the routines coded differently. There was no way to tell where code was duplicated or what code had to change when the business rules changed. It was complete chaos, all because there was no comprehensive view of the application.

In defense of the current team, the original development team (including the people in charge of the original design) was replaced. However, that just goes to show that everyone must understand the design of an application so that others, if needed, can take over and complete the application.

You should examine the architecture, at a minimum, at the deployment/component model and object model levels. There are obviously other levels to any application model, but you will concentrate on these because they most directly relate to how you will build the application.

Examining the Component/Deployment Model

Chapter 1, "Understanding Application Architecture: An Overview," discussed the advantages of a three-tier architecture, so I do not repeat them here. Instead, you will examine the application's components and how they are deployed using a three-tier architecture. Also, you will learn how this relates to one specific technology in .NET: remoting. Figure 3-1 shows the component/deployment model you will use for the NorthwindTraders application.

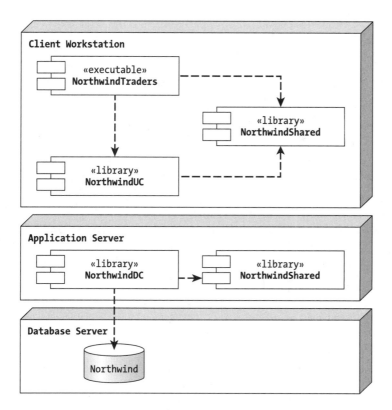

Figure 3-1. NorthwindTraders component/deployment model

First, notice that there is no connection between the client workstation and the application server. These objects run independently of one another. Second, note that the NorthwindShared assembly is on both the client and the server. This must be the exact same file on both machines. Why? Well, that takes a little bit of explaining and is a perfect introduction to .NET remoting.

How Objects Communicate Using Remoting

Chapter 2, "Building an N-Tier Application," gave a brief overview of remoting. This section introduces the actual mechanism of remoting and how it works. There are several different ways to use remoting, but the method you will use consists of calls made on the interfaces of the remote component. This is kind of a confusing topic for VB 6 developers because although VB has interfaces, no one really used them. In this scenario, they are mandatory. So to begin with, what is an interface?

An *interface* is a set of methods and properties that have no functionality. Yes, you read it right—they have no functionality. The response to this statement is usually, "Why the heck would I want to code something that does not work?" Good question. Before going further, let's look at a simple interface:

```
Public Interface ITest
    Function Add(int1 as Integer, int2 as Integer) As Integer
End Interface
```

The first thing everyone notices about an interface is that there is no body to the method signature. In other words, as mentioned, interfaces have no functionality. You cannot call interfaces directly because you cannot use them. Also, there is no scope declaration statement in front of the Add method signature—this is because everything in an interface is public. But how do you actually use the interface, and what is its part in making remote calls across process boundaries? Let's create a small sample application to demonstrate this.

Start Visual Studio (VS) .NET and create a new VB console application called *InterfaceExample*. Add the code in Listing 3-1.

Listing 3-1. The InterfaceExample Application

```
Module Module1

    Sub Main()
        Dim objAdd As New cAdd
        Dim objTip As New CalcTip
        Console.WriteLine("Processing cAdd Class.")
        ProcessNumbers(objAdd)
        Console.WriteLine("Processing CalcTip Class.")
        ProcessNumbers(objTip)
        Console.ReadLine()
    End Sub

    Private Sub ProcessNumbers(ByVal objI As ITest)
        Console.WriteLine(objI.Add(4, 5))
    End Sub
End Module

Public Interface ITest
    Function Add(ByVal int1 As Integer, ByVal int2 As Integer) As Integer
End Interface
```

```
Public Class cAdd
    Implements ITest

    Public Function Add(ByVal int1 As Integer, ByVal int2 As Integer) _
    As Integer Implements ITest.Add
        Return int1 + int2
    End Function
End Class

Public Class CalcTip
    Implements ITest

    Public Function Add(ByVal int1 As Integer, ByVal int2 As Integer) _
    As Integer Implements ITest.Add
        Return (int1 + int2) * 9.25
    End Function
End Class
```

This is an interface (ITest) that is implemented by the classes cAdd and CalcTip. A ProcessNumbers method takes as an argument an object of type ITest. This process calls the Add method of the interface and passes it the values 4 and 5, and the result outputs to the screen. Except, this is the problem: How did the numbers get added together when you know that there is no functionality in the ITest interface? The answer is that the functionality is invoked in the cAdd and CalcTip classes, not the ITest interface. Because cAdd and CalcTest implement the ITest interface, they are also of type ITest. Therefore, any method that can accept an object of type ITest can accept any object that implements the interface. In this example, the ProcessNumbers method knew nothing about either of the classes that were passed to it, but because the classes implement an interface that ProcessNumbers does know about, it can make calls on the methods that are visible to it. In this example there are two entirely different classes being passed to the same method and a call is being made on those classes. However, the ProcessNumbers method does not know that one class is different from the other because this method sees the same thing—an object of type ITest. It can only make calls on methods that are known through the ITest interface. If you place any other methods in either of these classes, you would not be able to call them from the ProcessNumbers method because they would not be part of the ITest interface. And that is how you are going to implement remoting.

By placing the interfaces into the NorthwindShared component, which is hosted on both the client and the server, you can make calls on objects that you do not know anything about! As long as your server objects implement an interface that the client knows about, the client objects can make calls against the server objects.

Using SOAP and Binary Messages

As mentioned in Chapter 2, "Building an N-Tier Application," when using a channel there are two formats in which the data can be serialized: as a Simple Object Access Protocol (SOAP) message or as a binary message. This section discusses the differences between the two in terms of tradeoffs you need to make as you start building the application. When working in an intranet, you should use the binary formatter because it creates a more compact message stream; a SOAP call contains a large amount of XML markup that adds to the size of the message stream. However, using the binary formatter presents a small problem: It serializes the version information contained in the object that is being serialized and all of the methods and attributes contained within the object (in contrast, for example, the XmlSerializer only serializes a class's public attributes). This makes deserializing the object that you pass somewhat problematic because you can only deserialize an object serialized this way with the same version of the object. There are two ways to handle this situation. The first way is to have the local class implement the ISerializeable interface, create your own serialization routines, and only serialize what you want. One of the properties of the BinaryFormatterSink class is the includeVersions property.

NOTE   The includeVersions property is not a well-documented property, and it is only available when using an HttpChannel for communication.

Setting the includeVersions to False strips the version information off of the message stream and does not require it to deserialize the object. However, this is a lot of work and requires that every object that needs to access your object perform these operations. A much simpler solution is to use a structure to pass information across the network. Structures are fairly small and can be included in the same file that contains the interface.

NOTE   This process is analogous to using a User Defined Type (UDT) to store object information in VB 6 and then serializing it into a string and deserializing it on the receiving end. In this instance as well, the UDT must be available on both the sending and receiving side.

You will use this method in your application to simplify the implementation.

Creating the Object Model

Creating an object model before constructing the application is extremely important. This provides several advantages for the entire team. Developers can understand where their piece of code fits into the overall scheme of things. It also helps point out any weaknesses in design before they become too much of a problem to fix. Another huge advantage is that everyone can see that a piece of code has been written to perform a specific task, and they can reuse that object. Reusable pieces of code are great, but developers have to know they exist to be able to use them!

This section presents two object models. Figure 3-2 contains a logical view of the user-centric objects. Figure 3-3 contains the physical implementation of the user-centric objects. The objects are grouped into four subsections in each model. For the purpose of this book, you will create all of the objects in the section that contains the Employee, Territory, and Region objects.

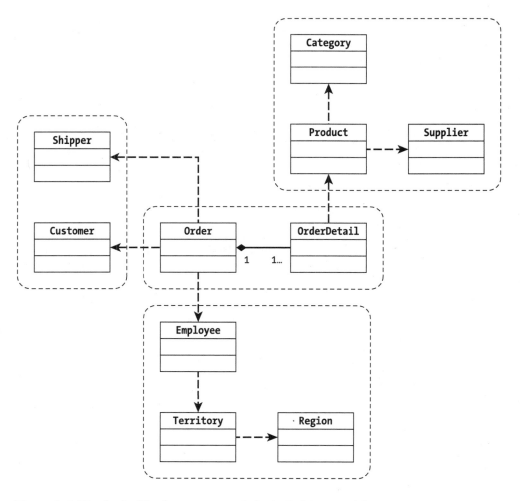

Figure 3-2. NorthwindTraders user-centric logical object model

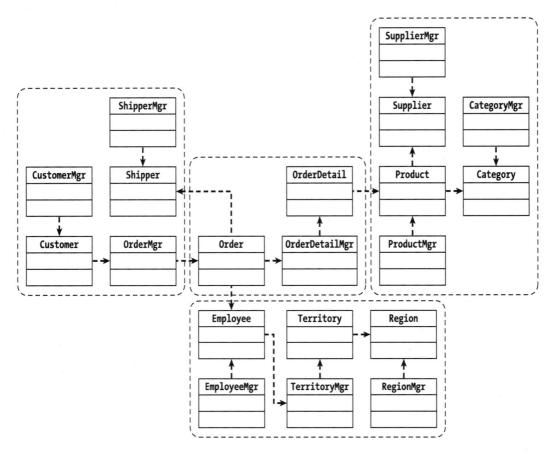

Figure 3-3. NorthwindTraders user-centric physical object model

Before getting into a discussion on the Unified Modeling Language (UML) model and what it implies, you should know how to derive an object model. As mentioned, you will use the Northwind database that comes with SQL Server. There are many theories for how to derive an object model, but for a business application you can derive the object model directly from the data model. If possible, you should try to create a one-to-one relationship between tables and objects. Figure 3-4 shows the tables and their relationships in the Northwind database.

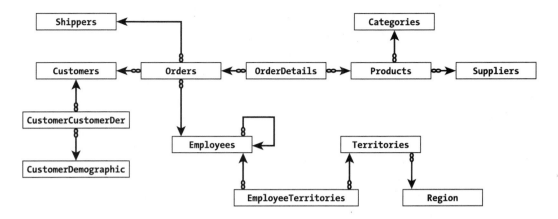

Figure 3-4. The Northwind database tables and relationships

By comparing the logical object model and the data model, you should be able to see this correlation. The only real deviation is that there are not any objects to represent the join tables. The logical object model is similar to the logical data model in that join tables are generally not displayed on a logical model. However, Figure 3-3 shows a series of objects with the extension *Mgr*. These objects help maintain relationships represented by one-to-many or many-to-many relationships in the data model. You should note that the objects maintain the same relationship between each other that the tables maintain.

 NOTE There are many reasons to have an object model that deviates from a data model, but you should do this with care. On the assumption that your data modeler understands the business, you must make sure that if you deviate, it is for a good reason. The objects must always model the business process or you are guaranteed to have problems later.

Understanding the UML Static Model

If you have not seen a UML static model before, this will require some explanation. Three basic types of relationships can occur between objects: dependencies, aggregations, and compositions. The differences between the three can often be just a matter of semantics; however, the implementation of these three types of relationships can make a big difference in the design of the object relationships:

A *dependency* is when one object has a relationship with another object in some way. It may be that one object instantiates another object or that one object may have a reference to the object. In an object model diagram, a dotted line with an arrow at the end denotes a dependency.

Aggregation is when one object (the client object) contains a reference to another object (the supplier object), but the supplier object does not depend on the client object for its lifetime. In terms of implementation, when a reference between objects is made ByRef, it is an aggregation. When the client object is destroyed, the supplier object remains because it was only referenced ByRef. In the object model diagram, a hollow diamond represents aggregation.

Composition is when the client object controls the lifetime of the supplier object. In terms of implementation, when a client object gets a reference (or creates a reference) to a supplier object, it is referenced ByVal. So, when a client object is destroyed, the supplier object is also destroyed. In the object model diagram, a filled-in diamond represents composition. In this object model, only the Order/Order Details relationship is represented this way. The reason is easy to understand: An order detail item must be part of an order, but it cannot exist on its own.

The question to ask now is, "What does this model imply about how the application will be built and what drawbacks do I face with this design?" You should almost always ask this question after you have finished a model. There is no such thing as a perfect model, so there are always decisions to make and things to understand about a model. I explain two implications.

You should first understand the implication in regard to the Region and Territory objects. The Territory object has a dependency on the Region object and not the other way around. So, you will always be able to discover the Region that a Territory is a part of, but you will not be able to discover the Territories contained within a Region. The Region object knows nothing about the Territory object in this instance. This affects the display of information to the user. In other words, using this model, you cannot show a screen that lists all of the Territories in each of the Regions. The reason why you would make this choice will become apparent after you understand the second implication of this part of the model.

The second implication involves the relationship between the Employee and Territory Manager. This relationship tells you that you can determine which territory an employee is in if you are looking at the employee, but you cannot tell which employees are part of a territory if you are looking at a territory. The reason why this design is OK is because this is an order-entry system—it is not a reporting system. In other words, it is a transactional system as opposed to a data-mining tool.

In a transactional system of this nature, you would normally start at the Order screen to take or enter an order. The employee who is taking the order would enter their name, so who cares what territory or region in which they are a part? You would need that type of information for month-end or year-end reports, so it is separate from this system.

NOTE An excellent book on the topic of objects and object-oriented design is *The Art Of Objects* by Yun-Tung Lau (Addison-Wesley, 2000). Although this book is a bit theoretical and is not for the faint of heart, it has everything you could ever want to know about objects and their relationships. A more down-to-earth book on applying UML is *UML Distilled* (Addison-Wesley, 1999). This is a quick-and-easy how-to manual that explains each of the diagrams used in UML modeling, how to use them, and what the notations mean.

Understanding the Data-Centric Object Model

In contrast to the user-centric object model, the data-centric object model is much simpler (see Figure 3-5).

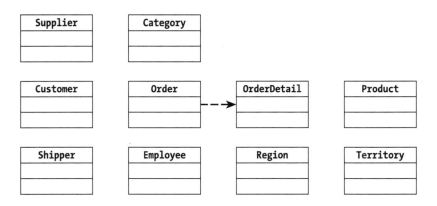

Figure 3-5. NorthwindTraders data-centric object model

These objects check business rules, and they save, delete, and retrieve information from the database. There are no relationships between these objects (except for the Order and Order Details). It is up to the application that consumes them to use them in whatever fashion it chooses. Again, you should note that this is not entirely true—there is the one relationship between the Order and Order

Detail objects. The reason for this is the composition of the objects. The Order Details do not know how to save themselves because they are part of an order. The Order object does know about the Order Details and knows how to save the order details. In terms of implementation, the Order Details object can save itself, but the information needs to come from the Order object.

Having examined the object models, you now have enough information to start building your application.

Creating the Shared Objects

To begin, you need to create the interfaces and structures that will allow your objects to communicate across the network. Then you can start building the data-centric objects. You will build this application vertically (that is, one piece of functionality at a time), so you need to start with the Region objects, then build the Territory objects, and finally build the Employee objects.

In the VS .NET Integrated Development Environment (IDE), select the Class1.vb file from the NorthwindShared project. Rename the file to *Structures.vb* and delete the class definition that is in the file by default. Now you should have a blank code module.

....

Option Explicit and Option Strict

Option Explicit requires that all variables be declared before they are used. This ensures that there are no untyped variables floating around.

Option Strict ensures that all values are explicitly cast from one type to another. For example, `intNum = "5"` would work with Option Strict off, but with Option Strict on, the code would read `intNum = Convert.ToInt32("5")`. This enforces type casting at design-time rather than having an error occur during runtime.

In VB6, Option Explicit needed to appear at the head of every code module. In .NET they do not. There is a setting for each of these options in the Options dialog box of VS .NET (under the Projects node), and they apply to all modules in a project. However, under certain circumstances this is not desirable (when using reflection specifically) and so you will need to add these declarations at the head of every module.

To declare these values, use the following syntax:

```
Option Explicit On
Option Strict On
```

....

Building the Structure

Next, let's create the structure used by the Region objects. Enter the following code in the Structures.vb code module:

```
Public Structure structRegion
    Public RegionID As Integer
    Public RegionDescription As String
End Structure
```

 NOTE I have named the structure *structRegion*, which follows my naming convention. It does not matter what naming convention you use; what is important is that you use the same naming convention everywhere and that the convention is well documented. It also helps if it makes sense….

Now you need to make a slight change to your structure. Change the structure declaration line to read as follows:

```
<Serializable()> Public Structure structRegion
```

The Serializable attribute allows the Common Language Runtime (CLR) to handle object serialization for you. You do not have to write your own routine to serialize the data in your object—the .NET Framework handles it all for you. Finally, you need to start organizing your code into namespaces. Namespaces make finding pieces of code easy and help speed up developer productivity. As you saw in Chapter 2, "Building an N-Tier Application," you can set the root namespace in the properties for a project, so now you will create additional namespaces within the project. You will create a new namespace called *Structures*, which contains all of your shared structures. Your code should look like Listing 3-2 when you are done.

Listing 3-2. The Structures Code Module

```
Option Explicit On
Option Strict On

Namespace Structures

    <Serializable()> Public Structure structRegion
        Public RegionID As Integer
        Public RegionDescription As String
    End Structure

End Namespace
```

Building the Interface

Now, add another code module to the NorthwindShared project called *Interfaces*. To do this, right-click the NorthwindShared project in the Solution Explorer and select Add ➤ Add Class and change the name to *Interfaces*. When the code module loads, delete the class declaration created by default. Enter the code in Listing 3-3 into the Interfaces code module.

Listing 3-3. The Interfaces Code Module

```
Option Explicit On
Option Strict On

Imports NorthwindTraders.NorthwindShared.Structures

Namespace Interfaces

    Public Interface IRegion
        Function LoadProxy() As DataSet
        Function LoadRecord(ByVal intID As Integer) As structRegion
        Sub Save(ByVal sRegion As structRegion, ByRef intID As Integer)
        Sub Delete(ByVal intID As Integer)
    End Interface

End Namespace
```

Let's look at each of these method signatures because they will form the basis of all of the communication across the network.

The LoadProxy method simply returns a dataset with all of the rows in a table. It may or may not return all of the columns of data—this depends on how many columns there are. You will look at this in more depth when you create the user interface.

The LoadRecord method returns the Region structure, which contains one entire record from the database. It accepts an ID as an argument because this is the type of value that is the key on the Regions table.

The Save method saves a single record. It takes a structure and an ID as arguments. You might be curious about the intID argument. You could return the ID by turning the Save method into a function as opposed to a subroutine. However, you will be modifying this routine to return a different type of value, which saves you from having to do more work than necessary.

The Delete method accepts a table key and deletes a record from the database.

NOTE   Many people use the terms *argument* and *parameter* interchangeably, but there is subtle difference between the two. A parameter is the type of variable that a method takes and is part of the method signature. An argument is the actual value passed to the method.

The Imports line allows you to avoid fully qualifying your structRegion reference. Without the imports line, you would have to enter the line to look like the following:

```
Function LoadRecord(ByVal intID As Integer) As Structures.structRegion
```

This could get tedious after a while, so use the imports line where it is needed to cut down on the amount of code you need to enter.

At this point, you have enough information to communicate across the network, so it is time to build the stored procedures and the data-centric business objects.

Creating the Stored Procedures

For security reasons, it is always best to use stored procedures to retrieve, save, and delete information in the database. The reasons why can fill a book on security all by themselves, so I only mention it briefly here. The type of attack this protects against is called a *SQL injection attack*.

NOTE   Until I started taking courses on security, I was unaware of the power of this attack and even that a database could be attacked this way. Although this book is not a security manual, it will point you in the right direction so you can get additional information.

SQL Injection Attacks

A SQL *injection attack* is an attack in which a malformed entry in a text field is turned into executable SQL code. Take the following example: You have a form with a textbox that searches for books in the database; users enter the title they want to find. The resulting SQL statement might look something like the following:

```
Select * From Books Where book_title = '" & txtTitle & '""
```

This simple SQL statement retrieves all of the rows from the books table where the title matches what the user entered. (This assumes the user entered a real book title.) Now, the user could enter the following text in the txtTitle field:

```
' Drop Table Books --
```

Your SQL statement will end up looking like the following:

```
Select * From Books Where book_title = '' Drop Table Books --
```

This drops the books table, which is not something you want to happen! Using stored procedures, parameters are always treated as strings and are never executed (unless you want them to be). This blocks a user from performing this type of attack.

If you are interested in protecting against this type of attack and other attacks, you should refer to the book *Writing Secure Code* by Michael Howard and David Leblanc (Microsoft Press, 2001).

For each object that you create, there should be, in general, four stored procedures. These stored procedures should perform the following operations: getting all records, getting one record, deleting a record, and saving a record. You can break the save stored procedure into an insert and update stored procedure, but it is really up to you. Listing 3-4 shows all of the stored procedures that you should execute against the Northwind database in SQL Server.

Listing 3-4. The Region Stored Procedures

```
--Retrieve all of the records from the Region table
CREATE PROCEDURE usp_region_getall
AS
SELECT  *
FROM    Region
go
--Retrieve a single record from the Region table
CREATE PROCEDURE usp_region_getone
@id int
AS
SELECT  *
FROM    Region
WHERE   RegionID = @id
go
```

```
--Delete a single record from the Region table
CREATE PROCEDURE usp_region_delete
@id int
AS
DELETE
FROM     Region
WHERE    RegionID = @id
go
--Save a record to the Region table (this includes both inserts and updates)
CREATE PROCEDURE usp_region_save
@id int,
@region varchar(50),
@new_id int OUTPUT
AS

IF @id = 0
  BEGIN
    SET @id = (SELECT MAX(RegionID)
    FROM Region) + 1

    INSERT INTO Region (RegionID, RegionDescription)
      VALUES (@id, @region)
  END
ELSE
  UPDATE Region
  SET     RegionDescription = @region
  WHERE      RegionID = @id

SET @new_id = @id
```

I like to name my stored procedures in the following format:

```
"usp_" + table name + "_" + operation
```

This tells you what the stored procedure is for and separates the stored procedures out from SQL Server's stored procedures (which all begin with *sp_*).

Some people may protest against the inclusion of both the insert and update statements in the single Save stored procedure. However, when creating a large application, it is easier for the database developer to write this than to have the developer code multiple parameters to multiple stored procedures. It also abstracts the save process from the objects. All the object has to do is pass the parameters and let the stored procedure figure out what to do with it. This does place a little bit of business logic into the stored procedure, but it sometimes may be worth it.

Creating the Data-Centric Object

In VS .NET, select the Class1 code module located in the NorthwindDC project. Rename the code module to *RegionDC.vb* and clear the code module. Add the following four Imports statement:

```
Imports NorthwindTraders.NorthwindShared.Interfaces
Imports NorthwindTraders.NorthwindShared.Structures
Imports System.Configuration
Imports System.Data.SqlClient
```

In Chapter 2, "Building an N-Tier Application," you created a reference to the NorthwindShared project, which allows you to import NorthwindTraders.NorthwindShared.Interfaces and Structures. The System.Configuration namespace reads the database connection string from the web.config file. The SqlClient namespace contains libraries used to access SQL Server.

Create the class declaration as follows:

```
Public Class RegionDC
    Inherits MarshalByRefObject

    Implements IRegion

End Class
```

TIP Microsoft made (besides other changes) one very cool change between release 1.0 and 1.1 of VS .NET. If you are using release 1.1, when you add the Implements IRegion line, all of the interfaces that are contained in IRegion will be automatically generated for you.

The first thing to notice about the RegionDC class is the MarshalByRefObject, which forms the basis for the RegionDC class. This allows the .NET Framework to create a proxy on the remote system. Without this statement, a runtime error would occur when the first remoting call is made. Next, you are implementing the IRegion interface you created earlier. When you first add this line of code, IRegion will be underlined, which denotes an error (this only applies to version 1.0 of the .NET Framework). If you have the Task List visible, you will see something that looks like Figure 3-6.

!	✓	Description	File
		Click here to add a new task	
!	⊛	'NorthwindTraders.NorthwindDC.RegionDC' must implement 'Function LoadProxy() As System.Data.DataSet' for interface 'NorthwindTraders.NorthwindSh:	C:\Documents and ...\RegionDC
!	⊛	'NorthwindTraders.NorthwindDC.RegionDC' must implement 'Function LoadRecord(intID As Integer) As NorthwindTraders.NorthwindShared.Structures.str	C:\Documents and ...\RegionDC
!	⊛	'NorthwindTraders.NorthwindDC.RegionDC' must implement 'Sub Delete(intID As Integer)' for interface 'NorthwindTraders.NorthwindShared.Interfaces.IR	C:\Documents and ...\RegionDC
!	⊛	'NorthwindTraders.NorthwindDC.RegionDC' must implement 'Sub Save(sRegion As NorthwindTraders.NorthwindShared.Structures.structRegion, ByRef int:	C:\Documents and ...\RegionDC

Figure 3-6. Interface implementation errors

Basically, it says you have not implemented the interface yet, and until you implement all of the methods, you will continue to see these errors.

> **NOTE** When you implement an interface, it is a contract that says your object implements *all* of the methods of the interface. This allows you to make the remote procedure call work.

Understanding Class Attributes

Before you can implement the interface, you need to set up the class attributes. I like to create regions for certain sections of code so that I can collapse them and get them out of the way.

> **CAUTION** When I use the term *regions*, I am talking about regions within the code, not the Region table in the Northwind database.

> **NOTE** At this point, it might be a good idea to look at the ClassGenerator application available for download from the Apress Web site (http://www.apress.com). This application makes the process of creating class attributes easier.

Create the following region and add the following attributes to the RegionDC class:

```
#Region " Private Attributes"
    Private mintRegionID As Integer
    Private mstrRegionDescription As String
#End Region
```

Next, you will create the public attributes of your class. You will create the RegionID as a read-only attribute and the RegionDescription as a read/write attribute. RegionID is set by your stored procedure in the database and should not be settable by outside objects. Create another region and the public properties, as shown in Listing 3-5.

Listing 3-5. The Public Attributes of the RegionDC Class

```
#Region " Public Attributes"
    Public ReadOnly Property RegionID() As Integer
        Get
            Return mintRegionID
        End Get
    End Property

    Public Property RegionDescription() As String
        Get
            Return mstrRegionDescription
        End Get
        Set(ByVal Value As String)
            mstrRegionDescription = Value
        End Set
    End Property
#End Region
```

Implementing the Interface

Now it is time to start implementing the IRegion interface. First you will implement the LoadProxy interface. In a class that has so few attributes, the advantage of the LoadProxy method is not apparent, but as you move into building the Employee object, it will become apparent. Enter the following code to declare the LoadProxy method (again, if you are using version 1.1, this will already be declared for you):

```
Public Function LoadProxy() As DataSet Implements IRegion.LoadProxy
End Function
```

The name of the method that implements the LoadProxy interface is not important. It is only important that the method signature is the same as the LoadProxy signature. However, for readability and as a convention, the names should be the same. Also, creating a method signature that matches the interface signature is not enough—you need to mark it as implementing the interface. To do that, you add the Implements IRegion.LoadProxy onto the end of your method signature. When you do that, there will be one less error line in the Task List.

Enter the following method stubs so that you can complete the implementation of the interface:

```
Public Function LoadRecord(ByVal intID As Integer) As structRegion Implements _
IRegion.LoadRecord
End Function

Public Sub Delete(ByVal intID As Integer) Implements IRegion.Delete
End Sub

Public Sub Save(ByVal sRegion As structRegion, ByRef intID As Integer) _
Implements IRegion.Save
End Sub
```

The LoadProxy Method

Now that you have implemented your interface methods, you will add some code to them, starting with the LoadProxy method. Add the code in Listing 3-6 to the LoadProxy method.

Listing 3-6. The LoadProxy Method

```
Dim strCN As String = ConfigurationSettings.AppSettings("Northwind_DSN")
Dim cn As New SqlConnection(strCN)
Dim cmd As New SqlCommand()
Dim da As New SqlDataAdapter(cmd)
Dim ds As New DataSet()

cn.Open()

With cmd
    .Connection = cn
    .CommandType = CommandType.StoredProcedure
    .CommandText = "usp_region_getall"
End With
```

```
da.Fill(ds)

cmd = Nothing
cn.Close()

Return ds
```

The first line of this code reads the web.config file to retrieve the database connection string. Normally, reading XML is a slow process compared to other types of file reads. However, reading the configuration file is fast because that file exists in memory when IIS starts. Everything else is a straightforward call to the database using the Command object and a data adapter to fill the dataset.

NOTE   For more information on making calls to a database, see *Database Programming with Visual Basic .NET*, Second Edition by Carsten Thomsen (Apress, 2002). This is a good solid introduction to using ADO.NET.

The LoadRecord Method

Now, you will implement the LoadRecord method. Enter the code in Listing 3-7 to the LoadRecord method of the RegionDC class.

Listing 3-7. The LoadRecord Method

```
Dim strCN As String = ConfigurationSettings.AppSettings("Northwind_DSN")
Dim cn As New SqlConnection(strCN)
Dim cmd As New SqlCommand()
Dim da As New SqlDataAdapter(cmd)
Dim ds As New DataSet()
Dim sRegion As structRegion

cn.Open()

With cmd
    .Connection = cn
    .CommandType = CommandType.StoredProcedure
    .CommandText = "usp_region_getone"
    .Parameters.Add("@id", intID)
End With
```

```
da.Fill(ds)

cmd = Nothing
cn.Close()

With ds.Tables(0).Rows(0)
    sRegion.RegionID = Convert.ToInt32(.Item("RegionID"))
    sRegion.RegionDescription = _
        Convert.ToString(.Item("RegionDescription"))
End With
ds = Nothing

Return sRegion
```

For compatibility, you convert the dataset to a structure and return the structure. Java is not able to easily read a dataset. Because you may use this call in an XML Web service later, you want to return a set of data that is easily understood by any application that can read an XML file. Although datasets are easily serialized into XML data, the XML structure can be extremely complicated. Another .NET application could read a serialized dataset easily, but an application written in another language may not be able to read it quite so easily. When you put a Web service interface on your application, you will need to return the information in a format that all languages can parse easily.

 NOTE   It is not that Java cannot understand a dataset, but for Java to use the dataset, it would have to perform extensive parsing of the SOAP envelope. Fortunately, because .NET was built with Web services in mind, .NET handles all of this transparently. Often in the enterprise, however, you need to develop with different platforms in mind.

Most of Listing 3-7 is similar to the code in the previous method except that you are now passing an ID into a stored procedure. There are six overloaded methods on the Command.Parameters.Add method, which you will explore as you create more commands that call stored procedures.

The Delete Method

Enter the code in Listing 3-8 into the Delete method of the RegionDC class.

Listing 3-8. The Delete Method

```
Dim strCN As String = ConfigurationSettings.AppSettings("Northwind_DSN")
Dim cn As New SqlConnection(strCN)
Dim cmd As New SqlCommand()

cn.Open()

With cmd
    .Connection = cn
    .CommandType = CommandType.StoredProcedure
    .CommandText = "usp_region_delete"
    .Parameters.Add("@id", intID)
    .ExecuteNonQuery()
End With

cmd = Nothing
cn.Close()
```

The only real difference in Listing 3-8 is that you actually execute the command on the Command object explicitly. In the prior blocks of code, the data adapter executed the Command object. You do not need the data adapter here because you are not retrieving data and you are not working with prepared datasets.

The Save Method

Lastly, you come to the Save method. To implement this method, add the code in Listing 3-9 to the Save method.

Listing 3-9. The Save Method

```
Dim strCN As String = ConfigurationSettings.AppSettings("Northwind_DSN")
Dim cn As New SqlConnection(strCN)
Dim cmd As New SqlCommand()

With sRegion
    Me.mintRegionID = .RegionID
    Me.RegionDescription = .RegionDescription
End With

cn.Open()
```

```
With cmd
    .Connection = cn
    .CommandType = CommandType.StoredProcedure
    .CommandText = "usp_region_save"
    .Parameters.Add("@id", mintRegionID)
    .Parameters.Add("@region", mstrRegionDescription)
    .Parameters.Add("@new_id", SqlDbType.Int).Direction = _
        ParameterDirection.Output
    .ExecuteNonQuery()
    intID = Convert.ToInt32(.Parameters.Item("@id").Value)
End With

cmd = Nothing
cn.Close()
```

This method implements a couple of new things, so let's examine different parts of this routine. First, you are taking the values from the sRegion structure and assigning them to your object's attributes. However, the RegionID value is being assigned to the private member variable, and the RegionDescription value is being assigned to the public member variable. This is because there are no business rules to check for a system-generated number. There are rules that need to be checked for the values entered by the user. You will see how this works in Chapter 5, "Building Business Objects" when you learn about business rules.

There is also a new usage of the Parameter object. The last Parameter Add method looks like the following:

```
.Parameters.Add("@new_id", SqlDbType.Int).Direction = _
    ParameterDirection.Output
```

You need to specify the parameter, but because you are not passing anything in, you do not have to specify a value. However, you do need to provide the data type of the variable you are adding. Finally, you need to set the direction equal to Output. By default, the parameter direction is Input.

Notice also how simple this routine is. The logic to determine how the save is done is in the database, so the code does not need to know how to save the object (using insert or update)—it just knows that it needs to call the Save method.

Creating the User-Centric Business Objects

Now that you have built the data-centric objects, you actually have something to call remotely. Before you add the user-centric object, though, you need a place to start putting your application constants.

The AppConstants Module

Add another class module to the NorthwindUC project and call it *AppConstants.vb*. Add the following code to the module:

```
Option Explicit On
Option Strict On

Public Class AppConstants
    Public Shared REMOTEOBJECTS As String = "http://localhost:80/Northwind/"
End Class
```

The REMOTEOBJECTS variable holds the path to your remote objects. If you are using another computer to host the remote objects, you will need to replace *localhost* with the correct computer name. Also, if for some reason your IIS server is using a port other than 80, you will need to change the port number as well. Notice that you declare it as a shared variable so that you never have to instantiate this class—you just need to reference it to get at the value of the variable.

NOTE Shared variables and methods are new to VB with the introduction of VB .NET. A *shared method* is one that can be called without instantiating the object (as with the AppConstants class you created earlier). A *shared variable* is a variable that exists across all instances of the object in which it is declared. It also does not require the class that it is declared in to be instantiated. The .NET Framework guarantees there will only ever be one instance of a shared variable or method during an application's lifetime.

Next, add the class shown in Listing 3-10 to the AppConstants module.

Listing 3-10. The ChangedEventArgs Class

```
Public Class ChangedEventArgs
    Public Enum eChange
        Added = 0
        Updated = 1
    End Enum

    Private meChange As eChange
```

```
    Public Sub New(ByVal ChangeEvent As eChange)
        meChange = ChangeEvent
    End Sub

    Public ReadOnly Property Change() As eChange
        Get
            Return meChange
        End Get
    End Property
End Class
```

You will use ChangedEventArgs for all of your objects to inform the presentation layer that a change has been made to the object and the type of change it is. This allows you to provide a generic method to respond to all of your object's events without being specific to a particular object. This is much the same way that .NET can respond to different objects using the same method—your method signatures will match from class to class. Also, this follows the .NET convention of using an object and a set of event arguments in another object as the signature for any actions that can occur on an object.

NOTE You can see an example of this by looking at the Click event of the button object. The Click event signature looks like the following: `ByVal sender As System.Object, ByVal e As System.EventArgs`. And remarkably enough, the BackColorChanged event signature of a form looks like this: `ByVal sender As System.Object, ByVal e As System.EventArgs`. They are identical, but the EventArgs contains different information. This is how your ChangedEventArgs class will operate.

The Region Class

The user-centric object is going to start as a duplicate of the data-centric object. You can copy a lot of code from one to the other.

In the NorthwindUC project, rename the Class1.vb code module to *Region.vb*. Next, add (or copy from the RegionDC.vb file) the code in Listing 3-11 into the Region code module.

Listing 3-11. The User-Centric Region Code Module

```
Option Strict On
Option Explicit On

Imports NorthwindTraders.NorthwindShared.Structures
Imports NorthwindTraders.NorthwindShared.Interfaces

Public Class Region

#Region " Private Attributes"
    Private mintRegionID As Integer = 0
    Private mstrRegionDescription As String = ""
#End Region

#Region " Public Attributes"
    Public ReadOnly Property RegionID() As Integer
        Get
            Return mintRegionID
        End Get
    End Property

    Public Property RegionDescription() As String
        Get
            Return mstrRegionDescription
        End Get
        Set(ByVal Value As String)
            mstrRegionDescription = Value
        End Set
    End Property
#End Region
End Class
```

There are a couple of changes in Listing 3-11, but they are all minor. The initialization of the private variables now reads as follows:

```
Private mintRegionID As Integer = 0
Private mstrRegionDescription As String = ""
```

This sets the mintRegionID variable to zero and the region description to an empty string when the class is instantiated.

Also, you do not need to import the sqlClient or the Configuration namespace or implement the IRegion interface. Finally, the Region class does not inherit from the MarshalByRef object because it will not be called from another application domain.

Now, add the following code to the beginning of the class:

```
Private mblnDirty As Boolean = False
Public Loading As Boolean
Private Const LISTENER As String = "RegionDC.rem"
Private msRegion As structRegion

Public Event ObjectChanged(ByVal sender As Object, _
    ByVal e As ChangedEventArgs)
```

The listener constant simply makes it easy for you to change the remote object to which you are connecting. This value will be used in several places in the class. The msRegion variable holds the original values that were returned to you from the database. This handles object state if the user presses the Cancel button after they have made changes. The ObjectChanged event will inform the presentation layer that a change has been made to your object—either that it has been added to the database or that the record has been updated. You can expand upon this later if you want.

Now add the following code at the bottom of the class:

```
Public ReadOnly Property IsDirty() As Boolean
    Get
        Return mblnDirty
    End Get
End Property
```

The IsDirty property determines whether the class has been edited. The Loading property signals the class that it is being loaded and that it should not mark itself as having been edited. You have not implemented the Loading property as a standard property; rather, it is just a public variable. You do not need to know when the value of the variable changes, so that would just add extra overhead.

Next, you need to implement the Loading property in the Region class. Edit the RegionDescription property so that it looks like the following:

```
Public Property RegionDescription() As String
    Get
        Return mstrRegionDescription
    End Get
    Set(ByVal Value As String)
        If mstrRegionDescription.trim <> Value Then
            If Not Loading Then
                mblnDirty = True
            End If
            mstrRegionDescription = Value
        End If
    End Set
End Property
```

All this code does is check to see if the new value is equal to the current value. If it is not, the code checks to see if you are loading. If you are loading, then the dirty flag will not be set; otherwise, the class will be marked as dirty.

Constructors

Now you need to create a couple of constructors for your class. Constructors are new to VB with the introduction of .NET. They allow you to pass parameters to an object at instantiation time. All objects in VB .NET have a constructor with them by default even if they are not visible in code.

The default constructor is a Sub New method with no code. It is not displayed in the class because it is assumed. If you create a constructor that takes arguments, the default constructor will no longer exist. If you need to have the default constructor after you have added a constructor that takes arguments, you must add the constructor with no arguments and no code.

NOTE If you do add a constructor with no arguments after you have added a constructor that takes arguments, you must be aware that a developer can instantiate your class and bypass any arguments you might be expecting.

Typically, you will not need to create your own constructor unless you have some specific setup that needs to occur when your class is instantiated. Here, you need to create a constructor because of the RegionID property. The property is read-only because you do not want it to be set by any outside calls once you have instantiated the object. So, by including it as a parameter to the constructor, you can set it, and it will not be changeable after that point.

You need to create two versions of your constructor. To do this, enter the following code in the Region class:

```
Public Sub New()
    'No code necessary right now
End Sub

Public Sub New(ByVal intID As Integer)
    mintRegionID = intID
End Sub
```

The first constructor, which takes no arguments, is the default constructor. You need this constructor so that your interface can create a new instance of this object to be able to add a new Region. You need the second constructor so that your RegionMgr class (which you will create next) can load Region objects that contain their Region IDs.

In VB .NET, constructors always have the name *New*—no matter what class the constructor is a part of.

NOTE   C# and other languages use the convention that the constructor has the same name as the class.

Overriding the ToString Method

You need to take care of one more basic method: the ToString method. The ToString method is a member of the Object class. If it is not overridden, it returns the fully qualified type of the object. You will override it for the purpose of filling a combo box. This might sound a little strange, but .NET's method of filling list and combo boxes is slightly different (OK, it is radically different) from VB 6. Add the method as follows:

```
Public Overrides Function ToString() As String
    Return mstrRegionDescription
End Function
```

This method is straightforward; it simply returns a string—any string you want it to return. When you add an object to a list control (most list controls), it will display the value returned by the ToString method. You will see exactly how this works when you start adding objects to list and combo boxes.

The LoadRecord Method

It is time to add the main methods that your class will implement. The methods you need to add are the Load, Delete, and Save methods because a class should be self-contained, or *encapsulated*. Although your Region manager will be able to load all of the objects contained within it, as you will see, when you get to larger objects it will not be able to load the entire object. It will only be able to load what is needed for a list or combo box. So, in this case, the Load method is not as important (although you will see that it does still play a part in helping the object maintain a consistent state).

Add the code in Listing 3-12 to the Region class.

Listing 3-12. The LoadRecord Method of the Region Class

```
Public Sub LoadRecord()
    Dim objIRegion As IRegion

    objIRegion = CType(Activator.GetObject(GetType(IRegion), _
AppConstants.REMOTEOBJECTS & LISTENER), IRegion)
    msRegion = objIRegion.LoadRecord(mintRegionID)
    objIRegion = Nothing

    LoadObject()
End Sub

Private Sub LoadObject()
    With msRegion
        Me.mintRegionID = .RegionID
        Me.mstrRegionDescription = .RegionDescription
    End With
End Sub
```

You start by declaring a variable of type IRegion. The most important line of Listing 3-12 is the Activator.GetObject line, which retrieves your reference to the remote object. Without it, there is no remote communication. (How this works and what it does exactly are topics for a complete book, so I will not go into it here. However, I recommend further reading about it if you use this method to communicate remotely.)

The first thing you pass to this call is the type of object you are going to be getting—in this case, an object that implements the IRegion interface. Next, you pass it the objectUri, which is simply the Uniform Resource Locator (URL) to your object and is contained in the REMOTEOBJECTS shared variable. When using Option Strict, you must convert the entire return value to the correct object type by using the CType statement. At this point you are able to make calls on the methods of the interface. Even if your remote object had other public methods (if you will remember, there are a couple of public properties that exist for the RegionDC class), you would not be able to call them because they were not implemented as part of the interface and you have not actually obtained a reference to your object. What you have done is obtained a reference to an object that you know nothing about except that it implements a specific interface that you know all about! That is why you are limited to making calls on the interface implementation only.

Finally, you load up the object from the structure that is returned. Note that the structure is a module-level variable, and you leave the values in it after you are done with it. You will see why in a little bit.

The Delete Method

Next, add the following code for the Delete method:

```
Public Sub Delete()
    Dim objIRegion As IRegion

    objIRegion = CType(Activator.GetObject(GetType(IRegion), _
 AppConstants.REMOTEOBJECTS & LISTENER), IRegion)
    objIRegion.Delete(mintRegionID)
    objIRegion = Nothing
End Sub
```

As with the previous method, this method just gets a reference to the remote object and makes a method call on the interface. You are not passing in the ID of the record to delete. The object is acting on itself and needs no outside intervention. This is another example of the encapsulation that you are trying to achieve.

The Save Method

This method is a little more involved (and this method will always be more involved than every other method in an object in a business application). Add the code shown in Listing 3-13 to the Region class.

Listing 3-13. The Save Method

```
Public Sub Save()
      'Only save the object if it has been edited
      If mblnDirty = True Then
           Dim objIRegion As IRegion
           Dim intID As Integer
           Dim sRegion As structRegion

           'Store the original ID of the object
           intID = mintRegionID

           'Assign the values of the object to a structure of
           'type structRegion
           With sRegion
                .RegionID = mintRegionID
                .RegionDescription = mstrRegionDescription
           End With

          'Obtain a reference to the remote object
          objIRegion = CType(Activator.GetObject(GetType(IRegion), _
          AppConstants.REMOTEOBJECTS & LISTENER), IRegion)

           'Save the object
           objIRegion.Save(sRegion, mintRegionID)
           objIRegion = Nothing

          'Check the original ID and see if it was a new object
          If intID = 0 Then
                'If it was, raise the event as an added
                RaiseEvent ObjectChanged(Me, New _
                ChangedEventArgs(ChangedEventArgs.eChange.Added))
          Else
                'If it was not, raise the event as an update
                RaiseEvent ObjectChanged(Me, New _
                ChangedEventArgs(ChangedEventArgs.eChange.Updated))
          End If
          'The object is no longer dirty
          mblnDirty = False
      End If
End Sub
```

Because this code is fully commented, let's only touch on one piece of code:

```
intID = mintRegionID
```

The comment with this line of code says, "Store the original ID of the object." But why? When you instantiate the object, if you call the default constructor, mintRegionID is zero. This tells the object that it is new and has not come from the database. So, if it is new, once you call the Save method of the interface, the value of mintRegionID will change. The Save method of the IRegion interface takes an ID ByRef. This means that the value will change automatically. So, after the Save method has been called, you have no way to determine if the object is new. Storing the state before the call allows you to determine this.

Finally, you raise the appropriate event to the calling code (in this case, the user interface) to tell the code that a change has been made. This may not make sense at this point because you are initiating the call in the user interface so you know if it is new, right? Well, it turns out that the form that makes this call is not the form that receives this event. This is an easy way for you to pass information between forms but let the objects handle the details.

NOTE It is good object-oriented practice to make sure an object is as self-aware as possible and can communicate information about itself. That means it has the ability to inform other objects when its state changes. In some cases (as you will see in the next chapter), you need helper classes to accomplish this.

Later on, you will be adding additional events to the class that will make your object more robust.

Creating Collection Classes

You will need to create one final class before you move on to the user interface: the RegionMgr class. The RegionMgr class manages a collection of your Region objects. Collection classes have changed significantly between VB 6 and VB .NET. It is still possible to use the collection object that was provided with VB 6 in the same manner under .NET. However, the .NET Framework also comes with some great collection classes from which you can inherit. These classes are more efficient in handling collections because they are built with specific purposes in mind. The two collection classes that you will probably use most often will be the CollectionBase and DictionaryBase classes. Each of these classes is for a specific purpose, and both have advantages and disadvantages. These collection classes (as well as others) are in the System.Collections namespace.

The CollectionBase Class

The CollectionBase class stores values that can be retrieved by index only. This class handles moving through a collection using a For..Next loop and is extremely efficient. However, you cannot use a key to find the item you want. It does, however, already implement an enumerator, so you can use a For..Each..Next loop to retrieve all the values without having to code it. Listing 3-14 contains an example of an object that inherits from the CollectionBase class.

Listing 3-14. A CollectionBase Example

```
Public Class CollectionTest
    Inherits System.Collections.CollectionBase

    Public Sub Add(ByVal obj As SomeObject)
        list.Add(obj)
    End Sub

    Public Function Item(ByVal Index As Integer) As SomeObject
        Return CType(list.Item(Index), SomeObject)
    End Function

    Public Sub Remove(ByVal Index As Integer)
        list.RemoveAt(Index)
    End Sub
End Class
```

As you can see from this example, the object itself is simple. The list object is a protected object that is internal to the CollectionBase. It is roughly analogous to the collection object in VB 6. The Add, Item, and Remove methods are the only methods you need to implement in your code (and technically you do not need to implement the Remove method). You need to implement the Add method because the base class does not know what type of object you are going to add. You need the Item method because the base class does not know what type of item it is returning. You need the Remove method because there are two ways to remove an item from the CollectionBase—Remove and RemoveAt. Also, each one is handled slightly differently. So, if you do not implement a Remove method, the only publicly available method to remove an object is the RemoveAt method.

The CollectionBase class has one major advantage to the other collection classes: It implements the IList interface. This may seem like a small thing, but you can bind any class that implements the IList interface to list boxes and combo boxes. Instead of looping through the entire collection, all you have to do is write the following lines of code:

```
ComboBox1.DataSource = objMgr
ComboBox1.DisplayMember = "FirstName"
```

All you have to do is assign the object to the DataSource. If the object overrides the ToString method, the combo box will be filled with whatever value is returned. If the ToString method is not overridden (of even if it is and you want to specify another property), simply assign the property you want to display to the DisplayMember property of the list control as you did in the second line of Listing 3-14.

The DictionaryBase Class

The DictionaryBase class provides a dictionary object. It is almost identical to the Scripting.Dictionary object in VBScript—with a couple of great improvements. The scripting object in VBScript was a key/value collection that could only contain simple data types. The .NET version of the DictionaryBase also holds a key/value pair, but the key can be anything and the value can be any type of object. In the typical VB 6 collection, if you tried to add a key that was numerical, you received an error unless you appended a string onto the end of the key, typically a *K*. With the DictionaryBase, the key can be numerical or character based; it is your choice. However, you cannot use the For..Next loop to return all of the values. You must use the For..Each..Next loop to retrieve these values. Unfortunately, the collection does not return the object that the collection holds. It returns a DictionaryEntry object, which adds a little overhead to the process, but not much. You will see an example of this as you start coding your forms.

CAUTION None of the collections guarantee that enumerating through the collection will return the items in the order you placed them into the collection. This may affect how you retrieve the information from a collection.

The DictionaryBase offers an extremely efficient means of retrieving an object based on the key that is passed to it. Because you are going to be using keys on all of your tables, you will be implementing the DictionaryBase class in your collection classes.

NOTE   If you need to implement a collection that can be searched by index or by key (which you cannot do with the DictionaryBase class), I recommend using the Collection object and implementing it as you would in VB 6. However, this is not nearly as efficient as .NET's built-in collection classes, and it does not implement the IList interface.

The RegionMgr Class

Now that you have a little background on collection classes, it is time to implement your RegionMgr collection class. In the same code module as the Region class, add the code in Listing 3-15 (add this outside of the Region class or you will get a syntax error).

Listing 3-15. The RegionMgr Collection Class

```
Public Class RegionMgr
    Inherits System.Collections.DictionaryBase

    Public Sub Add(ByVal obj As Region)
        dictionary.Add(obj.RegionID, obj)
    End Sub

    Public Function Item(ByVal Key As Object) As Region
        Return CType(dictionary.Item(Key), Region)
    End Function

    Public Sub Remove(ByVal Key As Object)
        dictionary.Remove(Key)
    End Sub
End Class
```

This code is almost identical to the CollectionBase class that I showed you in Listing 3-14, except that the DictionaryBase exposes a dictionary object to any inheriting classes. Also, as mentioned earlier, you are using a key to retrieve the objects and setting a key in the Add method.

> **NOTE** A common mistake is to set the object and key in the same order as in VB 6. This is the reverse of what it was in VB 6. Now, you pass in the key first and then the object that is being added to the collection. Hence, the term *key/value pair.*

Now you need to add a method to load your collection of Region objects. Add the code in Listing 3-16 to the RegionMgr class.

Listing 3-16. The Load Method of the RegionMgr Class

```
Private Sub Load()
    Dim objIRegion As IRegion
    Dim dRow As DataRow
    Dim ds As DataSet

    objIRegion = CType(Activator.GetObject(GetType(IRegion), _
    AppConstants.REMOTEOBJECTS & "RegionDC.rem"), IRegion)
    ds = objIRegion.LoadProxy()
    objIRegion = Nothing

    For Each dRow In ds.Tables(0).Rows
        Dim objRegion As New Region(Convert.ToInt32(dRow.Item("RegionID")))
        With objRegion
            .Loading = True
            .RegionDescription = _
                Convert.ToString(dRow.Item("RegionDescription")).Trim
            .Loading = False
        End With
        Me.Add(objRegion)
    Next

    ds = Nothing
End Sub
```

This code simply retrieves the dataset from the remote object, loops through it, and adds it to the collection. Notice that this method is private because if someone is going to instantiate this object, they are going to do it for the purpose of loading it. So why have them make two calls? Notice that you have not implemented a constructor yet; you will do this in the "Implementing the Singleton Pattern" section.

The next small block of code refreshes the collection from the database. At this point you might ask, "Why don't I just make the load method public and then I don't need a refresh routine?" This is a matter of convention. You do not want developers who are writing the interface to have to call the load routine to refresh the object. That could cause more problems than it would solve with developers calling the load routine right after instantiating the object. However, it is just a matter of personal preference. Add the refresh routine as follows:

```
Public Sub Refresh()
    dictionary.Clear()
    Load()
End Sub
```

The dictionary.Clear method is a method that is internal to the dictionary object that clears all of the objects contained within it.

Understanding Design Patterns

Design patterns are relatively new to VB developers because their full potential could not be explored in VB 6. Most design patterns really do require a full object-oriented language as opposed to an object-based language. Some design patterns could be implemented in VB 6, but it was often more trouble than it was worth. Volumes of material have been written about patterns and anti-patterns, and this book does not go into them.

 NOTE An excellent introduction and reference on the subject is *Design Patterns: Elements of Reusable Object-Oriented Software* Erich Gamma, Richard Helm, Ralph Johnson, and John Vlissides (Addison-Wesley, 1995). I recommended this book earlier to learn about objects, but it also discusses objects in terms of how to use them in design patterns.

A design pattern is a way of seeing how something works in a generic sense and being able to develop a framework for solving the problem. A popular example of a pattern—and one you are using all the time even though you might not realize it—is called the *Observer/Observed pattern*. This pattern says that one object can observe another object and that the object being observed can tell things about itself to the observer. Where do you think this pattern might be in use? Whenever a control raises an event to a form, the Observer pattern is in use. This is because the form observes the control, and the control tells the form about itself.

I am going to introduce my favorite pattern and perhaps the most useful pattern I have ever used—the Singleton pattern. You will recall from Chapter 2, "Building an N-Tier Application," that you set your remote objects to the Singleton mode as opposed to the SingleCall mode. In doing this, I said that there would only ever be one instance of the object created. That is exactly what the Singleton pattern offers you—and the implementation is simple. For the purposes of this application (and most applications I have worked on), you do not want more than one Region collection in memory at one time. After all, what do you gain by having multiple Region collections in memory except used memory? You may find the need to have multiple collections of certain objects in memory, such as a collection of order details because you may have multiple orders open at any given time. In a case such as that, the Singleton pattern would be more harmful than helpful. Using this pattern needs a lot of careful thought. It gives you a great deal in that you only ever have to go to the database once (unless you want to refresh the collection), but it does take some thought beforehand.

So, how does the Singleton pattern work? The principle is that the object instantiates itself and there is only ever one object during the course of application execution. It requires that there be no publicly available constructor that can be called.

Implementing the Singleton Pattern

To implement the Singleton pattern, add the code in Listing 3-17 to the RegionMgr class after the Inherits statement.

Listing 3-17. The RegionMgr Implementation of the Singleton Pattern

```
Private Shared mobjRegionMgr As RegionMgr

Public Shared Function GetInstance() As RegionMgr
    If mobjRegionMgr Is Nothing Then
        mobjRegionMgr = New RegionMgr()
    End If
    Return mobjRegionMgr
End Function

Protected Sub New()
    Load()
End Sub
```

Here you have done a number of things to make this work correctly. The first thing you did was declare an object of type RegionMgr as a shared module-level variable. This means that only one instance of this object will ever exist. By declaring it as private, you only allow access to it through the GetInstance method. Because the GetInstance method is shared, you do not have to do the following to instantiate the class:

```
Public Sub GetRegionMgr()
    Dim objRegionMgr As New RegionMgr()
End Sub
```

And, in fact, doing so will give you a syntax error because the constructor is now protected. It is only available to your object or any objects that inherit from your object.

The GetInstance method takes care of instantiating a new object if one does not already exist. And it always returns the reference to mobjRegionMgr regardless of whether it has to instantiate the object. The constructor takes care of calling the Load method when the object is first instantiated.

NOTE This causes a slight delay when getting a reference to this object the first time, but it saves having this delay every time you need a list of Regions. The delay only happens once here (and optionally at other times if you call the Refresh method).

The following example shows how you will get a reference to the RegionMgr object if you need it:

```
Public Sub GetRegionMgr()
    Dim objRegionMgr As RegionMgr
    objRegionMgr = objRegionMgr.GetInstance
End Sub
```

You now have a reference to the RegionMgr object, but you never once had to call the constructor.

NOTE One area this can help in is having the object registered with various other objects that can all respond to the events generated by the Singleton object. Although this might not be considered a best practice, it does save the interface developer from having to pass objects all over the place because the object that implements the Singleton pattern acts as a global object now.

Whew! You are now done with your business objects for the moment, and it is time to create the user interface and test your creation.

Creating the User Interface

Creating the user interface is generally the most time-consuming process when developing an application. First, you have to prototype the interface, then you have to build it, then you have to go back and rework it, and so on and so on. I introduce a few methods in this section to help you avoid (or at least lessen) the work necessary when building the user interface. At the beginning, though, there is slightly more work needed.

Two things every business application, regardless of the content of the application, needs to do are as follows: show lists of data and show data details for viewing and editing. Every developer has their own method of creating list screens and editing forms. This is great in that a developer can express their creativity, but the users tend to have a problem with it. They expect that if they are going to view one list, then every other list they view in the same application will have the same controls on the screen and will behave and look the same way. Consistency makes everyone happier and results in fewer calls to the help desk and fewer complaints by the user. No developer can probably honestly say they have not heard a user complain, "Why doesn't it work like this?" So, the key is consistency, and with consistency comes a lot less work on the part of the interface developer. To this end you will create two base forms, one for showing lists of information, the other for editing that information. All of the forms that you create afterward will inherit from one form or the other.

To being with, let's create the Multiple Document Interface (MDI) form that will serve as your framework.

 NOTE There has been a move in recent years to create Single Document Interface (SDI) applications. It is been my experience while developing for the enterprise that many users like to compare different things side by side and like to have multiple windows open. I see no need to move away from this paradigm as long as it is what my users want to see. After all, without users there can be no developers.

Double-click the Form1.vb class module in NorthwindTraders in the Solution Explorer. This brings up Form1 in the editor. Rename Form1.vb to *frmMain.vb*. Then, go to the Properties tab and change the IsMdiContainer to *True*. Change the

WindowState property to *Maximized*, and change the name property of the form to *frmMain*. If you have the Task List visible, the following error will display:

```
'Sub Main' was not found in 'NorthwindTraders.UserInterface.Form1'.
```

To correct this error, double-click this entry in the Task List and select NorthwindTraders.frmMain from the Startup Object dialog box that appears and click OK. That removes the error.

Next, you add a test menu to your MDI container so that you can launch your forms from it for testing purposes. Add a MainMenu control to the form and add a single menu item called *Test*. The menu should look like the menu in Figure 3-7.

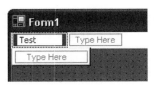

Figure 3-7. frmMain MainMenu Test MenuItem

Creating the ListBase Form

You can now start adding your base forms. As with VB 6, the best way to show lists of information is still with the listview control. In .NET, the listview control has been vastly improved so that you can format individual items and subitems independently of any other items on the row. This is an awesome capability that many of you who used VB 6 fought to try and make happen with custom controls and fancy Application Programming Interface (API) tricks that never worked very well. Add a new form to the NorthwindTraders project and call it *frmListBase*. To do this, right-click the NorthwindTraders project and select Add ➤ Add Windows Form and name it *frmListBase.vb*. When you are done adding controls to the form, it should look like the form in Figure 3-8.

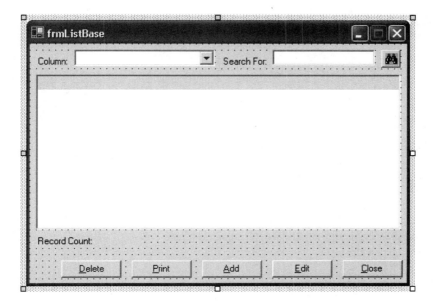

Figure 3-8. The completed frmListBase

Add the controls to the form as listed in Table 3-1.

Table 3-1. The ListBase Form Controls and Properties

Control	Control Name	Control Text
Label		Column:
Combobox	cboColumn	[Empty]
Label		Search For:
Textbox	txtSearch	[Empty]
Button*	btnFind	
Listview	lvwList	
Button	btnDelete	&Delete
Button	btnPrint	&Print
Button	btnAdd	&Add
Button	btnEdit	&Edit
Button	btnClose	&Close

Table 3-1. The ListBase Form Controls and Properties (Continued)

Control	Control Name	Control Text
ContextMenu	ctmListBase	N/A
ContextMenu	ctmEdit	&Edit
ContextMenu	ctmDelete	&Delete
Label	lblRecordCount	Record Count:

* You can find a binoculars image in the Visual Studio .NET folder
  \Common7\Graphics\Bitmaps\ Tlbr_W95 folder.

Next, set the properties for the different controls according to Table 3-2.

Table 3-2. Additional Control Properties

Control	Property	Value
lvwList	ContextMenu	ctmListBase
lvwList	FullRowSelect	True
lvwList	MultiSelect	False
lvwList	View	Details
cboColumn	DropDownStyle	DropDownList
frmListBase	MaximizeBox	False
txtSearch	Anchor	Top, Left, Right
btnFind	Anchor	Top, Right
lvwList	Anchor	Top, Left, Bottom, Right
lblRecordCount	Anchor	Left, Bottom
btnDelete	Anchor	Bottom, Right
btnPrint	Anchor	Bottom, Right
btnAdd	Anchor	Bottom, Right
btnEdit	Anchor	Bottom, Right
btnClose	Anchor	Bottom, Right

CAUTION   Although the users may want to have the ability to maximize a form, remember that in an MDI application, when one form is maximized, all of the forms are maximized. This has the undesirable effect of maximizing the edit screen even when you do not want it to be maximized.

Now, return to frmMain, double-click the test menu item to get to the code module, and add the following code above the Windows Forms Designer–generated code:

```
Private mfrmListBase As frmListBase
```

Then enter the following code in the MenuItem1_Click method:

```
mfrmListBase = New frmListBase()
mfrmListBase.MdiParent = Me
mfrmListBase.Show()
```

In .NET, you must use code to set a form as an MDI child, as you can see here. Also, remember that unlike VB 6, forms are now true objects. If you declare a form in a method and run it, when the method execution ends, so does your object's lifetime. In practical terms this means that unless you are displaying a form using the ShowDialog() method, you will need to declare it as a module-level variable.

You should now be able to run the application and click the Test menu item, which should cause your base list form to display. The controls on the form should remain in the correct position and move as the form is resized. In the next section, you will inherit from your base form so that you can actually load some data. Then you will come back and make some more changes to your base form.

Inheriting the ListBase Form

In the NorthwindTraders project, right-click the project and select Add ➤ Inherited Form. Call the form *frmRegionList* and click the Open button. An inheritance window will display, as shown in Figure 3-9.

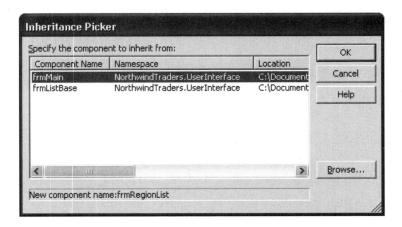

Figure 3-9. Inheritance Picker window

Double-click the frmListBase from the list of available forms. The new form will be displayed in the VS .NET IDE, as shown in Figure 3-10.

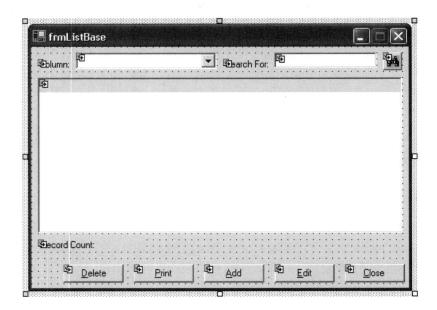

Figure 3-10. frmRegionList form, inherited from the frmListBase form

Notice that all of the controls on the form now have a little blue arrow in the top-left corner. This denotes that these controls have been inherited.

CAUTION When using inherited forms in the same application as the form you are inheriting from, the form you are inheriting from must be compiled before a subclassed form can be rendered. You may have to build the application before the subclassed form is displayed. Also, if you have a problem with your code in the base form, you will have numerous errors when you try to display your subclassed form in the design environment.

Change the form caption to read *Region List*. Next, add the following three lines to the top of the frmRegionList code module:

```
Option Explicit On
Option Strict On

Imports NorthwindTraders.NorthwindUC
```

Also, take note that the inherits line does not read *System.Windows.Forms.Form*. Instead, it now reads *NorthwindTraders.frmListBase*.

TIP You do not have to add an inherited form using the Add ➤ Inherited Window menu item. You can simply add a Windows form and change the class from which the form inherits.

The RegionList Form

Add the following module-level reference to the frmRegionList class:

```
Private mobjRegionMgr As RegionMgr
```

Create a new method called *LoadList* by adding the code in Listing 3-18.

Listing 3-18. The LoadList Method

```
Private Sub LoadList()
    Dim objRegion As Region
    Dim objDictEnt As DictionaryEntry

    lvwList.BeginUpdate()
```

```
        If lvwList.Columns.Count = 0 Then
            With lvwList
                .Columns.Add("Region Description", CInt(.Size.Width / 1) - 8, _
    HorizontalAlignment.Left)
            End With
        End If

        lvwList.Items.Clear()

        mobjRegionMgr = mobjRegionMgr.GetInstance

        For Each objDictEnt In mobjRegionMgr
            objRegion = CType(objDictEnt.Value, Region)
            Dim lst As New ListViewItem(objRegion.ToString)
            lst.Tag = objRegion.RegionID
            lvwList.Items.Add(lst)
        Next

        lvwList.EndUpdate()
        lblRecordCount.Text = "Record Count: " & lvwList.Items.Count
    End Sub
```

There are many things going on here, so let's start at the top. First you create a variable for a Region object and another variable for a DictionaryEntry object. As mentioned, the For..Each..Next loop used to loop through the RegionMgr class actually returns a DictionaryEntry object. The BeginUpdate method of the listview pauses the redrawing of the listview as you are adding objects to it. Next, you set up the listview by adding the correct number of columns and sizing them. Then you clear the listview and call the GetInstance method of RegionMgr object, which returns a reference to a fully loaded RegionMgr object. Next, you loop through the RegionMgr collection and add the text that you need to a listviewitem object. Notice that the first line of the For..Each..Next loop reads as follows:

```
objRegion = CType(objDictEnt.Value, Region)
```

To actually get the contents of the DictionaryEntry object, you need to access the value property and convert this to the object of the correct type. You store the ID for the Region object in the tag property of the listview item because it is easy to retrieve. Finally, you add the listviewitem to the listview, and after you are done adding all of your Region objects, you call the EndUpdate method of the listview, which allows the listview to redraw itself.

Lastly, you will call the LoadList method from the frmRegionList form constructor (this will be the last line of the constructor). To do this, expand the

Windows Forms Designer–generated code region of the frmRegionList code
module and change the Public Sub New constructor to look like the following:

```
Public Sub New()
    MyBase.New()

    'This call is required by the Windows Form Designer.
    InitializeComponent()

    'Add any initialization after the InitializeComponent() call
    LoadList()
End Sub
```

The reason why you are calling this from the constructor and not from the
form load event is because you need to have the listview filled before you call the
Load method of the base form. This will be explained when you implement the
ability to search through the listview for a specific item (in the "Implementing the
Find Functionality" section).

The final change you need to make before you test your region object is to
change the reference in frmMain to point to your frmRegionList form instead of
the frmListBase form. Change the code to read as follows:

```
Private mfrmRegionList As frmRegionList

Private Sub MenuItem1_Click(ByVal sender As System.Object, _
ByVal e As System.EventArgs) Handles MenuItem1.Click
    Cursor = Cursors.WaitCursor
    mfrmRegionList = New frmRegionList()
    mfrmRegionList.MdiParent = Me
    mfrmRegionList.Show()
    Cursor = Cursors.Default
End Sub
```

Creating the Remoting Channel

You need to add one last bit of code to make this work. You need to create the
channel to communicate with your remote objects. To do this, import the following
two namespaces into frmMain:

```
Imports System.Runtime.Remoting.Channels
Imports System.Runtime.Remoting.Channels.Http
```

These two namespaces contain the classes that facilitate the communication over a remoting channel. Add this module-level variable declaration to frmMain:

```
Private chan As HttpChannel
```

This is the actual channel that you will register with the ChannelServices object. Open the Windows Forms Designer–generated code region and locate the constructor. Then add the following code:

```
'Add any initialization after the InitializeComponent() call
Dim props As New Collections.Specialized.ListDictionary()
props.Add("useDefaultCredentials", True)
chan = New HttpChannel(props, New BinaryClientFormatterSinkProvider(), New _
BinaryServerFormatterSinkProvider())
ChannelServices.RegisterChannel(chan)
```

This code does a couple of things. First it creates a ListDictionary object to which you can add properties recognized by the HttpChannel. The only property you are interested in here is the useDefaultCredentials property, which you set to *True*. This allows your Windows identity to be passed over the network to IIS in such a manner that IIS can impersonate your identity. Next, you declare the new channel, pass in your property dictionary, and specify that you want to serialize the data using a binary formatter. The last step to make this work is to register the channel with the ChannelServices object.

Finally, you need a way to unregister the channel when the user exits the application. To do this, enter the following code that will run when the application closes:

```
Private Sub frmMain_Closed(ByVal sender As Object, _
ByVal e As System.EventArgs) Handles MyBase.Closed
    ChannelServices.UnregisterChannel(chan)
End Sub
```

Building and Deploying the Application

The final step you need to take is to actually build the assemblies. Select Build ➤ Build Solution from the main menu. You should see the following in the Output window at the bottom of the IDE:

```
--------------------- Done ---------------------
    Build: 4 succeeded, 0 failed, 0 skipped
```

At this point you need to go to the bin directory located under the NorthwindDC project folder and copy the NorthwindDC.dll and NorthwindShared.dll files to the c:\inetpub\wwwroot\Northwind\bin folder (or wherever you set this up in Chapter 2, "Building an N-Tier Application"). You should now be able to run the application by clicking the Run button (or F5 depending on the developer template you selected).

Click the Test menu item on the main menu. The window that appears should look identical to the window in Figure 3-11.

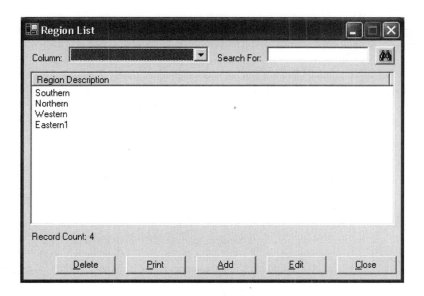

Figure 3-11. The Region List from the Northwind database

Now that you have this working, it is time to start making some enhancements.

Adding Some Basic Functionality

What would you expect to find on a form like this? You probably want the column drop-down to contain a list of columns and the find functionality to work. You might also like to have a list that can be sorted by clicking the column header. Because the Print button is going to be on all of these list forms, maybe you can find a way to have it print the contents of the list, regardless of what is contained in it. You will add all of these touches in the following sections to finish your coding of the base form.

Implementing the Find Functionality

To implement the find functionality, go into the frmListBase form and add the following code:

```
Private Sub frmListBase_Load(ByVal sender As Object, _
ByVal e As System.EventArgs) Handles MyBase.Load
    Dim i As Integer

    For i = 0 To lvwList.Columns.Count - 1
        cboColumn.Items.Add(lvwList.Columns(i).Text)
    Next
    If cboColumn.Items.Count > 0 Then
        cboColumn.SelectedIndex = 0
    End If
End Sub
```

This code cycles through the columns in the listview and adds the column header text to the cboColumn drop-down list. Because the LoadList method is called during the execution of the constructor in the subclassed form, the listview is completely set up and filled by the time the Load method of the base class is called.

The actual code to perform the search is simplistic. If you wanted to make this more powerful, you could enhance it by using regular expressions, which provide a great deal of power.

NOTE The .NET Framework has an extremely powerful regular expression engine. The System.Text.RegularExpressions namespaces contain all of the classes that you can use to handle regular expressions. Regular expressions allow for pattern matches as well as other good features. A great e-book that explains regular expressions is *Regular Expressions with .NET* by Daniel Appleman, which is available from http://www.desaware.com.

To implement the find functionality, which will be specific to the column that the user selects, you simply have to do the following:

- Get the index number of the column the user wants to search

- Check the specific subitem property that corresponds to the index of the column

- Make the search case insensitive by converting everything to uppercase

- Selecting the item

- Making sure the item is visible

The code to actually do this is quite simple. Enter code in Listing 3-19 into the frmListBase form.

Listing 3-19. The Find Method

```
Private Sub btnFind_Click(ByVal sender As System.Object, _
ByVal e As System.EventArgs) Handles btnFind.Click
    Dim i As Integer
    Dim lst As ListViewItem

    i = cboColumn.SelectedIndex

    For Each lst In lvwList.Items
        If _
lst.SubItems(i).Text.ToUpper.StartsWith(txtSearch.Text.ToUpper) Then
            lst.Selected = True
            lst.EnsureVisible()
            Exit For
        End If
    Next

    lvwList.Focus()
End Sub
```

Now, every form you create that displays lists of items can be searched by column. You can also extend this functionality to include filtering capabilities.

Adding Sorting Functionality to the ListView

Sorting a listview in .NET is not the same as it is in VB 6. In VB 6 the capability was built in to the listview. All you had to do was to make sure it was sorted in the right order based on the column clicked. In .NET, you have to provide your own sorting capability. This process involves creating a class that implements the IComparer interface. You will see how to implement the code in this section.

Add a new code module to the NorthwindTraders project and call it *UIutilities*. You will use this class as a repository for code that can be helpful in multiple locations.

By placing your column sorting routine here, you can use this routine for any listview in your entire application. After you have added this module, delete the template declaration and enter the code in Listing 3-20 for your comparer class.

Listing 3-20. The ListViewColumnSorter Class

```
Public Class ListViewColumnSorter
    Implements System.Collections.IComparer

    Private mintSortCol As Integer = 0
    Private mobjOrder As SortOrder = SortOrder.None
    Private mobjCompare As CaseInsensitiveComparer

    Public Sub New()
        mobjCompare = New CaseInsensitiveComparer()
    End Sub

    Public Function Compare(ByVal x As Object, ByVal y As Object) As Integer _
    Implements _
    IComparer.Compare
        Dim intResult As Integer
        Dim lvwItem1 As ListViewItem
        Dim lvwItem2 As ListViewItem

        lvwItem1 = CType(x, ListViewItem)
        lvwItem2 = CType(y, ListViewItem)

        intResult = mobjCompare.Compare(lvwItem1.SubItems(mintSortCol).Text, _
        lvwItem2.SubItems(mintSortCol).Text)

        If (mobjOrder = SortOrder.Ascending) Then
            Return intResult
        Else
            If (mobjOrder = SortOrder.Descending) Then
                Return (-intResult)
            Else
                Return 0
            End If
        End If
    End Function
```

```
    Public Property SortColumn() As Integer
        Get
            Return mintSortCol
        End Get
        Set(ByVal Value As Integer)
            mintSortCol = Value
        End Set
    End Property

    Public Property Order() As SortOrder
        Get
            Return mobjOrder
        End Get
        Set(ByVal Value As SortOrder)
            mobjOrder = Value
        End Set
    End Property
End Class
```

In this code, the Compare function does all the work. It takes two values (which are listview items in this case), compares them (ignoring case), and returns a value indicating if the first value was equal to, larger, or smaller than the second value. It then returns this comparison value. The rest of the class is designed so that you know how to return the comparison result.

The SortColumn property is just a convenient way for you to store the last selected column so that you know whether to sort the column ascending or descending when it has been clicked.

Next, go back to the frmListBase form and add the following module-level declaration:

```
Private lvwColumnSorter As ListViewColumnSorter
```

Next, add the following to lines to the frmListBase constructor (below the InitializeComponent call):

```
lvwColumnSorter = New ListViewColumnSorter()
Me.lvwList.ListViewItemSorter = lvwColumnSorter
```

NOTE Any code you add to a form constructor should always be added at the end of the constructor. Anytime a call to the base class new method is made (via the MyBase.New call), it *must* be the first call of the constructor or else you will receive a syntax error. The InitializeComponent call actually sets up all of the controls on the form, so it defeats the purpose to try to run any of your own code before the form's controls actually exist.

Add the code in Listing 3-21 to the frmListBase form. This handles the ColumnClick method of the listview.

Listing 3-21. The ColumnClick Method

```
Private Sub lvwList_ColumnClick(ByVal sender As Object, _
ByVal e As System.Windows.Forms.ColumnClickEventArgs) _
Handles lvwList.ColumnClick
    If (e.Column = lvwColumnSorter.SortColumn) Then
        If (lvwColumnSorter.Order = SortOrder.Ascending) Then
            lvwColumnSorter.Order = SortOrder.Descending
        Else
            lvwColumnSorter.Order = SortOrder.Ascending
        End If
    Else
        lvwColumnSorter.SortColumn = e.Column
        lvwColumnSorter.Order = SortOrder.Ascending
    End If

    Me.lvwList.Sort()
End Sub
```

This code is almost identical to what you would find in VB 6 to control the direction of the sort. You check to see if the column the user clicked has already been sorted. If it has been sorted, you check to see if it has been sorted as ascending or descending. Whatever it is, you reverse the sort order. If the column has not been sorted, you sort it in ascending order. The Sort method actually instructs the listview to sort itself.

Every form that inherits from the base list form now has a sortable listview.

Implementing the Print Functionality

In this section you will implement some basic printing functionality. It does not use Crystal Reports (the reporting tool that comes with VS). It is a generic routine to print the contents of the listview. The reason for it is that it is dynamic and does not have to be set up with all of the overhead that is needed for Crystal Reports.

NOTE I am not a graphics specialist and I am not in the habit of rolling my own print routines, but I think the knowledge comes in handy. You should be able to extend this routine fairly easily.

Import the System.Drawing and System.Drawing.Printing namespaces in the header of the frmListBase form. Then add the following module-level declaration:

```
Private WithEvents mobjPD As PrintDocument
Private mstrTitle As String
Private mintPrintCount As Integer
```

The mstrTitle variable holds the title of the form for use in printing on the header of your custom report. The mintPrintCount variable holds the current record that you are printing and allows you to continue to the next record after you reach the bottom of the page. Next, add the code in Listing 3-22, which creates the btnPrint.Click method.

Listing 3-22. The Print Method

```
Protected Overridable Sub btnPrint_Click(ByVal sender As System.Object, _
ByVal e As System.EventArgs) Handles btnPrint.Click
    Dim PPD As PrintPreviewDialog = New PrintPreviewDialog()

    mobjPD = New PrintDocument()
    PPD.Document = mobjPD
    PPD.WindowState = FormWindowState.Maximized
    PPD.PrintPreviewControl.AutoZoom = False
    PPD.PrintPreviewControl.Zoom = 1.0
    PPD.ShowDialog()
End Sub
```

First you create a new Print Preview dialog box and then you create a new print document, which is the actual graphic rendered on the screen. Next, you associate the print document with the Print Preview dialog box.

TIP This method is declared as Protected Overridable as opposed to Private. The reason for this is that you might not want to print a generic report for all of your list screens. You might want a fancy Crystal Report or some other type of report. By declaring your method this way, you can alter the btnPrint_Click method to do something else in a subclassed form.

This code causes the Print Preview dialog box to be displayed, but it has nothing to do with the actual printing of the information into the dialog box. The PrintDocument object raises an event called *PrintPage*. It is this event that you need to respond to print your custom information. Enter the code in Listing 3-23 into the frmListBase form. There is quite a bit of code, so let's go over it in detail in just a moment.

Listing 3-23. The PrintPage Method

```
Private Sub mPD_PrintPage(ByVal sender As Object, ByVal e As _
System.Drawing.Printing.PrintPageEventArgs) Handles mobjPD.PrintPage
    Try
        Dim printFont As New Font("Arial", 10)
        Dim titleFont As New Font("Arial", 12, CType(FontStyle.Underline + _
FontStyle.Bold, FontStyle), GraphicsUnit.Pixel)
        Dim headerFont As New Font("Arial", 24, FontStyle.Bold, _
GraphicsUnit.Pixel)
        Dim headerLineHeight As Single = headerFont.GetHeight(e.Graphics)
        Dim lineHeight As Single = printFont.GetHeight(e.Graphics)
        Dim lPos As Single = e.MarginBounds.Left
        Dim yPos As Single = e.MarginBounds.Top
        Dim intLength As Integer
        Dim i, j As Integer

        'Print the header
        e.Graphics.DrawString("List Report", headerFont, Brushes.Black, _
lPos, yPos)
        yPos += headerLineHeight
        lPos += 3
```

```vb
        'Print the Maintenance report type
        e.Graphics.DrawString(mstrTitle, printFont, Brushes.Black, lPos, yPos)

        yPos += lineHeight * 2

        'Reset the left margin
        lPos = e.MarginBounds.Left

        'Print the header columns
        For i = 0 To lvwList.Columns.Count - 1
            e.Graphics.DrawString(lvwList.Columns(i).Text, titleFont, _
Brushes.Black, lPos, yPos, New StringFormat())
            If i < lvwlist.Columns.Count - 1 Then
                lPos += 150
            End If
        Next

        'Print the data to the report
        For i = mintPrintCount To lvwList.Items.Count - 1
            yPos += lineHeight
            lPos = e.MarginBounds.Left
            If lvwList.Items(i).Text.Length > 20 Then
                intLength = 20
            Else
                intLength = lvwList.Items(i).Text.Length
        End If
        e.Graphics.DrawString(lvwList.Items(i).Text.Substring(0, intLength), _
printFont, Brushes.Black, lPos, yPos, New StringFormat())
        For j = 1 To lvwList.Columns.Count - 1
            lPos += 150
            If lvwList.Items(i).SubItems(j).Text.Length > 20 Then
                intLength = 20
            Else
                intLength = lvwList.Items(i).SubItems(j).Text.Length
            End If
            e.Graphics.DrawString( _
lvwList.Items(i).SubItems(j).Text.Substring(0, intLength), printFont, _
Brushes.Black, lPos, yPos, New StringFormat())
            Next
```

```
                    'If there are more pages, continue
                    If yPos > e.MarginBounds.Bottom Then
                         e.HasMorePages = True
                         Exit For
                    Else
                         mintPrintCount += 1
                    End If
            Next
        Catch exc As Exception
             MessageBox.Show(exc.Message, "Print Error", MessageBoxButtons.OK, _
    MessageBoxIcon.Error)
        End Try
    End Sub
```

The real power in this routine is PrintPageEventArgs, which allows you to
control virtually every aspect of the printed page—from the font you use to the
page on which you print.

Now that you have all the code, let's examine the different parts of the code, so
you understand what is going on:

```
Dim printFont As New Font("Arial", 10)
Dim titleFont As New Font("Arial", 12, CType(FontStyle.Underline + _
FontStyle.Bold, FontStyle), GraphicsUnit.Pixel)
Dim headerFont As New Font("Arial", 24, FontStyle.Bold, GraphicsUnit.Pixel)
Dim headerLineHeight As Single = headerFont.GetHeight(e.Graphics)
Dim lineHeight As Single = printFont.GetHeight(e.Graphics)
Dim lPos As Single = e.MarginBounds.Left
Dim yPos As Single = e.MarginBounds.Top
Dim intLength As Integer
Dim i, j As Integer
```

The printFont, titleFont, and headerFont variables just store font information
for printing. The Font constructor has several overloaded methods for creating
fonts. (Refer to the MSDN documentation for additional information.) The
headerLineHeight variable holds the height of a line in $1/100^{th}$-inch increments. It
gets this height by calling the GetHeight method of the font object, which takes a
Graphics object as its argument. The same operation happens for the lineHeight,
which is the height of the line onto which you will print your data. The lPos and
yPos variables hold the left-margin bounds and top-margin bounds, respectively.
By default, the margin bounds are one inch, so these variables will both hold the

value 100. The intLength variable holds the length in characters of a value that you want to write to a page. (I did not want to write a routine that examined the widths of columns and resized them on the fly. I wanted to use a standard width that will apply to everything.)

NOTE   As mentioned earlier, you could improve a great deal about this routine, but it is a solid, generic starting point from which you can write your own print routines. Some improvements might include page numbers and additional header and footer information.

The DrawString method of the Graphics object allows you to draw text onto the page:

```
'Print the header
e.Graphics.DrawString("List Report", headerFont, Brushes.Black, lPos, yPos)
yPos += headerLineHeight
lPos += 3

'Print the Maintenance report type
e.Graphics.DrawString(mstrTitle, printFont, Brushes.Black, lPos, yPos)

yPos += lineHeight * 2

'Reset the left margin
lPos = e.MarginBounds.Left
```

In this case, you are simply drawing the words *List Report* using the font chosen as the headerFont (in this case, a 24-point Arial font in bold) with a black brush and the position specified. Then you increase your horizontal position on the page by adding the height of the line you just printed to your current location. Next, you add a slight indent to the page to print the report type because the alignment is slightly off. Then, you draw the report title using the printFont font. Next you move down horizontally on the page by the equivalent of two lines in height and you reset the left position to be equal to that of the left page margin.

The following block of code prints your column captions in the chosen font. After each column header is printed, the vertical position increases by 1.5 inches (this equates to about 20 characters):

```
'Print the header columns
For i = 0 To lvwList.Columns.Count - 1
    e.Graphics.DrawString(lvwList.Columns(i).Text, titleFont, Brushes.Black, _
    lPos, yPos, New StringFormat())
    If i < lvwlist.Columns.Count - 1 Then
        lPos += 150
    End If
Next
```

Listing 3-24 prints your data to the page.

Listing 3-24. Printing Your Data

```
'Print the data to the report
For i = mintPrintCount To lvwList.Items.Count - 1
    yPos += lineHeight
    lPos = e.MarginBounds.Left
    If lvwList.Items(i).Text.Length > 20 Then
        intLength = 20
    Else
        intLength = lvwList.Items(i).Text.Length
    End If
    e.Graphics.DrawString(lvwList.Items(i).Text.Substring(0, intLength), _
    printFont, Brushes.Black, _
    lPos, yPos, New StringFormat())
    For j = 1 To lvwList.Columns.Count - 1
        lPos += 150
        If lvwList.Items(i).SubItems(j).Text.Length > 20 Then
            intLength = 20
        Else
            intLength = lvwList.Items(i).SubItems(j).Text.Length
        End If
        e.Graphics.DrawString(lvwList.Items(i).SubItems(j).Text.Substring(0, _
        intLength), _
        printFont, Brushes.Black, lPos, yPos, New StringFormat())
    Next

    'If there are more pages, continue
    If yPos > e.MarginBounds.Bottom Then
        e.HasMorePages = True
        Exit For
    Else
        mintPrintCount += 1
    End If
Next
```

The mintPrintCount variable starts off the loop where the last run through the procedure left off. The first line increases the line position by one line and then resets the left print position to the left margin. Then you check to see how long the text that is in the listitem that you are trying to print is. If the text is greater than 20 characters, you set the length to 20 characters. If it is fewer than 20 characters, you get the actual length of the text. Then you print the text to the page. Then you loop through the subitems.

First, you increase the vertical position by one column, then you perform a text length check again, and finally you draw the text to the page. Next, you check the horizontal position to see if you are within the bounds of the bottom margin. If you are outside the bounds of the bottom margin, set the HasMorePages to *true*. This instructs the print document to add another page and begin the printing process for the next page. If you have more room on the page, increase the mintPrintCount variable so that when you eventually run out of lines to print on, you know where to continue in your list of records.

Finally, you have the error handler:

```
Catch exc As Exception
    MessageBox.Show(exc.Message, "Print Error", MessageBoxButtons.OK, _
    MessageBoxIcon.Error)
End Try
```

The last thing you need to add is the ability for your inheriting classes to set the title of the report. You can best accomplish this by creating a new constructor in the frmListBase form. Add the constructor shown in Listing 3-25.

Listing 3-25. The New frmListBase Constructor

```
Public Sub New(ByVal ReportTitle As String)
    MyBase.New()

    'This call is required by the Windows Form Designer.
    InitializeComponent()

    'Add any initialization after the InitializeComponent() call
    mstrTitle = ReportTitle
    lvwColumnSorter = New ListViewColumnSorter()
    Me.lvwList.ListViewItemSorter = lvwColumnSorter
End Sub
```

Once you add this to the form, you can go back and edit the frmRegionList constructor so that the MyBase.New line reads as follows:

```
MyBase.New("Regions")
```

The base list form now has the ability to print any information placed in it. This only works for about five or six columns of data. After that, you will run off the printed page. However, because of the need for application speed, you will not be adding more than five or six columns to any of the list forms. This will become more apparent when you begin developing more advanced classes. Running the print routine (by clicking the Print button) produces the result shown in Figure 3-12.

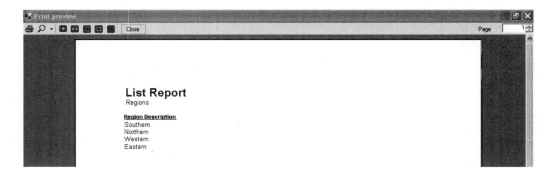

Figure 3-12. The list report

Adding Some Finishing Touches...

You need to handle the resizing of the listview columns when the form is resized. And you also add a line above the command buttons on your list form. To do this, add the code in Listing 3-26 to the frmListBase.Paint event.

Listing 3-26. The frmListBase Paint Method

```
Private Sub frmListBase_Paint(ByVal sender As Object, _
ByVal e As System.Windows.Forms.PaintEventArgs) Handles MyBase.Paint
    Dim i As Integer
    'Resize the columns in the listview
    For i = 0 To lvwList.Columns.Count - 1
        lvwList.Columns.Item(i).Width = CInt((lvwList.Size.Width / _
        lvwList.Columns.Count) - 6)
    Next
    'Clear the line that we drew previously
    Me.CreateGraphics.Clear(Me.BackColor)
```

```
'Draws the line above the buttons
Me.CreateGraphics.DrawLine(New Pen(Color.Black, 1), _
            lvwList.Location.X, btnDelete.Location.Y - 10, _
            lvwList.Location.X + lvwList.Size.Width, _
            btnDelete.Location.Y - 10)
End Sub
```

Next you need to set the tab order for the form. In .NET this is a simple matter. Switch to the design view of frmListBase, then select View ➤ Tab Order from the main menu, and set the tab order as shown in Figure 3-13.

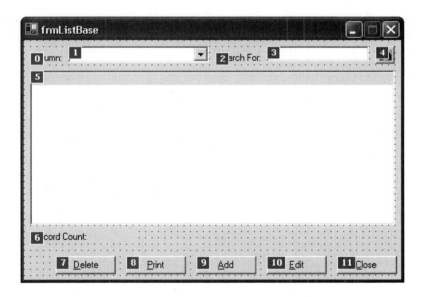

Figure 3-13. List base tab order

Finally, set the CancelButton property of the form to *btnClose*.

Next you need to group your buttons and context menus so they can be easily used by the forms that are going to inherit from this form. And you need to implement the Close button functionality.

The code to close the form is simple. Add this code to the frmListBase form:

```
Private Sub btnClose_Click(ByVal sender As Object, _
ByVal e As System.EventArgs) Handles btnClose.Click
    Close()
End Sub
```

Add the following code for the btnAdd button click event:

```
Protected Overridable Sub AddButton_Click(ByVal sender As Object, _
ByVal e As System.EventArgs) Handles btnAdd.Click
End Sub
```

Note here that you have made this routine Protected and Overridable so that it can be overridden by forms that inherit from this form.

TIP Technically, you should set this method as MustOverride because you are not actually implementing any functionality. However, because of the nature of visual inheritance, it is impossible for .NET to display an inherited form unless all of the MustOverride methods are overridden. It is easier to use the Overridable keyword.

Add the following blocks of code to handle the Delete button and the Edit button click events (as well as the context menu versions of these buttons):

```
Protected Overridable Sub DeleteButton_Click(ByVal sender As Object, _
ByVal e As System.EventArgs) Handles btnDelete.Click, ctmDelete.Click
End Sub

Protected Overridable Sub EditButton_Click(ByVal sender As Object, _
ByVal e As System.EventArgs) Handles btnEdit.Click, ctmEdit.Click, _
lvwList.DoubleClick
End Sub
```

Notice that each of these events handles the button click and the context menu click. Additionally, the EditButton_Click method handles the listview double-click event. This is possible because the same method signature is used for both events. At this point you have a fully working form that can display a list of information from the database and can print this list. You can search through the listview for a piece of information, and you can select that information and ensure that it is visible in the listview window. You can resize the form, and you can close the form. And all it took is 374 lines of code, with 200 of those lines having been generated by the .NET Framework!

This functionality never needs to be implemented ever again. That is the real power of what you have implemented so far. And if the user wants to see a change in the interface, you only need to make the change in the base form and it instantly spreads to all of the forms that inherit from the base form.

Now you need to add the functionality to add and edit your regions.

 NOTE   You need to add this functionality before you test the delete functionality because of the referential integrity that currently exists within the database. Do not worry—you will get to this functionality eventually!

Creating the Add/Edit Form

You will create a base edit form from which all of your other edit forms will inherit. As with the base list form, this form will implement some functionality that you want all of your edit forms to implement but that you do not want to write the same code for again and again. A typical edit form has a collection of textboxes, combo boxes, check boxes, and so on from which the user can make selections. Edit forms typically have OK and Cancel buttons as well. Some edit forms have Help buttons, others do not. Most support the concept of cut, copy, and paste and other standard operations. You need to code some of this functionality for every edit form; it just is not generic enough. But other things are generic enough to work with any control or layout; you will put this functionality into your base edit form.

Creating the Base Edit Form

To start, add a new form to the NorthwindTraders project and call the form *frmEditBase*. For the moment you are only going to add a couple of buttons and set some basic properties. You will come back and add additional functionality once you have your edit form working. When you are done adding the controls in Table 3-3, the form should look like the form in Figure 3-14.

Table 3-3. The frmEditBase Controls

Control	Control Name	Control Text
Button	btnCancel	&Cancel
Button	btnOK	&OK

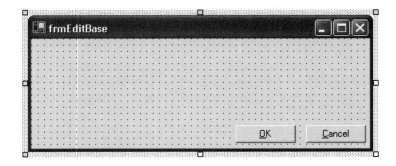

Figure 3-14. The frmEditBase form

Next, set the properties of the controls as shown in Table 3-4.

Table 3-4. frmEditBase Control Properties

Control	Property	Value
btnOK	Anchor	Bottom, Right
btnCancel	Anchor	Bottom, Right
btnOK	Modifiers	Protected
btnCancel	Modifiers	Protected
frmEditBase	AcceptButton	btnOK
frmEditBase	CancelButton	btnCancel
frmEditBase	FormBorderStyle	FixedSingle
frmEditBase	MaximizeBox	False
frmEditBase	MinimizeBox	False
frmEditBase	StartPosition	CenterParent

NOTE When dealing with visual inheritance, you should set all of the controls to Protected. .NET exhibits some interesting behavior when it comes to resizing forms that inherit from another form (in terms of control positions). Although setting the control modifiers to Protected allows the inheriting form to modify the controls, it helps avoid several problems with the positioning of controls.

Add the following code in frmEditBase to close the form:

```
Private Sub btnCancel_Click(ByVal sender As System.Object, _
ByVal e As System.EventArgs) Handles btnCancel.Click
    Close()
End Sub
```

Now you have a basic, generic edit form with which you can work. Select Build ➤ Build Solution from the main menu so that you can inherit from the frmEditBase form.

Creating the Region Edit Form

In the NorthwindTraders project, add an inherited form. Call it *frmRegionEdit* and select frmEditBase to be the form from which it will be inheriting. Your Region object is simple in that it only has one property that you can edit—the region description—so this will be a simple form (which is always a good place to start).

NOTE As a technical architect, I have found that it is easier to have developers new to the language perform simple tasks . By having a form from which they can inherit, they pick up the visual standards easily, and they can examine the base form to see some coding standards that are in use throughout the application. Too often I have seen projects take the new guys, who know little about anything, and throw them into the deep end of the application. Building them up a little at a time allows them to become grounded in the application standards.

Change the form text to read *Region [Detail]* and then add a label and a textbox to the frmRegionEdit form, with the properties shown in Table 3-5.

Make sure when you are placing the label and the textbox on the form that you leave about a quarter inch of space between the label and the textbox. You will not use this space now, but you will take advantage of it in Chapter 5, "Building Business Objects." When you are done, your form should look like the form in Figure 3-15.

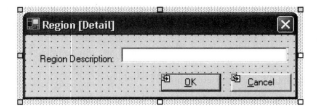

Figure 3-15. Region edit form

Normally you should set the tab order, in relation to the buttons, so that the OK button gets the focus before the Cancel button. However, because you only have one textbox on this form, that will prove to cause a problem later. So for this particular form, you will set the tab order according to Table 3-6.

Table 3-6. The frmRegionEdit Tab Order

Control	Tab Order
lblRegionDescription	0
txtRegionDescription	1
btnOK	3
btnCancel	2

Implementing the Edit Form

Now it is time to implement the form. Go to the code module of the frmRegionList form. Add two module-level variables to the frmRegionList class—one for the edit form and another for the region class—as in the following:

```
Private WithEvents mfrmEdit As frmRegionEdit
Private WithEvents mobjRegion As Region
```

Next, from the Class Name drop-down, select the (Overrides) entry. This provides you with a list of all of the methods that your form can override. From the list, select the AddButton_Click method. Now modify the AddButton_Click method to look like method in Listing 3-27.

Listing 3-27. The AddButton_Click Method

```
Protected Overrides Sub AddButton_Click(ByVal sender As Object, _
ByVal e As System.EventArgs)
    If mfrmEdit Is Nothing Then
        Cursor = Cursors.WaitCursor
        mobjRegion = New Region()
        mfrmEdit = New frmRegionEdit(mobjRegion)
        mfrmEdit.MdiParent = Me.MdiParent
        mfrmEdit.Show()
        Cursor = Cursors.Default
    End If
End Sub
```

This code checks to see if the mfrmEdit variable has been instantiated, and, if it has not been instantiated, you instantiate it and display it after passing in a reference to the mobjRegion variable. You only want to have one edit form open at a time.

NOTE   This is basically a design issue. For forms that maintain simple lists of information, users rarely need to have more than one form open at a time. When you build more complicated parts of an application that require side-by-side comparisons, then this method will not work. But why deal with the complexity when you do not have to?

For the moment, this generates a syntax error for frmRegionEdit(mobjRegion). This is because you have not altered the constructor for the frmRegionEdit form yet, but you will do that in a moment. When you do alter it, you will be passing in the mobjRegion variable ByRef. your list form needs to know that a region has been added or edited so that you can update the list (and the manager class) appropriately. Next, select mfrmEdit from the Class Name drop-down list and select the Closed method from the Method Name drop-down list. In the Closed method, add the single line of code to make it appear like the following code:

```
Private Sub mfrmEdit_Closed(ByVal sender As Object, _
ByVal e As System.EventArgs) Handles mfrmEdit.Closed
    mfrmEdit = Nothing
End Sub
```

You are simply setting the mfrmEdit variable to *Nothing* because even though the frmRegionEdit form may have been closed by way of the edit form, your list form still has a reference to it, so it is not removed from memory until you make this call. Next, select the mobjRegion entry from the Class Name drop-down, and select ObjectChanged from the Method Name drop-down. Edit the method so that it looks like Listing 3-28.

Listing 3-28. The ObjectChanged Method

```
Private Sub mobjRegion_ObjectChanged(ByVal sender As Object, _
ByVal e As NorthwindTraders.NorthwindUC.ChangedEventArgs) Handles _
mobjRegion.ObjectChanged
    Dim lst As ListViewItem
    Dim objRegion As Region = CType(sender, Region)

    Select Case e.Change
        Case ChangedEventArgs.eChange.Added
            mobjRegionMgr.Add(objRegion)
            lst = New ListViewItem(objRegion.RegionDescription)
            lst.Tag = objRegion.RegionID
            lvwList.Items.Add(lst)
            lblRecordCount.Text = "Record Count: " & lvwList.Items.Count
        Case ChangedEventArgs.eChange.Updated
            For Each lst In lvwList.Items
                If Convert.ToInt32(lst.Tag) = objRegion.RegionID Then
                    lst.Text = objRegion.RegionDescription
                    Exit For
                End If
            Next
    End Select
End Sub
```

If the region has been added, you simply add the Region object to the manager, and then you add the item to the listview and reset the record count. If the region has been updated, you need to loop through the listview looking for the item that was updated. Once you find it, you update the text to be equal to the new value of RegionDescription.

Switch to the frmRegionEdit code module and add the following Imports statement:

```
Imports NorthwindTraders.NorthwindUC
```

Add the following declaration to the frmRegionEdit class:

```
Private mobjRegion As Region
```

Next, alter the constructor so that it reads as follows:

```
Public Sub New(ByRef objRegion As Region)
    MyBase.New()

    'This call is required by the Windows Form Designer.
    InitializeComponent()

    'Add any initialization after the InitializeComponent() call
    mobjRegion = objRegion
End Sub
```

Your constructor now accepts an object of type Region ByRef so that any events raised by your object can be reported back to the list form. Add the code in Listing 3-29 to the frmRegionEdit form.

Listing 3-29. The frmRegionEdit_Load Method

```
Private Sub frmRegionEdit_Load(ByVal sender As Object, _
ByVal e As System.EventArgs) Handles MyBase.Load
    If mobjRegion.RegionID > 0 Then
        txtRegionDescription.Text = mobjRegion.RegionDescription.Trim
    End If
End Sub
```

First you check to see if the ID is greater than zero. If it is, then the object actually contains some information, so you should load your form. Otherwise, you need to skip this code because it will cause errors when you try to assign *Nothing* to the text property of the textbox. You should note that you need to call the Trim method on the region description because the database field is set up as an nchar field.

NOTE   I have never been able to figure out why the Northwind database is set up in the fashion that it is. In the case of the RegionDescription field, this field should be a varchar field—and, in most cases, character fields should be varchar fields. They take up less space in the database, and it alleviates the need to trim all of the strings. The only real reason to use a char field is when the value will always be the same length.

TIP The *n* in front of a variable type in SQL Server indicates that the value will be stored as a Unicode value. This is crucial for international applications or for any applications that will hold characters from a character set other than the default character set on the machine.

At this point, you should be able to run the application and click the Add button while on the frmRegionList form. This should open your edit form, albeit empty at this point. Go back to the frmRegionList form, select the (Overrides) option from the Class Name drop-down, and select the EditButton_Click method from the Method Name drop-down list. Edit this method so that it looks like the method shown in Listing 3-30.

Listing 3-30. The EditButton_Click Method

```
Protected Overrides Sub EditButton_Click(ByVal sender As Object, _
ByVal e As System.EventArgs)
    If mfrmEdit Is Nothing Then
        If lvwList.SelectedItems.Count > 0 Then
            mobjRegion = mobjRegionMgr.Item(lvwList.SelectedItems(0).Tag)
            mobjRegion.LoadRecord()
            mfrmEdit = New frmRegionEdit(mobjRegion)
            mfrmEdit.MdiParent = Me.MdiParent
            mfrmEdit.Show()
        End If
    End If
End Sub
```

First you are checking to see if the edit form has already been instantiated. If it has not been, you get a reference to the region that the user selected. Next you check to see if the user has selected an item to edit; if they have, then you call the LoadRecord routine, which refreshes the data from the database to ensure that the user is editing the latest record.

 NOTE For the moment, this does not seem smart. You already have the data in memory, why load it again? When you get to some of the larger objects for which you will only partially instantiate them, this LoadRecord method will be the only way you have of getting all of the information about an object from the database.

You then instantiate the edit form and pass it in the fully loaded Region object.

Saving the Object's Changes

Now you can open the form in an edit or add mode; it is time to actually be able to add records and edit records. Before you can save a record, you have to be able to update the object with information from the form. You do this in the Validated event for each of the controls. In this case you are working with only one control, the txtRegionDescription textbox, so you only need one method. Add this method and the OK button click method, as shown in Listing 3-31, to the frmRegionEdit form.

Listing 3-31. The txtRegionDescription_Validated Method

```
Private Sub txtRegionDescription_Validated(ByVal sender As Object, _
ByVal e As System.EventArgs) Handles txtRegionDescription.Validated
    Dim txt As TextBox

    txt = CType(sender, TextBox)
    mobjRegion.RegionDescription = txt.Text
End Sub

Private Sub btnOK_Click(ByVal sender As System.Object, _
ByVal e As System.EventArgs) Handles btnOK.Click
    If mobjRegion.IsDirty Then
        mobjRegion.Save()
    End If
    Close()
End Sub
```

The txtRegionDescription.Validated event occurs just before the control loses focus. At this point you are just setting the RegionDescription property of the object with the value in the textbox. In later chapters you will modify this behavior. The btnOk.Click event checks to see if the object is dirty. If it is, you call the Save method on the object and the value saves to the database. Then the form closes.

Deleting an Object

At this point, the edit form is working, and you can add and edit values in the region form. The last thing you need to implement before moving on is the ability to

delete a region. In the code module for the frmRegionList form, select the
(Overrides) entry from the Class Name drop-down list and then select
the DeleteButton_Click method from the Method Name drop-down. Edit the
DeleteButton_Click method so that it looks like the method in Listing 3-32.

Listing 3-32. The DeleteButton_Click Method

```
Protected Overrides Sub DeleteButton_Click(ByVal sender As Object, _
ByVal e As System.EventArgs)
    Dim objRegion As Region
    Dim dlgResult As DialogResult
    If lvwList.SelectedItems.Count > 0 Then
        objRegion = mobjRegionMgr.Item(lvwList.SelectedItems(0).Tag)
        dlgResult = MessageBox.Show("Do you want to delete the " _
        & objRegion.RegionDescription & " region?", _
        "Confirm Delete", MessageBoxButtons.YesNo, MessageBoxIcon.Question)
        If dlgResult = DialogResult.Yes Then
            objRegion.Delete()
            mobjRegionMgr.Remove(objRegion.RegionID)
            lvwList.SelectedItems(0).Remove()
            lblRecordCount.Text = "Record Count: " & lvwList.Items.Count
        End If
    End If
End Sub
```

First you check to see if an object has been selected, and if one has, then you
get a reference to the selected item in the listview. Then you check to see if the user
really wanted to delete the object. If they do, then you call the Delete method on
the Region object. This is the actual call that will delete the object from the database.
Next you remove the Region from the RegionMgr object. Then you remove the
item from the listview and reset the record count.

Now you can add, edit, and delete records from the database. However, if you
try to delete one of the original values, you will get a SQL Exception error. Do not
worry about this yet; you will handle it in the next chapter, which covers error handling
in an enterprise application.

Summary

In this chapter you have built a working application that spans three tiers. To review, you have accomplished the following:

- Created the interfaces and structures necessary to pass data across a network

- Built an object to retrieve, save, and delete data from a database

- Built an encapsulated business object that is aware of whether it has been edited

- Inherited from the CollectionBase class to build your own collection class to manage your objects

- Built a reusable form for listing records that can be printed, searched, and sorted

- Inherited from a base list form to display information from the database for your specific needs

- Built a reusable form for editing records

- Inherited from this base edit form so that you can edit your object

- Deployed your components to IIS

That is a lot of work for one chapter! However, you have also started to understand how you can build code specifically for the purpose of reusing it by creating generic routines that can adapt to the data given them (you will see more of this in Chapter 10, "Using Reflection"). You have also seen how easy it is to build and deploy all of the tiers needed for a three-tier application. In later chapters you will expand on this concepts to make your objects more robust.

In the next chapter you will see how to implement centralized error handling in an enterprise application. This goes far beyond the concepts of the Try..Catch..Finally block in that you will implement methods to inform technical support that an error has occurred at the moment that it occurs.

CHAPTER 4

Handling Errors
with Class

WE HAVE ALL BEEN THERE. It is Friday afternoon, you have just released the application to the users, and within three hours you are already fielding phone calls from users because your application is popping up error messages. And what is worse is that the application is crashing, and in some cases it is crashing Windows or affecting other applications. So what happened? You tested your application. You fixed all the bugs you found. You fixed all the bugs the testers found. You thought you had all the errors handled. As any developer can tell you—and you probably know as well—there is no way to solve (or even find) every defect before you release an application. The best you can do is to handle the errors in a graceful manner. Does that mean including error handling in every single routine? Although some people might crucify me for this, the answer is not necessarily. In fact, you generally should not have any error handlers in business objects (I explain why later in the chapter). This chapter presents you with a lot of reusable code that can handle errors elegantly—no matter what the error is.

There is a wrong way and a right way to fail out of an application, and this chapter shows you how to fail the right way—with style. When you are done, your application will be able to report an error directly to technical support. You will know that a user encountered an error at the same time the user encounters it. You will be able to track error occurrence metrics and get detailed information about errors that occurred—in many cases, getting the exact line that caused the error.

Understanding Visual Basic 6 Error Handling Structures

Visual Basic (VB) 6 used the On Error Goto construct—or, for those developers who like to play with fate, the On Error Resume Next construct. Although ASP developers were forced to use the On Error Resume Next statement, it is a generally accepted axiom that there is no good reason to use anything other than the On Error Goto structure when writing a VB 6 application. For reference, the On Error Goto structure looks like the following:

```
Private Sub Example()
    On Error Goto errHandler
    'Some code here
    Exit Sub
errHandler:
    Msgbox err.Number & " " & err.description
End Sub
```

There is one big problem with this code (well, there are several problems with this code), which can turn this into spaghetti code in a second: There is no easy way to include cleanup code. For example, if you opened a connection to the database at the top of the routine and an error occurred in the middle of the routine before closing the connection, the application would never get to the code that closes the connection. The way developers handled this was with the following code:

```
Private Sub Example()
    On Error Goto errHandler
    'Some code here
Cleanup:
    'Some cleanup code here
Exit Sub
errHandler:
    Msgbox err.Number & " " & err.Description
    Goto Cleanup
End Sub
```

This is not a very elegant solution, and using Goto statements is the beginning of spaghetti code, so it will only get worse. You cannot really nest error handlers in a VB 6 routine. You can include multiple error handlers, but that becomes messy. .NET solves these problems and gives you an elegant way of handling errors. For VB developers, it brings you in line with other development languages.

Understanding VB .NET Error Handling Structure

.NET uses the Try..Catch..Finally structure. You can nest these structures, which can handle multiple types of errors with ease. The structure looks like the following:

```
Private Sub Example()
    Try
        'Some code
    Catch
        'Code to handle the error
    Finally
        'Cleanup code here -- this always run, regardless of whether an error
        'occurs
    End Try
End Sub
```

The other form of this type of structure is identical except that there are multiple Catch blocks. This looks like the following:

```
Private Sub Example()
    Try
        'Some code
    Catch excNull as ArgumentNullException
        'Code to handle this specific exception
    Catch excZero as DivideByZeroException
        'Code to handle a divide by zero error
    Catch
        'Code to handle any other errors
    Finally
        'Cleanup code here -- this always run, regardless of whether an error
        'occurs
    End Try
End Sub
```

There can be as many Catch blocks as needed. The Try block always runs; the Catch block only runs when there is an error, and the Finally block always runs.

TIP Any variables declared in the Try..Catch..Finally blocks are block-level variables. Therefore, if you declare a variable in the Try block, it will not be in scope in the Finally block. Any variable that must be accessed in a different block must be declared before the Try block.

Using the .NET Exception Class

The base class that all exceptions inherit from is the Exception class. The Exception class has the properties described in Table 4-1.

Table 4-1. Exception Properties

Property	Description
HelpLink	The link to the help file associated with the error
InnerException	The exception that caused the current exception
Message	The error message
Source	The application that caused the error
StackTrace	Call stack up to the point where the error was thrown
TargetSite	The method that threw the current exception

The Exception class supports several other properties and methods, but those in Table 4-1 are the only ones you need to be concerned with in this chapter. There are two classes that inherit from this base Exception class that are of interest to you as well. These are the ApplicationException class and the SystemException class. The ApplicationException class is the base class from which almost all application exceptions inherit. You should use this class to indicate that an application caused the errors. The operating system or Common Language Runtime (CLR) uses the SystemException class to inform an application that the system threw an error. The MSDN documentation recommends that applications do not throw or handle SystemException errors. The only difference between these classes is an initial numeric value.

NOTE   Other Exception classes inherit directly from the Exception class, but you should not be concerned with these for this chapter. For more information, search for "Exception Hierarchy" in the MSDN documentation.

The ApplicationException class is the class that you will inherit from for your custom application errors.

Determining What Happened

Handling an error is only part of the issue. So you handled all the errors and the application did not crash. So what? Handling an error only means you popped up a message box with a description of the error, but the user still cannot use the application. And most error messages are not helpful at all. How often are users getting a particular type of error? What were they doing when they got the error? How does this help the development staff? The answer is that it does not.

Some developers got smart and put the method and function names in the header of the error message. And they put some sophisticated debugging information in the message. But that requires the user to take a screenshot or report all of that debugging information to the technical support person over the phone. Users do not dislike anything more than helping you fix an application that should not have had bugs anyway. Not only are they inconvenienced by having an error, but it becomes their responsibility to help fix it.

 NOTE Although displaying debugging information might be considered OK within an enterprise, it is generally not a good idea. The more information attackers have about an error, the easier it is for them to exploit the error. Generally, you should hide the details about an error from the users. However, taking this approach limits the amount of information that a user can report to you about an error.

As you will see next, there is an easy, efficient way to overcome the problem of not having enough information with which to debug an error—both for an individual application and as a method that can be easily implemented throughout an enterprise.

Storing Error Information

One difference between an in-house application and a commercial application is the response of the development team when errors in the application are found. In an in-house application, errors are typically noted and scheduled to be fixed in a release or two. If developers cannot find a workaround and the error is critical, they must fix it immediately. In a commercial application, this is not the case. The best that can happen is that the error is reported and you, as the user, hope that it eventually gets fixed because you do not have any control over a commercial application. If it is a problem that affects your business, you cannot really count on a quick fix.

Another difference is how the errors get logged. In a commercial application, there is no real log for errors that occur and no real way to track those errors. The development team of a commercial application must rely on the users correctly reporting errors. If the user tells you that an error occurred but cannot give you the circumstances in which it occurred, finding it is going to be difficult. An in-house application, on the other hand, has a number of advantages in this area. The application is run on a network you control and connected to a database you control. You can also write error handling routines that will benefit the entire enterprise.

SEI-CMM

The Carnegie Mellon University in conjunction with the U.S. government developed the Software Engineering Institute Capability Maturity Model (SEI-CMM). The purpose of this institute, and the SEI-CMM specifically, was to create a disciplined approach to software development. One of the main tenets in the CMM is the process of capturing metrics for quality assurance. These metrics range from code development estimates to the number of bugs found and the number of bugs fixed. It also covers many other metrics—too many to mention here.

Many organizations are now switching to the SEI-CMM model because it is a proven method for reducing costs and improving quality. Because tracking bugs is crucial to gathering metrics, this chapter becomes an integral part of any enterprise software development.

To learn more about the SEI-CMM, visit the Carnegie Mellon Web site at `http://www.sei.cmu.edu/cmm/cmm.sum.html`.

To track bugs, you will store the application errors in a database table. Storing errors in a database table allows the development team to keep accurate metrics on the errors generated by the application. It also allows the development team to find and fix errors faster than having to rely on a user reading the error information to a technical support person. And, using this method gives the development team the chance to be notified that a user had an error at the same time that the error occurred. How many enterprise applications do you know of that have this capability built in?

However, other types of errors can occur that will prevent application errors from being logged. These errors can range from network errors to server errors to database errors. What do you do then? You use the Windows Event Log. This log stores application and system information—including errors. But in VB 6 developers could not take a lot of advantage of it unless they used the Win32 Application Programming Interface (API), which was troublesome at times. The .NET

Framework provides the System.Diagnostic namespace for dealing with the Windows Event Log.

The next section discusses the specific classes in the System.Diagnostic namespace. Now that you have had a brief introduction to handling errors in the enterprise, it is time to start writing your own custom, generic error handler. The first step is to set up your database.

Setting Up the Database

First, you need to add a table to the database that will store unexpected application errors. Execute the SQL statement in Listing 4-1 against the Northwind database in the Query Analyzer.

Listing 4-1. Creating the application_errors Table

```
CREATE TABLE application_errors (
error_id int IDENTITY (1, 1) PRIMARY KEY NOT NULL,
username varchar(50) NOT NULL,
error_message varchar(200) NOT NULL,
error_time smalldatetime NOT NULL,
 stack_trace varchar(4000) NULL)
```

NOTE I come from the database design camp that advocates using a surrogate primary key on every table. I also like to make each of the primary keys an identity field with a seed of one and an increment of one. There are many data architects that advocate using natural keys. It is an age-old argument that I will not even try to argue or answer here!

NOTE *Surrogate* keys are artificial keys that have no relationship to the data within the table. *Natural* keys are keys created from the data within the table. Natural keys are usually multiple column keys that can be unwieldy. Surrogate keys are mandatory in dimensional database design (the type of model used for data warehouses).

Next you need to create the stored procedure through which information will be saved to this table. Execute the SQL in Listing 4-2 to create the stored procedure.

Listing 4-2. The usp_application_errors_save Stored Procedure

```
CREATE PROCEDURE usp_application_errors_save
@user_name varchar(50),
@error_message varchar(200),
@error_time smalldatetime,
@stack_trace varchar(4000)
AS
INSERT INTO application_errors
  (username, error_message, error_time, stack_trace)
  VALUES
  (@user_name, @error_message, @error_time, @stack_trace)
```

You now have the ability to save your application errors in the database. It is time to actually create the classes responsible for capturing and saving errors.

Creating the LogError Classes

These classes have dual responsibilities. The first responsibility is to send error information to the data-centric business object so that the error can be logged to the database. The second responsibility is to store the data in a custom Windows Event Log, which your class will also be responsible for creating. As part of this responsibility, it also retrieves errors from the event log, formats them in a file, and sends an e-mail to technical support with the contents of the event log. It then clears the event log. Although this might seem like a lot of work, all of this is generic enough to be reusable on any application with no modifications.

The LogErrorDC Class

First you need to create the data-centric business object to pass the data to this stored procedure. But before you do that, you need to create an interface to the LogErrorDC class, just as with any other object that needs to communicate across a remoting channel. Add the following interface to the Interfaces.vb code module in the NorthwindShared project:

```
Public Interface ILogError
    Sub Save(ByVal exc As Exception)
End Interface
```

> **NOTE** Although the class you are creating only allows the application to store the error, it is a simple matter to extend the interface and the classes so that the application can read from this log as well. However, this ability is not something that should be available to most applications. This type of error log is for development and maintenance people only.

In the NorthwindDC project, add a class module and call it *LogErrorDC*. Add the following code to the header of the LogErrorDC code module:

```
Imports System.Data.SqlClient
Imports System.Configuration
Imports NorthwindTraders.NorthwindShared.Interfaces
```

Next, modify the LogErrorDC class so that it contains the code shown in Listing 4-3.

Listing 4-3. The LogErrorDC Class

```
Public Class LogErrorDC
    Inherits MarshalByRefObject

    Implements ILogError

    Public Sub Save(ByVal exc As Exception) Implements ILogError.Save
        Dim strCN As String = _
ConfigurationSettings.AppSettings("Northwind_DSN")
        Dim cn As New SqlConnection(strCN)
        Dim cmd As New SqlCommand()

        cn.Open()
```

```
        With cmd
            .Connection = cn
            .CommandType = CommandType.StoredProcedure
            .CommandText = "usp_application_errors_save"
            .Parameters.Add("@user_name", _
            System.Security.Principal.WindowsIdentity.GetCurrent.Name)
            .Parameters.Add("@error_message", exc.Message)
            .Parameters.Add("@error_time", Now)
            If exc.StackTrace = "" Then
                .Parameters.Add("@stack_trace", DBNull.Value)
            Else
                .Parameters.Add("@stack_trace", exc.StackTrace)
            End If
        End With

        cmd.ExecuteNonQuery()
        cmd = Nothing
        cn.Close()
        cn = Nothing
    End Sub
End Class
```

Notice again that this class inherits from the MarshalByRef class because you need to create a proxy object on the local machine when this method is called. You implement the ILogError class by implementing its only subroutine, Save.

NOTE The Exception class implements the ISerializable interface. This means you can pass exceptions over the network with no additional work necessary. However, this does not apply to classes that inherit from the Exception class. If you want to be able to pass custom exceptions across the network, they will also need to implement the ISerializable interface.

The Save routine is a straightforward call to the database to pass your exception information. One call you have not seen before is the following:

```
System.Security.Principal.WindowsIdentity.GetCurrent.Name
```

This simply retrieves the name of the user currently logged onto the machine. But, because you are actually on a remote machine, you might think it would retrieve the name of the user who was logged onto the remote machine, not your logon. You would be right, except that in your web.config file you set the Identity Impersonate flag equal to true, so for the space of this transaction Windows believes you are the person logged onto this machine. You could use the user_name function in SQL Server to automatically add this information into the application_errors table when you add a record, but this method makes the functionality a little more flexible. The other thing to note is the If..Then statement around the stack trace variable:

```
If exc.StackTrace = "" Then
     .Parameters.Add("@stack_trace", DBNull.Value)
Else
     .Parameters.Add("@stack_trace", exc.StackTrace)
End If
```

Even though you have set the stack_trace column in the database to nullable, you cannot pass in an empty string value or else SQL Server returns an error saying that it expected a value. Therefore, if the value can be an empty string, you need to check for it and pass in the value of DBNull. For some reason SQL Server recognizes this, but not an empty string.

The last thing you need to do is to modify the web.config file. Add another wellknown tag to reference the LogErrorDC class (below the existing wellknown tag) as follows:

```
<wellknown mode="Singleton"
   type="NorthwindTraders.NorthwindDC.LogErrorDC,_NorthwindDC"
   objectUri="LogErrorDC.rem"/>
```

Now you need to add the class that is going to be responsible for the bulk of the work.

The LogError Class

In the NorthwindUC project, add a class module called *LogError*. This class performs a simple operation: It sends an exception to the data-centric object for storage in the database. Delete the empty class declaration and add the code shown in Listing 4-4 to the LogError code module.

Listing 4-4. The LogError Class

```
Option Explicit On
Option Strict On

Imports NorthwindTraders.NorthwindShared.Interfaces

Namespace ErrorLogging

    Public Class LogError

        Private Const LISTENER As String = "LogErrorDC.rem"

        Public Sub New()
        End Sub

        Public Sub New(ByVal exc As Exception)
            LogException(exc)
        End Sub

        Public Sub LogException(ByVal exc As Exception)
            Dim objILog As ILogError

            objILog = CType(Activator.GetObject(GetType(ILogError), _
        AppConstants.REMOTEOBJECTS & LISTENER), ILogError)
            objILog.Save(exc)
            objILog = Nothing
        End Sub

    End Class

End Namespace
```

The empty constructor is available in case you want to declare an object before you send it the exception. The second constructor is so that you can pass the exception at object instantiation time, and finally the LogException routine passes the application exception to the data-centric objects.

Next you need to create the class that will handle the Windows Event Log and all of the other overhead of logging an error locally.

Creating the LogErrorEvent Class

This class is responsible for the bulk of your error logging code. Your LogErrorEvent class is going to use the Singleton pattern because you only need to ever have one instance of this object in memory. Your class raises two events: one to inform the interface that an error was logged and one to inform the interface that the event log was cleared. You will also use constants for the event log name and the error log file so that it makes it easier to reuse this object (of course, the ultimate in reusability is to make these properties, but that is a change I will let you make). Add the class in Listing 4-5 to the ErrorLogging namespace in the LogError code module.

Listing 4-5. The LogErrorEvent Class

```
Public Class LogErrorEvent
    Private Shared mobjLogErrEvent As LogErrorEvent

    Public Event ErrorLogged()
    Public Event ErrorsCleared()

    Private Const EVENTLOGNAME As String = "Northwind"
    Private Const ERRORFILENAME As String = "NorthwindErrors.xml"

    Public Shared Function getInstance() As LogErrorEvent
        If mobjLogErrEvent Is Nothing Then
            mobjLogErrEvent = New LogErrorEvent()
        End If
        Return mobjLogErrEvent
    End Function

    Protected Sub New()
    End Sub
End Class
```

Next, you need to add code to create your custom event log if it does not exist. Add the following code to the constructor:

```
Dim objEventLog As New EventLog()

If Not objEventLog.Exists(EVENTLOGNAME) Then
    objEventLog.CreateEventSource(EVENTLOGNAME, EVENTLOGNAME)
End If
```

Here you create a new EventLog object that gives you a reference to the Windows Event Log. Then you check to see if the Northwind event log exists. If it does not exist, you create the event log and specify that the application that is the source of events in this log is the Northwind application. This object will be checked every time the application throws the first error that needs to be stored in the event log, so you are always sure that the event log exists.

Although the event log provides the ability to store a lot of information about the event that was logged, you are going to largely ignore this capability. Instead, you are going to store the information about your errors in an Extensible Markup Language (XML) format in the message section of the event log. There are several reasons why you are going to do this:

- It is easier to read the information about the exception.

- It is easier to manipulate given .NET's built-in support for XML.

- It is easier to serialize into a file.

- You can pick out specific pieces of information quickly.

To be able to do this, you need to create a structure you can use to store your exception information. Create the following structure in the LogError code module as part of the ErrorLogging namespace (but outside of other classes):

```
<Serializable()> Public Structure structLoggedError
    Public UserName As String
    Public ErrorTime As Date
    Public Source As String
    Public Message As String
    Public StackTrace As String
End Structure
```

Now that you have your structure, and knowing that you are going to turn it into an XML format, you need to add another Imports statement:

```
Imports System.Xml.Serialization
```

The System.Xml.Serialization namespace contains several libraries to help you serialize and deserialize data to and from XML. You will also need to add one more Imports statement:

```
Imports System.IO
```

The System.IO namespace contains a class library called *StringWriter*. This class inherits from the System.IO.TextWriter class, which is an object that can be passed to the Serialize method of the XML class. But, because you want to serialize the data to a string so that you can write the string to the event log, you have to take a roundabout way to get there. You need to serialize the data to a StringBuilder object, which you can then turn into a string.

Logging the Error

Add the routine in Listing 4-6 to the LogErrorEvent class and then examine it.

Listing 4-6. The LogErr Method

```
Public Sub LogErr(ByVal exc As Exception)
    Dim objEventLog As New EventLog()
    Dim objErr As structLoggedError
    Dim xmlSer As New XmlSerializer(GetType(structLoggedError))
    Dim strB As New System.Text.StringBuilder()
    Dim txtWriter As New StringWriter(strB)
    Dim strText As String

    With objErr
        .UserName = System.Security.Principal.WindowsIdentity.GetCurrent.Name
        .ErrorTime = Now
        .Source = exc.Source
        .Message = exc.Message
        .StackTrace = exc.StackTrace
    End With

    xmlSer.Serialize(txtWriter, objErr)
    strText = strB.ToString

    objEventLog.WriteEntry(EVENTLOGNAME, strText, EventLogEntryType.Error)
    objEventLog = Nothing

    RaiseEvent ErrorLogged()
End Sub
```

Because this code introduces a couple of new things, let's examine each block of code:

```
Dim objEventLog As New EventLog()
Dim objErr As structLoggedError
Dim xmlSer As New XmlSerializer(GetType(structLoggedError))
Dim strB As New System.Text.StringBuilder()
Dim txtWriter As New StringWriter(strB)
Dim strText As String
```

The first line retrieves a reference to the Windows Event Log. The second line declares a variable for your structure, which holds your error information. The third line declares the XmlSerializer that accepts the type of object you will be serializing. The XmlSerializer needs this information ahead of time so that it knows how to handle the data you will be passing to it.

Using the StringBuilder Class

The StringBuilder class is a useful class for a variety of reasons. One reason is how it manages memory. Strings, by their nature are immutable—that is, once a string is created in memory, it cannot be changed. For example, look at the following two lines of code:

```
Dim strName as String = "John"
strName += "Smith"
```

It looks as though I have simply added the word *Smith* onto the end of the string variable called *strName*. But, if strings are immutable, then that is not what really happened here. What happens when you perform this operation is that .NET creates a temporary string variable large enough to hold the entire value of the variable plus the string you are adding to it. It places the contents of the second call into this temporary variable, destroys the strName variable, and re-creates it in the correct size. It then copies the contents of the temporary variable into the new variable named strName. Obviously this is an involved process, especially if you are performing operations on thousands of strings. The StringBuilder class can size itself dynamically without having to go through this entire process, which makes it a fast string processor.

A StringBuilder object serves as the data store for the StringWriter. That means you can serialize a structure using the Serialize method of the Xml class and store that data in a StringWriter object. You can then take the StringBuilder object that is storing that information and convert it to a true string object, as you can see in the following code from the middle of Listing 4-6:

```
xmlSer.Serialize(txtWriter, objErr)
strText = strB.ToString
objEventLog.WriteEntry(EVENTLOGNAME, strText, EventLogEntryType.Error)
```

Here, you serialize the data to the txtWriter object, which is of type StringWriter and then you can call the ToString method of the StringBuilder object to return the contents of the StringBuilder object in a string format. You then take this information and store it in the Northwind event logs message property.

NOTE The event log can store a limited amount of information. Figure 4-1 shows the properties page of the Windows Application Event Log. Note the maximum log size of 512KB. Although you can configure this manually, you should leave the settings at their defaults.

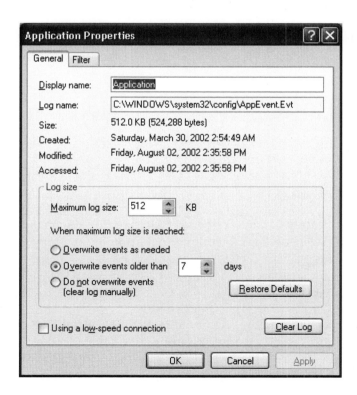

Figure 4-1. The Windows Application Event Log properties page

Now you can store your error in the event log. Next you need to be able to retrieve this information from the event log.

Retrieving the Error Log

Add the method in Listing 4-7 to the LogErrorEvent class.

Listing 4-7. The RetrieveErrors Method

```
Public Function RetrieveErrors() As structLoggedError()
    Dim objEL As New EventLog(EVENTLOGNAME)
    Dim objEntry As EventLogEntry
    Dim errArray(objEL.Entries.Count - 1) As structLoggedError
    Dim i As Integer = 0
    Dim xmlSer As New XmlSerializer(GetType(structLoggedError))

    For Each objEntry In objEL.Entries
        Dim txtReader As New StringReader(objEntry.Message)
        errArray(i) = CType(xmlSer.Deserialize(txtReader), structLoggedError)
        i += 1
        txtReader = Nothing
    Next
    objEL = Nothing
    Return errArray
End Function
```

Let's examine this code so you can see exactly what is happening. The following line retrieves a reference to your specific event log:

```
Dim objEL As New EventLog(EVENTLOGNAME)
```

This next line creates an array variable of type structLoggedError to store the XML information from the event log. You dimension it to the number of errors stored in the event log:

```
Dim errArray(objEL.Entries.Count - 1) As structLoggedError
```

The following block of code loops through the entries in the event log. First you create a new StringReader object that accepts a string. Remember that the information store for a StringReader object is a StringBuilder object. The next line deserializes the string into a structLoggedError structure:

```
For Each objEntry In objEL.Entries
    Dim txtReader As New StringReader(objEntry.Message)
    errArray(i) = CType(xmlSer.Deserialize(txtReader), structLoggedError)
    i += 1
    txtReader = Nothing
Next
```

Reporting the Errors

Finally, you need to add the code to send these errors to the technical support personnel. To do this, you need to get a reference to the System.Web namespace, which is not available by default when you create a Windows Forms application. To get this reference, right-click the NorthwindUC project and select Add Reference. Then select the System.Web.dll entry from the .NET tab. Once you have done that, add an Imports line at the top of the LogError code module, as shown here:

```
Imports System.Web
```

You also need to add one additional class. For .NET to be able serialize the XML directly to a file, it needs to have a class that it can serialize—just passing it an Array type will cause a runtime error. So let's add a simple one-line class that you can use to serialize your errors to the LogError code module:

```
Public Class CustomErrors
    Public ErrArray() As structLoggedError
End Class
```

Now add the method in Listing 4-8 to the LogErrorEvent class.

Listing 4-8. The SendErrors Method

```
Public Sub SendErrors(ByVal errArray() As structLoggedError)
    Dim objAllErrors As New CustomErrors()
    Dim xmlFileSer As New XmlSerializer(GetType(CustomErrors))
    Dim dirPath As Environment
    Dim strPath As String = _
        dirPath.GetFolderPath(Environment.SpecialFolder.LocalApplicationData)
    Dim fStream As New FileStream(strPath & "\" & ERRORFILENAME, _
        FileMode.Create)
    Dim email As New Mail.MailMessage()
    Dim emailAttach As Mail.MailAttachment
```

```
        objAllErrors.ErrArray = errArray
        xmlFileSer.Serialize(fStream,Objallerrors)
        fStream.Close()
        xmlFileSer = Nothing
        emailAttach = New Mail.MailAttachment(strPath & "\" & ERRORFILENAME)
        With email
            .From = "user.name@somewhere.com"
            .To = "tech.support@somewhere.com"
            .Subject = "Northwind Error Log"
            .Priority = Web.Mail.MailPriority.High
            .Attachments.Add(emailAttach)
        End With
        Mail.SmtpMail.Send(email)
        Kill(strPath & "\" & ERRORFILENAME)
        ClearErrors()
End Sub
```

The first line of this code declares your CustomErrors class, which you will serialize to an XML file. Then you tell the XmlSerializer what type of object it will be serializing:

```
Dim objAllErrors As New CustomErrors()
Dim xmlFileSer As New XmlSerializer(GetType(CustomErrors))
```

The following line gets the location of the place where you will store your temporary file:

```
Dim strPath As String = _
    Environment.GetFolderPath(Environment.SpecialFolder.LocalApplicationData)
```

The Environment class is a very special, very cool class that has a multitude of uses. It can tell you everything you need to know about the system. All of the class's members are shared, so it never needs to be instantiated.

NOTE   See the MSDN documentation for the Environment class. This class can provide a lot of help in dealing with the local environment, and it is one of the better-documented classes.

The GetFolderPath method can retrieve a variety of special Windows folders. (I chose this because many companies lock down user machines, but the folders in the Documents and Settings folder for the current user are generally not locked down.)

Next, you declare a FileStream variable that holds a reference to your temporary file. Notice that the file is opened using FileMode.Create. This destroys a file with the same name if it exists and creates a new one. The MailMessage class is the class that actually constructs the e-mail, and the MailAttachment class stores a reference to the file that you will be attaching. The MailMessage class can store a collection of MailAttachment objects so that you can attach multiple files to an e-mail:

```
Dim fStream As New FileStream(strPath & "\" & ERRORFILENAME, FileMode.Create)
Dim email As New Mail.MailMessage()
Dim emailAttach As Mail.MailAttachment
```

The next block of code stores your array of messages in a CustomErrors variable. The object is then serialized to the temporary file and the file stream is closed. Finally, you create an e-mail attachment and attach the temporary file that contains your XML serialized errors:

```
objAllErrors.ErrArray = errArray
xmlFileSer.Serialize(fStream, objAllErrors)
fStream.Close()
xmlFileSer = Nothing
emailAttach = New Mail.MailAttachment(strPath & "\" & ERRORFILENAME)
```

Lastly, you set the e-mail properties, attach the attachments, and send the e-mail. To send the e-mail, you call the Send method of the SmtpMail object. This is a shared method, so the object does not have to be instantiated. Finally, you delete the temporary file and clear the errors from the error log:

```
With email
.From = "user.name@somewhere.com"
.To = "tech.support@somewhere.com"
.Subject = "Northwind Error Log"
.Priority = Web.Mail.MailPriority.High
.Attachments.Add(emailAttach)
End With
Mail.SmtpMail.Send(email)
Kill(strPath & "\" & ERRORFILENAME)
ClearErrors()
```

NOTE The From properties and To properties must have valid e-mail addresses. If only the To property has a valid e-mail address, the e-mail still will not reach its intended recipient. This may be something that is network specific, but in all of my tests (on different networks) I have found this to be true.

CAUTION To send e-mail by the SmtpMail.Send method, you use the CDO objects on a user's machine. There are some known issues with this because not everyone has the CDO objects. At this time, the only way to guarantee that this will work is if Internet Information Server (IIS) is installed on the machine or the CDO objects have been installed in some other manner. To guarantee this works in an enterprise, it may be a better choice to write a small routine that automates Microsoft Outlook or whatever the standard e-mail client is. Note that if you do this, you still do not have to change the routine, just plug in a different class to this method!

You will notice that the last line of code calls the ClearErrors method, which you have not yet created, so let's go ahead and do that now and then test this class. Add the following code to the LogErrorEvent class:

```
Public Sub ClearErrors()
    Dim objEventLog As New EventLog(EVENTLOGNAME)
    objEventLog.Clear()
    objEventLog = Nothing
    RaiseEvent ErrorsCleared()
End Sub
```

This routine simply gets a reference to our custom event log, calls the clear method on it, and raises the appropriate event. There is nothing to it!

Testing the LogErrorEvent Class

Now that you have a working class, let's try it. To do this you will create a small
console application and copy your code over to it. Open a new instance of the
.NET Integrated Development Environment (IDE) and select New ➤ Project from
the main menu. Select a Console Application project and call it *EventLogTest*. The
code window you are presented with looks like the following:

```
Module Module1
    Sub Main()

    End Sub
End Module
```

Copy all of the classes and structures in the ErrorLogging namespace, except
the LogError class, to this code module and paste it after the End Module statement.
Next, copy the Imports statement from the head of the LogError code module in
the NorthwindUC project to the console project (do not copy the Imports statement
for the NorthwindUC namespace). Finally, add a reference to the System.Web
namespace in your console application.

NOTE Make sure to change the From and To e-mail address (preferably
to an e-mail address you have access to so that you can see the results).
They can be the same value.

Now, modify the Sub Main procedure so that it looks like the procedure in
Listing 4-9.

Listing 4-9. The Sub Main Procedure

```
Sub Main()
    Console.WriteLine("Press the enter key to start the test")
    Console.ReadLine()
    Console.WriteLine("Throwing an error...")
    Try
        Throw New ApplicationException("My error")
    Catch exc As Exception
        Dim objEL As LogErrorEvent
        Dim errArray() As structLoggedError

        objEL = objEL.getInstance

        objEL.LogErr(exc)
          Console.WriteLine("Error has been logged. Press the enter key to " _
          & "continue.")
          Console.ReadLine()
          Console.WriteLine("Reading error log...")
          errArray = objEL.RetrieveErrors()
          Console.WriteLine("Errors Retrieved. Press the enter key to " _
          & "continue.")
          Console.ReadLine()
          Console.WriteLine("Sending Errors...")
          objEL.SendErrors(errArray)
          Console.WriteLine("Errors Sent. Press the Enter Key To Exit " _
          & "Application.")
          Console.ReadLine()
    End Try
End Sub
```

This code throws an error that is caught by the Catch block. Then a reference to the LogErrorEvent class is made and the error is passed to the LogErr method. Next you retrieve the error from the event log and then send the error. The reason why there are so many Readline statements is because these pause the application execution until you press a key. At this point, run the application and do the following:

1. When the error has been logged, check the event log (shown in Figure 4-2).

2. Open the error message and examine it (shown in Figure 4-3).

3. Press a key to continue the application until the end.

4. Examine the attachment in the e-mail you receive (shown in Figure 4-4).

 NOTE   If you already had the event log open, you may have to refresh the window to see the error.

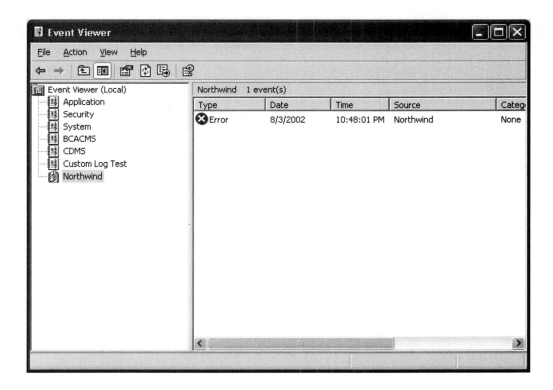

Figure 4-2. Event Viewer with the Northwind custom error log

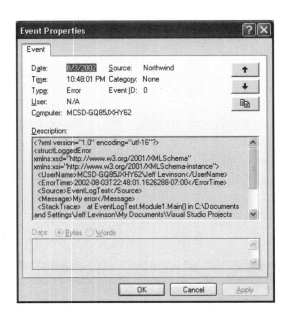

Figure 4-3. Your custom-generated event log entry

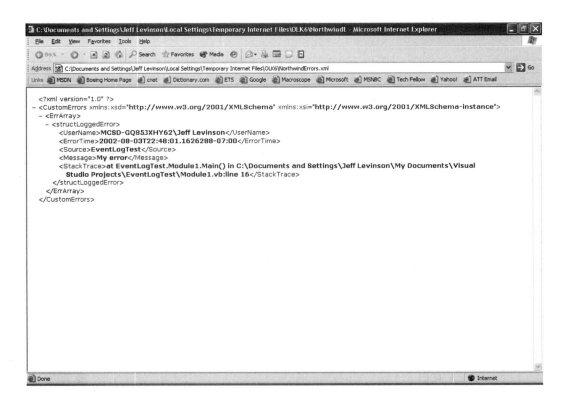

Figure 4-4. Custom error log file sent by e-mail

The important things here are the Message and the StackTrace. The StackTrace is extremely helpful in finding and debugging errors. If you go back and check the console application, line 16 is the line that threw the error. This makes it simple to find and fix errors.

Handling Errors in the Northwind Application

Now that you have your error handling classes and can save errors in either the database or the Windows Event Log, it is time to implement the functionality in your application. In a typical application you might have to put an error handling routine, like you are going to create, in every form of your application. Thanks to .NET and visual inheritance, you have a convenient place to put your code—our base classes. For the purposes of this application, you will add your error handling routine to the frmListBase form and the frmEditBase form. You will also add it to the main form, frmMain. Add the method in Listing 4-10 to the frmListBase form.

Listing 4-10. The LogException Method

```
#Region " Error Logger"
    Protected Sub LogException(ByVal exc As Exception)
        Dim objLogErr As New NorthwindUC.ErrorLogging.LogError()

        Try
            objLogErr.LogException(exc)
            MessageBox.Show("The NorthwindTrader application generated " _
            & "the following error:" & ControlChars.CrLf & exc.Message, _
            "NorthwindTrader Error", MessageBoxButtons.OK, _
            MessageBoxIcon.Error)
        Catch excNew As Exception
            Dim objErrorEvent As NorthwindUC.ErrorLogging.LogErrorEvent
            objErrorEvent = objErrorEvent.getInstance
            objErrorEvent.LogErr(exc)
            objErrorEvent.LogErr(excNew)
            objErrorEvent = Nothing
            MessageBox.Show("The NorthwindTrader application generated " _
            & "the following critical error: " & excNew.Message, _
            "NorthwindTrader Error", MessageBoxButtons.OK, _
            MessageBoxIcon.Error)
        Finally
            objLogErr = Nothing
        End Try
    End Sub
#End Region
```

The method is declared as protected so that you can access it from the forms that inherit from your base form. This routine tries to log the exception that was generated to the database. If an error occurs during the logging of the exception to the database, you can usually be guaranteed that it is a network connection or database connection issue (or some other issue that involves calling remote components). However, you do not want to lose the original error, so you log both errors to the event log and inform the user that a more serious error occurred. It is simple and elegant. Any Windows application can use this code (at least the code that logs to the event log).

NOTE   In an actual production environment, it would make more sense to split the database logging mechanism and the event log logging mechanism into two classes in different files, but for these purposes it will work fine. This is because it makes the code more reusable; not every application will have a database with this table in it.

Add the code in Listing 4-10 to the frmEditBase and the frmMain form as well. Next you are going to add a little interface so that the users can send the errors that are in the event log to technical support.

CAUTION   It is easy to automatically send the errors via e-mail to technical support whenever an error occurs; however, with all of the issues surrounding privacy and information being sent with or without the user's permission, this could be problematic. Even though this is an enterprise application, you still do not want to violate that privacy. This is a personal choice, but if in doubt, have your company define these policies explicitly so you do not violate any of their privacy guidelines.

At this point, you can go back into the user interface and add error handling code in your application. I recommend that every routine (except the constructors) have a Try..Catch block if that routine is in the user interface (this includes the base forms). To add the Try..Catch blocks, enter the following code in every routine:

```
Try
    'Your routines code
Catch exc As Exception
    LogException(exc)
End Try
```

NOTE If, as in the MenuItem1_Click method in frmMain, you turn the cursor into an hourglass, it makes sense to include a Finally block and in the Finally block turn the cursor back into the default cursor. This saves you the embarrassment of having the cursor looking like an hourglass after an error occurred when there is no processing occurring.

Fortunately there is not a lot to retrofit right now so this process is fairly painless. Make sure to avoid adding error handling code in the txtRegionDescription_Validated event in the frmRegionEdit form. Until the next chapter, you are going to leave any error that occurs here unhandled because you will be performing some special error handling for the validated events.

 NOTE Some developers claim you do not have to include error handling in every routine. They may want to put an error handler only in code that is directly executed by the user. Further, if a method was called by another method, only the original method needs the error handler. However, how do you know all of the methods called by all of the other methods in the application? And what happens if the error occurred in an event raised by a class to which you did not have access? So, why take the chance? If there is an error handler in every routine, there is almost no chance of the application crashing without warning and without reporting the error that caused it to terminate.

Creating the ErrorReporting Form

Now that you have a way to retrieve the application errors from the Windows Event Log, you need to give the users a way to send you those errors when they occur. To start with, add a new form to the NorthwindTraders project called *frmReportErrors*. When you are done adding controls to the form, the form should look like the form in Figure 4-5.

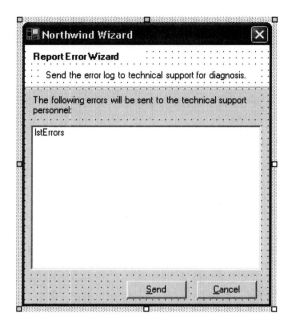

Figure 4-5. Report Error Wizard form

Add the controls in Table 4-2 to the form.

Table 4-2. Report Error Wizard Controls

Control	Control Name
Groupbox	
Label	
Label	
Label	
Listbox	lstErrors
Button	btnSend
Button	btnCancel

Set the properties for these controls according to Table 4-3.

Table 4-3. The Report Error Wizard Control Properties

Control Name	Property	Value
grpHeader	Backcolor	White
lblWizardLabel	Text	Report Error Wizard
lblWizardLabel	Font	Bold
lblInfo	Text	Send the error log to technical support for diagnosis.
lblOperation	Text	The following errors will be sent to the technical support personnel:
btnSend	Text	&Send
btnCancel	Text	&Cancel
frmReportErrors	FormBorderStyle	FixedSingle
frmReportErrors	MaximizeBox	False
frmReportErrors	MinimizeBox	False
frmReportErrors	Text	Northwind Wizard

Import the ErrorLogging namespace using the following line:

```
Imports NorthwindTraders.NorthwindUC.ErrorLogging
```

Next, add the following module-level variables:

```
Private mobjLogErr As LogErrorEvent
Private mobjErrArray() As structLoggedError
```

Before adding any other code into this form, let's copy and paste the LogException method from one of the base classes. It would probably be embarrassing for your error reporting form to cause the application to fail because of an unhandled error!

In the form load event, you will retrieve your errors and place them in the listbox. To do this, add the code in Listing 4-11 to frmReportErrors.

Listing 4-11. The frmReportErrors_Load Method

```
Private Sub frmReportErrors_Load(ByVal sender As Object, _
ByVal e As System.EventArgs) Handles MyBase.Load
    Dim i As Integer

    Try
        mobjLogErr = mobjLogErr.getInstance
        mobjErrArray = mobjLogErr.RetrieveErrors

        For i = 0 To mobjErrArray.Length - 1
            lstErrors.Items.Add(mobjErrArray(i).Message)
        Next

        If lstErrors.Items.Count = 0 Then
            btnSend.Enabled = False
        End If
    Catch exc As Exception
        LogException(exc)
    End Try
End Sub
```

This code simply retrieves the array of errors and loops through them to add them to the listbox. If there are no items in the array, it means there were no errors, so just disable the Send button.

Next, add the code in Listing 4-12 to implement the btnSend_Click method so that technical support can actually get the errors.

Listing 4-12. The btnSend_Click Method

```
Private Sub btnSend_Click(ByVal sender As Object, _
ByVal e As System.EventArgs) Handles btnSend.Click
    Try
        Cursor = Cursors.WaitCursor
        mobjLogErr.SendErrors(mobjErrArray)
    Catch exc As Exception
        LogException(exc)
    Finally
        Cursor = Cursors.Default
        Me.Close()
    End Try
End Sub
```

This code simply calls the SendErrors method of the LogErrorEvent. Finally, to finish the form, add the following two methods:

```
Private Sub btnCancel_Click(ByVal sender As Object, _
ByVal e As System.EventArgs) Handles btnCancel.Click
    Try
        Close()
    Catch exc As Exception
        LogException(exc)
    End Try
End Sub

Private Sub frmReportErrors_Closed(ByVal sender As Object, _
ByVal e As System.EventArgs) Handles MyBase.Closed
    Try
        mobjLogErr = Nothing
        mobjErrArray = Nothing
    Catch exc As Exception
        LogException(exc)
    End Try
End Sub
```

The Cancel button click event simply closes the form, and the Closed event cleans up any of your variables. That is it for the errors form.

NOTE   This form only displays a list of error messages, with no other information. Extending this form to be able to show the actual information about the exception that is being sent to technical support should be easy if you desire to let them see this information. Remember, the more information an attacker has about vulnerabilities in your system, the easier it will be to take advantage of them. Of course, if an attacker is actually on the user's system, they probably already have access to the event log!

To implement the form, let's hard-code a menu item (you will create a dynamic menu structure in Chapter 5, "Building Business Objects," when you clean up the user interface). Go back into frmMain and add a new menu item called *Report Errors*. Double-click the new Report Errors menu item to create the MenuItem.Click event in the code module and alter the method so that it looks like the method in Listing 4-13.

Listing 4-13. Method to Display the Application Errors

```
Private Sub MenuItem2_Click(ByVal sender As System.Object, _
ByVal e As System.EventArgs) Handles MenuItem2.Click
    Dim objReportErrors As frmReportErrors

    Try
        objReportErrors = New frmReportErrors()
        objReportErrors.ShowDialog()
    Catch exc As Exception
        LogException(exc)
    Finally
        objReportErrors = Nothing
    End Try
End Sub
```

NOTE   Your menu control name may not be the same, but it does not matter. As you will notice, I am not following any particular naming convention at this point because you are going to fix most of this work in Chapter 5, "Building Business Objects."

Because you are showing this form using the ShowDialog() method, you do not need to declare this form as a module-level variable.

Testing the NorthwindTraders Exception Storing

Now that you have all of your error handling capabilities in place, it is time to see what happens when you throw an exception that gets stored to the database. But before you can do anything, you need to rebuild the data-centric and shared assemblies and redeploy them to the IIS server.

For the purposes of this test only, modify the LoadList method of the frmRegionList form by adding the following line immediately after the Try statement:

```
Throw New Exception("My Error Test")
```

After you have redeployed the remote assemblies, run the application. When you try to open up the Region List form, you will receive the error shown in Figure 4-6.

Figure 4-6. Error test

Assuming that there were no other errors, this will be the only error that is displayed and the form will then be displayed with an empty list. So now that you have an error, let's look at what it stored in the database. Figure 4-7 shows the exception as stored in the application_errors table.

error_id	username	error_message	error_time	stack_trace
74	MCSD-GQ85JXHY62\Jeff Levinson	My Error Test	8/4/2002 8:11:00 AM	at NorthwindTraders.UserInterface.frmRegionList.LoadList() in C:\Documents and Settings\Jeff Levinson\My Documents\Visual Studio Projects\Northwind\NorthwindTraders\frmRegionList.vb:line 61

Figure 4-7. The exception as stored in application_errors table

Remember to remove the exception you added for this test!

Summary

This chapter covered basic error handling structures and briefly examined the base Exception class. It also reviewed strategies and reasons for enterprise error handling structures and why they are different. You created a flexible, robust, and extensible set of classes for handling and storing almost every conceivable error. In addition, the application can report those errors to technical support regardless of the status of the database.

Using the strategies for error handling in this chapter, the technical support response time of any organization has the potential to become much faster and more efficient.

In the next chapter, you will start looking at the important part of any application—business rules. You will examine what they are, how to handle them, and how to report violations to the user. You will examine object state, make your objects more aware of their own state, and give them the ability to communicate that state to the user interface.

CHAPTER 5

Building Business Objects

WHILE BUILDING BUSINESS APPLICATIONS and overseeing the development of them, I have seen many applications go awry because of the poor construction of the business objects. The rules that the business objects are supposed to implement are not implemented correctly, the rules are implemented in the user interface, or the rules are implemented solely in the database. Each of these three issues has brought more than one system to its knees. I have seen application development cancelled during construction, and I have seen applications scrapped after the construction was complete because of a failure of the business objects. When most of us think of an application, we think about the data the application accesses and the user interface through which the user enters and views information. The truth of the matter is this: These are not the application. The database is a repository for information; it does not do a lot of processing (in some cases, none at all, which is not necessarily right either). The user interface is a window to the data. In a perfect world, the user interface does not do any processing except display the information. The business logic, which is the application, should perform the bulk of the processing of information.

This chapter concentrates on building business objects in such a way that they can verify business rules and report useful information to the user. There are many parts to this process; it is not a cut-and-dried process. However, once you have implemented the business rules correctly, you can reuse the majority of the code with only slight modifications. The .NET Framework provides some mechanisms to help you trap and report errors—no matter what the user interface is. You will start by going back and modifying your code that retrieves Regions because it is a small block of code and it will be easy to understand. Then you will move on to building the Employee business objects where you will see more complicated rule processing.

Exploring Business Rule Types

There are two types of business errors: One is a *constraint error*, which generally controls the size and type of the data so that it can actually fit into the database, and the second type of error is a *business rule*. Database constraint errors generally consist of the appropriate data type and the length of that data type. For example, you cannot put a string into a numeric column; or, if a field is defined as a varchar(10), you could not insert a value with more than 10 characters. A business rule is something along the following lines: An employee is set to receive a raise and the business has put a rule in place that a pay raise cannot be more than 7 percent at a time. The user entering the pay raise percentage accidentally enters 9 percent. The application should capture this and return it to the user as an error. Another example of a business rule may not seem so obvious—the format of data, such as an e-mail address. A business rule might require that the e-mail address is in a valid format. This is something that is difficult, if not impossible, to verify in a database and has nothing to do with data types or lengths.

Reporting Business Rule Violations

So how do you capture these rules? If you have written business objects in Visual Basic (VB) 6, you will remember that the way errors were reported to the user was with the Err.Raise statement. Typically, you would have a list of constants that defined error numbers and another list of constants that defined error messages. Catching the error meant putting an error handler in the routine, checking the number of the error (and do not forget subtracting the vbObjectError value!), and using a message box to display the error to the user. Some developers became clever and added icons to the left or right of a label or textbox in their own custom control that they could use to display error messages to the user in the form of a tooltip. Microsoft has been good at listening to the desires of the development community. And it really listened during the development of .NET. Microsoft now provides the error provider control that you can use to display error information to the user. There are no more errors in message boxes. However, the error provider control is only a tool, which means it can be used in both an efficient and inefficient manner. Consider the following situation:

Your user John is sitting at your application and working on a form with a combination of 30 textboxes and/or combo boxes that he needs to fill out. He finishes filling out the form and clicks the OK button. The form comes back with a message telling John that he made an error in textbox 3. He fixes it and clicks the OK button again. The form comes back with a message telling John he made an error in combo box number 6. He fixes it and clicks the OK button again. It comes back with an error, again and again and again until he fixes all of the errors.

Over the years, many developers have been on the receiving end of an irate user who has been in this situation. In this chapter you will fix this problem the right way, with a reusable set of routines.

 CAUTION If you trap a business rule in the user interface, you *must* also trap it in the data-centric business objects. Not doing so may pose some security issues, but another issue is that other applications may use your objects and they will not be going through your interface!

Creating Your First Rule

When trapping for business rule violations, it is a good idea to map out what those business rules are. For your Region objects, you are going to use database constraints because this is a simple object and there are no true business rules. It will give you a good chance to understand how business rules work.

There are only two rules you can check for at this time—one is for zero-length strings and the other is for values longer than the allowable value. You do not want to allow a zero-length string into a column that does not accept nulls because a zero-length string defeats the purpose of this. If you enter a zero-length string into the RegionDescription column, that is not a null value, and you would end up with a region with no name—obviously something you do not want. So, you can come up with two different error classes, one to handle values longer than the maximum length and one to handle a zero-length string values.

Working with .NET Exception Classes

.NET includes a large number of built-in exception classes. Microsoft recommends you use these exception classes when you can and create new exception classes only when you need to throw an exception that does not exist. To get a list of all of the .NET Framework exception classes, select Debug ➤ Exceptions. You will see a dialog box similar to Figure 5-1.

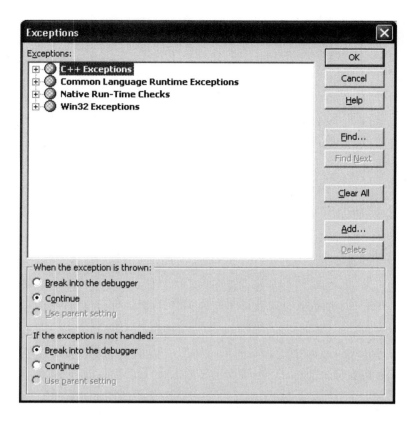

Figure 5-1. .NET Framework Exceptions dialog box

The Exceptions list may be slightly different depending on the languages you added during installation. Expanding the Common Language Runtime Exceptions list item and then the System item displays a tree that looks like Figure 5-2.

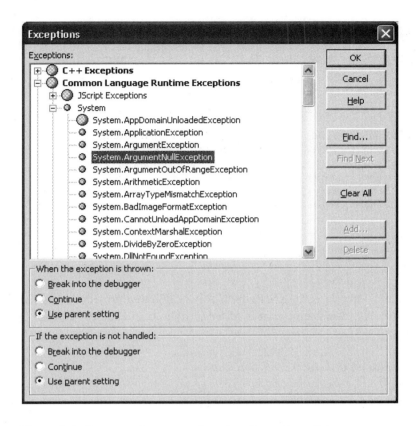

Figure 5-2. Common Language Runtime Exceptions list

Using this dialog box, you can search for all different types of .NET exceptions. Get to know this list; it will cut down on your development time because you will not be duplicating exceptions that already exist.

Creating the Error Classes

You will have to create your own error classes to handle a maximum length exception and a zero-length string exception.

 NOTE Microsoft has developed a set of exception handling libraries called the *Exception Management Application Block*. But a set of libraries is really just scratching the surface. It is a set of code you can also use to implement your own exception classes, and it is designed as a framework. Microsoft also includes the source code and best practices for its use. If you are creating large-scale applications or a repository of enterprise application errors, this is probably a good source of code and/or information.

To begin, add a new class module to the NorthwindShared project and call it *Errors*. Delete the class declaration that is added by default and add the code in Listing 5-1.

Listing 5-1. The MaximumLengthException Class

```
Option Strict On
Option Explicit On

Namespace Errors

    Public Class MaximumLengthException
        Inherits ApplicationException

        Public Sub New(ByVal MaxLength As Integer)
            MyBase.New("The maximum length for this value is " _
            & MaxLength.ToString & " characters.")
        End Sub
    End Class

End Namespace
```

All of your custom errors will be placed in the Errors namespace so that you can find them easily. Here you are creating an exception class called *MaximumLengthException* using .NET's exception naming standards (the error name followed by the word *Exception*). Your constructor accepts the maximum length you are allowing for the rule and creates a message to pass in to the base class constructor. This exception is now reusable by any piece of data that might violate this rule. Now you need to add one more exception to catch zero-length strings (empty strings). To do this, enter the following code in the Errors namespace:

```
Public Class ZeroLengthException
    Inherits System.ApplicationException

    Public Sub New()
        MyBase.New("A value must be entered for this item.")
    End Sub
End Class
```

Creating the BusinessErrors Class

As mentioned earlier, you need to have a way to report multiple errors from the data-centric business logic to the user interface instead of one error at a time. The easiest way to do this is to pass an array of errors to the user interface. However, you need an easy way to add values to the array so that you are not calling ReDim Preserve all the time. To this end, you will create a new class called *BusinessErrors*. Before you do this, though, you need to create a new structure to hold your collection of errors. In the Structures code module in the NorthwindShared project, add the following structure:

```
<Serializable()> Public Structure structErrors
    Public errProperty As String
    Public errMessage As String
End Structure
```

Next, add an Imports statement at the top of the Errors code module to import the Structures namespace:

```
Imports NorthwindTraders.NorthwindShared.Structures
```

Create the class shown in Listing 5-2 in the Errors code module in the Errors namespace.

Listing 5-2. The BusinessErrors Class

```
<Serializable()> Public Class BusinessErrors
    Inherits System.Collections.CollectionBase
```

```
        Public Sub Add(ByVal strProperty As String, ByVal strMessage As String)
            Dim obj As New structErrors()
            obj.errProperty = strProperty
            obj.errMessage = strMessage
            list.Add(obj)
            obj = Nothing
        End Sub

        Public Function Item(ByVal Index As Integer) As structErrors
            Return CType(list.Item(Index), structErrors)
        End Function

        Public Sub Remove(ByVal Index As Integer)
            list.RemoveAt(Index)
        End Sub
End Class
```

In Listing 5-2, you are inheriting from the CollectionBase object because you will only need to loop through these items using a For..Next loop—you do not have to access anything by key. You will pass in the property that caused the error and the error message and add them to the list. You could require that a structError object be passed in, but that would require the user of this object to do a lot of extra work all over the place (the object would have to create a structure variable, assign the properties, and then pass the structure to the collection class). As it is, the work happens in only one place. Everything else is part of a standard collection class. Now it is time to start implementing your new class.

Adding Business Rules to the Data-Centric Object

Before you begin trapping rules, you need to import the Errors namespace. Add the following line in the header of the RegionDC code module:

```
Imports NorthwindTraders.NorthwindShared.Errors
```

Next, add the following variable declaration in the header of the RegionDC class:

```
Private mobjBusErr As BusinessErrors
```

Now, in the Save routine, add the following line of code below the Dim statements but above the sRegion with statement:

```
mobjBusErr = New BusinessErrors()
```

Now you are ready to begin handling the rule violations.

The only property you are checking for business rule violations on is the RegionDescription property because the RegionID property is read-only. To review, this is what your RegionDescription property currently looks like:

```
Public Property RegionDescription() As String
    Get
        Return mstrRegionDescription
    End Get
    Set(ByVal Value As String)
        mstrRegionDescription = Value
    End Set
End Property
```

Because you are going to be trapping for the violations when the property is set, you are only concerned with the Set block. All of your business rule checks will occur in a Try..Catch block, so start by altering the Set block of code so that it looks like the following:

```
Try
    mstrRegionDescription = Value
Catch exc As Exception
    mobjBusErr.Add("Region Description", exc.Message)
End Try
```

The Catch block of your routines will be used to catch any business violations you throw. When the error is thrown, you set the property name and pass in the exception message and then continue on your way.

To perform your validations, let's add the following If..Then..Else statement right below the Try statement:

```
If Value.Length = 0 Then
    Throw New ZeroLengthException
Else
    If Value.Length > 50 Then
        Throw New MaximumLengthException(50)
    End If
End If
```

Now you have all the rules in place to validate, and you can trap the violations.

NOTE   Examining the code, you will notice it is only going to catch one violation per rule. In other words, when an exception is thrown, you do not go back and check any of the additional rules. This is easier to handle than trying to catch multiple errors per property. As you will see when you get to the user interface, it is easier for you and less confusing for the user if you only handle one error per property.

Retrieving Business Rules

Next you will add another method that is extremely useful in large business applications—the GetBusinessRules method. This method has one purpose: to return a set of all of the rules implemented by the class. There are two good reasons for doing this. The first is that it makes sense in many applications to be able to inform the user of all of the rules of an object when they are performing data entry. The second reason is to allow other applications that may use your objects to be able to retrieve a list of your objects rules. Although these rules should be published in application documentation, it is often advantageous to allow the object to be self-describing.

NOTE   This is not truly a self-describing object, although it looks like one right now. It is not self-describing because first you have to duplicate your business rules, and second, the object does not really examine itself. Chapter 10, "Using Reflection," shows you how to create a truly self-aware class in terms of business rules.

Add the following code to implement this method into the RegionDC class:

```
Public Function GetBusinessRules() As BusinessErrors
    Dim objBusRules As New BusinessErrors()
    With objBusRules
        .Add("Region Description", "The value cannot be null.")
        .Add("Region Description", "The value cannot be more than 50 " _
        & "characters in length.")
    End With

    Return objBusRules
End Function
```

This method creates a BusinessErrors object and adds all of the errors that can occur in your object to it. It then returns this collection of errors to the calling code. To allow this method to be accessible from the client code, you need to add another method to your IRegion interface. To do this, alter the IRegion interface in the Interfaces code module so that it reads as follows:

```
Public Interface IRegion
    Function LoadProxy() As DataSet
    Function LoadRecord(ByVal intID As Integer) As Structures.structRegion
    Function Save(ByVal sRegion As structRegion, _
    ByRef intID As Integer) As BusinessErrors
    Sub Delete(ByVal intID As Integer)
    Function GetBusinessRules() As BusinessErrors
End Interface
```

You made two changes to this interface. The first change is to the Save routine, which is now a function that returns a BusinessErrors object. The second change is the addition of the GetBusinessRules function. Once you incorporate these changes, you will have a couple of syntax errors until you import the following namespace into the Interfaces code module:

```
Imports NorthwindTraders.NorthwindShared.Errors
```

NOTE This change is why you returned the ID of the saved record as a ByRef value.

Return to the RegionDC class and alter the GetBusinessRules function so that it implements the interface function you just created. To do this, change the signature line of the method to read as follows:

```
Public Function GetBusinessRules() As BusinessErrors _
Implements IRegion.GetBusinessRules
```

Returning Errors during the Save

Before you can report errors to the user interface, you need to alter your Save routine (at this point you have an error caused by your altering of the IRegion Interface)—first so that it matches your interface signature and second so that it actually returns your collection of errors. Alter the Save method signature to read as follows:

```
Public Function Save(ByVal sRegion As structRegion, _
    ByRef intID As Integer) As BusinessErrors Implements IRegion.Save
```

The way this code is currently structured, the following events will take place when you try to save your object:

1. The BusinessErrors object is instantiated.

2. The public RegionDescription property will have its value set.

3. Any error will cause an error to be added to the BusinessError object.

The last thing you need to do is to respond to any business rules that were violated during the setting of the properties. To do this, add the following code to check to see if there were any errors (add this code after the With sRegion block in place of the code that is already there):

```
If mobjBusErr.Count = 0 Then
    cn.Open()

    With cmd
        .Connection = cn
        .CommandType = CommandType.StoredProcedure
        .CommandText = "usp_region_save"
        .Parameters.Add("@id", mintRegionID)
        .Parameters.Add("@region", mstrRegionDescription)
        .Parameters.Add("@new_id", SqlDbType.Int).Direction = _
        ParameterDirection.Output
        .ExecuteNonQuery()
        intID = Convert.ToInt32(.Parameters.Item("@id").Value)
    End With

    cmd = Nothing
    cn.Close()
End If


Return mobjBusErr
```

The only change here is the addition of the If..Then statement and the addition of the Return line. The If statement checks to see if any errors were thrown. If you did, then you skip the block of code that calls the database; otherwise you save the data to the database. Finally, you return the collection of errors. On the user interface side, you will check the count of errors to see if you need to do anything with the object that is returned to you. Now you are ready to move on to the user-centric objects.

Adding Business Rules to the User-Centric Object

When you add business rules to the user-centric objects, you expect to have these rule violations reported to the user interface immediately. For that reason, the only rules you should place here are the database constraint rules. The reason for this is that the real business rules can be quite involved and may necessitate some checks against the database or even other systems. Also, changes to the database structure are rare, but changes to the business rules can occur on a daily or weekly basis. Therefore, it is best to place the business rules in only one place.

NOTE   Placing database constraint business rules in the user-centric objects is optional, but if you have a lot of users, this helps cut down on the server load by only allowing calls to be made when the data is at least within the database constraint limits. Also, these rule violations will be returned to the user when they leave the current field in which they are working.

Using the BrokenRules Class

In the best situation, an object should be self-aware and should be able to report information about itself to other objects that consume it. A well-known author named Rockford Lhotka wrote a book called *Visual Basic 6.0 Business Objects* (Wrox Press, 1998) in which he builds just such an object. In this book he creates a class called the BrokenRules class. I read this book many years ago, and it became the book I always used as a reference. This section presents an updated version of the BrokenRules class, which behaves in a slightly different way but with the same purpose.

Add a new class to the NorthwindUC project and call it *BrokenRules*. This class is a specialized collection class that inherits from the DictionaryBase class. This class keeps track of the rules that have been broken in a user-centric object. Enter the code in Listing 5-3 in the BrokenRules module.

Listing 5-3. The BrokenRules Class

```
Option Strict On
Option Explicit On

Public Class BrokenRules
    Inherits System.Collections.DictionaryBase

    Public Event RuleBroken(ByVal IsBroken As Boolean)

    Public Sub BrokenRule(ByVal strProperty As String, ByVal blnBroken As _
Boolean)
        Try
          If blnBroken Then
                dictionary.Add(strProperty, blnBroken)
          Else
                dictionary.Remove(strProperty)
          End If
        Catch
          'Do Nothing
        Finally
            If dictionary.Count > 0 Then
                RaiseEvent RuleBroken(True)
            Else
                RaiseEvent RuleBroken(False)
            End If
        End Try
    End Sub

    Public Sub ClearRules()
        dictionary.Clear()
    End Sub
End Class
```

This class works as follows:

1. The class is instantiated when the object that it is checking the rules for is instantiated.

2. When a property is set, if it breaks a rule, the BrokenRule method is called with a value of True.

3. When a property is set, if it does not break a rule, the BrokenRule method is called with a value of False.

4. If the rule had previously been broken, but it is no longer broken, then that value will be cleared from the dictionary object.

5. If the rule had never been broken, it is passed with a value of False and the code tries to remove the value from the dictionary. Because the value was not in the dictionary, an exception will be thrown. This is the exception you catch and ignore.

6. Finally, you check the count of the broken rules and raise the RuleBroken event with the appropriate flag.

TIP   The Catch block is included because if no Catch block is available to handle the error, even though the Finally block runs, the exception is not cleared from memory. To try this, when you have completed the coding in this chapter, comment out the Catch block and break a rule in the user interface to see what happens.

The ClearRules routine simply clears all of the rules from the dictionary object. You use this because every time you go back to the database to load an individual record, you want to reset any rules that have been previously broken. You will see this when you implement the BrokenRules class in the next section.

Implementing The BrokenRules Class

Now you need to implement the BrokenRules class in your Region class. The first thing you need to do is to declare the BrokenRules class using the WithEvents keyword so you can receive the message from the RuleBroken event. Add the following module-level declaration in the Region class:

```
Private WithEvents mobjRules As BrokenRules
```

Now you need to create an event in the Region class so that you can pass on this message to the user interface. To do this, create the following event:

```
Public Event BrokenRule(ByVal IsBroken As Boolean)
```

Now you need to respond to the RuleBroken event and pass this information on to the user interface. Add the following code to take care of this:

```
Private Sub mobjRules_RuleBroken(ByVal IsBroken As Boolean) _
Handles mobjRules.RuleBroken
    RaiseEvent BrokenRule(IsBroken)
End Sub
```

This code simply passes the value that was given to the Region object up to the user interface. The last thing you need to do is to instantiate the mobjRules variable. Alter *both* of the constructors so that they look like the following:

```
Public Sub New()
    mobjRules = New BrokenRules()
    mobjRules.BrokenRule("Region Description", True)
End Sub

Public Sub New(ByVal intID As Integer)
    mobjRules = New BrokenRules()
    mintRegionID = intID
End Sub
```

Notice that in the Sub New() constructor, you broke the Region Description rule. That is a new object and you do not know what will go there, but you do know that it requires at least one property that needs to be set, so on instantiation you mark the RegionDescription property as invalid.

NOTE   All properties that do not have default values (discussed later) should be broken. The logic behind this is the following: You do not want an object to be marked as valid until all of the values are set according to the rules. By breaking the rule to begin with, you ensure the object will not be valid until the property is set to a valid value.

However, for the constructor being called for an existing object that you are loading from the database, you can assume the rules have not been violated.

NOTE   There may be some controversy over this. If your application was used to put things into the database, the assumption is that you checked the values. There is also an assumption that if the value violated the database constraints (which is all you are checking for here), it would not have been allowed in the first place. I prefer not to waste processing power, especially as you start building objects with many more properties.

This is all the infrastructure that needs to be created to inform the user interface that the object has one or more broken rules; now you need a way to trap those rules.

Trapping Business Rule Violations

Because you are accessing the custom exceptions you created in the Errors namespace, you need to import that namespace into this module:

```
Imports NorthwindTraders.NorthwindShared.Errors
```

Now you will alter the RegionDescription Set code block. Listing 5-4 shows the original code for the RegionDescription property.

Listing 5-4. The Original RegionDescription Property

```
Public Property RegionDescription() As String
    Get
        Return mstrRegionDescription
    End Get
    Set(ByVal Value As String)
        If mstrRegionDescription.trim <> Value Then
            If Not Loading Then
                mblnDirty = True
            End If
            mstrRegionDescription = Value
        End If
    End Set
End Property
```

Add the rules you specified in the data-centric class first (in this case, it is a simple copy and paste) so that the RegionDescription property Set block of code now has the following additions (place this code right below the Set line, just as in the data-centric class):

```
If Value.Length = 0 Then
    Throw New ZeroLengthException
Else
    If Value.Length > 50 Then
        Throw New MaximumLengthException(50)
    End If
End If
```

Now, this code will not quite do it for you because once an error is thrown, it will be passed right up to the user interface. However, you want to make sure the object knows that it broke a rule (or did not break a rule) by passing the appropriate information to the BrokenRules class. To do this, wrap the code in a Try..Catch block. Listing 5-5 shows the entire modified RegionDescription property.

Listing 5-5. The Modified RegionDescription Property

```
Public Property RegionDescription() As String
    Get
        Return mstrRegionDescription
    End Get
    Set(ByVal Value As String)
        Try
            If Value.Length = 0 Then
                Throw New ZeroLengthException
            Else
                If Value.Length > 50 Then
                    Throw New MaximumLengthException(50)
                End If
            End If
            If mstrRegionDescription.trim <> Value Then
                mstrRegionDescription = Value
                If Not Loading Then
                    mobjRules.BrokenRule("Region Description", False)
                    mblnDirty = True
                End If
            End If
        Catch exc As Exception
            mobjRules.BrokenRule("Region Description", True)
            mstrRegionDescription = Value
            mblnDirty = True
            Throw exc
        End Try
    End Set
End Property
```

Let's take a look at what is happening here and why. The beginning of the Set block looks the same as the RegionDC class. This is to be expected because there are no rules other than database constraints for which you are checking. After all of the business rules are checked, the code changes a little. First, you check to see if the value entered is already equal to the value that you had. The trim method is necessary because the field is declared as a char field in the database:

```
If mstrRegionDescription.trim <> Value Then
```

If it is, you do not want to mark the object as dirty if it has not really changed. If the values are different, then you want to set the module-level value equal to the value that was passed in (at this point, it has not broken any rules, so it is allowed):

```
mstrRegionDescription = Value
```

If you are loading the object, then you want to skip marking anything as dirty or playing with the BrokenRules class because it is unnecessary. If you are not loading the object, though, you need to let the BrokenRules class know that if there is a broken rule for this property that it is no longer broken and should be removed:

```
mobjRules.BrokenRule("Region Description", False)
```

You also know at this point that the object changed, so you need to set the dirty flag:

```
mblnDirty = True
```

Next comes the Catch block. First you catch the fact that an exception was thrown and you break the rule for that property in the BrokenRules object:

```
mobjRules.BrokenRule("Region Description", True)
```

CAUTION   It is especially important to note that whatever you call the property when you pass it to the BrokenRule method does not matter. What does matter is that you use the same name for a single property. The reason for this is that this is the key in the dictionary object in the BrokenRules object!

Then you set the property to a value you know violates the business rules (in almost all cases it should probably be the value that was passed in because that triggered the rule violation in the first place):

```
mstrRegionDescription = Value
mblnDirty = True
```

Then you set the IsDirty flag to true. Why do you do that? Why don't you leave both of those properties alone? The answer takes some explaining. If you do not do either of these things, then this is what will happen when the user enters an invalid value:

1. The invalid value will be passed to the Region object.

2. It will violate one of the business rules.

3. Code execution will jump to the Catch block.

4. The rule will be marked as broken.

5. The error will be rethrown to the user interface.

Nowhere in these steps did the value of mstrRegionDescription change. The only thing that effectively occurred was that the RegionDescription property was marked as having a broken rule. Now, assume that the user said, "Whoops," and either does an undo or types the same entry. In that case, the following steps would take place:

1. The valid value will be passed to the Region object.

2. It will not violate any of the business rules.

3. It will be compared with the module-level RegionDescription variable.

4. There will be *no* difference between the two values.

5. Code execution continues back in the user interface.

Although the value in the object will be correct (because it never changed), the object will not be marked as dirty and there will be a rule broken for the RegionDescription property. The user interface will never be able to determine that everything is OK. That is a problem. So by setting the property to an invalid value and marking it as dirty, the user interface knows that the object has changed somehow (this is useful so you can ask a user if they really want to close a form and lose their changes), and the property is different than what was originally entered. If the original value is put back in, it will not match the internal value.

The Save routine will not run if there is a broken rule, so you should add the code in to make that a reality because the class will not do it on its own!

Modify the Save routine so that the entire routine is in an If…Then statement that reads as follows:

```
Public Sub Save()
    If mobjRules.Count = 0 Then
        'Original code here
        .
        .
        .
    End If
End Sub
```

Now the Save routine will not run if there are any broken rules. And finally you need to add one read-only property called *IsValid*. This property lets another object check the status of this object. Listing 5-6 shows the code for this property.

Listing 5-6. The IsValid Property

```
Public ReadOnly Property IsValid() As Boolean
    Get
        If mobjRules.Count > 0 Then
            Return False
        Else
            Return True
        End If
    End Get
End Property
```

This way you can always check the status of your object, which you will do in the next section.

Returning Business Rules to the User Interface

In the previous section you added a GetBusinessRules method to your data-centric objects. You need to implement a routine in the user-centric objects that can retrieve this data for you. Then you need to implement a form that you can use to display this information to the user.

Add the code for the GetBusinessRules method in Listing 5-7 to the Region class.

Listing 5-7. The GetBusinessRules Method

```
Public Function GetBusinessRules() As BusinessErrors
    Dim objIRegion As IRegion
    Dim objBusRules As BusinessErrors

    objIRegion = CType(Activator.GetObject(GetType(IRegion), _
    AppConstants.REMOTEOBJECTS & LISTENER), IRegion)
    objBusRules = objIRegion.GetBusinessRules
    objIRegion = Nothing

    Return objBusRules
End Function
```

This routine calls the GetBusinessRules method on the remote object and returns a BusinessErrors collection, which you then return to the user interface.

Displaying Business Rules to the User

The entire purpose of returning your objects' rules to the user interface is so the user can see all of the possible rule combinations at once. It is too difficult to continually modify these rules in a help file or anywhere else, but as a developer makes changes to the rules in the classes, they should be able to easily update the GetBusinessRules routine. In this way, a user running the application will always have access to the latest rules that apply to a certain screen.

Creating the Business Rules Form

Now you need to create a form that you can use to display business rules from any object you create. To do this, add a new form to the NorthwindTraders project and call it *frmBusinessRules*. When you are done adding controls, your form should look like Figure 5-3.

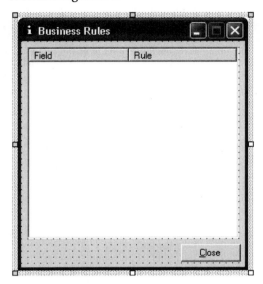

Figure 5-3. The Business Rules form

Add the controls listed in Table 5-1.

Table 5-1. The Business Rules Form Controls

Control	Name
Listview	lvwList
Button	btnClose

Next, set the properties for the controls according to Table 5-2.

Table 5-2. The Business Rules Form Control Properties

Control	Property	Value
frmBusinessRules	Text	Business Rules
frmBusinessRules	MaximizeBox	False
frmBusinessRules	Icon	MSGBOX04.ICO
lvwList	View	Details
lvwList	Columns Collection	Add ColumnHeader1
lvwList	Columns Collection	Add ColumnHeader2
ColumnHeader1	Text	Field
ColumnHeader2	Text	Rule
lvwList	Anchor	Top, Left, Right, Bottom
btnClose	Text	&Close
btnClose	Anchor	Right, Bottom

Add the following code to the top of the frmBusinessRules code module:

```
Option Explicit On
Option Strict On

Imports NorthwindTraders.NorthwindShared.Errors
```

Next, modify the constructor so that it reads as follows:

```
Public Sub New(ByVal objBE As BusinessErrors)
    MyBase.New()

    'This call is required by the Windows Form Designer.
    InitializeComponent()

    'Add any initialization after the InitializeComponent() call
    LoadListView(objBE)
End Sub
```

The LoadListView method (shown in Listing 5-8) comes next. This method takes your BusinessErrors object and populates the listview with the contents.

Listing 5-8. The LoadListView Method

```
Private Sub LoadListView(ByVal objBusErr As BusinessErrors)
    Dim i As Integer

    For i = 0 To objBusErr.Count - 1
        Dim lst As New ListViewItem(objBusErr.Item(i).errProperty)
        lst.SubItems.Add(objBusErr.Item(i).errMessage)
        lvwList.Items.Add(lst)
    Next
End Sub
```

Next, add the two methods shown in Listing 5-9, one to respond to the Close button click event and the other to respond to the form Paint event. This event occurs when the user resizes the form—it resizes the listview columns for you.

Listing 5-9. Additional BusinessRules Methods

```
Private Sub frmBusinessRules_Paint(ByVal sender As Object, _
ByVal e As System.Windows.Forms.PaintEventArgs) Handles MyBase.Paint
    Dim i As Integer

    For i = 0 To lvwList.Columns.Count - 1
        lvwList.Columns.Item(i).Width = CInt((lvwList.Size.Width / _
        lvwList.Columns.Count) - 6)
    Next
End Sub

Private Sub btnClose_Click(ByVal sender As Object, _
ByVal e As System.EventArgs) Handles btnClose.Click
    Close()
End Sub
```

You now have a form that can display business rules, regardless of which object generated the business rules that you are going to display.

Updating the Base Edit Form

Now let's edit the frmEditBase form so that you can display the business rules from any of the edit forms you will create. Add a new button to the frmEditBase form and set the following properties for it according to Table 5-3. The form should look like Figure 5-4 when you are done.

Table 5-3. The frmEditBase Rules Modification

Control	Property	Value
Button	Name	btnRules
btnRules	Modifiers	Protected
btnRules	Anchor	Bottom, Left
btnRules	Text	Empty String
btnRules	Size	24,23
btnRules	Image	MSGBOX04.ICO

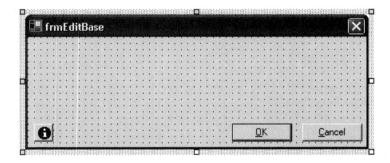

Figure 5-4. frmEditBase with the btnRules button

When you are done, rebuild the solution so that the changes are reflected in the frmRegionEdit form.

TIP One of the hazards of using a base form is that when you position a control on the form, it needs to be visible in any of the forms that are inheriting from it. When you look at the frmRegionEdit form, you will probably not be able to find the btnRules button. One simple solution to this problem is to go to the frmRegionEdit form, and select the btnRules from the object drop-down list (as shown in Figure 5-5). Then, set the location to 0,0 and you will be able to move it to the correct position.

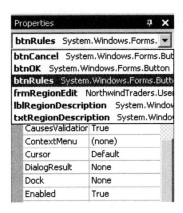

Figure 5-5. Object drop-down list

In the frmRegionEdit form, double-click the btnRules button to create the btnRules_Click method and modify the method to match the code in Listing 5-10.

Listing 5-10. The btnRules_Click Method

```
Private Sub btnRules_Click(ByVal sender As System.Object, _
ByVal e As System.EventArgs) Handles btnRules.Click
    Dim frmRules As New frmBusinessRules(mobjRegion.GetBusinessRules)
    frmRules.ShowDialog()
    frmRules = Nothing
End Sub
```

You are all done. At this point you have finished making changes to the data-centric objects and shared objects so it is time to build the solution and deploy the server-side assemblies. To do this, simply build the application and copy the NorthwindDC.dll and NorthwindShared.dll files to the C:\inetpub\wwwroot\Northwind\bin folder—or wherever you placed the directory that links to the virtual directory in Internet Information Server (IIS). You can now run the application and test to see if the business rules form can be displayed. The result should be identical to what is shown in Figure 5-6.

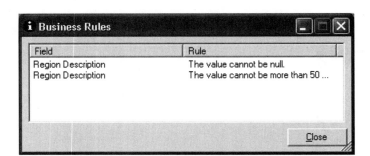

Figure 5-6. Completed Business Rules form

Responding to Object Changes in the User Interface

You have implemented business rules in your objects; now it is time to tell the users about the state of the objects they are accessing. Microsoft has provided a great new control called the *ErrorProvider*. The control is simple: It displays an icon (any icon you want) next to whatever control chooses to use it. You add the ErrorProvider control to the form level, and it is available to all of the controls on the form. In general, there are few good reasons to have more than one error provider on a single Windows form.

TIP One reason to have more than one error provider on a Windows form is that you want to display different icons depending on the type of error or some other notification besides an error.

Implementing the ErrorProvider Control

To begin with, add an ErrorProvider control to your base edit form. Go to the frmEditBase form in design view. Double-click the ErrorProvider control in the Toolbox. Once you have done that, the form should look like Figure 5-7.

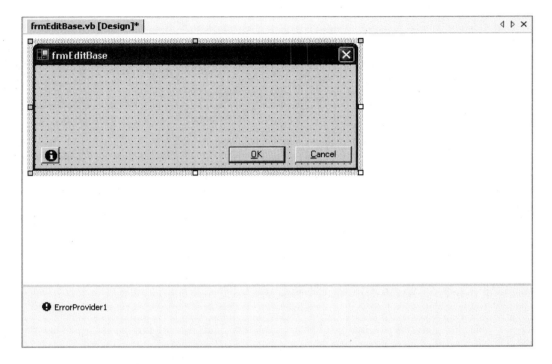

Figure 5-7. ErrorProvider on the frmEditBase form

Rename the control to *erpMain*. The ErrorProvider control has the properties shown in Table 5-4.

Table 5-4. The ErrorProvider Control Properties

Property	Description
BlinkRate	The rate at which the icon blinks (in milliseconds)
BlinkStyle	Has the following values: BlinkIfDifferent: If the error provider is not cleared and a new message is set, the icon will blink. AlwaysBlink: Icon always blinks. NeverBlink: Icon never blinks.
DataMember	The specific pieces of data to which the provider is bound
DataSource	The data source to which the control is bound
Icon	The icon that is displayed. The default icon is an exclamation mark.
Modifiers	Public, Protected, Friend, and Private

Alter any of the properties to suit your needs, but you must change the Modifiers property to Protected. This is so it can be accessed by all of your forms that inherit from the frmEditBase. Once you have done this, rebuild the solution so that your frmRegionEdit form reflects this change.

Displaying Errors to the User

Now let's edit the frmRegionEdit form so that you can take advantage of the self-aware object. Change the mobjRegion variable declaration so that it now handles events:

```
Private WithEvents mobjRegion As Region
```

Select mobjRegion from the Class Name drop-down list and select the BrokenRule event from the Method Name drop-down list. Modify the method that is created so that it looks like the method in Listing 5-11.

Listing 5-11. The BrokenRule Method Implemented

```
Private Sub mobjRegion_BrokenRule(ByVal IsBroken As Boolean) _
Handles mobjRegion.BrokenRule
    If IsBroken Then
        btnOK.Enabled = False
    Else
        btnOK.Enabled = True
    End If
End Sub
```

All you are doing here is checking to see if a rule is broken, and if it is, you disable the OK button; if there are no broken rules, you enable the OK button.

CAUTION Some people use the absolute least amount of code necessary. For instance, the code in Listing 5-11 could be reduced to one line of code: btnOk.Enabled = Not IsBroken. But what if you need to take other actions that are dependant on the state of the object? In some cases, the least amount of code presents the most problems later.

Next you need to edit your Region Description textbox properties. When you select the txtRegionDescription textbox, there will be two new properties available to you in the Properties window. One property reads *IconAlignment On erpMain* (change this property value to *MiddleLeft*), and the other property reads, *IconPadding on erpMain*. The first property just selects where the icon will be displayed in relationship to the control, and the second property sets the padding around the icon. Set the icon alignment to the left side of the control if you like to see errors lined up uniformly as opposed to icons being displayed at the end of the control (which is the default). There is a third property associated with the error provider control, the Error property, which is displayed in the Properties window as *Error on erpMain*. Setting this property causes the error icon to be displayed. This is the property you will be setting in code to make the error icon appear next to your txtRegionDescription textbox.

TIP The development team should use the same Integrated Development Environment (IDE) settings for the entire project. It is often good to test, with your projects settings, the placement of the error icon. Then you can devise a standard that says there must be *X* number of grid dots between the labels and the edit controls.

Now you need to edit the txtRegionDescription_Validate event so you can actually reflect the state of your object in the user interface. Modify the txtRegionDescription_Validate method so that it looks like the code in Listing 5-12.

Listing 5-12. The Modified txtRegionDescription_Validated Method

```
Private Sub txtRegionDescription_Validated(ByVal sender As Object, _
ByVal e As System.EventArgs) Handles txtRegionDescription.Validated
    Dim txt As TextBox = CType(sender, TextBox)

    Try
        mobjRegion.RegionDescription = txt.Text
        erpmain.SetError(txt, "")
    Catch exc As Exception
        erpmain.SetError(txt, "")
        erpmain.SetError(txt, exc.Message)
    End Try
End Sub
```

The first line converts the sender object into a textbox object. Then you enclose the property Set method in a Try..Catch block because now, if the value is invalid, an exception will be thrown. If it is valid, you simply clear the error. If the value is invalid, then you first need to clear the error. The reason for this is that if there was an error before, and you set a new error, the error icon will still be displayed, but it will only display the original error. Then you set the new error.

 TIP   Setting the error equal to an empty string clears the error icon.

The last thing you need to do is to disable the OK button if this form is opened as the result of the user clicking the Add button on the frmRegionList form. The reason for this is that your object is declared and instantiated in the frmRegionList form. Therefore, even though the object breaks its rules, the event is not reported to the edit form because the edit form has not been instantiated yet. And, when the user elects to add a record, they will start with an empty object that contains at least one broken rule, so it is invalid.

To do this, add the following line at the end of the constructor in the frmRegionList form:

```
If Not mobjRegion.IsValid Then
    btnOK.Enabled = False
End If
```

You are done! To test the results, run the application and do the following:

1. Select a Region from the Region List form and click Edit.

2. Delete the value in the Region Description textbox and tab out of the control.

3. You should see an error icon, and when you put your mouse over it, it should tell you that a value must be entered for this item and the OK button should be disabled.

4. Then, enter more than 50 characters in the Region Description textbox and tab out of the control.

5. You should see an error icon that tells you that the maximum length is 50 characters and the OK button is still disabled.

6. Enter a valid value and tab out of the text box.

7. The OK button should become enabled and you should be able to save the object.

Handling Edit Cancellations

The last thing you have to cover is rolling back your objects' state if a user cancels an edit. The main reason to do this is for consistency. Your project standard is to load an individual record from the database every time the user wants to edit a record. This, in part, negates the need to roll back changes. However, it is never a good idea to leave an object in an invalid state. After every single edit in the user interface, a property is set in your user-centric objects. If the user cancels their actions, the object will not be valid because the information will not match the data in the database.

Chapter 3, "Creating the Application Infrastructure," mentioned that the purpose of the msRegion variable in the Region class was going to be used to help maintain object state in case the user clicked a Cancel button. Here you will implement that functionality, which is surprisingly simple. Add the following new method to the Region class in the Region.vb module:

```
Public Sub Rollback()
    LoadObject()
End Sub
```

This method calls the LoadObject method, which loads the class members from the module-level structure. This returns the object to the state it was in before the edit began.

Finally, you need to make sure users do not accidentally lose any changes. Also, if they do want to lose their changes, you need to roll back the changes by calling the Rollback method of your Region object. To do this, add the code in Listing 5-13 to the frmRegionEdit form.

Listing 5-13. The frmRegionEdit_Closing Method

```
Private Sub frmRegionEdit_Closing(ByVal sender As Object, _
ByVal e As System.ComponentModel.CancelEventArgs) Handles MyBase.Closing
    Dim dlgResult As DialogResult

    Try
        If mobjRegion.IsDirty Then
            dlgResult = MessageBox.Show("The Region information has " _
            & "changed, do you want to exit without saving your changes?", _
            "Confirm Cancel", MessageBoxButtons.YesNo, _
            MessageBoxIcon.Question)

            If dlgResult = DialogResult.No Then
                e.Cancel = True
            Else
                mobjRegion.Rollback()
            End If
        End If
    Catch exc As Exception
        LogException(exc)
    End Try
End Sub
```

This code checks to see if the object is dirty (if the user clicked OK to close the form, the dirty flag is set back to false after the change). If it is dirty, you ask the user if they really want to exit and lose their changes. If they answer no, you set the Cancel property for the form to True, which stops the form from closing. If they do want to lose their changes, you call the Rollback method. That is all there is to it.

NOTE You may want to ask the user if they want to save their changes before they exit the form and give them the option of clicking Yes, No, or Cancel. You can do this, but it is just a bit more involved. To do it, you need to call the code in the btnOK_Click method, check to see if there were any business errors from the data-centric object, and then cancel the close if there were and close the form if not.

Summary

In this chapter you have built a complete system for trapping and displaying business rule violations to the user interface. You have done this by creating your own exceptions that inherit from .NET's base exception class and by making your objects self-aware. You have seen the powerful and reusable BrokenRules class to keep track of your objects' state. Through this class you have given an object the ability to tell any of the objects' consumers that the object is valid or invalid.

The user now has a quick, easy, and powerful way to see the rules that they have broken and all of the objects' rules if they want to. In Chapter 10, "Using Reflection," you will take this class and turn it into a truly self-aware class!

In the next chapter you will take a break from your objects and concentrate on the user interface. You will implement the standard cut, copy, paste, find, and select all methods that seem to be missing from most internal business applications. You will also create a dynamic menu structure, add a status bar, and dynamically add and remove resources.

CHAPTER 6

Creating the Windows User Interface

UP TO THIS POINT you have built a set of self-aware business objects and the forms needed to display the values returned by those business objects. You will now move on to developing the mechanisms that you will use to build the user interface. You can do many things to give the user a good experience with your application. In this chapter you will concentrate on building not only a functional user interface but one that looks good. This includes incorporating icons, displaying the application's status on a status bar, and providing basic Windows functionality that users often take for granted. More than anything your goal should be to create an application that users enjoy using.

NOTE   To many people—developers included—a good application is one that performs the job it is designed to do. A successful application, on the other hand, is one that is well liked and used by many people. *Successful* and *good* are two different terms that make a huge difference in a corporation. I have seen applications that developers would consider to be good fail (in the sense that nobody used it, and they went back to the old way of doing things); therefore, they were not successful. The best application is one that is good and successful. To make a successful application, it has to be an application that not only meets the users' needs but is also something that they like and want to use.

One piece of basic functionality you will implement is the ability to cut, copy, or paste from a menu or toolbar or by using the control keys. Part of this is easy to accomplish (creating the Control key combination functionality) because it is built in to almost all of the text editing controls. Part of this is more difficult to accomplish (accessing the functionality from a toolbar or menu) because although there is a Cut, Copy, or Paste method that you can invoke on a control that inherits from the Textbox base class, not all controls have this functionality. You will create this functionality for virtually any control you want.

You will also incorporate a menu that is dynamically loaded from the database, a toolbar, and a status bar. The status bar will be able to display messages from forms in your application and icons when there is an error. You will also be able to display the status of specific keys (such as the Num Lock and Caps Lock keys) on the status bar using the owner-drawn property of a panel.

In short, this chapter shows you some methods for building a great user interface.

Building a Dynamic Menu Structure

In Visual Basic (VB) 6 there were few options when it came to building menu structures. Although you could add menus dynamically, the top-level menu item had to exist first. You could not make all of the menu items in a group invisible, so hiding unneeded menu items was difficult at best. The .NET Framework provides several options because it is fully object oriented. The MainMenu control is just another object you are adding and removing other objects from—and because of this you truly have full control over the menu.

There are always differing points of view when it comes to creating a dynamic menu structure. To make this work, it is assumed that the application can connect to the database. If the application cannot connect, then the application may load, but the menu will not. And this creates problems. In some cases, applications are built to work offline. If that is the case, then this design will not work and the menu structure should be hard-coded into the executable. The major advantage to a dynamic menu structure is functional security. In other words, you can control access to the application's functions by just not giving access to the specific menu items. With a static structure, you must traverse the MainMenu object and disable specific menu items.

NOTE A MenuItem object cannot be referenced by name through the MenuItemsCollection because it implements the IList, ICollection, and IEnumerable interfaces only. This presents a great deal of problems when it comes to referencing individual menu items dynamically. There is not a tag property or even a name property (that you can reference anyway), so the only way to figure out what menu item you are on is by recursively traversing the entire menu structure and examining the text property! My suggestion would be to either extend the MainMenu class or purchase a control such as the Infragistics UltraWinToolbars, which allows you to reference menu items by key.

In the following sections, you will dynamically create a menu structure from information stored in the database. For this application (and most sales/orders/ inventory applications) to work, the user must be connected to the database. You will create one menu table and two routines, one of which is a recursive routine to load all submenus. You will also create a data-centric menu class and a user-centric menu class.

NOTE   You can expand these menu classes later to create full-fledged security classes that control access to specific parts of the application.

Setting Up the Database

To begin, let's create the menu table in the database. Open the SQL Query Analyzer, enter the SQL in Listing 6-1, and execute it. Table 6-1 defines the menu table's columns.

Listing 6-1. The Menu Table

```
Use Northwind
CREATE TABLE menus (
    menu_id int identity(1,1) primary key,
    menu_under_id int null foreign key references menus(menu_id),
    menu_order int not null,
    menu_caption varchar(30) not null,
    menu_shortcut varchar(5),
    enabled int default(1) check(enabled in (0,1)),
    checked int default(0) check(checked in (0,1)))
```

Table 6-1. Menu Table Column Definitions

Column	Definition
menu_id	Primary key, identity.
menu_under_id	References the primary key. This controls whether the menu item is a submenu under the referenced menu.
menu_order	Controls the order that a menu appears in the specified menu. For example, if there are three menu items under the File menu, the value here controls the order the items appear under the File menu.
menu_caption	Represents the text displayed on the menu item.
menu_shortcut	Represents the shortcut associated with the menu item.
enabled	Sets whether the menu is enabled or disabled by default. The default is yes (1).
checked	Sets whether the menu item has a check displayed next to it. The default is no (0).

TIP Using a self-referencing table makes it possible to create a recursive routine to load the menu structure. This saves you from having to write an inordinate amount of code to load your menu structure.

Next, add the menu items in Table 6-2, which form the basis for your menu structure. (When you are entering these items, I have assumed that the ID numbers will be generated in numerical order starting at 1. I have included the menu ID and the caption of the menu item so that you know the menu item it is supposed to be under.)

Table 6-2. Menu Table Data

menu_under_id	menu_order	menu_caption	menu_shortcut	enabled	checked
null	1	&File	NULL	1	0
null	2	&Edit	NULL	1	0
null	3	&Maintenance	NULL	1	0
null	4	&Window	NULL	1	0
null	5	&Help	NULL	1	0
1 (&File)	1	E&xit	NULL	1	0
2 (&Edit)	1	Cu&t	CtrlX	1	0
2 (&Edit)	2	&Copy	CtrlC	1	0
2 (&Edit)	3	&Paste	CtrlV	1	0
2 (&Edit)	4		NULL	1	0
2 (&Edit)	5	Select Al&l	NULL	1	0
2 (&Edit)	6	&Find...	CtrlF	1	0
2 (&Edit)	7	Find &Next	F3	1	0
3 (&Maintenance)	1	&Region	NULL	1	0
3 (&Maintenance)	2	&Territories	NULL	1	0
3 (&Maintenance)	3	&Employees	NULL	1	0
4 (&Window)	1	&Cascade	NULL	1	0
4 (&Window)	2	&Tile	NULL	1	0
18 (&Tile)	1	&Horizontal	NULL	1	0
18 (&Tile)	2	&Vertical	NULL	1	0
5 (&Help)	1	&Report Errors	NULL	1	0
5 (&Help)	2	&About	NULL	1	0

This gives you the following menu structure:

&File

  E&xit

&Edit

  Cu&t Ctrl+X

  &Copy Ctrl+C

  &Paste Ctrl+V

  Select Al&l

  &Find Ctrl+F

  Find &Next F3

&Maintenance

  &Region

  &Territories

  &Employees

&Window

  &Cascade

  &Tile

    &Horizontal

    &Vertical

&Help

  &Report Errors

  &About

Now you will create the stored procedure to retrieve the menu items. Execute the following SQL statement against the Northwind database:

```
Use Northwind
Go
CREATE PROCEDURE get_menu_structure
AS
SELECT *
FROM    menus
ORDER BY menu_under_id, menu_order
```

Creating the Menu Objects

Next you will add the data-centric menu class, which retrieves this menu structure. Before you do that however, you need to create a new interface for your menu class. Modify the Interfaces code module so that it contains the following new interface:

```
Public Interface IMenu
    Function GetMenuStructure As DataSet
End Interface
```

Add a new class to the NorthwindDC project and call it *MenuDC*. Add the code from Listing 6-2 to the MenuDC code module.

Listing 6-2. The MenuDC Class

```
Option Strict On
Option Explicit On

Imports NorthwindTraders.NorthwindShared.Interfaces
Imports System.Configuration
Imports System.Data.SqlClient

Public Class MenuDC
    Inherits MarshalByRefObject

    Implements IMenu

    Public Function GetMenuStructure() As DataSet _
    Implements IMenu.GetMenuStructure
        Dim strCN As String = ConfigurationSettings.AppSettings("Northwind_DSN")
        Dim cn As New SqlConnection(strCN)
        Dim cmd As New SqlCommand()
        Dim da As New SqlDataAdapter(cmd)
        Dim ds As New DataSet()

        cn.Open()

        With cmd
            .Connection = cn
            .CommandType = CommandType.StoredProcedure
            .CommandText = "get_menu_structure"
        End With
```

```
            da.Fill(ds)

            cmd = Nothing
            cn.Close()

            Return ds
        End Function
End Class
```

Once you have added this code, rebuild the NorthwindDC project (which also causes the NorthwindShared project to be rebuilt) and copy the resulting two assemblies (NorthwindDC.dll and NorthwindShared.dll) to the bin folder in the directory to which the Internet Information Server (IIS) virtual directory points.

Because you have added another object that you need to reference on the data-centric side, you need to add the following tag to the web.config file:

```
<wellknown mode="Singleton"
    type="NorthwindTraders.NorthwindDC.MenuDC, NorthwindDC"
    objectUri="MenuDC.rem"/>
```

Add this tag in the same section as the wellknown tag for the RegionDC object. Save the web.config file.

Next, add a class to the NorthwindUC project called *UIMenu*. This class passes the menu structure to the user interface. Add the code from Listing 6-3 to the UIMenu code module.

Listing 6-3. The UIMenu Class

```
Option Strict On
Option Explicit On

Imports NorthwindTraders.NorthwindShared.Interfaces

Public Class UIMenu
    Private Shared mUIMenu As UIMenu

    Public Shared Function getInstance() As UIMenu
        If mUIMenu Is Nothing Then
            mUIMenu = New UIMenu ()
        End If
        Return mUIMenu
    End Function
```

```
    Protected Sub New()
        'Do nothing
    End Sub

    Public Function GetMenuStructure() As DataSet
        Dim objIMenu As IMenu
        Dim ds As DataSet

        objIMenu = CType(Activator.GetObject(GetType(IMenu), _
        AppConstants.REMOTEOBJECTS & "MenuDC.rem"), IMenu)
        ds = objIMenu.GetMenuStructure
        objIMenu= Nothing

        Return ds
    End Function
End Class
```

As with the RegionMgr class, this class uses the Singleton pattern. The reason for this is simple—you only want to have to load up the menu information once.

NOTE   As mentioned earlier, you can alter this class to help control functional access. Once you do that, you do not want to make multiple trips to the database to get this information, so making this object a Singleton is the right choice. You will not be expanding upon this class in this chapter, but on the assumption that you can, you should leave this as a Singleton.

Now you have the dataset to use in creating your user interface's menu, you will actually create the menu structure. All of the code you will add now should be added to the frmMain class. To create the function that will actually handle the menu item click events, add the following code:

```
Private Sub MainMenu_Click(ByVal sender As System.Object, _
ByVal e As System.EventArgs)

End Sub
```

For the moment, you are not going to add any code to this method, but it needs to be here. Notice also that this method handles no events right now.

NOTE Note the choice of the method name. I chose this name because it is consistent with the names .NET gives to methods. It is also a self-documenting name. The name of the method no longer matters in VB .NET gives you great latitude—but it also gives you enough rope to hang yourself with....

Add the following import statement to the frmMain code module:

```
Imports NorthwindTraders.NorthwindUC
```

Add the following module-level variable declaration in the frmMain class:

```
Private mdsMenuLoad As DataSet
```

The mdsMenuLoad dataset stores the dataset returned to you by the UIMenu object while you are loading up the menu structure.

NOTE The choice to use a module-level variable to hold the dataset while you load the data is a personal choice. Because of how you are loading the data, it saves you from having to continually pass the dataset to the method that is using it, but it decreases the modularity of your code.

Now you will add the two routines that actually load the menu items and examine them in detail. To begin, add the LoadMenus routine in Listing 6-4 to the frmMain class. You will examine the code afterward.

Listing 6-4. The LoadMenus Routine

```
Private Sub LoadMenus()
    Try
        Dim objMenu As UIMenu
        objMenu = objMenu.getInstance

        mdsMenuLoad = objMenu.GetMenuStructure

        Dim dv As New DataView(mdsMenuLoad.Tables(0))
        Dim drv As DataRowView
```

```
        dv.RowFilter = "menu_under_id is null"
        dv.RowStateFilter = DataViewRowState.CurrentRows

        For Each drv In dv
            Dim mnuHeader As New _
            MenuItem(Convert.ToString(drv.Item("menu_caption")))
            AddItems(mnuHeader, Convert.ToInt32(drv.Item("menu_id")))
            MainMenu1.MenuItems.Add(mnuHeader)
        Next
    Catch exc As Exception
        LogException(exc)
    End Try
End Sub
```

The first three lines of code declare the menu object, get a reference to the menu object, and retrieve the dataset with the menu structure in it from the database. The next line declares something you have not seen before, a DataView object:

```
Dim dv As New DataView(mdsMenuLoad.Tables(0))
```

The DataView object is exactly what it sounds like—a view of your data. However, this view acts exactly as a view in SQL Server. You can filter your dataset using a SQL Where clause so that you only see a portion of your data. It is similar to the Filter method of the recordset object in ADO. The constructor of the DataView object accepts the table of data from which you are creating the view. The next line declares a DataRowView object, which is the object that traverses the rows of data once you have filtered them in the DataView object. The next two lines filter the data that is accessed by the DataView object:

```
dv.RowFilter = "menu_under_id is null"
dv.RowStateFilter = DataViewRowState.CurrentRows
```

You are looking for rows where the menu_under_id is null, which means you are looking for top-level menu items. The next line tells the DataView you want this filter to be applied to all of the rows currently available to the DataView object.

NOTE   There are many different things you can do with the DataView object, and this chapter only touches on a few of its aspects. A good reference on the subject is *Database Programming with Visual Basic .NET Second Edition* by Carsten Thomsen (Apress, 2002). It would be worth your time and effort to get to know this object better, especially if you deal with databases frequently.

The next block of code actually does the work of creating your menu structure:

```
For Each drv In dv
    Dim mnuHeader As New _
    MenuItem(Convert.ToString(drv.Item("menu_caption")))
    AddItems(mnuHeader, Convert.ToInt32(drv.Item("menu_id")))
    MainMenu1.MenuItems.Add(mnuHeader)
Next
```

This code loops through all of the rows in the DataView object. In this case, it is limited to looping through the top-level menu items. First, it creates a new MenuItem object, which takes the menu caption as an argument to its constructor. Second, you call the AddItems method (you will create this method next), which is responsible for adding all of the subitems to a top-level menu. It is the AddItems method, which is recursive. This method takes a menu and a menu ID as arguments. Finally, once the AddItems method is done running, you add the top-level menu item to the MainMenu1 control.

Now it is time to add the routine that does all the work—the AddItems method. Add the code from Listing 6-5 to the frmMain class, and then you will examine what is occurring.

Listing 6-5. The AddItems Method

```
Private Sub AddItems(ByVal mnuTop As MenuItem, ByVal intMenuID As Integer)
    Dim dr As DataRowView
    Dim dv As New DataView(mdsMenuLoad.Tables(0))

    Try
        dv.RowFilter = "menu_under_id = " & intMenuID
        dv.RowStateFilter = DataViewRowState.CurrentRows
        If dv.Count > 0 Then
            For Each dr In dv
                Dim mnuItem As New _
                MenuItem(Convert.ToString(dr.Item("menu_caption")))
                If Not IsDBNull(dr.Item("menu_shortcut")) Then
                    mnuItem.Shortcut = _
                    CType([enum].Parse(GetType(Shortcut), _
                    Convert.ToString(dr.Item("menu_shortcut"))), _
                    Shortcut)
                End If
```

```
              If Convert.ToInt32(dr.Item("enabled")) = 0 Then
                    mnuItem.Enabled = False
              Else
                    mnuItem.Enabled = True
              End If

              If Convert.ToInt32(dr.Item("checked")) = 0 Then
                    mnuItem.Checked = False
              Else
                    mnuItem.Checked = True
              End If

              AddItems(mnuItem, Convert.ToInt32(dr.Item("menu_id")))
              AddHandler mnuItem.Click, AddressOf MainMenu_Click
              mnuTop.MenuItems.Add(mnuItem)
          Next
      End If
  Catch exc As Exception
      LogException(exc)
  End Try
End Sub
```

Let's examine this code to find out what this routine is doing, starting with the method signature. The AddItem method accepts a menu item and a menu ID. The menu that is passed in is a menu with submenu items. The menu ID is the ID of the menu that has been passed to it. For example, during the fourth iteration of the LoadMenus method, the &Window menu item is passed in with the menu ID of 4 because that is its key in the database:

```
Private Sub AddItems(ByVal mnuTop As MenuItem, ByVal intMenuID As Integer)
    Dim dr As DataRowView
    Dim dv As New DataView(mdsMenuLoad.Tables(0))
```

Next you filter the DataView rows so that you only get the menus that come under the menu that you passed in. Continuing with the previous example, when you perform this filter by using the ID of 4, you come up with the &Cascade and &Tile menu items:

```
dv.RowFilter = "menu_under_id = " & intMenuID
dv.RowStateFilter = DataViewRowState.CurrentRows
```

Then you check to see if the count of rows is greater than zero. If it is, then you know there are menu items under the menu item that you passed in, and you loop through them:

```
If dv.Count > 0 Then
    For Each dr In dv
```

For each menu item you find, do the following:

1. Create a new menu item.

2. Check to see if the menu_shortcut column has data in it.

3. If it does, then add a shortcut to the menu item.

To add a shortcut you take your string entry (which matches the enumerated entry for the shortcut keys) and turn it into an enumerated shortcut type. Notice that you are calling the parse method on the [enum] object. This is a static method, so you can call it on any [enum] object:

```
Dim mnuItem As New MenuItem(Convert.ToString(dr.Item("menu_caption")))
If Not IsDBNull(dr.Item("menu_shortcut")) Then
    mnuItem.Shortcut = _
    CType([enum].Parse(GetType(Shortcut), _
    Convert.ToString(dr.Item("menu_shortcut"))), Shortcut)
End If
```

 TIP   One of the cool features of .NET is the ability to turn an enumerated value into its string equivalent and vice versa. You can find more about this in the MSDN documentation under the Enum.Parse method.

Next you check to see if the menu item should be enabled and if the menu item should be checked:

```
If Convert.ToInt32(dr.Item("enabled")) = 0 Then
     mnuItem.Enabled = False
Else
     mnuItem.Enabled = True
End If


If Convert.ToInt32(dr.Item("checked")) = 0 Then
     mnuItem.Checked = False
Else
     mnuItem.Checked = True
End If
```

After that, you call the AddItems method again, but this time with the menu item that was just created and the ID of this menu item. Using the previous example, the second time through the &Windows menu item, this value would be &Tile and the menu ID would be 18. When this routine started again, it would note that there were two menu items under &Tile, and these would be added as submenus to &Tile:

```
AddItems(mnuItem, Convert.ToInt32(dr.Item("menu_id")))
```

This next block of code delegates the responsibility of handling the menu item's click event to the MainMenu_Click method (which you created previously). Then you add the menu item to the top-level menu item:

```
AddHandler mnuItem.Click, AddressOf MainMenu_Click
mnuTop.MenuItems.Add(mnuItem)
```

NOTE Because the AddItem routine is called recursively before you get to these two lines, you are guaranteed that all of the menus that belong below your top-level menu will be added before these two lines of code are called.

The last step you need to perform to make this routine work is to call the LoadMenus method from the constructor of frmMain. Edit the constructor so that the LoadMenus call comes at the end of the constructor method as follows:

```
LoadMenus()
```

Finally, before you run this routine for the first time, you need to delete the two temporary menu items that we have created.

You should now be able to run the application, and when you do, you should have a fully loaded menu structure that duplicates what you have placed in the database. However, there is no functionality at this point, so you will add that now. Modify the MainMenu_Click method so it matches the method shown in Listing 6-6.

Listing 6-6. MainMenu_Click Method

```
Private Sub MainMenu_Click(ByVal sender As System.Object, _
ByVal e As System.EventArgs)
    Dim mnu As MenuItem = CType(sender, MenuItem)

    Select Case mnu.Text
        Case "&Regions"
            LoadRegion()
        Case "&Report Errors"
            LoadErrors
        Case "E&xit"
            Close()
    End Select
End Sub
```

Note that you will receive an error when you enter the LoadRegion and LoadError methods, because you have not added them yet. This code converts the sender object, which is a MenuItem object in this routine into a MenuItem object. Then you perform a select case on the text to find out what was clicked and you respond appropriately.

NOTE It is usually my preference to place one-line or two-line commands directly in the Select Case statement. However, if other code will be accessing this functionality, you should move them to individual routines. First, it means you do not have to duplicate code, and second, it makes for a much cleaner Select Case block.

Next, let's create the LoadRegion method. The easiest way to do this is to change the name of a routine you have already created and add a few more lines of code. The current method that launches the Region list form looks like the code in Listing 6-7.

Listing 6-7. Current Code to Launch the Region List

```
Private Sub MenuItem1_Click(ByVal sender As System.Object, _
ByVal e As System.EventArgs)
    Try
        Cursor = Cursors.WaitCursor
        mfrmRegionList = New frmRegionList()
        mfrmRegionList.MdiParent = Me
        mfrmRegionList.Show()
    Catch exc As Exception
        LogException(exc)
    Finally
        Cursor = Cursors.Default
    End Try
End Sub
```

Alter the method signature to read as follows:

```
Private Sub LoadRegion()
```

Also, alter the MenuItem2_Click method so that the signature now reads as follows:

```
Private Sub LoadErrors()
```

After doing this, everything should run fine. The menu should load up, and selecting Maintenance ➤ Regions should load the frmRegionList form.

NOTE You have not added the functionality for the Territories or Employees yet. You will add this functionality in Chapter 7, "Revisiting Objects and Rules," and Chapter 9, "Understanding Server-Side Business Rules."

Implementing Cut, Copy, and Paste Functionality

You implement the cut, copy, and paste functionality as part of the textbox control. So why is it that so few VB 6 applications (or any other internal enterprise applications) do not have an edit menu with Cut, Copy, and Paste options (for simplicity throughout the rest of this chapter, I will call these options *edit functionality*)? Simply put, implementing the functionality took a lot of work and planning in VB 6. With .NET, this becomes a nonissue. And because of your application's architecture, implementing it becomes even easier.

So, how is the edit functionality that a menu or toolbar provides different from the textbox implementation of it? There is no difference in functionality (both use the Clipboard to hold data), but you need to be able to target the control that has the focus and to be able to invoke that call without being in the form on which the control is located. There are many different ways to implement this, but the solution covered in this section is probably the simplest to implement. This solution involves creating an interface that provides method signatures for your edit methods.

NOTE   Interfaces are available for use in VB 6, but they are slightly more difficult to implement. Many developers did not use interface inheritance in VB 6, and they overlooked this solution.

TIP   If you are only using textboxes and richtextboxes, then this entire setup is unnecessary because you can call the cut, copy, or paste method of the control to perform the needed functionality. However, this does not allow you to implement the functionality for a control such as a combo box or a listbox like this method of implementation will allow.

All your MDI form has to do is to check to see if the active form implements the ICutCopyPaste interface you will create. The real issue is not how to implement the edit functionality for a textbox, but how to make this functionality extensible for other types of controls and to access that functionality using the menu items.

NOTE Because there are so many permutations of the Undo method, describing how to implement it would take many more pages to explain. Consider that the undo must be available if you press the Backspace key, perform a cut or paste operation, highlight text, press any key, and so on. If you decide to create your own routines to handle the Undo, it should be fairly easy for you to extend this code.

So let's create your interface and implement it. Add a new class module to the NorthwindTraders project and call it *UIInterfaces*. Delete the class module code that is created by default and add the code in Listing 6-8 to the UIInterfaces module.

Listing 6-8. The UIInterface Module

```
Option Explicit On
Option Strict On

Public Interface ICutCopyPaste
    Sub Cut()
    Sub Copy()
    Sub Paste()
End Interface
```

In the frmEditBase form, add the following implementation line:

```
Implements ICutCopyPaste
```

Let's start by implementing the Cut method. Add the code in Listing 6-9 to the frmEditBase class and afterward, you will walk through it.

TIP If you are using Visual Studio .NET (VS .NET) 1.1, the methods will have already been created for you so you will just need to modify the methods to match those in Listing 6-10.

Listing 6-9. The Cut Method

```
Public Sub Cut() Implements ICutCopyPaste.Cut
    Dim txt As TextBoxBase

    If TypeOf ActiveControl Is TextBoxBase Then
        txt = CType(ActiveControl, TextBoxBase)
        txt.Cut
    End If
End Sub
```

The first thing that occurs is a check of the type of the active control. In this case, you are only implementing the cut routine if the control derives from the TextBoxBase class.

NOTE You can easily edit this functionality to work for the textbox part of a drop-down list. But even this can be tricky because you have to check the style of the combo box before you can make it work (Cut does not work on a drop-down listbox).

Once you have confirmed that it is a type of TextBoxBase control, you perform the conversion to a TextBoxBase control so that you can manipulate the object correctly. Next you call the following line of code:

```
txt.Cut
```

This line simply invokes the Cut method on the TextBoxBase control.

Now you will implement the Copy method. To do this, add the code in Listing 6-10 to the frmEditBase class.

Listing 6-10. The Copy Method

```
Public Sub Copy() Implements ICutCopyPaste.Copy
    Dim txt As TextBoxBase

    If TypeOf ActiveControl Is TextBoxBase Then
        txt = CType(ActiveControl, TextBoxBase)
        txt.Copy
    Else
        Clipboard.SetDataObject(ActiveControl.Text)
    End If
End Sub
```

Here you are doing something slightly different because this method only copies data. Again, you are checking to see if this is a TextBoxBase—but for a slightly different reason. If it is a type of TextBoxBase, you convert the object again and send the selected text to the Clipboard. However, if it is not a type of TextBoxBase, you simply send the value of the text property of the control to the Clipboard. This is fairly simple to get away with because almost every control that a user could be editing will have the text property.

NOTE In specific instances, you may have to modify this code because of controls that may not have a text property or when you need to copy something other than text.

Next you need to implement the last and final method of the interface, the Paste method. Add the code in Listing 6-11 to the frmEditBase class.

Listing 6-11. The Paste Method

```
Public Sub Paste() Implements ICutCopyPaste.Paste
    Dim txt As TextBoxBase

    If TypeOf ActiveControl Is TextBoxBase Then
        txt = CType(ActiveControl, TextBoxBase)
        txt.Paste
    End If
End Sub
```

Again, this code is easy to implement. You only run this code if the active control is a type of TextBoxBase. You are simply calling the Paste method of the control.

Now every form that inherits from your frmEditBase form automatically implements the ICutCopyPaste interface. Now you need to hook up this functionality to the frmMain menu click events. Add the code in Listing 6-12 to the frmMain form.

Listing 6-12. The CutCopyPaste Method

```
Private Sub CutCopyPaste(ByVal strMenu As String)
    Dim objCCPU As ICutCopyPaste
    Dim t As System.Type

    If ActiveMdiChild Is Nothing Then Exit Sub
    Try
        t = ActiveMdiChild.GetType
        If Not t.GetInterface("ICutCopyPaste") Is Nothing Then
            objCCPU = CType(Me.ActiveMdiChild, ICutCopyPaste)

            Select Case strMenu
                Case "Cu&t"
                    objCCPU.Cut()
                Case "&Copy"
                    objCCPU.Copy()
                Case "&Paste"
                    objCCPU.Paste()
            End Select
        End If
    Catch exc As Exception
        LogException(exc)
    End Try
End Sub
```

This routine invokes the methods on your interface contained in the base edit form class. Let's look at some of this code in detail:

```
Dim objCCPU As ICutCopyPaste
Dim t As System.Type
```

The objCCPU is the declaration of your interface through which you will access all of your interface calls. Just as with the remoting calls, you are operating on the interface definitions not directly on your base class. The t variable is declared so that you can examine the form upon which you want to operate, as you will see next:

```
t = ActiveMdiChild.GetType
If Not t.GetInterface("ICutCopyPaste") Is Nothing Then
    objCCPU = CType(Me.ActiveMdiChild, ICutCopyPaste)
```

The first line retrieves the type information from your object so that you can examine it. Next, you call the GetInterface method that, in one of its overloaded methods, accepts the string name of the interface for which you are querying. If the interface is implemented by the object you are testing, then you will receive that type back. If it is not implemented, you will get nothing back.

NOTE Reflection is an extremely powerful tool that should not be overlooked. Although you are not truly using the reflection namespace classes here, this is a method of reflection. Chapter 10, "Using Reflection," covers reflection in detail.

If the interface is implemented, you can assign the object to your interface variable by performing a conversion on it. After that, you simply invoke the specific methods on the interface.

Now you need to hook up this method to the menu click event. Edit the MainMenu_Click event so that the following Case statement is added to the Select Case statement:

```
Case "Cu&t", "&Copy", "&Paste"
    CutCopyPaste(mnu.Text)
```

That was not too painful, and every form you create after this that inherits from the base edit form automatically has this functionality.

TIP This may seem like a roundabout way of implementing an edit functionality interface, but it is really the most reusable way to do this. This set of methods gives you the ability to implement editing capabilities on any control that you want because you can control all of the aspects of what actually takes place during the cut or paste process.

Implementing Select All Functionality

Just to demonstrate how easy it is to go back and modify this code once it has been created, you are going to implement the Select All method that you added to your menu.

To do this, start by editing the ICutCopyPaste interface to include the following method signature:

```
Sub SelectAll()
```

Then add the code in Listing 6-13 to the frmEditBase class.

Listing 6-13. The SelectAll Method

```
Public Sub SelectAll() Implements ICutCopyPaste.SelectAll
    Dim txt As TextBoxBase

    If TypeOf ActiveControl Is TextBoxBase Then
        txt = CType(ActiveControl, TextBoxBase)
        txt.SelectAll()
    End If
End Sub
```

This code calls the SelectAll method on the TextBoxBase control, which takes care of the work for you. Now you need to update your main form to invoke this method. Edit the Select Case statement in the MainMenu_Click method in the frmMain class so that it looks like the following:

```
Case "Cu&t", "&Copy", "&Paste", "Select Al&l"
    CutCopyPaste(mnu.Text)
```

Next, edit the CutCopyPaste routine by adding the following Case statement to the Select Case block:

```
Case "Select Al&l"
    objCCPU.SelectAll()
```

Now you should be able to click the Select All menu item to select all of the text in a textbox or richtextbox on any edit form. Of course you only have the one right now, but it works for everything.

Implementing Find Functionality

Implementing the find functionality is a little different because your find functionality should only work on the list forms, not the edit forms. To start this, let's add a new interface to the UIInterfaces code module. Create the following interface called *IFind*:

```
Public Interface IFind
    Sub Find()
    Sub FindNext()
End Interface
```

Next, add this Implements line to the frmListBase class:

```
Implements IFind
```

Now add the Find method to the frmListBase class:

```
Public Sub Find() Implements IFind.Find
End Sub
```

 NOTE Again, if you are using VS .NET version 1.1, this method will have already been added for you as soon as you enter the Implements line.

To make life easy, you can move all of the code from the btnFind_Click method to the Find method and then call the Find method from the btnFind_Click event, like this:

```
Private Sub btnFind_Click(ByVal sender As System.Object, _
ByVal e As System.EventArgs) Handles btnFind.Click
    Find()
End Sub
```

Now, add the FindNext routine as shown in Listing 6-14. The code first checks to see if anything is selected. If there is not anything selected, you cannot possibly perform a find next, so you just exit the routine. If you do have an item selected, you get the index of the selected item and start looking for the next available match. If you find it, we select it and make it visible.

Listing 6-14. The FindNext Method

```
Public Sub FindNext() Implements IFind.FindNext
    Dim i, j, k As Integer
    Dim lst As ListViewItem

    If lvwList.SelectedItems.Count = 0 Then Exit Sub

    Try
        i = cboColumn.SelectedIndex
        k = lvwList.SelectedItems(0).Index + 1

        For j = k To lvwList.Items.Count - 1
            lst = lvwList.Items(j)
            If _
lst.SubItems(i).Text.ToUpper.StartsWith(txtSearch.Text.ToUpper) Then
                lst.Selected = True
                lst.EnsureVisible()
                Exit For
            End If
        Next
    Catch exc As Exception
        LogException(exc)
    End Try
End Sub
```

You can choose to extend these routines by adding message boxes or status bar messages when an item is not found. You can also alter these to search through all of the columns without the user having to pick a column. But these are basic, solid routines for searching through a listview.

Next, go to the frmMain form and add the method in Listing 6-15, which works exactly like the CutCopyPaste method created earlier. You are going to cheat a little because your application is the only one calling the Find and FindNext methods. Your routine accepts a value of 1 or anything else to determine whether to call the Find or FindNext methods. You could create an enumeration, but you do not need it for such a simple routine being called in only one place.

Listing 6-15. Implementing the Find/FindNext Method in the MDI Form

```
Private Sub Find(ByVal intType As Integer)
    Dim objFind As IFind
    Dim t As System.Type

    If ActiveMdiChild Is Nothing Then Exit Sub
    Try
        t = ActiveMdiChild.GetType
        If Not t.GetInterface("IFind") Is Nothing Then
            objFind = CType(Me.ActiveMdiChild, IFind)
            If intType = 1 Then
                objFind.Find()
            Else
                objFind.FindNext()
            End If
        End If
    Catch exc As Exception
        LogException(exc)
    End Try
End Sub
```

This method checks to see if the IFind interface is implemented by the child form. If it is, it calls the Find or FindNext method on the interface. Finally, edit the Select Case statement in the MainMenu_Click event by adding the following Case statement:

```
Case "&Find..."
    Find(1)
Case "Find &Next"
    Find(0)
```

This finishes implementing the Select All and Find functionality. As you can see, extending either of these interfaces is extremely simple and requires little work. It is little things like these that impress users (of course, a working application is a pretty good trick also).

Adding a Toolbar

Implementing a toolbar in .NET is essentially the same as it was in VB 6. You are just going to add a simple toolbar and a couple buttons. To begin, select the toolbar object while you have frmMain in design mode. Along with the toolbar, you need to add an ImageList control to hold the images your toolbar will display. When you are done adding both of those items, your screen should look like Figure 6-1.

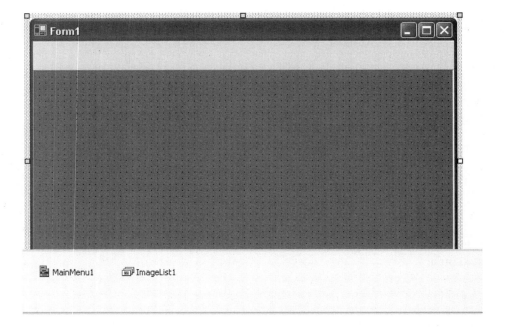

Figure 6-1. MDI form with a toolbar and ImageList control

Add the Cut, Copy, Paste, and Find images to the image control so that it looks like Figure 6-2.

NOTE The images, if you installed them, are located in Microsoft Visual Studio .NET\Common7\Graphics\Bitmaps\Tlbr_W95. If you did not install these images, pick any four small bitmaps you want.

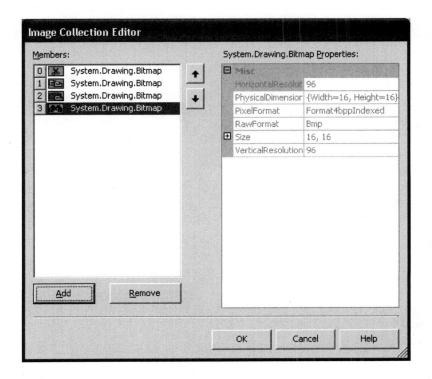

Figure 6-2. ImageList Image Collection Editor

Now you have to add buttons to the toolbar and associate them with the images you just loaded. First, rename the toolbar control (currently named toolbar1) to tlbMain. In the property list for the toolbar, select the imagelist property drop-down and select ImageList1. Next, select the ellipses next to the Buttons property. Add four buttons to the toolbar and set the properties according to Table 6-3.

Table 6-3. The Toolbar Buttons

Control	Name	Image
ToolbarButton	tlbCut	Scissors
ToolbarButton	tlbCopy	Double Page
ToolbarButton	tlbPaste	Clipboard and Paper
ToolbarButton	tlbFind	Binoculars

When you are finished, you will have a toolbar with four buttons and four images similar to what is in Figure 6-3.

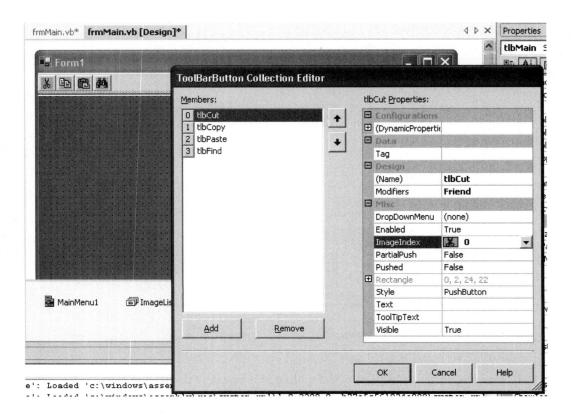

Figure 6-3. ToolBarButton Collection Editor

Finally, you need to add the code to hook up your buttons with your functions. Go to the code module for frmMain and add the method shown in Listing 6-16.

Listing 6-16. The Toolbar Button Event Handler

```
Private Sub tlbMain_ButtonClick(ByVal sender As Object, _
ByVal e As System.Windows.Forms.ToolBarButtonClickEventArgs) _
Handles tlbMain.ButtonClick

    Select Case tlbMain.Buttons.IndexOf(e.Button)
        Case 0
            CutCopyPaste("Cu&t")
```

```
        Case 1
                CutCopyPaste("&Copy")
        Case 2
                CutCopyPaste("&Paste")
        Case 3
                Find(1)
    End Select
End Sub
```

ToolBarButtonClickEventArgs provides the button that was clicked. One annoying thing about .NET is that you cannot access the name of the object, so you have to resort to using the index of the toolbar button that was clicked. Obviously, this has some drawbacks to it—namely that if you add a button before any of your existing buttons, you have to rework this routine.

TIP If you examine the MSDN documentation on information about the toolbarbutton class, it shows an example similar to this in that it uses the indexOf in the Select Case statement. I am not a big fan of this method. My preferred method is to add tooltip text to each of the buttons on the toolbars and then reference this text in the Select Case statement. In this way, the position of the toolbars does not matter.

Implementing a StatusBar

A status bar is something you see on almost every application. It displays a variety of information about the application as it is running. Implementing a status bar in .NET is similar to implementing a status bar in VB 6, so this section covers this topic briefly. However, you will spend a little bit of time adding and removing icons dynamically from the status bar and sending messages to the status bar using your MDI child forms, which is a little more difficult than in VB 6. Also, in .NET there is no longer a setting on the status bar for Num Lock or Caps Lock status to be displayed. In .NET, you need to do this using an owner-drawn panel. You will see one method for implementing this functionality using the same style as in VB 6.

To add the status bar to frmMain, double-click the status bar icon in the Toolbox. The status bar appears at the bottom of the form. Change the name of the status bar from *StatusBar1* to *sbrMain*. The default property for ShowPanels is false, which is similar to the Simple Mode in VB 6. Change this property to *True*. Even though it looks like there is one panel on the status bar at this point, there really are not any, so let's add a couple of panels. Select the Panels collection of the sbrMain control, add the panels, and set the properties of the panels according to Table 6-4. Table 6-5 describes the purpose of each panel.

Table 6-4. The sbrMain Panels

Panel	AutoSize	Style	Minimum Width	Width
pnlStatus	Spring	Text	100	
pnlUser	Contents	Text	10	10
pnlErrors	Contents	Text	10	10
pnlCapsLock	None	OwnerDraw	50	50
pnlNumLock	None	OwnerDraw	50	50
pnlDate	Contents	Text	10	10

Table 6-5. Purpose of Each Panel

Panel	Function
pnlStatus	Displays the status of application operations
pnlUser	Displays the user logged on to the system
pnlErrors	Displays an icon if there are errors in the windows event log that have not been reported to technical support
pnlCapsLock	Displays the status of the Caps Lock key
pnlNumLock	Displays the status of the Num Lock key
pnlDate	Displays the current date

The application user and the date will probably not change during the application session (or there are some overworked users), so you can set those in the constructor for the form. Add the following code at the end of the constructor for frmMain:

```
pnlDate.Text = Now.ToShortDateString
pnlUser.Text = Security.Principal.WindowsIdentity.GetCurrent.Name
```

The first line takes the date (returned by the Now method), converts it to a short date string format, and displays it in the date panel. The second line retrieves the name of the user currently logged onto the client machine where the application is being run.

Creating the Owner-Drawn Panels

Next you will take care of the owner-drawn panels. There are a couple of things to note about the owner-drawn panels before getting into this. The StatusBar object raises an event called *DrawItem*. This method actually paints the graphics onto the object. In this case you will be drawing text graphics, but you can draw anything on the object. The event is raised whenever the status bar is refreshed in any manner (either through text changes to a panel, form resizing, or other such changes). The graphics you are placing on the object must be in this event and no other event. If the graphics are not drawn in this event, then whenever this event is called, the graphics there will be erased.

NOTE   These notes apply to all owner-drawn controls. One control you may find useful to set as owner drawn is a MenuItem control, which allows you to place graphics to the left of the MenuItem.

Now that you know these few rules, let's go over what is necessary to determine the status of the Caps Lock and Num Lock keys. If you look at the KeyUp or KeyDown events for frmMain, you will notice you can determine which key was pressed by checking the enumerated values of the KeyEventArgs object.

NOTE   For a full reference of this object and the enumerators, see the "Keys Enumeration" section in the MSDN documentation.

However, you cannot check to see if the Caps Lock is engaged or if the Num Lock is engaged. To do this, you need to call a Win32 API function. The specific function is the GetKeyState function. Calling a Win32 API function in .NET is fairly simple, but you must realize that the Win32 API is not managed code. Although this will not affect your application, it is something to note. In the UIUtilities code module, create a class called *Win32APIcalls*. Next, add the function call for the GetKeyState function. Your code will look like the following when you are done:

```
Public Class Win32APIcalls

    Public Declare Function GetKeyState Lib "user32" _
    Alias "GetKeyState" (ByVal nVirtKey As Long) As Integer

End Class
```

NOTE   An easy way to get the list of Win32 API calls available to you is by using the Win32 API Viewer that shipped with VS 6.

You can set the nVirtKey argument by using the Keys.Capslock and Keys.Numlock enumerated values. The integer value returned by the GetKeyState function represents the key and the state of the key. The last bit of the value specifies the state of the key. Take the following example:

The GetKeyState function returns the value 65408 if the Caps Lock key is off and 65409 if the Caps Lock key is on. The number 65408 translates into the binary value of 1111111110000000. The number 65409 translates into the binary value of 1111111110000001. Notice that the only difference is the last bit.

TIP   You can check this by setting the following line of code in the frmMain.KeyDown event: `MessageBox.Show(Win32APIcalls. GetKeyState(Keys.CapsLock).ToString)`. Make sure you set the KeyPreview property of frmMain to True.

Using this information, you can set the values in your status bar. Before you begin, you need to set the KeyPreview property of the MDI form (frmMain) to True. This allows your form to respond to specific key events. Without this, the MDI Form would never know that the Caps Lock or Num Lock key had been pressed. Then add the code from Listing 6-17 to frmMain. Afterward, you will examine the code line by line.

Listing 6-17. Drawing Owner-Drawn Panels

```
Private Sub sbrMain_DrawItem(ByVal sender As System.Object, _
ByVal sbdevent As System.Windows.Forms.StatusBarDrawItemEventArgs) _
Handles sbrMain.DrawItem

    Dim intValue(0) As Integer
    Dim ba As BitArray
    Dim fnt As New Font(New FontFamily("Arial"), 10, FontStyle.Regular)
    Dim strText As String
    Dim clr As Color
```

```
    If sbdevent.Panel Is pnlCapsLock Then
        intValue(0) = Win32APIcalls.GetKeyState(Keys.CapsLock)
        ba = New BitArray(intValue)
        strText = "CAPS"
        If ba.Item(0) = False Then
            clr = Color.DarkGray
        Else
            clr = Color.Black
        End If
    End If

    If sbdevent.Panel Is pnlNumLock Then
        intValue(0) = Win32APIcalls.GetKeyState(Keys.NumLock)
        ba = New BitArray(intValue)
        strText = "NUM"
        If ba.Item(0) = False Then
            clr = Color.DarkGray
        Else
            clr = Color.Black
        End If
    End If

    sbdevent.Graphics.DrawString(strText, fnt, New SolidBrush(clr), _
    sbdevent.Graphics.VisibleClipBounds.Location.X, _
    sbdevent.Graphics.VisibleClipBounds.Location.Y)
End Sub
```

There are many things going on in this block of code, so let's examine the code. First, this code is called for every owner-drawn item on the status bar, which explains some of this code. The intValue integer array holds the return value from the GetKeyState function. The reason you are storing this value in a one-dimensional array is because of the constructor for the BitArray object. The BitArray object is used for exactly what you think it is used for—it holds an array of bits. By placing your return integer value into a BitArray, you can more easily examine the individual bits of the return value. There are other ways to examine the individual bits, such as using AND and OR bitwise operations on the return value, but this way gives you a more precise way to examine the values (it is also my preference, but how you do this does not really matter). The Font object is the font you will use to draw your text into the owner-drawn panels. The strText value holds the text string you will draw, and the clr variable holds the color of the text you will draw.

Next you check to see which panel you are going to be drawing. If you determine it is the Caps Lock panel, you call the following:

```
intValue(0) = Win32APIcalls.GetKeyState(Keys.CapsLock)
ba = New BitArray(intValue)
```

The first line assigns the return value of your call to GetKeyState to the integer array. The second line instantiates the BitArray object. One of the overloaded methods of the constructor accepts an integer value, and another overloaded method accepts an integer array. The key is that the method that accepts a single integer value dimensions the BitArray and does nothing else. Passing in an integer array converts the values stored in the array to their binary representation.

CAUTION   One interesting effect of converting an integer value to a BitArray is that it reverses the values because of an AND operation. Therefore, when you pass in a value of 65408 (1111111110000000), it translates to 0000000111111111. This makes your job a little easier because you only need to check the first bit.

NOTE   The binary values you have seen so far have been 16-bit values even though in .NET an integer is a 32-bit value. The rest of the bits are set to zero and are unimportant because the value you are working with really is a 16-bit value.

Next you start by setting the text you are going to draw in the panel. Then you check the first bit in your BitArray object to see if it is set. If it is False, then the Caps Lock is not pressed, so you want to draw the *CAPS* text in dark gray. If it is True, then you want to draw it in black. The same block of code is repeated again, but this time you check for and make the correct settings for the Num Lock key:

```
strText = "CAPS"
If ba.Item(0) = False Then
     clr = Color.DarkGray
Else
     clr = Color.Black
End If
```

This is the last bit of code:

```
sbdevent.Graphics.DrawString(strText, fnt, New SolidBrush(clr), _
sbdevent.Graphics.VisibleClipBounds.Location.X, _
sbdevent.Graphics.VisibleClipBounds.Location.Y)
```

This code draws your string value onto the panel. The arguments it takes, as you can see here, are the string to draw, the font to draw it in, the brush to use (with the color to use for the brush), and the location to draw it. The VisibleClipBounds property figures out where to draw the text. There are other location properties available through StatusBarDrawItemEventArgs, but it is much easier to use this one because it does not require any additional calculations.

Finally, there is only one thing left to do—trigger the DrawItem event when the user presses the Caps Lock or Num Lock key. The code to do this is pretty straightforward:

```
Private Sub frmMain_KeyDown(ByVal sender As Object, _
ByVal e As System.Windows.Forms.KeyEventArgs) Handles MyBase.KeyDown
    If e.KeyCode = Keys.CapsLock Or e.KeyCode = Keys.NumLock Then
        sbrMain.Refresh()
    End If
End Sub
```

Add this code to the frmMain class and give the application a try. It should produce the results as shown in Figure 6-4 (probably with a different username).

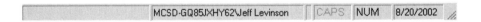

Figure 6-4. Completed status bar with owner-drawn panels

Dynamically Adding and Removing Icons

With .NET, you can compile resources directly into the assembly. This is similar to a resource file in VB 6, but everything is directly accessible through the assembly using reflection. The actual process for setting up and accessing the resources is pretty simple. The first step is to add the resource to the assembly.

NOTE The resources do not have to be in the same assembly from which you are calling them. It is the case in this section, but it is just as easy to create an assembly to store resource information separately.

Right-click the NorthwindTraders project and select Add Existing Item. Navigate to the directory where the standard icons that are installed with VS are stored.

NOTE   The default folder is C:\Program Files\Microsoft Visual Studio .NET\Common7\Graphics\Icons\Computer.

Select the icon with the W95MBX01.ICO filename. The icon looks like the following:

Next, right-click the newly added resource and select Properties. Set the Build Action property to Embedded Resource. This instructs the compiler to include the icon in the assembly when it is built.

Next, import the System.IO and System.Reflection namespaces into the frmMain code module. Then add the method shown in Listing 6-18 to the frmMain class.

Listing 6-18. The ShowErrorIcon Method

```
Private Sub ShowErrorIcon()
    Dim asm As [Assembly] = [Assembly].GetExecutingAssembly
    Dim iStream As Stream

    iStream=asm.GetManifestResourceStream _
    ("NorthwindTraders.UserInterface.W95MBX01.ICO")
    pnlErrors.Icon = New Icon(iStream)
End Sub
```

So, what is going on here? The first line gets a reference to the assembly that is currently running—in this case it will be the NorthwindTraders assembly. Then you grab the stream of information that represents the resource for which you are looking. You are searching for the W95MBX01.ICO resource, but note you have to fully qualify the name or else you will not find the resource. Finally, you create an icon out of the stream using one of the overloaded methods of the Icon class.

Next, you need to alter your LogErrorEvent class so that you can find out if there are any errors when the application starts. Let's alter the LogErrorEvent class by adding the following method:

```
Public Function ErrorCount() As Integer
    Dim objEL As New EventLog(EVENTLOGNAME)
    Return objEL.Entries.Count
End Function
```

Now you have a simple function that tells you if there are any errors stored in the Windows Event Log. To use this information, though, you need to call it from frmMain as soon as the form is loaded. Add the following declaration to the general declarations section of the frmMain class:

```
Private WithEvents mobjEventLog As ErrorLogging.LogErrorEvent
```

Next, alter the constructor for frmMain so that the following line of code is added after the LoadMenus call:

```
mobjEventLog = mobjEventLog.getInstance
```

Now you just need to create the following method to handle the frmMain.Load event:

```
Private Sub frmMain_Load(ByVal sender As Object, _
ByVal e As System.EventArgs) Handles MyBase.Load
    If mobjEventLog.ErrorCount > 0 Then
        ShowErrorIcon()
    End If
End Sub
```

Lastly, you need to handle the events raised by the mobjEventLog object. Add the following two methods to the frmMain class:

```
Private Sub mobjEventLog_ErrorLogged() Handles mobjEventLog.ErrorLogged
    ShowErrorIcon()
End Sub

Private Sub mobjEventLog_ErrorsCleared() Handles mobjEventLog.ErrorsCleared
    pnlErrors.Icon = Nothing
End Sub
```

Now that you have all the code added, you can test it just to make sure it works. If you already have some errors stored in the Windows Event Log, the error icon should display as soon as the application runs. If not, you can alter one line of code temporarily to throw an error. Alter the LoadRegion method so that the line immediately after the Try statement reads as follows:

```
Throw New Exception("Test")
```

Next, edit the LogException method in frmMain so that the line immediately following the Try statement throws the same exception as previously.

Now, run the application and try to load the Regions. You should receive a critical error message and a red icon should appear in the status bar. Selecting the Report Errors menu item from the Help menu should display the frmReportErrors form with two errors in it as in Figure 6-5.

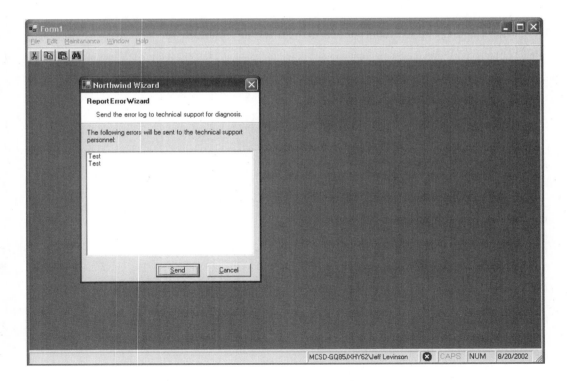

Figure 6-5. Error list and error icon

Click the Send button, and the Report Errors form should close and the error icon should be removed from the status bar.

Once you are done with the test, remember to remove the two errors you created for these tests.

Summary

In this chapter you explored some aspects of enhancing the user interface by providing some basic Windows functionality. You learned how to create a dynamic structure using data stored in the database and you hooked up those menu items to specific methods in your MDI form. In addition, you notified the user that unreported errors are in the Windows Event Log and you learned how to draw status bar panels with whatever you want on them. You also learned how to include resources in an assembly and how to reference those resources.

In the next chapter, you will add the functionality to display and edit the territories in the database. You will also look at how the choices you made earlier in the design process directly affect how you physically code your objects and how they actually relate to each other.

CHAPTER 7

Revisiting Objects and Rules

IN CHAPTER 3, "Creating the Application Infrastructure," you created your first set of business objects, which you used to retrieve data for the application's regions. If you remember the object model presented in Chapter 3 (included in Figure 7-1 for reference), then you will notice the Territory object's dependency on the Region object.

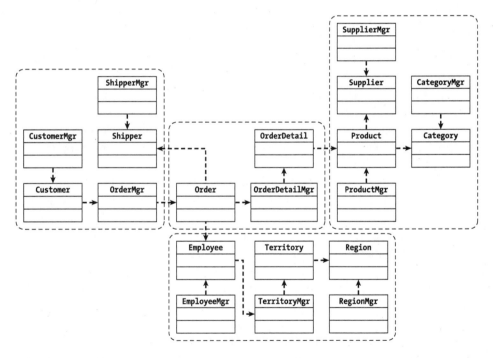

Figure 7-1. NorthwindTraders application's user-centric physical object model

You saw the effect of this design decision on your application and how it affects the abilities of your application. In this chapter you will see how to code this type of relationship between objects.

NOTE   There are a number of excellent books on objects and object-oriented relationships. Some of the best books are part of the Addison-Wesley Object Technology Series. The book that I have found most useful in understanding object theory is *The Art Of Objects: Object-Oriented Design and Architecture* by Yun-Tung Lau (Addison-Wesley, 2000).

Determining Object Relationships

The first step in determining the relationships between objects is to figure out what you want to do with your objects because their purpose determines your design. When I was having a design issue one day, a project manager of mine said he looks at objects this way: If I was a car dealer working to sell a car, a tire would not be an object to me—the car would be an object because that is what is important to me. I would not care what the tire on the car is; however, if I was a mechanic working on the car, then the tire would be an object because I care who made it, what it is made out of, what its size is, and so on.

The same principle, which is just a matter of perspective, also applies to the Territory and Employee objects. If you look at the system from the employee perspective, then each employee is associated with one or more territories. Or, you can reverse that relationship and say that a territory has one or more employees (an employee is a part of a territory). Also, you could represent this relationship by relating the employee to the TerritoryMgr or by relating the territory to the EmployeeMgr. Again, it depends on how you want to display these objects to the user. For your purposes, when you build the Employee class, you will relate the employee to one or more territories and not vice versa. The reason for this is mostly logical. It just does not seem right that you assign an employee to a territory from the territory screen, but you would assign an employee to a territory when you are on the Employee screen because you are editing information about an employee.

The next thing is to determine when and why you would need a relationship. For example, when using the program, I do not particularly care which territory an employee belongs to. But when I run reports, I might want to create a report that summarizes what the sales were in a particular territory or region—for that I definitely need that relationship. But, you are not creating the reports from objects in your application—you are creating the reports from your database, so that object relationship is not as important. Another thing to think about is when you might need a piece of information. If I load up an Employee object and I need to know everything there is to know about the employee immediately after I load the employee object, then I need to examine my relationships more carefully because the Employee object would be an aggregate of almost everything. I would be telling myself that I do not want and cannot use my Employee object without knowing everything about the employee—that would make the Employee object an aggregate of everything. This is something that is independent of the interface; it is a rule that should be enforced in the business objects, but oftentimes how you design your interface determines these relationships. I have yet to find someone who has said that there is a hard and fast rule to these things. I believe object design is as much an art as a science, which means no two people will ever build object relationships the same way. This has worked for me on several large scale projects—it is not the only way you can do it, but it allows for a great deal of flexibility and is easily extended later without affecting other parts of your application.

The other thing to remember is the purpose of the application. This is an inventory system; it is not an HR system. The Employee, Territory, and Region objects are small parts of the system. If you did not know what region or territory an employee was part of, it probably would not affect your ability to create an invoice. The same goes for the employee with respect to an order. Many ordering systems use the Internet today, and there are no employees associated with an order when ordering from an Internet application. Regardless of anything else, the purpose of the application must always be foremost in creating object relationships.

NOTE I have presented a couple of small arguments on how objects are related to each other. This is mostly so that you can see the type of thinking that must go into object-oriented design. I have often had long, confusing discussions with other developers as I was working on a system over precisely these types of issues. Theory is wonderful, and it does help, but determining how and when to relate an object is the key.

Most of the objects in this object model are for the purposes of filling combo boxes. For example, the Region list will fill a combo box on the territories edit form so that you can associate a region with a territory. The territories will fill a list box on the employee edit form so that you can associate an employee with one or more territories and so on. You can even look at the employee/orders relationship the same way. These objects simply associate themselves with other objects. Even the relationship between the Order object and the Order Detail object can work this way. However, the Order Detail objects cannot exist without their associated Order object.

Building the Territory Classes

With that said, let's start building the Territory objects. As before, you need to create your four stored procedures for performing all of your operations in the database. Execute the SQL in Listing 7-1 against the Northwind database.

Listing 7-1. The Territory Stored Procedures

```
USE northwind
go
CREATE PROCEDURE usp_territory_delete
@id nvarchar(20)
AS
DELETE
FROM  Territories
WHERE TerritoryID = @id
go
CREATE PROCEDURE usp_territory_getall
AS
SELECT  *
FROM    Territories
go
CREATE PROCEDURE usp_territory_getone
@id nvarchar(20)
AS
SELECT  *
FROM  Territories
WHERE TerritoryID = @id
go
CREATE PROCEDURE usp_territory_save
@id nvarchar(20),
@territory nchar(50),
@region_id int,
@new bit
AS
IF @new = 1
   INSERT INTO Territories (TerritoryID, TerritoryDescription, RegionID)
      VALUES (@id, @territory, @region_id)
ELSE
   UPDATE  Territories
   SET TerritoryDescription = @territory,
       RegionID = @region_id
   WHERE TerritoryID = @id
```

You will notice that the Territories table does not have a numeric, auto-generated identifier as a key. Although I do not agree with this approach—because it leaves the burden of creating a primary key value on the user and because it can be any value the user wants—you will leave it as is because that is the way the database was constructed. Once you have created all of the stored procedures, it is time to create the structure and the interface. Then you will create the data-centric business object.

 CAUTION Having a user-created key on a table can cause an incredible amount of problems in code. You will see why this is a problem later in the "Creating the frmTerritoryList Form" section. I have said it before and I will say it again: All keys in a database should be surrogate keys because it makes everyone's life easier.

Creating the Territory Structure

To create the structure and the interface, edit the Structures.vb code module and add the following structure:

```
<Serializable()> Public Structure structTerritory
    Public TerritoryID As String
    Public TerritoryDescription As String
    Public RegionID As Integer
    Public IsNew as Boolean
End Structure
```

Notice that you have added a property that does not exist in the database: the IsNew property. In the case of the Region class, it was easy to determine if you were going to perform a save or an update because you could check to see if the ID was zero. Because the TerritoryID is a string, you cannot check it. You also cannot check to see if it is an empty length string because the user needs to set it if it is new—that is one of the rules your object will implement. The only way to have the save stored procedure perform the right operation is to set this flag.

Creating the Territory Interface

Next you need to create the interface for this object. Add the following interface to the Interfaces.vb code module:

```
Public Interface ITerritory
    Function LoadProxy() As DataSet
    Function LoadRecord(ByVal strID As String) As structTerritory
    Function Save(ByVal sTerritory As structTerritory) _
    As BusinessErrors
    Sub Delete(ByVal strID As String)
    Function GetBusinessRules() As BusinessErrors
End Interface
```

Notice that this interface is almost identical to the IRegion interface except for the LoadRecord, Delete, and Save signatures. The difference between these three signatures is the structure that is either passed or returned and the data type of the integer. Also, in the case of the Save method, you do not need to return the ID because that is set by the user. In the next chapter, when you work on reducing your redundant code, this will come into play.

Creating the TerritoryDC Object

Because this object is materially like the Region object, you will see the code in Listing 7-2 and examine the differences afterward. Add a new class to the NorthwindDC project and call it *TerritoryDC*. Next, add the code from Listing 7-2.

Listing 7-2. The TerritoryDC Object

```
Option Strict On
Option Explicit On

Imports NorthwindTraders.NorthwindShared.Interfaces
Imports NorthwindTraders.NorthwindShared.Structures
Imports NorthwindTraders.NorthwindShared.Errors
Imports System.Configuration
Imports System.Data.SqlClient

Public Class TerritoryDC
    Inherits MarshalByRefObject

    Implements ITerritory

    Private mobjBusErr As BusinessErrors
```

```
#Region " Private Attributes"
    Private mstrTerritoryID As String
    Private mstrTerritoryDescription As String
    Private mintRegionID As Integer
#End Region

#Region " Public Attributes"

    Public Property TerritoryID() As String
        Get
            Return mstrTerritoryID
        End Get
        Set(ByVal Value As String)
            Try
                If Value Is Nothing Then
                    Throw New ArgumentNullException("Territory ID")
                End If

                If Value.Length = 0 Then
                    Throw New ZeroLengthException()
                End If

                If Value.Length > 20 Then
                    Throw New MaximumLengthException(20)
                End If

                mstrTerritoryID = Value
            Catch exc As Exception
                mobjBusErr.Add("Territory ID", exc.Message)
            End Try
        End Set
    End Property
    Public Property TerritoryDescription() As String
        Get
            Return mstrTerritoryDescription
        End Get
        Set(ByVal Value As String)
            Try
                If Value Is Nothing Then
                    Throw New ArgumentNullException("Territory Description")
                End If
```

```vb
                    If Value.Length = 0 Then
                        Throw New ZeroLengthException()
                    End If

                    If Value.Length > 50 Then
                        Throw New MaximumLengthException(50)
                    End If

                    mstrTerritoryDescription = Value
                Catch exc As Exception
                    mobjBusErr.Add("Territory Description", exc.Message)
                End Try
            End Set
        End Property


        Public Property RegionID() As Integer
            Get
                Return mintRegionID
            End Get
            Set(ByVal Value As Integer)
                Try
                    If Value = 0 Then
                        Throw New ArgumentNullException("Region")
                    End If

                    mintRegionID = Value
                Catch exc As Exception
                    mobjBusErr.Add("Region", exc.Message)
                End Try
            End Set
        End Property
#End Region

    Public Function LoadProxy() As DataSet Implements ITerritory.LoadProxy
        Dim strCN As String = ConfigurationSettings.AppSettings("Northwind_DSN")
        Dim cn As New SqlConnection(strCN)
        Dim cmd As New SqlCommand()
        Dim da As New SqlDataAdapter(cmd)
        Dim ds As New DataSet()

        cn.Open()
```

```
    With cmd
        .Connection = cn
        .CommandType = CommandType.StoredProcedure
        .CommandText = "usp_territory_getall"
    End With

    da.Fill(ds)

    cmd = Nothing
    cn.Close()

    Return ds
End Function

Public Function LoadRecord(ByVal strID As String) As _
structTerritory Implements ITerritory.LoadRecord
    Dim strCN As String = ConfigurationSettings.AppSettings("Northwind_DSN")
    Dim cn As New SqlConnection(strCN)
    Dim cmd As New SqlCommand()
    Dim da As New SqlDataAdapter(cmd)
    Dim ds As New DataSet()
    Dim sTerritory As structTerritory

    cn.Open()

    With cmd
        .Connection = cn
        .CommandType = CommandType.StoredProcedure
        .CommandText = "usp_territory_getone"
        .Parameters.Add("@id", strID)
    End With

    da.Fill(ds)

    cmd = Nothing
    cn.Close()

    With ds.Tables(0).Rows(0)
        sTerritory.TerritoryID = Convert.ToString(.Item("TerritoryID"))
        sTerritory.TerritoryDescription = _
        Convert.ToString(.Item("TerritoryDescription"))
        sTerritory.RegionID = Convert.ToInt32(.Item("RegionID"))
    End With
```

```
            ds = Nothing

        Return sTerritory
    End Function

    Public Sub Delete(ByVal strID As String) Implements ITerritory.Delete
        Dim strCN As String = ConfigurationSettings.AppSettings("Northwind_DSN")
        Dim cn As New SqlConnection(strCN)
        Dim cmd As New SqlCommand()

        cn.Open()

        With cmd
            .Connection = cn
            .CommandType = CommandType.StoredProcedure
            .CommandText = "usp_territory_delete"
            .Parameters.Add("@id", strID)
            .ExecuteNonQuery()
        End With

        cmd = Nothing
        cn.Close()
    End Sub

    Public Function Save(ByVal sTerritory As structTerritory) _
    As BusinessErrors Implements ITerritory.Save
        Dim strCN As String = ConfigurationSettings.AppSettings("Northwind_DSN")
        Dim cn As New SqlConnection(strCN)
        Dim cmd As New SqlCommand()
        Dim intNew As Integer
        mobjBusErr = New BusinessErrors()

        With sTerritory
            Me.TerritoryID = .TerritoryID
            Me.TerritoryDescription = .TerritoryDescription
            Me.RegionID = .RegionID
        End With

        If mobjBusErr.Count = 0 Then

            If sTerritory.IsNew Then
                intNew = 1
            Else
                intNew = 0
            End If
```

```
        cn.Open()

        With cmd
            .Connection = cn
            .CommandType = CommandType.StoredProcedure
            .CommandText = "usp_territory_save"
            .Parameters.Add("@id", mstrTerritoryID)
            .Parameters.Add("@territory", mstrTerritoryDescription)
            .Parameters.Add("@region_id", mintRegionID)
            .Parameters.Add("@new", intNew)
            .ExecuteNonQuery()
        End With

        cmd = Nothing
        cn.Close()
    End If

    Return mobjBusErr
End Function

Public Function GetBusinessRules() As BusinessErrors _
Implements ITerritory.GetBusinessRules
    Dim objBusRules As New BusinessErrors()
    With objBusRules
        .Add("Territory ID", "The value cannot be null.")
        .Add("Territory ID", "The value cannot be more than 20 " _
        & "characters in length.")
        .Add("Territory Description", "The value cannot be null.")
        .Add("Territory Description", "The value cannot be more " _
        & "than 50 characters in length.")
        .Add("Region", "The value cannot be null.")
    End With

    Return objBusRules
    End Function
End Class
```

That is a lot of code, but after this you will not have to type in that much code at one time for the rest of the project! The biggest change in Listing 7-2 is the Save method. Because you already know what the ID of the new record is, you do not have to pass it back. Aside from this, this code is almost identical to the code for the RegionDC class.

Building the User-Centric Territory Classes

The next thing you need to do is to build the user-centric Territory classes. This is where you have to implement the choice you made concerning the object relationships. The user-centric business objects are coupled with the user interface. It is not a tight coupling, but many times you make choices to support your own user interfaces. If you make this object loosely coupled and another application wants to use your user-centric business objects, they may not realize they need to instantiate the Region objects on their own and therefore your Territory object will not be complete. So, you will create an association between this class and the Region class because it is a simple starting point. Because this class is an aggregate of another class, you will see some slightly different behavior in your class.

Creating the Territory Class

Add a new class module to the NorthwindUC project called *Territory.vb*. As before, add the following code to the top of the Territory.vb code module:

```
Option Strict On
Option Explicit On

Imports NorthwindTraders.NorthwindShared.Structures
Imports NorthwindTraders.NorthwindShared.Interfaces
Imports NorthwindTraders.NorthwindShared.Errors
Imports NorthwindTraders.NorthwindShared
```

Now, let's start adding code to your Territory class.

```
Private WithEvents mobjRules As BrokenRules
Private mblnDirty As Boolean = False
Public Loading As Boolean
Private Const LISTENER As String = "TerritoryDC.rem"
Private msTerritory As structTerritory

Private mblnNew As Boolean

Public Event BrokenRule(ByVal IsBroken As Boolean)
Public Event ObjectChanged(ByVal sender As Object, _
ByVal e As ChangedEventArgs)
```

A new variable in the preceding code (if you compare this to the Region class) is the mblnNew variable. This is the flag you will set to indicate whether the object is new. Besides that change, the code is the same so far. This is the reason for using the generic object to pass back your object in the ObjectChanged event; you can copy and paste it everywhere without making a single change to the signature.

NOTE   In the next chapter you will see how you can reduce a large amount of redundancy within the two classes you have created so far (the Region and Territory classes). It allows you to create a standard base class that can be used by everything and that ensures you have implemented the BrokenRules class and several other things you have determined as mandatory for your classes.

Add the following private member attributes to the Territory class:

```
#Region " Private Attributes"
    Private mstrTerritoryID As String = ""
    Private mstrTerritoryDescription As String = ""
    Private mobjRegion As New Region
#End Region
```

Notice that instead of a RegionID variable you have an instance of the Region object. This is the actual object dependency and it forces you to load and refresh your object in a slightly different way. Add the public attributes of your class as shown in Listing 7-3.

Listing 7-3. Public Attributes of the Territory Class

```
#Region " Public Attributes"

    Public Property TerritoryID() As String
        Get
            Return mstrTerritoryID
        End Get
        Set(ByVal Value As String)
            Try
                If Value Is Nothing Then
                    Throw New ArgumentNullException("Territory ID")
                End If
```

```
                        If Value.Length = 0 Then
                            Throw New ZeroLengthException()
                    Else
                            If Value.Length > 20 Then
                                Throw New MaximumLengthException(20)
                            End If
                    End If

                    If mstrTerritoryID <> Value Then
                        mstrTerritoryID = Value
                        If Not Loading Then
                            mobjRules.BrokenRule("Territory ID", False)
                            mblnDirty = True
                        End If
                    End If
                Catch exc As Exception
                    mobjRules.BrokenRule("Territory ID", True)
                    mstrTerritoryID = Value
                    mblnDirty = True
                    Throw exc
                End Try
            End Set
        End Property

        Public Property TerritoryDescription() As String
            Get
                Return mstrTerritoryDescription
            End Get
            Set(ByVal Value As String)
                Try
                    If Value Is Nothing Then
                        Throw New ArgumentNullException("Territory Description")
                    End If

                    If Value.Length = 0 Then
                        Throw New ZeroLengthException()
                    Else
                            If Value.Length > 50 Then
                                Throw New MaximumLengthException(50)
                            End If
                    End If
```

```
                If mstrTerritoryDescription <> Value Then
                    mstrTerritoryDescription = Value
                    If Not Loading Then
                        mobjRules.BrokenRule("Territory Description", False)
                        mblnDirty = True
                    End If
                End If
            Catch exc As Exception
                mobjRules.BrokenRule("Territory Description", True)
                mstrTerritoryDescription = Value
                mblnDirty = True
                Throw exc
            End Try
        End Set
    End Property

    Public Property Region() As Region
        Get
            Return mobjRegion
        End Get
        Set(ByVal Value As Region)
            Try
                If Value Is Nothing Then
                    Throw New ArgumentNullException("Region")
                End If

                If Not Value Is mobjRegion Then
                    mobjRegion = Value
                    If Not Loading Then
                        mobjRules.BrokenRule("Region", False)
                        mblnDirty = True
                    End If
                End If
            Catch exc As Exception
                mobjRules.BrokenRule("Region", True)
                mobjRegion = Value
                mblnDirty = True
                Throw exc
            End Try
        End Set
    End Property
#End Region
```

This follows the exact same pattern as the one you used when you created your Region object, except for the inclusion of a Region object here. Notice that you are using a property for the Region object that accepts a Region object ByVal. In actual practice, however, this is a reference type and so it is passed by reference. You will see this once you are done creating this object and you test it. It should be noted that the Region objects associated using this property will not be destroyed if you destroy this object. You should only do this type of setup for object relationships that consist of dependencies, rather than true aggregations. In a true aggregation, the supplier object (Region) would be created by the client object (Territory).

TIP One of the great powers of this type of setup is the consistency of the code. You do not have to do anything radically different from one class to the other, which helps make maintenance incredibly easy. It also makes reading the code fairly easy because if you understand it in one place, you understand it in all places.

Next, add the IsDirty and IsValid properties (or copy them from the Region object) as shown in Listing 7-4.

Listing 7-4. The IsDirty and IsValid Methods

```
Public ReadOnly Property IsDirty() As Boolean
    Get
        Return mblnDirty
    End Get
End Property

Public ReadOnly Property IsValid() As Boolean
    Get
        If mobjRules.Count > 0 Then
            Return False
        Else
            Return True
        End If
    End Get
End Property
```

Although the IsDirty and IsValid classes remain the same, the constructors will be slightly different. Add the constructors as shown in Listing 7-5.

Listing 7-5. The Territory Class Constructors

```
Public Sub New()
    mblnNew = True
    mobjRules = New BrokenRules()
    mobjRules.BrokenRule("Territory ID", True)
    mobjRules.BrokenRule("Territory Description", True)
    mobjRules.BrokenRule("Region", True)
End Sub

Public Sub New(ByVal strID As String)
    mblnNew = False
    mobjRules = New BrokenRules()
    mstrTerritoryID = strID
End Sub
```

In the first constructor, you set the New flag to true, which is the indicator to the stored procedure to execute the correct block of code when you go to save your object. Also, in this method, you set all of the properties as broken because they are all required and none of them have defaults. The second constructor is similar to the Region constructor except that you set the New flag to false because any changes will indicate an update to the object, not a new object. Also, notice you do not break any rules. The reason for this is that it is assumed you will load your object with valid values, so this saves a bunch of unneeded processing. Also, you have a backup system here because if you assign properties that are invalid, the rules will be broken for you.

Add the ToString function as follows:

```
Public Overrides Function ToString() As String
    Return mstrTerritoryDescription
End Function
```

The ToString function remains the same, except that you now return the Territory Description. Next, add the LoadRecord routine. You will recall that this routine is used either to fully load the record if it is only partially loaded or to refresh the object from the database so that when a user goes to edit the record, they are editing the latest record. Add the LoadRecord method as shown in Listing 7-6.

Listing 7-6. The LoadRecord Method

```
Public Sub LoadRecord()
    Dim objITerritory As ITerritory
    Dim sTerritory As structTerritory
    Dim objRegionMgr As RegionMgr

    objITerritory = CType(Activator.GetObject(GetType(ITerritory), _
    AppConstants.REMOTEOBJECTS & LISTENER), ITerritory)
    sTerritory = objITerritory.LoadRecord(mstrTerritoryID)
    objITerritory = Nothing

    With sTerritory
        Me.mstrTerritoryID = .TerritoryID
        Me.mstrTerritoryDescription = .TerritoryDescription.Trim
    End With

    objRegionMgr = objRegionMgr.GetInstance
    mobjRegion = objRegionMgr.Item(sTerritory.RegionID)

    sTerritory = Nothing
End Sub
```

This method is similar to the Region class's LoadRecord method except for the addition of the RegionMgr object. The advantage of creating the RegionMgr object as a Singleton object is apparent. If you have not loaded the RegionMgr object at this point, it is loaded. Then you retrieve an object from the Manager. If the object is loaded, then you do not have to go to the database to get the object. See the sidebar "Singleton Object Dangers" for additional information.

Singleton Object Dangers

You need to be aware of a couple of things with Singleton objects and aggregation. What if there was a new Region added to the database and the current Territory you were working with was updated so that it was assigned to this new Region? And what if the old Region had been deleted? This scenario is not likely in this situation, but let's look at what you would have to do to take care of this problem.

First, when the updated Territory information is received from the database, you would need to check the value of the RegionID against the value of the RegionID in the Region object. If they matched, then there is no problem and you can just call the Load method on the aggregate object. If they did not match, well, this is where it gets sticky. First, you would need to get a reference to the RegionMgr object and check to see if the object was in the collection. If it is in the collection, then there is no problem. You just assign that Region object to your Territory object and call the Load method on it. If it was not there, you would need to call the Refresh method on the RegionMgr object and then get a reference to the new Region and assign it to your Territory object.

Although all of this works great, there is the small problem in that your objects are no longer loosely coupled. Instead they are tightly bound and one object needs to know everything about the other object. Of course, this is precisely what an aggregate is, but remember that it is your choice as to whether you aggregate your objects. There are no hard and fast rules, and this type of scenario demands that you examine your object relationships carefully before you begin coding.

Next is the Delete method, which again is the same except for the object that is being deleted. Add the code for this method as shown in Listing 7-7.

Listing 7-7. The Territory Delete Method

```
Public Sub Delete()
    Dim objITerritory As ITerritory

    objITerritory = CType(Activator.GetObject(GetType(ITerritory), _
    AppConstants.REMOTEOBJECTS & LISTENER), ITerritory)
    objITerritory.Delete(mstrTerritoryID)
    objITerritory = Nothing
End Sub
```

Next, add the Save method shown in Listing 7-8 to the Territory class.

Listing 7-8. The Territory Save Method

```
Public Sub Save()
    If mobjRules.Count = 0 Then
        If mblnDirty = True Then
            Dim objITerritory As ITerritory
            Dim sTerritory As structTerritory

            With sTerritory
                .TerritoryID = mstrTerritoryID
                .TerritoryDescription = mstrTerritoryDescription
                .RegionID = mobjRegion.RegionID
                .IsNew = mblnNew
            End With
```

```
            objITerritory = _
            CType(Activator.GetObject(GetType(ITerritory), _
            AppConstants.REMOTEOBJECTS & LISTENER), ITerritory)

            objITerritory.Save(sTerritory)
            objITerritory = Nothing

            If mblnNew Then
                mblnNew = False
                RaiseEvent ObjectChanged(Me, New _
                ChangedEventArgs(ChangedEventArgs.eChange.Added))
            Else
                RaiseEvent ObjectChanged(Me, New _
                ChangedEventArgs(ChangedEventArgs.eChange.Updated))
            End If
        End If
    End If
End Sub
```

The only difference between this method and the Save method in the Region class is that you check the value of the mblnNew flag instead of checking to see if the ID is equal to 0. Note also that you have to manually set the New flag to false once the object has been saved. The last two methods, GetBusinessRules and BrokenRules, are the same (shown in Listing 7-9). Add these methods to the Territory class.

Listing 7-9. The GetBusinessRules and BrokenRules Methods

```
Public Function GetBusinessRules() As BusinessErrors
    Dim objITerritory As ITerritory
    Dim objBusRules As BusinessErrors

    objITerritory = CType(Activator.GetObject(GetType(ITerritory), _
    AppConstants.REMOTEOBJECTS & LISTENER), ITerritory)
    objBusRules = objITerritory.GetBusinessRules
    objITerritory = Nothing

    Return objBusRules
End Function


Private Sub mobjRules_RuleBroken(ByVal IsBroken As Boolean) _
Handles mobjRules.RuleBroken
    RaiseEvent BrokenRule(IsBroken)
End Sub
```

Adding the TerritoryMgr Class

Next you need to add the TerritoryMgr class. This class is also a Manager class, but it is not a Singleton. The reason for this is that you do want to know what territories the employee is a part of, so every employee you load needs to have its own collection of territories. Listing 7-10 shows the code for the TerritoryMgr class. Add this code to the Territory.vb code module.

Listing 7-10. The TerritoryMgr Class

```
Public Class TerritoryMgr
    Inherits System.Collections.DictionaryBase

    Public Sub New
        Load
    End Sub

    Public Sub Add(ByVal obj As Territory)
        dictionary.Add(obj.TerritoryID, obj)
    End Sub

    Public Function Item(ByVal Key As Object) As Territory
        Return CType(dictionary.Item(Key), Territory)
    End Function

    Public Sub Remove(ByVal Key As Object)
        dictionary.Remove(Key)
    End Sub

    Private Sub Load()
        Dim objITerritory As ITerritory
        Dim dRow As DataRow
        Dim ds As DataSet
        Dim objRegionMgr As RegionMgr

        objITerritory = CType(Activator.GetObject(GetType(ITerritory), _
        AppConstants.REMOTEOBJECTS & "TerritoryDC.rem"), ITerritory)
        ds = objITerritory.LoadProxy()
        objITerritory = Nothing

        objRegionMgr = objRegionMgr.GetInstance
```

```
            For Each dRow In ds.Tables(0).Rows
                Dim objTerritory As New _
                Territory(Convert.ToString(dRow.Item("TerritoryID")))
                With objTerritory
                    .Loading = True
                    .TerritoryDescription = _
                    Convert.ToString(dRow.Item("TerritoryDescription")).Trim
                    .Region = _
                    objRegionMgr.Item(Convert.ToInt32(dRow.Item("RegionID")))
                    .Loading = False
                End With
                Me.Add(objTerritory)
            Next

            ds = Nothing
    End Sub
End Class
```

The differences to note in the Load method revolve around the RegionMgr object. As with the Load method in the Territory class, you need to get a reference to the RegionMgr object. Remember that the RegionMgr object is a shared object, so if the Regions have been loaded prior to this, the reference is established very quickly; otherwise the information must be retrieved from the database. Then, as you load the Territory objects, you assign a Region object based on the key, which in this case, is the RegionID that you pulled back and you returned to your Territory object. Because you are assigning the Region objects to your Territory objects in this way, you do not need to instantiate a new Region object for every Territory object that you instantiate. This makes the load process fairly quick.

Now that you have added the code, you need to make another entry in the web.config file. Add the following tag so that you can access the TerritoryDC object:

```
<wellknown mode="Singleton"
    type="NorthwindTraders.NorthwindDC.TerritoryDC, NorthwindDC"
    objectUri="TerritoryDC.rem"/>
```

Creating the Territory User Interface

You are ready to create the user interface for your Territory object. First, add a new, inherited form to the NorthwindTraders project and call it *frmTerritoryList.vb*. When the Inheritance Picker form displays, select the frmListBase form.

CAUTION Visual inheritance has a requirement at design-time. Often one form will inherit from another, but when you try to view the inherited form you get an error saying that the form cannot be loaded in the designer. There are a number of different error messages you can get when this occurs, but what it comes down to is that there is a problem in the base form. This is usually caused by some requirement of the constructor that has not been met. The inherited form must be able to compile at design-time! One way of making sure this requirement is met is to always have the default constructor in the base form and just overload it.

Creating the frmTerritoryList Form

Before you do anything else, you need to alter the constructor on the frmTerritoryList class so that the call to MyBase.New includes the title of the Territory List. It should look like the following:

```
MyBase.New("Territories")
```

This form is fairly similar to the frmRegionList form. There are no major differences between the two forms (except for the properties), so go ahead and add the code in Listing 7-11 to your list form (note that I have not included the Windows Forms Designer–generated code).

Listing 7-11. The frmTerritoryList Code Module and Class

```
Option Explicit On
Option Strict On

Imports NorthwindTraders.NorthwindUC

Public Class frmTerritoryList
    Inherits.UserInterface..frmListBase

    Private mobjTerritoryMgr As TerritoryMgr
    Private WithEvents mfrmEdit As frmTerritoryEdit
    Private WithEvents mobjTerritory As Territory

    Public Sub New()
        MyBase.New("Territories")
```

```
                    'This call is required by the Windows Form Designer.
                    InitializeComponent()

                    'Add any initialization after the InitializeComponent() call
                    LoadList()
            End Sub
#Region " Windows Form Designer generated code "
'Form overrides dispose to clean up the component list.
        Protected Overloads Overrides Sub Dispose(ByVal disposing As Boolean)
            If disposing Then
                If Not (components Is Nothing) Then
                    components.Dispose()
                End If
            End If
            MyBase.Dispose(disposing)
        End Sub

        'Required by the Windows Form Designer
        Private components As System.ComponentModel.IContainer

        'NOTE: The following procedure is required by the Windows Form Designer
        'It can be modified using the Windows Form Designer.
        'Do not modify it using the code editor.
        <System.Diagnostics.DebuggerStepThrough()> Private Sub InitializeComponent()
            components = New System.ComponentModel.Container
        End Sub

#End Region
    Private Sub LoadList()
            Dim objTerritory As Territory
            Dim objDictEnt As DictionaryEntry

            Try
                lvwList.BeginUpdate()

                If lvwList.Columns.Count = 0 Then
                    With lvwList
                        .Columns.Add("Territory ID", CInt(.Size.Width / 1) - 8, _
                        HorizontalAlignment.Left)
                        .Columns.Add("Territory Description", CInt(.Size.Width _
                        / 1) - 8, HorizontalAlignment.Left)
                        .Columns.Add("Region", CInt(.Size.Width / 1) - 8, _
                        HorizontalAlignment.Left)
                    End With
                End If
```

```
        lvwList.Items.Clear()

        mobjTerritoryMgr = New TerritoryMgr()

        For Each objDictEnt In mobjTerritoryMgr
            objTerritory = CType(objDictEnt.Value, Territory)
            Dim lst As New ListViewItem(objTerritory.TerritoryID)
            lst.SubItems.Add(objTerritory.TerritoryDescription)
            lst.SubItems.Add(objTerritory.Region.RegionDescription)
            lvwList.Items.Add(lst)
        Next

        lvwList.EndUpdate()

        lblRecordCount.Text = "Record Count: " & lvwList.Items.Count
    Catch exc As Exception
        LogException(exc)
    End Try
End Sub

Protected Overrides Sub AddButton_Click(ByVal sender As Object, _
ByVal e As System.EventArgs)
    Try
        If mfrmEdit Is Nothing Then
            mobjTerritory = New Territory()
            mfrmEdit = New frmTerritoryEdit(mobjTerritory)
            mfrmEdit.MdiParent = Me.MdiParent
            mfrmEdit.Show()
        End If
    Catch exc As Exception
        LogException(exc)
    End Try
End Sub

Private Sub mfrmEdit_Closed(ByVal sender As Object, _
ByVal e As System.EventArgs) Handles mfrmEdit.Closed
    mfrmEdit = Nothing
End Sub

Private Sub mobjTerritory_ObjectChanged(ByVal sender As Object, _
ByVal e As ChangedEventArgs) _
Handles mobjTerritory.ObjectChanged
    Try
        Dim lst As ListViewItem
        Dim objTerritory As Territory = CType(sender, Territory)
```

261

```
            Select Case e.Change
                Case ChangedEventArgs.eChange.Added
                    mobjTerritoryMgr.Add(objTerritory)
                    lst = New ListViewItem(objTerritory.TerritoryID)
                    lst.SubItems.Add(objTerritory.TerritoryDescription)
                    lst.SubItems.Add(objTerritory.Region.RegionDescription)
                    lvwList.Items.Add(lst)
                    lblRecordCount.Text = "Record Count: " _
                    & lvwList.Items.Count
                Case ChangedEventArgs.eChange.Updated
                    For Each lst In lvwList.Items
                        If lst.Text = objTerritory.TerritoryID Then
                            lst.SubItems(1).Text = _
                            objTerritory.TerritoryDescription
                            lst.SubItems(2).Text = _
                            objTerritory.Region.RegionDescription
                            Exit For
                        End If
                    Next
            End Select

            lvwList.Sort()
        Catch exc As Exception
            LogException(exc)
        End Try
    End Sub


    Protected Overrides Sub EditButton_Click(ByVal sender As Object, _
    ByVal e As System.EventArgs)
        Try
            If mfrmEdit Is Nothing Then
                If lvwList.SelectedItems.Count > 0 Then
                    mobjTerritory = _
                    mobjTerritoryMgr.Item(lvwList.SelectedItems(0).Text)
                    mobjTerritory.LoadRecord()
                    mfrmEdit = New frmTerritoryEdit(mobjTerritory)
                    mfrmEdit.MdiParent = Me.MdiParent
                    mfrmEdit.Show()
                End If
            End If
        Catch exc As Exception
            LogException(exc)
        End Try
    End Sub
```

```
    Protected Overrides Sub DeleteButton_Click(ByVal sender As Object, _
    ByVal e As System.EventArgs)
        Try
            Dim objTerritory As Territory
            objTerritory = mobjTerritoryMgr.Item(lvwList.SelectedItems(0).Text)
            objTerritory.Delete()
            mobjTerritoryMgr.Remove(objTerritory.TerritoryID)
            lvwList.SelectedItems(0).Remove()
            lblRecordCount.Text = "Record Count: " & lvwList.Items.Count
        Catch exc As Exception
            LogException(exc)
        End Try
    End Sub
End Class
```

 CAUTION   The one thing to note about this code is the mobjTerritory_ObjectChanged method. If you look at the updated block, you will notice that you are not updating the TerritoryID even though it is a value the user can edit. This is one reason using a key of this type is a terrible idea. I cannot stress that enough. By changing the primary key, you have no identifier by which you can determine what value was changed, so you cannot update the value in the list (or any other place where it might be used for that matter). I do not address how to take care of this because it can be complicated (especially if you have a composite primary key), but be aware that primary keys should be values that the user does not have access to change. This makes your life a lot easier.

Creating the *frmTerritoryEdit* Form

Next, add an inherited edit form to the NorthwindTraders project and call it *frmTerritoryEdit.vb*. This form should inherit from your frmEditBase form. There are going to be a couple of errors at this point because you have not added your code to the frmTerritoryEdit form. Let's take care of those errors by adding the necessary controls to the edit form and by adding the code you need. When you are done adding controls, the edit form looks like Figure 7-2. Table 7-1 lists the controls and their properties.

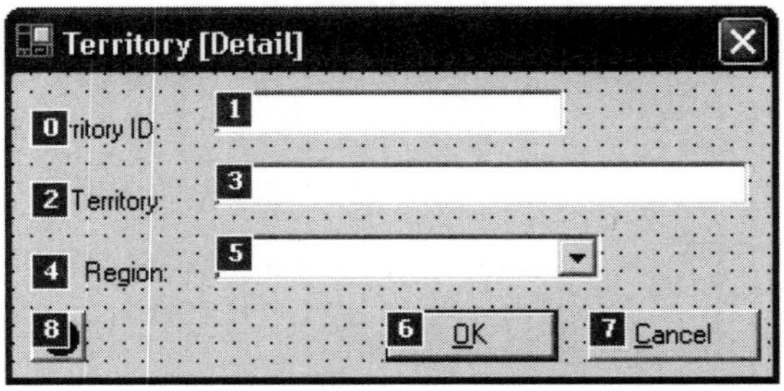

Figure 7-2. Territory edit form

Table 7-1. The Territory Edit Form Controls

Control	Name	Text	Style
Form	frmTerritoryEdit	Territory [Detail]	
Label	lblID	Territory ID:	
Label	lblTerritory	Territory:	
Label	lblRegion	Region:	
Textbox	txtTerritoryID		
Textbox	txtTerritory		
Combobox	cboRegion		DropDownList

The other controls have already been added by way of the base edit form. Set the tab order according to Figure 7-2. Remember to set the IconAlignment on erpMain property for all of the edit fields to MiddleLeft. Also, set the text alignment for the labels to the bottom right.

Add the following code to the frmTerritoryEdit.vb code module header:

```
Option Strict On
Option Explicit On

Imports NorthwindTraders.NorthwindUC
```

Declare a private module-level variable for the Territory object:

```
Private WithEvents mobjTerritory As Territory
```

Modify the constructor so it reads as follows (note that this is almost identical to the frmRegionEdit form):

```
Public Sub New(ByRef objTerritory As Territory)
    MyBase.New()

    'This call is required by the Windows Form Designer.
    InitializeComponent()

    'Add any initialization after the InitializeComponent() call
    mobjTerritory = objTerritory

    If Not mobjTerritory.IsValid Then
        btnok.Enabled = False
    End If
End Sub
```

Next, add the code in Listing 7-12 to handle the form's Load event.

Listing 7-12. The frmTerritoryEdit_Load Method

```
Private Sub frmTerritoryEdit_Load(ByVal sender As Object, _
ByVal e As System.EventArgs) Handles MyBase.Load
    Dim DictEnt As DictionaryEntry
    Dim objRegion As Region
    Dim objRegionMgr As RegionMgr

    Try
        objRegionMgr = objRegionMgr.GetInstance
        For Each DictEnt In objRegionMgr
            objRegion = CType(DictEnt.Value, Region)
            cboRegion.Items.Add(objRegion)
        Next

        If mobjTerritory.TerritoryID <> "" Then
            txtTerritoryID.Text = mobjTerritory.TerritoryID
            txtTerritory.Text = mobjTerritory.TerritoryDescription
            cboRegion.SelectedItem = mobjTerritory.Region
        End If
    Catch exc As Exception
        LogException(exc)
    End Try
End Sub
```

First, this method gets a reference to the RegionMgr object and loops through it to add all of the objects to the combo box. Next, it checks to see if this is a new record because if it is a new record, there is no reason to get anything from the object. If it is an existing record, you set the fields so they contain the proper values. Note the following two lines:

```
cboRegion.Items.Add(objRegion)
    .
    .
cboRegion.SelectedItem = mobjTerritory.Region
```

As mentioned in a previous chapter, the value used to fill combo and list boxes when adding an object to them is the value returned by the ToString method. Once the value has been added to the combo box, it is easily selectable by setting the SelectedItem property to the object that you want to select. You no longer have to loop through the combo or list box looking for a string.

 TIP   As a fun test, you can comment out the ToString method in the Region object and look at what fills the combo box. This is not very helpful, but when you do see it, you will remember what you forgot to do!

At this point, there is just about enough code to be able to bring up the territory list and to be able to open the edit form. Before you can do that, however, you need to modify the frmMain form. In the MainMenu_Click method, add the following Case statement:

```
Case "&Territories"
    LoadTerritories()
```

Next, add a module-level variable for the territory list form as follows:

```
Private mfrmTerritoryList As frmTerritoryList
```

Finally, add the LoadTerritories routine as shown in Listing 7-13.

Listing 7-13. The LoadTerritories Method

```
Private Sub LoadTerritories()
    Try
        Cursor = Cursors.WaitCursor
        mfrmTerritoryList = New frmTerritoryList()
        mfrmTerritoryList.MdiParent = Me
        mfrmTerritoryList.Show()
    Catch exc As Exception
        LogException(exc)
    Finally
        Cursor = Cursors.Default
    End Try
End Sub
```

Up to this point, there is one thing omitted from the code that loads your list forms, and you have probably discovered what it is by now: You can load up multiple list forms for the same item. To ensure there is only one list form for a particular item that is ever loaded, you need to modify your code a little bit. Let's modify the code in frmMain that loads the territory list form. First, change the module-level form variable to be a WithEvents variable. The reason for this is that you need to capture the Closed event that the form generates. Enter the following code to handle the Closed event:

```
Private Sub mfrmTerritoryList_Closed(ByVal sender As Object, _
ByVal e As System.EventArgs) Handles mfrmTerritoryList.Closed
    mfrmTerritoryList = Nothing
End Sub
```

Next, modify the LoadTerritories method to check and see if an instance of your variable already exists. Modify the Try block so that it looks like the following:

```
If mfrmTerritoryList Is Nothing Then
    Cursor = Cursors.WaitCursor
    mfrmTerritoryList = New frmTerritoryList
    mfrmTerritoryList.MdiParent = Me
    mfrmTerritoryList.Show()
Else
    mfrmTerritoryList.Focus()
End If
```

Now you are guaranteed that only one instance of your territory list form will ever exist at one time. If a user tries to load the form when it has already loaded, the form will get the focus and be moved to the front of all of the other forms. Now you are ready to run the code.

Before running the code, make sure to rebuild the solution and copy the NorthwindDC and the SharedObjects to the directory that is pointed to by the virtual Internet Information Server (IIS) directory! When you have that done, run the application so that you can examine some of the concepts discussed.

When the application loads, open the Territory screen by selecting Territories from the Maintenance menu. Notice all of the Region entries that say *Eastern*. Next, close this window and open the Region list screen from the Maintenance menu. Select the Eastern region and edit it so that it reads *Eastern1*. Close these windows and go back to the Territory list. Notice that everything that did read *Eastern* now reads *Eastern1*. All this occurs because you referenced the Region objects instead of instantiating your own.

NOTE   This is what I meant earlier when I said that even though the property set is ByVal, it is really ByRef in this case!

It is up to you if you want to go back and change *Eastern1* to *Eastern*. Next, select one of the Territory items for editing. Note the combo box values and the selected value. Close all of this and let's go back to adding code to the edit form.

Now you will add the validated events for the three edit fields. These are identical to the one validated event that you created before in the Region edit form, with only a slight difference for the combo box. Listing 7-14 shows the validated events.

Listing 7-14. The Territory Edit Form Validated Events

```
#Region " Validate Events"

    Private Sub txtTerritoryID_Validated(ByVal sender As Object, _
    ByVal e As System.EventArgs) Handles txtTerritoryID.Validated
        Dim txt As TextBox = CType(sender, TextBox)

    Try
        mobjTerritory.TerritoryID = txt.Text
        erpmain.SetError(txt, "")
```

```
        Catch exc As Exception
            erpmain.SetError(txt, "")
            erpmain.SetError(txt, exc.Message)
        End Try
    End Sub

    Private Sub txtTerritory_Validated(ByVal sender As Object, _
    ByVal e As System.EventArgs) Handles txtTerritory.Validated
        Dim txt As TextBox = CType(sender, TextBox)

        Try
            mobjTerritory.TerritoryDescription = txt.Text
            erpmain.SetError(txt, "")
        Catch exc As Exception
            erpmain.SetError(txt, "")
            erpmain.SetError(txt, exc.Message)
        End Try
    End Sub

    Private Sub cboRegion_Validated(ByVal sender As Object, ByVal e As _
    System.EventArgs) Handles cboRegion.Validated
        Dim cbo As ComboBox = CType(sender, ComboBox)

        Try
            mobjTerritory.Region = CType(cbo.SelectedItem, Region)
            erpmain.SetError(cbo, "")
        Catch exc As Exception
            erpmain.SetError(cbo, "")
            erpmain.SetError(cbo, exc.Message)
        End Try
    End Sub

#End Region
```

The cboRegion_Validated method uses a combo box object, but notice the line of code that assigns the value in the combo box to the Region value in your Territory object. You need to perform a conversion on the SelectedItem so that you can assign it to the Territory object.

TIP I have enclosed the validate events in a Validate Events region. It is a good idea to put like groups of methods together into a region so that they do not get in your way—especially when the coding is completed and you are 99-percent positive that there are no errors within that block of code. Who wants to keep looking at the same code when it is not important in the context of what you are trying to accomplish at the time?

Next, add the code for the btnOK.Click method as shown in Listing 7-15. This code is identical to the code in the frmRegionEdit form except that it works on an object.

Listing 7-15. The btnOK_Click Method

```
Private Sub btnOK_Click(ByVal sender As System.Object, _
ByVal e As System.EventArgs) Handles btnOK.Click
    Try
        If mobjTerritory.IsDirty Then
            mobjTerritory.Save()
        End If
        Close()
    Catch exc As Exception
        LogException(exc)
    End Try
End Sub
```

Finally, add the code in Listing 7-16 to handle the BrokenRules and GetBusinessRules events.

Listing 7-16. Handling the Broken Rules and Business Rules Events

```
Private Sub mobjRegion_BrokenRule(ByVal IsBroken As Boolean) _
Handles mobjTerritory.BrokenRule
    If IsBroken Then
        btnOK.Enabled = False
    Else
        btnOK.Enabled = True
    End If
End Sub
```

```
Private Sub btnRules_Click(ByVal sender As System.Object, _
ByVal e As System.EventArgs) Handles btnRules.Click
    Dim frmRules As New frmBusinessRules(mobjTerritory.GetBusinessRules)
    frmRules.ShowDialog()
    frmRules = Nothing
End Sub
```

At this point, you can now add, edit, delete, and print the territories.

Summary

In this chapter you have examined object relations in the overall application architecture. You have seen how to aggregate objects, and you have seen how to use a Singleton object to its fullest potential. Most obviously, you have added a second set of classes to your application. This is important because it has bearing on the next chapter.

In the next chapter you will look at ways to reduce duplicated code. Also, you have seen that there is a lot of code to enter for simple, basic tasks. In the next chapter you will also create a set of enterprise templates that you can use to avoid having to rewrite all of this code. This lessens the amount of code you need to write in any application.

CHAPTER 8

Reusing Code

UP TO THIS POINT, you have written a fair amount of code. In fact, if you do a line count, you will find out that it comes to about 3,624 lines of code (this includes blank lines and Windows Forms–generated code, but not comments). That is a lot of work for just two sets of classes that retrieve only two tables worth of data. In this chapter you will look at two ways of reducing the amount of code that your application needs. First, you will consolidate some of the code in your user-centric classes, and you will create a base class that you can use in your user-centric objects. After you do that, you will set up a couple of enterprise templates so that you can add standard blocks of code and just edit the parts you need to edit. In this manner, you might add 1,000 lines of code, but you only have to type about 50 lines. It makes for a much more streamlined development process, as you will see.

Reducing Redundant Code

Many times during an application's lifecycle, I have had the occasion to say something such as, "We use that code everywhere." That one statement means that I have redundant code. Sometimes, during the design phase, it is not always easy to figure out exactly what code will be redundant and what code will not be. Contrary to popular belief, development just is not that cut and dried. I like to review two completed sets of code for two functions that work fairly similar. By looking at these sets of code, I can figure out exactly what code needs to be moved around and changed and reduced. Any further in the process than this generally requires a lot of rework and is not a good idea. If you catch these things too late, it is often just better to count it as a lesson learned, add it to the change management log, and move on. Obviously you would like to avoid this situation altogether, but no matter how many times you think you have got it right, you will always miss a little something.

Visual Basic .NET (VB .NET) gives VB 6 developers a whole new world for removing redundant code. Through inheritance and interfaces you can cut down on a great deal of duplicate code. You have already seen this in action with the power of visual inheritance and even something as simple as inheriting from the dictionary base. So, you will now complete your own code reduction exercise. The first step to doing this is to list all of the routines and variables from the two pieces of code you want to compare. If they are similar, then you also want to add how they are different. If they are very different, then it does not make much difference. To keep it simple, you will examine the Territory and Region objects only by creating the list in Table 8-1.

Table 8-1. Method Comparison Table

Region	Territory	Notable Difference
Delete	Delete	ID is an integer in one, a string in the other
LoadRecord	LoadRecord	
mobjRules_RuleBroken	mobjRules_RuleBroken	None
Save	Save	
GetBusinessRules	GetBusinessRules	The remoting object on which the call is made
IsDirty	IsDirty	None
IsValid	IsValid	None
Loading	Loading	None
mblnDirty	mblnDirty	None
BrokenRule (Event)	BrokenRule (Event)	None
ObjectChanged (Event)	ObjectChanged (Event)	The object being passed

NOTE   A good, easy way to do this comparison is to switch to the Class View tab on the Solution Explorer. This gives you a view similar to the view in Figure 8-1 where it is easy to see all of the information you need to review.

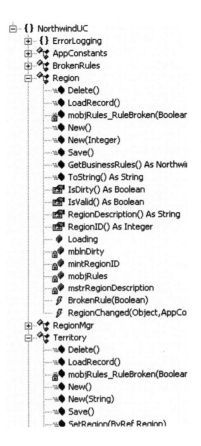

Figure 8-1. Solution Explorer's Class View tab

You will notice that Table 8-1 only lists the methods and properties that you could conceivably consolidate. You cannot consolidate constructors, the ToString method, or the properties. You want to create a generic set of reusable code that is reusable by all of the objects you will create from here on out. The methods with no notable difference are not at all similar. What they do may be similar, but they call different objects on the server and therefore they are not good candidates to consider. So, that leaves you with only a few things you can consolidate, but it will make a huge difference.

NOTE An important method to note in Table 8-1 is the Delete method. I listed this as an example because you cannot consolidate it—nor would you really want to consolidate it. The reason you cannot consolidate it is because of the ID passed to the remote objects to retrieve the record. If you use an Identity column as the ID on all of the tables, then you could conceivably consolidate the Delete method because it does not return any information. The reason why you would not want to consolidate it is because it is a method that is part of the object as opposed to something that acts on the object, so you do not really want to move this code outside of your object.

Consolidating the User-Centric Classes

Let's start consolidating your code by creating another class module called *BusinessBase* in the NorthwindUC project. Because you are taking duplicate code and adding it to this class, this will be an easy and painless process (well, mostly painless). Copy the code for each of the methods and properties that have no differences in Table 8-1 to the new BusinessBase class. When you are done, your BusinessBase class should look like the class in Listing 8-1.

Listing 8-1. The BusinessBase Class

```
Option Explicit On
Option Strict On

Public Class BusinessBase
    Private mblnDirty As Boolean = False
    Public Loading As Boolean
    Private WithEvents mobjRules As BrokenRules

    Public Event ObjectChanged(ByVal sender As Object, _
    ByVal e As ChangedEventArgs)

    Public Event BrokenRule(ByVal IsBroken As Boolean)

    Public ReadOnly Property IsDirty() As Boolean
        Get
            Return mblnDirty
        End Get
    End Property
```

```
    Public ReadOnly Property IsValid() As Boolean
        Get
            If mobjRules.Count > 0 Then
                Return False
            Else
                Return True
            End If
        End Get
    End Property

    Private Sub mobjRules_RuleBroken(ByVal IsBroken As Boolean) _
    Handles mobjRules.RuleBroken
        RaiseEvent BrokenRule(IsBroken)
    End Sub
End Class
```

Before doing anything else, you need to make one decision—do you want to allow a developer to instantiate this class? In this case the answer is easy—no, you do not. The reason is that this is a helper class, and it cannot operate on its own. So before going any further, add the MustInherit keyword between the words *Public* and *Class* in the class declaration.

Now you have to change some of the declarations so that your variable and method scopes are OK. For every method or property you need to access in your subclassed object, you need to change scope declarations from *Private* to *Protected*. In this case, you need to access only two variables: the mblnDirty variable and the mobjRules variable. So, change the scope from *Private* to *Protected* for these two variables. Next, alter just the Region class for right now by having it inherit from the BusinessBase class:

```
Public Class Region
    Inherits BusinessBase
```

This immediately causes several things to be underlined as errors. Do not worry. If you look at the Task List, you will notice that the only errors it shows are that different variables, methods, and events conflict with each other. Simply delete them. Every piece of code you moved to the BusinessBase class needs to be deleted from the Region class because it inherits from the BusinessBase class. Once you are done with this, you will find out that you still have a problem. The error you will see in the Task List is the following:

```
Derived classes cannot raise base class events.
```

Uh-oh. How do you fix this? The answer is you cannot, but you can work around it. You can get around it by creating a method in the base class that you can call and have it raise the event for you. In the base class, create a method called *CallChangedEvent* and code it as follows:

```
Protected Sub CallChangedEvent(ByVal sender As Object, _
ByVal e As ChangedEventArgs)
    RaiseEvent ObjectChanged(sender, e)
End Sub
```

Next, in the Save method of the Region object (because that is where the errors occurred), change the two RaiseEvent statements to look like the following:

```
If intID = 0 Then
    CallChangedEvent(Me, New _
        ChangedEventArgs(ChangedEventArgs.eChange.Added))
Else
    CallChangedEvent(Me, New _
        ChangedEventArgs(ChangedEventArgs.eChange.Updated))
End If
```

This simple change eliminates your problem, so you are good to go.

Now, perform all of these steps for the Territory class (with the exception of the intID, which is not needed in the Territory class). Your base business class now consists of 27 lines of code that you never need to write again. And you have already, with just these two classes, reduced the amount of code by 27 lines. Although this does not seem like a lot, consider a project with 100 classes (which is still a fairly small amount of classes)—this would then have reduced the number of lines of code by 2,700 lines! That is a big difference. But you can do better still.

The GetBusinessRules method is redundant. Although it does call a different remote object, that is just a value that you append onto the end of the REMOTEOBJECTS path. If you look at the GetBusinessRules method in the Region class, you will see the code in Listing 8-2.

Listing 8-2. The GetBusinessRules Method of the Region Class

```
Public Function GetBusinessRules() As BusinessErrors
        Dim objIRegion As IRegion
        Dim objBusRules As BusinessErrors

        objIRegion = CType(Activator.GetObject(GetType(IRegion), _
        AppConstants.REMOTEOBJECTS & LISTENER), IRegion)
        objBusRules = objIRegion.GetBusinessRules
        objIRegion = Nothing

        Return objBusRules
    End Function
```

You have used the IRegion interface to get a reference to the GetBusinessRules function of the remote objects. You definitely want to consolidate this call because it operates on an object and is not really a part of an object. To do this, you need to make a change to your Region and Territory interfaces. Go to the Interfaces code module in the NorthwindShared project. Listing 8-3 shows the Region and Territory interfaces.

Listing 8-3. The Region and Territory Interfaces

```
Public Interface ITerritory
        Function LoadProxy() As DataSet
        Function LoadRecord(ByVal strID As String) As structTerritory
        Function Save(ByVal sTerritory As structTerritory) _
        As BusinessErrors
        Sub Delete(ByVal strID As String)
        Function GetBusinessRules() As BusinessErrors
    End Interface

    Public Interface IRegion
        Function LoadProxy() As DataSet
        Function LoadRecord(ByVal intID As Integer) As structRegion
        Function Save(ByVal sRegion As structRegion, ByRef intID As Integer) _
        As BusinessErrors
        Sub Delete(ByVal intID As Integer)
        Function GetBusinessRules() As BusinessErrors
    End Interface
```

The similarities are immediately obvious upon comparing the two interfaces. Both the LoadProxy and GetBusinessRules methods are identical. To consolidate these methods, add a new Interface called *IBaseInterface* and add the method signatures to it as shown in Listing 8-4.

Listing 8-4. IBaseInterface

```
Public Interface IBaseInterface
    Function LoadProxy() As DataSet
    Function GetBusinessRules() As BusinessErrors
End Interface
```

Next, alter the IRegion and ITerritory interfaces so they both inherit from IBaseInterface. Delete the LoadProxy and GetBusinessRules methods from each of these interfaces. At this point you should not have any errors. Now, what does this have to do with consolidating the GetBusinessRules method in your objects? Now that the GetBusinessRules method is included in a base class, your call on the GetBusinessRules method can be performed on the IBaseInterface interface instead of on the IRegion or ITerritory interfaces. This allows you to create a generic routine that can make this call as long as the interface inherits from the IBaseInterface interface.

First, add the following two Imports statements to the top of the BusinessBase code module:

```
Imports NorthwindTraders.NorthwindShared.Interfaces
Imports NorthwindTraders.NorthwindShared.Errors
```

Move the GetBusinessRules method to the BusinessBase class and alter the code so that it is identical to the code in Listing 8-5.

Listing 8-5. The GetBusinessRules Method

```
Public Function GetBusinessRules() As BusinessErrors
    Dim objInterface As IBaseInterface
    Dim objBusRules As BusinessErrors

    objInterface = CType(Activator.GetObject(GetType(IBaseInterface), _
    AppConstants.REMOTEOBJECTS & LISTENER), IBaseInterface)
    objBusRules = objInterface.GetBusinessRules
    objInterface = Nothing

    Return objBusRules
End Function
```

Now you still have one problem here—the Activator.GetObject line, in particular the Listener constant. You do not have a listener constant in the base class and you do not have a value to put into it at this point anyway. You need to make this dynamic, but how? The answer lies in the constructor that you will create for this class. Add the following private variable and constructor to the BusinessBase class as shown in the following code:

```
Private mstrListener As String

Public Sub New(ByVal RemotePath As String)
    mstrListener = RemotePath
End Sub
```

And alter the Activator.GetObject line to read as follows:

```
objInterface = CType(Activator.GetObject(GetType(IBaseInterface), _
AppConstants.REMOTEOBJECTS & mstrListener), IBaseInterface)
```

This causes several errors also, so let's go back and edit the constructors for the Region object so they read as follows:

```
Public Sub New()
    MyBase.New(LISTENER)
    mobjRules = New BrokenRules()
    mobjRules.BrokenRule("Region Description", True)
End Sub

Public Sub New(ByVal intID As Integer)
    MyBase.New(LISTENER)
    mobjRules = New BrokenRules()
    mintRegionID = intID
End Sub
```

Notice that both methods now have a new first line that reads as follows:

```
MyBase.New(LISTENER)
```

Make the same change for the Territory object so that the first line of its constructors now reads as follows:

```
MyBase.New(LISTENER)
```

The last two changes are fairly simple: Delete the GetBusinessRules method from the Region and Territory classes and move the `mobjRules = New BrokenRules()`

statement from the constructors in the Region and Territory classes to the constructor in the BusinessBase class. At this point you should be able to run the application with no problems at all. Your count of reusable code lines is now up to 41. And with that, you are done consolidating the user-centric classes.

NOTE   The purpose of doing this is not just so that you reuse code. Although that is a laudable goal itself, it also allows you to place code that does one thing in one place. But more importantly than that, it gives your application a true, overall architecture. Every type of object in your application will now behave in substantially the same way. This makes maintenance a lot easier, and it makes adding new functionality to the entire application easier.

Adding a Configuration File

This may seem like a strange heading to place in this chapter, but it is not. I have already demonstrated the use of an application configuration file with the Internet Information Server (IIS) remoting objects. You have seen that you can store application-specific parameters and retrieve them quite easily. So why would you want to create yet another configuration file for your local objects? How often have you had to create one build for test and another for development and yet another for a demonstration environment? Or how many times have you had to change the code if a server location changed or any number of other reasons? The answer is probably a lot.

The addition of a configuration file is just as simple and straightforward as it is for the web.config file. Your configuration file for the local objects is going to store the Uniform Resource Locator (URL) of your remote objects. To begin with, add a configuration file to the NorthwindTraders project. To do this, select Project ➤ Add New Item and select the Application Configuration File entry. Leave the filename as *App.config*. Edit the App.config file so that it looks identical to the Extensible Markup Language (XML) in Listing 8-6.

Listing 8-6. The App.config File

```
<?xml version="1.0" encoding="utf-8" ?>
<configuration>
  <appSettings>
    <add key="Northwind_IIS"
     value="http://localhost:80/Northwind/"/>
  </appSettings>
</configuration>
```

Now you need to edit the code in the NorthwindUC AppConstants class. The code change is quite simple, but before you edit the code, import the System.Configuration namespace into the heading of the code module. The original code is as follows:

```
Public Class AppConstants
    Public Shared REMOTEOBJECTS As String = "http://localhost:80/Northwind/"
End Class
```

Edit the code so that it looks like the following:

```
Imports System.Configuration
Public Class AppConstants
    Public Shared REMOTEOBJECTS As String = _
    ConfigurationSettings.AppSettings("Northwind_IIS")
End Class
```

You are done. But you might be asking yourself one question now: "Why did you add an application configuration file to the NorthwindTraders project instead of the NorthwindUC project?" Well, the answer is that the NorthwindTraders project is the startup project and therefore it is the application, not the NorthwindUC assembly.

Each application can have only one application configuration file, which is why you did not rename it. However, there is also a different reason you did not rename it—the file is renamed when it is deployed. To see this, run the application and then check the bin folder of the NorthwindTraders project. You will now see a configuration file called *NorthwindTraders.exe.config*. By default, configuration files are renamed to the application executable file name plus the .config extension.

With this change you can now change the location of your IIS server and your data server without recompiling and redistributing the application. All you have to do is send out an updated configuration file—it is much simpler now!

Creating Enterprise Templates

Enterprise templates are one means for an organization to help implement standards by way of policy files, custom help files, and prototype code modules and projects. Three distinct parts comprise enterprise templates, as shown in Table 8-2.

Table 8-2. Template Components

Template Item	Description
Solution/project template	This is a predefined solution or project that contains all of the code module prototypes.
Project item template	This is a template for a single type of project item. These are the items that are displayed when you select Project ➤ Add New.
Policy file	This is an XML document that can be used to control the use of items within a project template. It can also be used to hook up custom help to the individual items in a project. The Template Descriptor Language is used when creating this document.

In this section you will look briefly at creating a simple project template and then you will dive into creating individual Project Item templates. You will not be covering policy files here. The Template Descriptor Language is an extensive language and the policy file is a huge file with many intricacies. There is enough information needed to be able to create a good policy file to fill another book and it is beyond the scope of this book (see the sidebar "Enforcing Architecture in the Enterprise").

Enforcing Architecture in the Enterprise

The goal of corporations in the current environment is to do things better, faster, and cheaper. That seems like common sense, but software development has largely been immune to two of these three things: better and cheaper. But what do *better* and *cheaper* mean? The definition of *better* has slowly evolved. *Better* used to mean that the product did cooler things or was more functional than a like product. In my experience, *better* has now come to mean simpler, standardized, and easy to maintain. The third part of that statement, easy to maintain, is where cheaper comes in. So how do enterprise templates affect this shift in thinking?

Enterprise templates allow for several things:

- They provide a starting point for the application architecture.

- They provide guidance for using that architecture.

- In some cases they can solve basic problems based on the experiences of other developers.

- They can also enforce enterprise standards and ensure conformity to the enterprise's chosen infrastructures.

Contrary to what some people may think, you do not need to have a different architecture for every n-tier application you build. You do not need to rethink the underlying portions of this architecture for every project. A handful of basic designs can be customized to your needs rather than having to build complete new designs. Using policy files, help that is specific to an architecture type and an organization can be included directly in the Integrated Development Environment (IDE), which means the learning curve for a particular architecture is smaller if the documentation is written correctly.

Finally, with policy files, an organization can say, "This is how we want our applications to be structured because it makes it easier to maintain." This is where you can save a great deal of headache. How many times have you been asked to work on a project temporarily (about two weeks) only to find out that it is going to take you two weeks to get up to speed on the project? Now what if you could move to a project and you understand the whole thing because it is the same architecture you were using on your other project? Corporations should be able to put policy files to good use, but I suspect it will not be until Microsoft comes up with a much easier way to create a policy file.

Creating a Solution/Project Template

To begin, you will create a generic template that outlines what you have worked up to at this point. Your solution template will contain a project for business rules, data-centric and user-centric business logic, shared objects, and a user interface. You will also add some basic, generic code to your application that can serve as the foundation for any other projects that choose to use your application design. Open Visual Studio and select File ➤ New ➤ Project. Next, expand the Other Projects node in the New Project dialog box and select the Enterprise Template Projects folder. From the Templates listed, select the Enterprise Template Project template and change the project name to *NTierApplication*. Finally, click OK.

This creates an empty solution with one node that has a different icon from those you have seen before, the template icon. This serves as the solution template to which you will add your projects. To add the projects, follow these steps:

1. Right-click this node and select Add ➤ New Project.

2. Select the Enterprise Template Project node.

3. Select the Enterprise Template Project template.

4. Name the Project *DataCentricProjects* and click OK.

Repeat these steps four more times using the following project names:

- UserCentricProjects

- SharedObjectsProjects

- BusinessRuleProjects

- UserInterfaceProjects

When you are finished, you should have a solution structure that looks like Figure 8-2.

Figure 8-2. The solution/project template structure

What you have done here is create a hierarchy of templates: one solution template with five project templates. You now need to flesh out the project templates so they contain actual projects. Before you start incorporating any of your code, you will just create some empty projects. To do this, follow these steps:

1. Right-click the BusinessRuleProjects node and select Add ➤ New Project.

2. Select the Visual Basic Projects node and select the Class Library template.

3. Name the project *BusinessRules* and click OK.

Repeat these steps for the DataCentricProjects node, the SharedObjectsProjects node, and the UserCentricProjects node. Name them as the nodes are, but with the word *Projects* at the end. For the UserInterfaceProjects node, follow the same steps but select the Windows Application template instead of the Class Library template. When you are done, your Solution Explorer pane should look like Figure 8-3.

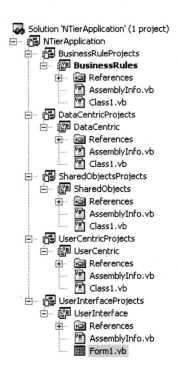

Figure 8-3. The template with all the projects

At this point you need to add some real functionality into these templates and create the correct relationships among them so that the developers who use this template do not have to do it themselves.

TIP Creating templates can be a time-consuming task. To make things easier, only include those items that do not require code changes to make them work. If code changes are going to be required, then you are wasting your time, but it is a good idea to put TODO comments in the code with instructions on how to complete a section.

The BusinessRules project is going to remain empty at this point because you have not yet learned about reflection (you will in Chapter 10). You can come back and update this template once you have worked through Chapter 10. You will add some functionality that every application can use (and coincidentally it will be things you have already coded). You will add the following basic items to your template:

- Error logging functionality

- BrokenRules class

- BusinessBase class

- Application configuration file

- Basic interfaces and structures

- EditBase and ListBase forms

- Contents of the UIUtilities and UIInterfaces code modules

Navigate to the NorthwindTraders folder in Windows Explorer and copy the following files to the \NTierApplication\UserInterfaceProjects\UserInterface folder (located with the other Visual Studio projects):

- frmBusinessRules.vb and frmBusinessRules.resx

- frmEditBase.vb and frmEditBase.resx

- frmListBase.vb and frmListBase.resx

- UIInterfaces.vb

- UIUtilities.vb

- App.config

Next, in the UserInterface project in the IDE, right-click the UserInterface node and select Add ➤ Add Existing Item. Make sure to change the Files of Type drop-down list to All Files, then select all of the files you just copied to this directory. This causes a few errors to be displayed in the Task List, but you will fix those in a little bit.

Now, navigate to the NorthwindUC folder in Windows Explorer and copy the following files to the \NTierApplication\UserCentricProjects\UserCentric folder:

- AppConstants.vb

- BrokenRules.vb

- BusinessBase.vb

- LogError.vb

Next, in the UserCentric project in the IDE, right-click the UserCentric node and select Add ➤ Add Existing Item, then select all of the files you just copied to this directory. Then delete the Class1.vb file from the project.

Now, navigate to the NorthwindShared folder in Windows Explorer and copy the following files to the \NTierApplication\SharedObjectsProjects\SharedObjects folder:

- Structures.vb

- Errors.vb

- Interfaces.vb

Next, in the SharedObjects project in the IDE, right-click the SharedObjects node and select Add ➤ Add Existing Item, then select all of the files you just copied to this directory. Then delete the Class1.vb file from the project.

Finally, navigate to the NorthwindDC folder and copy the LogErrorDC.vb file to the \NTierApplication\DataCentricProjects\DataCentric folder. Add this file to the DataCentric project and delete the Class1.vb file associated with this project.

Now you have to clean up your code (which mostly consists of adding references and changing Imports statements) before you create a template out of your projects. Add the References for each project based on Table 8-3.

Table 8-3. Template Project References

Project	References These Projects/Assemblies
UserInterface	UserCentric, SharedObjects, System.Runtime.Remoting
UserCentric	SharedObjects, System.Web
DataCentric	SharedObjects, System.Runtime.Remoting

You can get rid of most of the problems with the code fairly easily. Select Edit ➤ Find and Replace ➤ Replace in Files and enter *NorthwindTraders.NorthwindShared* in the Find box and enter *SharedObjects* in the Replace With box. Make sure to look in the entire solution. This leaves you with four errors. To fix these, perform a Find and Replace again and find *NorthwindUC* and replace it with *UserCentric*. Now you are error free, but you want to clean up a few more things.

In the Interfaces.vb code module, delete the ITerritory, IRegion, and IMenu interfaces. In the Structures.vb code module, delete the structRegion and structTerritories structures.

The last step you have to take is to associate a policy file with this template and these projects. You will take a shortcut and instead of creating your own, you will use one that already exists and just rename it. To do this, follow these steps:

1. Right-click the NTierApplication template node and select Properties.

2. Select the ellipsis next to the Policy File property.

3. Right-click the DAP.TDL file in the Select a TDL File dialog box and select Copy.

4. Right-click in the window and select Paste.

5. Rename the file to *NTierApplication.TDL*.

6. Double-click the icon of the NtierApplication.TDL file.

7. Click Yes when the dialog box to reload the projects is displayed and then save the solution.

Now that you have a clean project that has all the right references and a policy file, you can create your template.

TIP   Before you create a template, it is a good idea to back up the solution so that you can come back and change it easily later. You will see that the generation of the template is troublesome enough, and you do not want to have to repeat the steps you just took.

Close the IDE and navigate to the solution folder in Windows Explorer (this is usually My Documents\Visual Studio Projects\NTierApplication). Copy the entire folder and paste it in the EnterpriseFrameworks\Policy folder (located at C:\Program Files\Microsoft Visual Studio .NET 2003\ EnterpriseFrameworks\Projects). This is where you now have to follow these steps:

1. In the NTierApplication Solution folder, delete the .suo and .eto files.

2. In each of the project template folders, delete the .eto file.

3. In each of the project folders, delete the \bin and \obj folders.

4. Edit the NTierApplication.etp file using a text editor and delete all of the lines with the <GUIDPROJECTID> tag (there will be five in this file).

5. Edit each of the project .etp files using a text editor and delete the line with the <GUIDPROJECTID> tag (there will be only one line in these files).

NOTE   The .suo extension stands for *Solution User Options*. This file contains all of the customizations you have made to the project solution. The .eto extension stands for *Enterprise Template Options*. But you cannot create any choices at this point that alter this file (at least, I have not been able to do so).

Once you have finished all of those edits, you are done with the enterprise template; however, you need a way to be able to see it in the New Project dialog box in Visual Studio. To arrange that, navigate to the ProxyProjects folder (\Microsoft Visual Studio .NET 2003\EnterpriseFrameworks\ProxyProjects) and follow these steps:

1. Copy the proxyprojectsvb.vsdir file and paste it into the same folder.

2. Rename the file to a descriptive name, in this case *customtemplates.vsdir*.

3. Edit the file with Notepad.

4. Delete all the lines in the file except the first line.

5. Change the path on this line (which currently reads ..*Projects\Visual Basic Simple Distributed Application\Visual Basic Simple Distributed Application.etp*) to ..*Projects\NTierApplication\NTierApplication.etp*.

6. After the first GUID number you will see a vertical bar followed by another number (usually #5003). Change this number to #6000.

7. After this number is another vertical bar followed by a 1. Change this to 0. (This is the position that the template shows up in the templates list. Using 0 places it first). The file should now contain only the following line (without the line breaks), although your GUID number may be different:

```
..\Projects\NTierApplication\NTierApplication.etp|
{AE77B8D0-6BDC-11d2-B354-0000F81F0C06}|#6000|0|#5004|
{AE77B8D0-6BDC-11d2-B354-0000F81F0C06}|122|0|Project
```

8. Save and close the file.

Just to make sure this worked, open Visual Studio and select New ➤ Project and select the NTierApplication template from the Enterprise Templates node. You will see the entire structure of the project.

Creating a Project Item Template

You can have a solution template, but what about all of those code modules you had to create? For that you have to do something slightly different.

NOTE It would be nice if Microsoft makes some changes in a later release of Visual Studio because adding in project item templates could be "wizardized." However, you can accomplish most of this with text editing and copying and pasting.

The rest of this chapter walks you through creating a single user-centric template item. This will give you enough of an idea for you to create your own project item templates. To begin with, let's look at the items you can add to a VB project (see Figure 8-4).

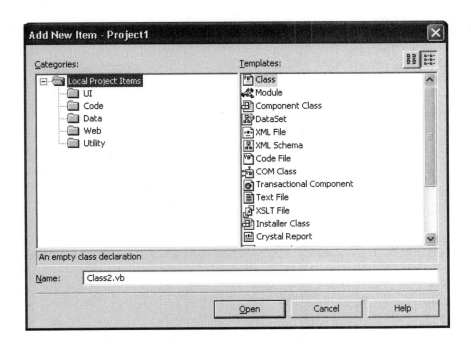

Figure 8-4. The Add New Item dialog box, VB project items

Next, Figure 8-5 shows the folder structure in the Microsoft Visual Studio .NET folder (this structure starts under the Microsoft Visual Studio .NET\VB7 folder).

Two things should be immediately obvious. First, the Local Project Items in the Add New Item dialog box in Figure 8-4 corresponds with the Local Project Items folder in Figure 8-5. Secondly, although the folder structure shows a partial list in Figure 8-4, the items on the Templates side of the Add New Item dialog box in Figure 8-4 correspond with the folders listed under the VBWizards folder in Figure 8-5.

Figure 8-5. Partial folder structure, Visual Studio .NET folders

Examining a Template Item

Look in the Local Project Items folder and you will see one file that has special importance—the LocalProjectItems.vsdir file. This is the same type of file as the one you modified earlier for the solution template, but now you will examine what one line from this file looks like and represents:

```
..\Class.vsz|{164B10B9-B200-11D0-8C61-00A0C91E29D5}|#3020|20|#3021|{164B10B9-B200-
11D0-8C61-00A0C91E29D5}|4510| |Class.vb
```

Table 8-4 shows the breakdown of the line.

Table 8-4. Local Project Item Directory File Line Breakdown*

Item	Description
..\	This shows a relative path from the file to the wizard parameter file.
Class.vsz	This is the name of the wizard parameter file.
GUID	This stands for *Global Unique Identifier*, which is used internally by .NET. It also can be blank.
#3020	This points to a description for the item name, or it can be a string.
20	This is the order the item shows up in the list (10, 20, 30, 40, and so on). The lowest numbered item is first.
#3021	This points to a description that shows in the gray box below the project items, or it can be a string.
GUID	This stands for *Global Unique Identifier*, which is used internally by .NET. It points to a DLL file that contains icons.
4510	This is the resource ID for the icon located in the file specified by the previous GUID.
[blank]	These are flags to indicate whether certain fields should be enabled or disabled in the Add New dialog box.
Class.vb	This is the default file name that is generated.

* For more information on the vsdir file, see the MSDN help topic "VSdir files."

With the information in Table 8-4, you have enough knowledge to do some copying and pasting to achieve your desired template.

Creating the UserCentric Project Item Template

For the moment, create a new Windows application, which you will use to examine your templates as you create them. Next you are going to start making some edits to some files and directories. First, go to the Microsoft

Visual Studio .NET\Vb7\VBProjectItems\Local Project Items folder and edit the LocalProjectItems.vsdir file. Take the following steps to modify the LocalProjectItems file:

1. Copy the line that starts with the word *Resources* and paste it as a new line on the next line.

2. Change the word *Resources* to *Custom*.

3. Change the #3109 entry on that line to *Custom*.

4. Change the order from 60 to 70.

5. Save and close the file.

This just created a new folder called *Custom* in the Add New Item dialog box in Visual Studio, which you will see after you make these next few changes. Now that you have your own folder that shows up in the Add New dialog box, it would probably be a good idea to actually create that folder so that Visual Studio has a folder to reference. Take these steps to create this folder:

1. Create a new folder in the Local Project Items folder and call it *Custom*.

2. Go into the Code folder located in the same directory and copy the LocalCodeProjectItems.vsdir file to the Custom folder.

3. Rename the LocalCodeProjectItems.vsdir file to *LocalCustomProjectItems.vsdir*.

4. Edit the LocalCustomProjectItems.vsdir file and delete everything in the file except the first line which begins with ..\..*Class.vsz*.

5. Save and close the file.

To see what you have done so far, go into the IDE and select Add New Item from the project file. In the Add New Item dialog box, click the Custom folder. You will see the dialog box in Figure 8-6.

Before moving on, go back and edit the LocalCustomProjectItems.vsdir file and change *Class.vsz* to *UserCentric.vsz*. Then save and close the file.

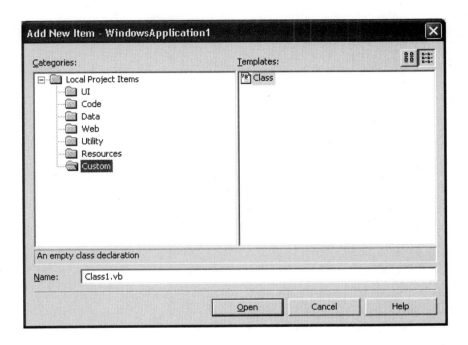

Figure 8-6. Your first customization to the project items

Setting Up the UserCentric Template

Next, you need to actually create the template that you will place in this Custom folder. If you recall the relative path in front of the UserCentric.vsz line in the LocalCustomProjectItems.vsdir file (..\..\), you will notice that it points to two directories above your current folder. If you go to that directory (VBProjectItems), you will see one file for each class that shows up in the Project Items dialog box. To make your life easier, copy the Class.vsz file, paste it, and rename it to *UserCentric.vsz*. If you open this file for editing file (which you need to do), it will look like Figure 8-7.

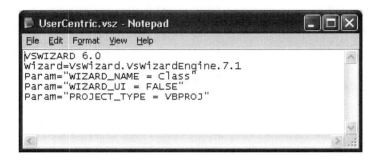

Figure 8-7. The UserCentric.vsz file

The only line you need to be concerned about is the first Param line. Change the value from *Class* to *UserCentric*. Then save and close the file.

NOTE   For more information on this file, see the MSDN help topic "vsz files."

Now, this file is pointing to a folder called *UserCentric* in the VBWizards folder (Microsoft Visual Studio .NET\Vb7\VBWizards). Because this folder does not exist yet, you need to create it. The easiest way to do this is to copy the Class folder, paste it, and rename it to *UserCentric*. If you look in this folder you will find two subfolders, the Scripts and Templates folders. You are interested in the Templates folder. In this folder you will find another folder named 1033 and in this folder you will find a file called *Class.vb*. This is the template you need to replace with your own template, but before you do, open the file and take a look. You will find the following two lines of code:

```
Public Class [!output SAFE_ITEM_NAME]

End Class
```

The [!output SAFE_ITEM_NAME] code is the name you give the code module in Visual Studio when you add it to your project. As you will see next, it plays a large part when using templates (you can close this file when you are done).

So, to begin creating the actual file you will use, add a new class to the Windows application you created earlier. Next, open the Northwind solution and copy all of the Region code module, including the RegionMgr class (from the NorthwindUC project), and paste it into the empty class (deleting the default class that was created in this code module) in your new project. Now that you have done that, you should have a code module that is identical to the Region code (and a bunch of errors, but you are only using this temporarily). You need to edit this file so that it is useful as a template.

Now, you need to make some assumptions here that you should keep in mind as you are creating a template. The first is that you are creating these templates to help you with the rest of your application right now, but you want the project item template to be usable to anyone who creates a project based on your NTierApplication template that you created earlier in the chapter. To this extent, and knowing that you are following a common naming convention, you can create the code for the template by modifying the code you pasted so that it looks like Listing 8-7.

Listing 8-7. Code for the UserCentric Project Item Template

```
Option Strict On
Option Explicit On

Imports SharedObjects.Structures
Imports SharedObjects.Interfaces
Imports SharedObjects.Errors

Public Class [!output SAFE_ITEM_NAME]
    Inherits BusinessBase

    'TODO: Set this value to point to your Remote Object URI
    'Private Const LISTENER As String = xxxx

    Dim ms[!output SAFE_ITEM_NAME] as struct[!output SAFE_ITEM_NAME]

#Region " Private Attributes"

#End Region

#Region " Public Attributes"

#End Region

    Public Sub New()
        MyBase.New(LISTENER)
        mobjRules = New BrokenRules
        'TODO: Break any business rules here
    End Sub
```

```
Public Sub New(ByVal intID As Integer)
    MyBase.New(LISTENER)
    mobjRules = New BrokenRules
    mint[!output SAFE_ITEM_NAME]ID = intID
End Sub

Public Overrides Function ToString() As String
    'TODO: Return the value that is to be displayed when this
    'item object is added to a list box
End Function

Public Sub LoadRecord()
    Dim objI[!output SAFE_ITEM_NAME] As I[!output SAFE_ITEM_NAME]

    objI[!output SAFE_ITEM_NAME] = _
    CType(Activator.GetObject(GetType(I[!output SAFE_ITEM_NAME]), _
    AppConstants.REMOTEOBJECTS & LISTENER), I[!output SAFE_ITEM_NAME])

    ms[!output SAFE_ITEM_NAME] = _
    objI[!output SAFE_ITEM_NAME].LoadRecord(mint[!output SAFE_ITEM_NAME]ID)

    objI[!output SAFE_ITEM_NAME] = nothing

    LoadObject()
End Sub

Private Sub LoadObject()
    'TODO: Assign the values from the module level structure to the object
End Sub

Public Sub Rollback()
    LoadObject()
End Sub

Public Sub Delete()
    Dim objI[!output SAFE_ITEM_NAME] As I[!output SAFE_ITEM_NAME]

    objI[!output SAFE_ITEM_NAME] = _
    CType(Activator.GetObject(GetType(I[!output SAFE_ITEM_NAME]), _
    AppConstants.REMOTEOBJECTS & LISTENER), I[!output SAFE_ITEM_NAME])

    objI[!output SAFE_ITEM_NAME].Delete(mint[!output SAFE_ITEM_NAME]ID)
    objI[!output SAFE_ITEM_NAME] = Nothing
End Sub
```

```vb
    Public Sub Save()
        If mobjRules.Count = 0 Then
            'TODO: Replace and uncomment as necessary
            If mblnDirty = True Then
                Dim objI[!output SAFE_ITEM_NAME] As I[!output SAFE_ITEM_NAME]
                Dim intID As Integer
                Dim s[!output SAFE_ITEM_NAME] as struct[!output SAFE_ITEM_NAME]

                'Store the original ID of the object
                intID = mint[!output SAFE_ITEM_NAME]ID

                'TODO: Assign the values from the object to the local structure
                'variable

                objI[!output SAFE_ITEM_NAME] = _
                CType(Activator.GetObject(GetType(I[!output SAFE_ITEM_NAME]), _
                AppConstants.REMOTEOBJECTS & LISTENER), _
                I[!output SAFE_ITEM_NAME])

                'TODO: Replace the local structure with the variable name
                objI[!output SAFE_ITEM_NAME].Save(s[!output SAFE_ITEM_NAME], _
                mint[!output SAFE_ITEM_NAME] ID)
                objI[!output SAFE_ITEM_NAME] = Nothing

                If intID = 0 Then
                    CallChangedEvent(Me, New _
                    ChangedEventArgs(ChangedEventArgs.eChange.Added))
                Else
                    CallChangedEvent(Me, New _
                    ChangedEventArgs(ChangedEventArgs.eChange.Updated))
                End If

                mblnDirty = False
            End If
        End If
    End Sub
End Class


Public Class [!output SAFE_ITEM_NAME]Mgr
    Inherits System.Collections.DictionaryBase

    Private Shared mobj[!output SAFE_ITEM_NAME]Mgr As _
    [!output SAFE_ITEM_NAME]Mgr
```

```vbnet
Public Shared Function GetInstance() As [!output SAFE_ITEM_NAME]Mgr
    If mobj[!output SAFE_ITEM_NAME]Mgr Is Nothing Then
        mobj[!output SAFE_ITEM_NAME]Mgr = New [!output SAFE_ITEM_NAME]Mgr
    End If
    Return mobj[!output SAFE_ITEM_NAME]Mgr
End Function

Protected Sub New()
    Load()
End Sub

Public Sub Add(ByVal obj As [!output SAFE_ITEM_NAME])
    dictionary.Add(obj.[!output SAFE_ITEM_NAME]ID, obj)
End Sub

Public Function Item(ByVal Key As Object) As [!output SAFE_ITEM_NAME]
    Return CType(dictionary.Item(Key), [!output SAFE_ITEM_NAME])
End Function

Public Sub Remove(ByVal Key As Object)
    dictionary.Remove(Key)
End Sub

Private Sub Load()
    Dim objI[!output SAFE_ITEM_NAME] As I[!output SAFE_ITEM_NAME]
    Dim dRow As DataRow
    Dim ds As DataSet

    'TODO: Replace the [Remote Object URI] with the actual URI
    objI[!output SAFE_ITEM_NAME] = _
    CType(Activator.GetObject(GetType(I[!output SAFE_ITEM_NAME]), _
    AppConstants.REMOTEOBJECTS & [Remote Object URI]), _
    I[!output SAFE_ITEM_NAME])
    ds = objI[!output SAFE_ITEM_NAME].LoadProxy()
    objI[!output SAFE_ITEM_NAME] = Nothing

    For Each dRow In ds.Tables(0).Rows
      'TODO: Replace "Identiy Column" in the line below with the name of
      'the identity column from the database
      Dim obj[!output SAFE_ITEM_NAME] As New _
      [!output SAFE_ITEM_NAME](Convert.ToInt32(dRow.Item("IdentityColumn")))
```

```
      With obj[!output SAFE_ITEM_NAME]
            .Loading = True
            'TODO: Assign values from the datarow to the object
            .Loading = False
      End With
      Me.Add(obj[!output SAFE_ITEM_NAME])
    Next


    ds = Nothing
  End Sub

  Public Sub Refresh()
      dictionary.Clear()
      Load()
  End Sub

End Class
```

That is quite a lot of code, but you will see how easy this makes your job once you implement the template. Of course, right now you have a boatload of errors, but do not worry about that as this is only a template! The one thing you should note is that you have used the [!output SAFE_ITEM_NAME] liberally here. Visual Studio will replace this tag wherever it is found in a code module when it is added. By using a standard naming convention you will only have to make one change and five additions once you actually use this template.

Finally, save this code module and exit Visual Studio. Navigate to the project folder you were just working in (if you did not rename the default project it is probably WindowsApplication1) and rename the code module from *Class1.vb* to *Class.vb*. Then, copy the file to the \VBWizards\User Centric\Templates\1033 folder you were working in earlier and overwrite the Class.vb file that is currently there.

Modifying the Policy File

There is only one little thing left that you need to do only one more little thing—modify the policy file. You will not see an in-depth explanation of what you are doing, but I am going to explain why because it is one of the great features of enterprise templates. Navigate to the \Microsoft Visual Studio .NET 2003\ EnterpriseFrameworks\Policy folder and double-click the NTierApplication.TDL file. This opens the file in Visual Studio's XML editor. The first thing you will notice is that this file is huge; the second thing you will notice if you try to switch to data view is that the file cannot be read correctly by Visual Studio! No matter, though.

For your purposes you need to do a Find and look for *projItemVBcodefile*. Listing 8-8 shows the block of code you will find.

Listing 8-8. The projItemVBCodeFile Element

```
<ELEMENT>
    <ID>projItemVBCodeFile</ID>
    <IDENTIFIERS>
        <IDENTIFIER>
            <TYPE>PROJECTITEM</TYPE>
            <IDENTIFIERDATA>
                <NAME>FileExtension</NAME>
                <VALUE>.vb</VALUE>
            </IDENTIFIERDATA>
        </IDENTIFIER>
    </IDENTIFIERS>
    <PROTOTYPES>
        <PROTOTYPE>[VB]\VBProjectItems\CodeFile.vsz</PROTOTYPE>
    </PROTOTYPES>
</ELEMENT>
```

Add the following prototype tag below the existing prototype tag:

```
<PROTOTYPE>[VB]\VBProjectItems\UserCentric.vsz</PROTOTYPE>
```

Then save and close the file. The policy file allows you to control the items that a developer can even add to a project. Because I have not gone into how to create elements that can be recognized by a policy file, you had to fake it by adding this in as another prototype of the CodeFile type.

NOTE For steps on how to add new elements that will be recognized by a policy file, see the MSDN documentation, "Walkthrough: Creating a New Enterprise Template."

So, all that you have done here is to give the developer the ability to add the UserCentric prototype to a template project.

Testing the Project Item Template

To test this project item, perform the following steps:

1. Open a new instance of the Visual Studio IDE.

2. Select File ➤ New ➤ Project.

3. Select the NTierApplication template from the Other Projects\Enterprise Template Projects node.

4. Select the UserCentric node in the Solution Explorer.

5. Right-click the node and select Add ➤ Add New Item.

6. Select the Custom folder under the Local Project Items folder and select the UserCentric Class template item.

7. Rename the item from *Class1.vb* to *Employee.vb* and click OK.

Once you do that, you will have about 50 errors in the Task List, but let's see just how easy it is to clean these errors up. To start with, go the SharedObjects project and open the Structures.vb code module. Add the following structure in the Structures namespace:

```
<Serializable()> Public Structure structEmployee
    Public EmployeeID As Integer
End Structure
```

Next, go to the Interfaces.vb code module and add the following interface to the Interfaces namespace:

```
Public Interface IEmployee
    Function LoadProxy() As DataSet
    Function LoadRecord(ByVal intID As Integer) As structEmployee
    Function Save(ByVal sEmployee As structEmployee, ByRef intID As Integer) _
    As BusinessErrors
    Sub Delete(ByVal intID As Integer)
    Function GetBusinessRules() As BusinessErrors
End Interface
```

Then, switch to the Employee.vb code module that you just added and uncomment the following line:

```
'Private Const LISTENER As String = xxxx
```

Enclose the *xxxx* in quotation marks so it looks like a string. Finally, in the Private Attributes region, add this declaration:

```
Private mintEmployeeID As Integer
```

And in the Public Attributes region, add this declaration:

```
Public ReadOnly Property EmployeeID() As Integer
    Get
        Return mintEmployeeID
    End Get
End Property
```

When you are all done with this, there will be only one error left. If you look at it, you will see that you only need to replace the text with the Uniform Resource Indicator (URI) of the remote objects.

Summary

This chapter has shown you a good deal about making your code reusable and easy to implement using consolidation techniques, templates, and a well-planned application configuration file. Although the process of creating a template can be long, you should be able to see the long-term benefit of implementing enterprise templates and project item prototypes. This helps not only with individual projects but also with enterprise architecture. Creating these templates allows a company to ensure that the application design is identical across the enterprise, and it ensures consistency and minimizes mistakes. It also allows for fast construction of even the most difficult distributed business applications as well as less ramp-up time for new developers.

 NOTE It is worthwhile to note that even though this chapter has not covered policy files, they can be a very powerful part of enterprise templates.

CHAPTER 9

Understanding Server-Side Business Rules

THIS BOOK HAS COVERED many major concepts up to this point. You have learned how to create business rules, respond to business rules, create special types of errors to report that your business rules have been broken, and package your code to be reusable. The last major concept you need to learn is the difference between client-side and server-side business rules. In a Windows application this is much more important than in a Web application. The reason for this is that almost everything in a Web application is checked on the server because that is the only place that real intelligence exists in a Web application. To be sure, you can check some rules on the client-side in a Web application, and ASP.NET certainly makes that 10 times easier than it was using ASP, but this idea holds true in most Web applications.

So, why check business rules in two places? Isn't this more work for the developer and a distribution of the business rules to boot? Yes, there is more work for the developer (although mostly in the area of copy and paste), and, yes, it does tend to distribute the business rules. However, you can separate business rules into two categories. The first is database constraint rules, and the second is rules based on the needs of the business. To answer the first question, you are checking rules in two places to reduce the load on the server. You would not want someone submitting a record to be saved if there was absolutely no possibility of that record being allowed in the database. It would be a waste of server time and might adversely impact the performance of the application in a large-scale environment. There is no hard-and-fast rule on what to check on the client side, and it is completely up to the software architect to break up these rules. The rules that get checked on the server side do have a hard-and-fast rule. The server-side rules that must be checked are any rules checked on the client-side plus any additional business rules that need to be checked. You have seen how to check rules, and that has not really changed on the server side, but reporting those rules is slightly different. In this chapter you will see how to report server-side rule violations back to the user interface. You will also see, for the first time, how to handle saving and deleting data in join tables. In addition, you will display and save image information in a SQL Server image data type from a picture box.

The Importance of Business Rules

In the course of creating enterprise business applications, first as a developer and then as an architect, I have always been amazed at the complexity and variety of business rules (and sometimes just how commonsense they are). The one thing you must always remember is that the business rules are everything. If data violates business rules, then it is bad data. Many times people do not like to acknowledge that there is bad data in their legacy or, even worse, in their modern systems.

One company that I worked for had a new system (less than two years old) that scheduled and monitored rail car shipments. This system also reported information about trip times. My first job there was to analyze this data so that the company could purchase or dispose of railcars so that they would be able to deliver product more efficiently. As I began to analyze the data, I found out that about one-third of the railcar shipment times were negative numbers. Apparently these railcars were traveling faster than the speed of light! In other cases, railcars that were part of the same train arrived at the same destination at different times. Huh? And, when I reported these findings to my supervisor, I was told to remove them from my equations or take the absolute value. This was the equivalent of dumping more than 36,000 shipment records to make the numbers look good to someone's supervisor. Needless to say, if the programmers who were responsible for creating the railcar-tracking program in the first place knew how to implement business rules, none of this would have been necessary.

From this short example, you can see just what kind of a disaster was brewing at this company because of the lack of business rules. In another application that I am working on (at the time of this writing), we are converting records from a legacy mainframe application to a new SQL Server/VB .NET application. In examining the data we have discovered that airplanes were sold in 100 and 101 A.D. In addition, maintenance parts for these airplanes were sold around the same time. Common sense would have been to put in a business rule that said an airplane could not be sold until at least after the Wright brothers flew! The data was easy to correct, but the mistake was avoidable with basic commonsense business rules.

Creating the Employee Stored Procedures

As before, creating the Employee stored procedures is a straightforward process. In addition to the four standard stored procedures (getone, getall, save, delete), there are several additional stored procedures. These stored procedures handle the

Employee/Territory relationship. However, you will note there are some additional complexities in your stored procedures now because you are handling relationships between tables. Because of this, you will look at these stored procedures one at a time. To begin with, execute the SQL in Listing 9-1 against the Northwind database.

Listing 9-1. The Employee Delete Stored Procedure

```
CREATE PROCEDURE usp_employee_delete
@id int
AS
DELETE
FROM  EmployeeTerritories
WHERE EmployeeID = @id

UPDATE Orders
SET EmployeeID = null
WHERE EmployeeID = @id

DELETE
FROM Employees
WHERE EmployeeID = @id
```

TIP You can handle some of these complexities by cascade updates and cascade deletes. Although these make programming the stored procedures easier, they can be difficult to manage (you do not always get the result you want because you are relying on a mechanism you do not really control). The choice to use cascading updates and deletes is entirely yours. I prefer not to use them because I like to have the maximum amount of control over my code that I can.

First, you need to delete or alter information in all of the related tables. You can delete the information in the EmployeeTerritory table, but you cannot just delete orders because an employee was deleted. So, because you are allowed to have an order that is not associated with an employee, you will just set the EmployeeID equal to null in the Orders table. In a real application, the employee would probably be marked as inactive in some way but never deleted. After all, you would want to keep track of the employees you have had and who was responsible for an order. Execute the SQL in Listing 9-2 against the Northwind database.

Listing 9-2. The Employee Getall Stored Procedure

```
CREATE PROCEDURE usp_employee_getall
AS
SELECT EmployeeID, LastName, FirstName, Title
FROM Employees
```

Second, this getall routine returns all of the rows in the Employees table, but it does not return all of the columns in the table. It returns enough information to fill a list (in this case your list form) and to load a single, full object. This is the reason that the name of the method that calls this stored procedure is called *LoadProxy* because you are not loading up a full object. Whenever you create a proxy object, that object must have the ability to fully load itself. In this case you are supplying the table key, so you know you can retrieve the full record from this.

The getone stored procedure, shown in Listing 9-3, retrieves a single employee, but it also returns additional information that is required because of the relationships of which this table is a part. Execute this SQL against the Northwind database.

Listing 9-3. The Employee getone Stored Procedure

```
CREATE PROCEDURE usp_employee_getone
@id int
AS
SELECT a.*, b.FirstName 'ReportsToFirstName', b.LastName 'ReportsToLastName',
b.Title
'ReportsToTitle'
FROM Employees a
LEFT OUTER JOIN Employees b ON a.ReportsTo = b.EmployeeID
WHERE a.EmployeeID = @id

SELECT TerritoryID
FROM EmployeeTerritories
WHERE EmployeeID = @id
```

This procedure looks a little different than what you have seen before. There are two select statements here. So how do you handle this? Well, the beauty of the dataset is that it simply creates multiple tables within the dataset. This allows you to return information from multiple tables with one call to the database. It also allows you to return the information without duplicating the records that are being returned. The first select statement returns a complete Employee object and to whom that employee reports. This is enough information to load up a proxy of another employee (the manager). The second select statement returns all of the territories with which an employee is associated.

CAUTION Be careful when using multiple select statements in a stored procedure. SQL Server is the only Relational Database Management System (RDBMS) that can return multiple result sets. This stored procedure would not work in Oracle. This can have an impact in the future if the database needs to be migrated to a different type of database. If you expect to perform this type of migration in the future, break this up into two separate stored procedures.

Saving an employee is a bit more complicated than saving a Region or a Territory. First, you are required to save the employee because you need the primary key from the Employees table to use in the EmployeeTerritories table. Then you need to save all of the territories in which an employee works. The solution to this is two stored procedures: one to save the employee and one to save the Employee/Territory relationship (this stored procedure can be called multiple times, one per related territory). Execute the save stored procedure (as shown in Listing 9-4) against the Northwind database.

Listing 9-4. The Employee Save Stored Procedure

```
CREATE PROCEDURE usp_employee_save
@id int,
@lname nvarchar(20),
@fname nvarchar(10),
@title nvarchar(30),
@courtesy nvarchar(25),
@birth datetime,
@hire datetime,
@address nvarchar(60),
@city nvarchar(15),
@region nvarchar(15),
@postal nvarchar(10),
@country nvarchar(15),
@phone nvarchar(24),
@extension nvarchar(4),
@photo image,
@notes ntext,
@reports int,
@photopath nvarchar(255),
@new_id int output
AS
IF @id = 0
```

```
BEGIN
    INSERT INTO Employees (LastName, FirstName, Title,
    TitleOfCourtesy, BirthDate, HireDate, Address, City, Region,
    PostalCode, Country, HomePhone, Extension, Photo, Notes,
    ReportsTo, PhotoPath)
    VALUES(@lname, @title, @title,
    @courtesy, @birth, @hire, @address, @city, @region,
    @postal, @country, @phone, @extension,
    @photo, @notes, @reports, @photopath)

    SET @new_id = (SELECT @@IDENTITY)
END
ELSE
    BEGIN
        UPDATE  Employees
        SET     LastName = @lname,
                FirstName = @fname,
                Title = @title,
                TitleOfCourtesy = @courtesy,
                BirthDate = @birth,
                HireDate = @hire,
                Address = @address,
                City = @city,
                Region = @region,
                PostalCode = @postal,
                Country = @country,
                HomePhone = @phone,
                Extension = @extension,
                Photo = @photo,
                Notes = @notes,
                ReportsTo = @reports,
                PhotoPath = @photopath
        WHERE   EmployeeID = @id

        SET @new_id = @id
    END
```

The save stored procedure is identical to the save stored procedures you have
already seen. But you have the added requirement of needing to save the territories
to which an employee is related. For this, enter the SQL in Listing 9-5.

Listing 9-5. The Employee Territory Relationship Stored Procedure

```
CREATE PROCEDURE usp_employee_territory_insert
@employee_id int,
@territory_id nvarchar(20)
AS
INSERT INTO EmployeeTerritories (EmployeeID, TerritoryID)
    VALUES (@employee_id, @territory_id)
```

Because you already have the code for an update in your save stored procedure, you only need to add one more stored procedure. Listing 9-6 shows this procedure. Execute this stored procedure against the Northwind database.

Listing 9-6. The Employee Territory Relationship Delete Stored Procedure

```
CREATE PROCEDURE usp_employee_territory_delete
@employee_id int
AS
DELETE
FROM EmployeeTerritories
WHERE EmployeeID = @employee_id
```

Because there are only two columns in the EmployeeTerritories join table, performing updates on the table is not worthwhile. The reason for this is that there is no single column primary key on the table. When you perform the update, you are updating the primary key. Although this is perfectly acceptable for a join table, it is just as easy to delete the record and re-create it.

NOTE You could argue quite easily that a single call to the database to update the record is more efficient, but I am *always* uncomfortable with an update that alters the primary key. Other than that, there really is no reason why you cannot have an employee territory update stored procedure.

Now that you have the stored procedures built, you can start looking at the business rules.

Determining the Business Rules

Business rules are not just those rules that violate business constraints; they are also the rules that violate common sense that the business may not think about. For instance, you may not allow any employees to be younger than 18. But what someone will often forget is that you cannot have a person with a birth date later in time than the current date. Things like this often get overlooked in applications. It is always best to get the business rules from the business community and then examine them yourself. So let's examine the rules for the Employee object.

NOTE This might seem like a business rule that is so obvious that it could not possibly be missed. But if you read the sidebar "The Importance of Business Rules" you will see that there were some fairly common sense business rules that seem to have gotten completely misplaced. If these types of rules are so common sense, then they should never be missed.

Database Constraints

As mentioned earlier, database constraints must also be considered rules or else an object can never be persisted if it violates those rules. Generally, you can break database column constraints (excluding referential integrity) into three categories: maximum length of a field, null fields, and allowable field values. Table 9-1 takes each piece of data and breaks out the rules that you must apply to that piece of data.

Table 9-1. Employees Table Data Constraint Rules

Column	Maximum Length	Nullable	Allowable Values
EmployeeID		No	
LastName	20	No	
FirstName	10	No	
Title	30	No*	
TitleOfCourtesy	25	Yes	(Mr., Mrs., Ms., Dr.)
BirthDate		No*	
HireDate		No*	
Address	60	No*	

Table 9-1. Employees Table Data Constraint Rules (Continued)

Column	Maximum Length	Nullable	Allowable Values
City	15	No*	
Region	15	Yes	
PostalCode	10	No*	
Country	15	No*	
HomePhone	24	No*	
Extension	4	Yes	
Photo		Yes	
Notes		Yes	
ReportsTo		Yes	
PhotoPath	255	Yes	

* The database as set up allows nulls in these columns, but you will disallow them in your business rules.

There are a couple of things to note about Table 9-1 as you look through it. The first is that there are no check constraints on the table that ensure values fall into a certain range. I have also added some allowable values for the TitleOfCourtesy field to demonstrate that type of business rule. So now that you have the database constraints figured out, let's move on to some real rules.

Business Rules

For simplicity, this section lists the business rules. This is probably not as comprehensive a list as you might find in a real application, but it will serve your purposes for this chapter:

- BirthDate

  - Cannot be older than 60 years old

  - Cannot be younger than 18 years old

  - Cannot be a date in the future

- HireDate

  - Cannot be more than two weeks in the future

  - Cannot be before 1976 (because that is when your company started)

- PhotoPath

  - Check for file

For your purposes, there are no additional business rules dealing with this object. Another rule, which you might be able to apply here (but because of the complexity you will not), is the phone number format based on the employee's region. If the employee is in Europe, the length and format would be different than if the employee resides in the United States or Canada. Rules like these are often overlooked, and for expediency, you will overlook them here as well.

Building the Employee Objects

After the previous chapter, you can see that the code is designed in a cookie-cutter fashion. This makes it faster to develop new classes and to maintain old classes. It makes bringing new developers onto a project and bringing them up to speed far easier than everyone going off and doing things their own way.

Development Teams

I worked on a project less than a year ago that had a team of about 10 developers on it. I was brought on about a year and a half into the project and by the time I left the project there was only one member of the original team left. Do not think for an instant that on any large project you will finish with the same team with which you started. In most cases it just is not practical or possible. Design your code with this in mind as well. There must be a cohesive, understandable overall architecture to any project.

In the case of the project that I was working on, every developer had a different way of writing the same piece of code. A lot of developers, including the developer I replaced, did not even document the code on which they were working. No one working on one part of the application was able to work on or understand a different part of the application. This means that every time you needed to move someone to a different part of the application, there was a huge learning curve. This ended up eating into the resources of the other developers and was in part responsible for causing the project to overrun the original estimates. There were also other problems that came out of everyone writing code their own way—the developers never worked as a team. This statement alone should be enough to make any developer understand the importance of a cohesive, overall architecture.

As you start building these objects, realize that there is another relationship you need to worry about: the territory relationship. Although there is no key in the Employees table for the territory, the territory is still a pertinent piece of information in relationship to the employee. You do not have to reference this information, but you need a way to add it into the database. Although you have already created the Territory object, you need a way to associate the territory with the employee. The nature of the relationship in the table indicates there is a many-to-many relationship between the employees and territories table. You already have the stored procedure to return the TerritoryIDs of those territories that the employee is associated with, but you do not return anything else. You will see how you handle this when you start creating your objects.

CAUTION   Before you start building the Employee objects, you have to do one thing first. When Microsoft created the original Northwind database, the photos of the employees stored in the photo column were added by way of an OLE control in Visual Basic 5 or 6. For this reason, header information for this control was stored in the photo column and cannot be read and displayed by any other means. You can download a zip file from the Apress website (http://www.apress.com) that contains a small program that I wrote to replace the bitmaps with bitmaps that have had the header information removed and can be read and displayed by any program. Simply run the LoadEmployeePics.exe file. The database needs to be on the same machine on which the program is running. The program connects to the SQL Server default instance using integrated authentication. Should you want to make any changes, the source code for the program is included with the application.

Employee Shared Objects

Once the photos have been updated, you can start building the Employee objects. These objects are considerably more complicated than what you have built up to this point. However, these objects in themselves are straightforward but do require a little bit of additional explanation, so we will go through them a little at a time.

As before, you will start off by building the interfaces and structures so that you can serialize your data and make calls across the network. Start off by adding the structure shown in Listing 9-7 to the structures namespace in the NorthwindShared assembly.

Listing 9-7. The structEmployee Structure

```
<Serializable()> Public Structure structEmployee
     Public EmployeeID As Integer
     Public LastName As String
     Public FirstName As String
     Public Title As String
     Public TitleOfCourtesy As String
     Public BirthDate As Date
     Public HireDate As Date
     Public Address As String
     Public City As String
     Public Region As String
     Public PostalCode As String
     Public Country As String
     Public HomePhone As String
     Public Extension As String
     Public Photo() As Byte
     Public Notes As String
     Public ReportsTo As Integer
     Public ReportsToFirstName As String
     Public ReportsToLastName As String
     Public PhotoPath As String
     Public Territories() As String
End Structure
```

You will notice two differences in this structure from your previous structures. The first is the Photo variable, and the second is the Territories variable. In SQL Server, an image data type is returned as a byte array. The Territories variable will need to hold the IDs of all of the territories with which the employee is associated. In addition, you are holding two additional properties that are not part of the Employees table: ReportsToFirstName and ReportsToLastName. These are necessary so that you have enough information to load an Employee object that represents a manager and to return enough information to fill a control to display this information to the user. You will see how you make use of this in the "Employee User-Centric Objects" section.

Next, create the interface you will use to make calls to your remote objects. Add the interface in Listing 9-8 to the Interfaces.vb code module in the NorthwindShared assembly.

Listing 9-8. The IEmployee Interface

```
Public Interface IEmployee
    Inherits IBaseInterface
    Function LoadRecord(ByVal intID As Integer) As structEmployee
    Function Save(ByVal sEmployee As structEmployee, _
        ByRef intID As Integer) As BusinessErrors
    Sub Delete(ByVal intID As Integer)
End Interface
```

This interface is identical to the other interfaces you have seen before. The last thing you have to do in the NorthwindShared assembly is to add your new business errors to the Errors namespace. Add the following errors to the Errors.vb code module.

The AllowedValuesException will be used when a value does not meet the requirements that you define for a check constraint:

```
Public Class AllowedValuesException
    Inherits System.ApplicationException

    Public Sub New(ByVal strValues As String)
        MyBase.New("The value must be one of the following: " & strValues)
    End Sub
End Class
```

The FutureDateException will be used for any date that cannot occur in the future:

```
Public Class FutureDateException
    Inherits System.ApplicationException

    Public Sub New()
        MyBase.New("This date can not occur in the future.")
    End Sub
End Class
```

The UnderAgeException will be used to handle any employees who are younger than the minimum hiring age. Note that this is a nonspecific age exception, so you can change the minimum age in your business object and still throw the same error:

```
Public Class UnderAgeException
    Inherits System.ApplicationException

    Public Sub New(ByVal intAge As Integer)
        MyBase.New("This person must be over " & intAge.ToString & ".")
    End Sub
End Class
```

Not to be discriminatory, but you have decided not to hire people older than a certain age, so you will create an error to handle this also:

```
Public Class OverAgeException
    Inherits System.ApplicationException

    Public Sub New(ByVal intAge As Integer)
        MyBase.New("This person cannot be over the age of " & intAge & ".")
    End Sub
End Class
```

This next exception informs you if you are trying to hire an employee on a date before the company was created:

```
Public Class BeforeCompanyCreatedException
    Inherits System.ApplicationException

    Public Sub New()
        MyBase.New("This date cannot occur before the date the " _
        & "company was created on (1 January 1976).")
    End Sub
End Class
```

Finally, you have an exception that will handle any invalid date that occurs in the future. It is designed to be fairly flexible but not to meet any specific needs:

```
Public Class SpecificFutureDateException
    Inherits System.ApplicationException

    Public Enum Unit
        Days = 0
        Weeks = 1
        Months = 2
        Years = 3
    End Enum

    Public Sub New(ByVal intPeriod As Integer, ByVal intUnit As Unit)
        MyBase.New("This date may not occur more than " _
        & intPeriod.ToString & " " & intUnit.ToString & ".")
    End Sub
End Class
```

Employee Data-Centric Object

Now that you have all of your shared objects constructed, it is time to build the data-centric Employee object. As you are building this class, keep in mind that for the first time you have the possibility of different errors occurring in the server-side business objects than the client-side business objects. Remember that you are only checking basic database constraints in the client-side business objects.

Listing 9-9 shows the header and attribute code for the data-centric Employee object. You will look at specific differences from the previous classes afterward. To start this process, add a new class to the NorthwindDC assembly called *EmployeeDC.vb*.

NOTE   To save typing, you can download the code for Chapter 9, which contains all the objects created in this chapter.

Listing 9-9. The Header and Properties of the EmployeeDC Class

```
Option Strict On
Option Explicit On

Imports NorthwindTraders.NorthwindShared.Interfaces
Imports NorthwindTraders.NorthwindShared.Structures
Imports NorthwindTraders.NorthwindShared.Errors
Imports System.Configuration
Imports System.Data.SqlClient

Public Class EmployeeDC
    Inherits MarshalByRefObject

    Implements IEmployee

    Private mobjBusErr As BusinessErrors

#Region " Private Attributes"

    Private mintEmployeeID As Integer
    Private mstrLastName As String
    Private mstrFirstName As String
    Private mstrTitle As String
    Private mstrTitleOfCourtesy As String
    Private mdteBirthDate As Date
    Private mdteHireDate As Date
    Private mstrAddress As String
    Private mstrCity As String
    Private mstrRegion As String
    Private mstrPostalCode As String
    Private mstrCountry As String
    Private mstrHomePhone As String
    Private mstrExtension As String
    Private mbytPhoto() As Byte
    Private mstrNotes As String
    Private mintReportsTo As Integer
    Private mstrPhotoPath As String
    Private mstrTerritory() As String

#End Region

#Region " Public Attributes"
```

```
Public ReadOnly Property EmployeeID() As Integer
    Get
        Return mintEmployeeID
    End Get
End Property

Public Property LastName() As String
    Get
        Return mstrLastName
    End Get
    Set(ByVal Value As String)
        Try
            'Test for null value
            If Value Is Nothing Then
                Throw New ArgumentNullException("Last Name")
            End If

            'Test for empty string
            If Value.Length = 0 Then
                Throw New ZeroLengthException()
            End If

            'Test for max length
            If Value.Length > 20 Then
                Throw New MaximumLengthException(20)
            End If

            mstrLastName = Value
        Catch exc As Exception
            mobjBusErr.Add("Last Name", exc.Message)
        End Try
    End Set
End Property

Public Property FirstName() As String
    Get
        Return mstrFirstName
    End Get
    Set(ByVal Value As String)
        Try
            'Test for null value
            If Value Is Nothing Then
                Throw New ArgumentNullException("First Name")
            End If
```

```
                         'Test for empty string
                         If Value.Length = 0 Then
                             Throw New ZeroLengthException()
                         End If

                         'Test for max length
                         If Value.Length > 10 Then
                             Throw New MaximumLengthException(10)
                         End If

                         mstrFirstName = Value
                     Catch exc As Exception
                         mobjBusErr.Add("First Name", exc.Message)
                     End Try
             End Set
     End Property

     Public Property Title() As String
         Get
             Return mstrTitle
         End Get
         Set(ByVal Value As String)
             Try
                         'Test for null value
                         If Value Is Nothing Then
                             Throw New ArgumentNullException("Title")
                         End If

                         'Test for empty string
                         If Value.Length = 0 Then
                             Throw New ZeroLengthException()
                         End If

                         'Test for max length
                         If Value.Length > 30 Then
                             Throw New MaximumLengthException(30)
                         End If

                         mstrTitle = Value
                     Catch exc As Exception
                         mobjBusErr.Add("Title", exc.Message)
                     End Try
             End Set
     End Property
```

```
Public Property TitleOfCourtesy() As String
    Get
        Return mstrTitleOfCourtesy
    End Get
    Set(ByVal Value As String)
        Try
            'Test for null value
            If Value Is Nothing Then
                Exit Property
            End If

            'Test for empty string
            If Value.Length = 0 Then
                mstrTitleOfCourtesy = Nothing
                Exit Property
            End If

            'Test for max length
            If Value.Length > 25 Then
                Throw New MaximumLengthException(25)
            End If

            'Test for specific values
            Select Case Value
                Case "Mr.", "Ms.", "Dr.", "Mrs."
                    'Do nothing
                Case Else
                    Throw New AllowedValuesException("Mr., Ms., " _
                    & "Dr., Mrs.")
            End Select

            mstrTitleOfCourtesy = Value
        Catch exc As Exception
            mobjBusErr.Add("Title Of Courtesy", exc.Message)
        End Try
    End Set
End Property

Public Property BirthDate() As Date
    Get
        Return mdteBirthDate
    End Get
```

```vbnet
            Set(ByVal Value As Date)
                Try
                    'Check for a future date
                    If Value > Now Then
                        Throw New FutureDateException()
                    End If

                    'Check for under 18
                    If DateDiff(DateInterval.Day, Value, Now) < (18 * 365) _
                    Then
                        Throw New UnderAgeException(18)
                    End If

                    'Check for over 67
                    If DateDiff(DateInterval.Year, Value, Now) > 67 Then
                        Throw New OverAgeException(67)
                    End If

                    mdteBirthDate = Value
                Catch exc As Exception
                    mobjBusErr.Add("Birth Date", exc.Message)
                End Try
            End Set
    End Property

    Public Property HireDate() As Date
        Get
            Return mdteHireDate
        End Get
        Set(ByVal Value As Date)
            Try
                'Check for a future date
                If Value > DateAdd(DateInterval.Day, 14, Now) Then
                    Throw New SpecificFutureDateException(2, _
                    SpecificFutureDateException.Unit.Weeks)
                End If

                'Check for before company creation date
                If Value < #1/1/1976# Then
                    Throw New BeforeCompanyCreatedException()
                End If
```

```vbnet
                mdteHireDate = Value
            Catch exc As Exception
                mobjBusErr.Add("Hire Date", exc.Message)
            End Try
        End Set
End Property


Public Property Address() As String
    Get
        Return mstrAddress
    End Get
    Set(ByVal Value As String)
        Try
                'Test for null value
                If Value Is Nothing Then
                    Throw New ArgumentNullException("Address")
                End If

                'Test for empty string
                If Value.Length = 0 Then
                    Throw New ZeroLengthException()
                End If

                'Test for max length
                If Value.Length > 67 Then
                    Throw New MaximumLengthException(67)
                End If

                mstrAddress = Value
            Catch exc As Exception
                mobjBusErr.Add("Address", exc.Message)
            End Try
        End Set
End Property


Public Property City() As String
    Get
        Return mstrCity
    End Get
    Set(ByVal Value As String)
        Try
                'Test for null value
                If Value Is Nothing Then
                    Throw New ArgumentNullException("City")
                End If
```

```
                        'Test for empty string
                        If Value.Length = 0 Then
                            Throw New ZeroLengthException()
                        End If

                        'Test for max length
                        If Value.Length > 15 Then
                            Throw New MaximumLengthException(15)
                        End If

                        mstrCity = Value
                    Catch exc As Exception
                        mobjBusErr.Add("City", exc.Message)
                    End Try
            End Set
    End Property

    Public Property Region() As String
        Get
            Return mstrRegion
        End Get
        Set(ByVal Value As String)
            Try
                        'Test for null value
                        If Value Is Nothing Then Exit Property

                        'Test for empty string
                        If Value.Length = 0 Then
                            mstrRegion = Nothing
                            Exit Property
                        End If

                        'Test for max length
                        If Value.Length > 15 Then
                            Throw New MaximumLengthException(15)
                        End If

                        mstrRegion = Value
                    Catch exc As Exception
                        mobjBusErr.Add("Region", exc.Message)
                    End Try
            End Set
    End Property
```

```vbnet
Public Property PostalCode() As String
    Get
        Return mstrPostalCode
    End Get
    Set(ByVal Value As String)
        Try
            'Test for null value
            If Value Is Nothing Then
                Throw New ArgumentNullException("Postal Code")
            End If

            'Test for empty string
            If Value.Length = 0 Then
                Throw New ZeroLengthException()
            End If

            'Test for max length
            If Value.Length > 10 Then
                Throw New MaximumLengthException(10)
            End If

            mstrPostalCode = Value
        Catch exc As Exception
            mobjBusErr.Add("Postal Code", exc.Message)
        End Try
    End Set
End Property

Public Property Country() As String
    Get
        Return mstrCountry
    End Get
    Set(ByVal Value As String)
        Try
            'Test for null value
            If Value Is Nothing Then
                Throw New ArgumentNullException("Country")
            End If

            'Test for empty string
            If Value.Length = 0 Then
                Throw New ZeroLengthException()
            End If
```

```
                        'Test for max length
                        If Value.Length > 15 Then
                             Throw New MaximumLengthException(15)
                        End If

                        mstrCountry = Value
                    Catch exc As Exception
                        mobjBusErr.Add("Country", exc.Message)
                    End Try
                End Set
            End Property


        Public Property HomePhone() As String
            Get
                    Return mstrHomePhone
            End Get
            Set(ByVal Value As String)
                    Try
                        'Test for null value
                        If Value Is Nothing Then
                             Throw New ArgumentNullException("Home Phone")
                        End If

                        'Test for empty string
                        If Value.Length = 0 Then
                             Throw New ZeroLengthException()
                        End If

                        'Test for max length
                        If Value.Length > 24 Then
                             Throw New MaximumLengthException(24)
                        End If

                        mstrHomePhone = Value
                    Catch exc As Exception
                        mobjBusErr.Add("Home Phone", exc.Message)
                    End Try
                End Set
            End Property
```

```
Public Property Extension() As String
      Get
            Return mstrExtension
      End Get
      Set(ByVal Value As String)
            Try
                  'Test for null value
                  If Value Is Nothing Then Exit Property

                  'Test for empty string
                  If Value.Length = 0 Then
                        mstrExtension = Nothing
                        Exit Property
                  End If

                  'Test for max length
                  If Value.Length > 4 Then
                        Throw New MaximumLengthException(4)
                  End If

                  mstrExtension = Value
            Catch exc As Exception
                  mobjBusErr.Add("Extension", exc.Message)
            End Try
      End Set
End Property

Public Property Photo() As Byte()
      Get
            Return mbytPhoto
      End Get
      Set(ByVal Value As Byte())
            If Value Is Nothing Then Exit Property

            mbytPhoto = Value
      End Set
End Property
```

```vb
Public Property Notes() As String
    Get
        Return mstrNotes
    End Get
    Set(ByVal Value As String)
        Try
            'Test for null value
            If Value Is Nothing Then Exit Property

            'Test for empty string
            If Value.Length = 0 Then
                mstrNotes = Nothing
                Exit Property
            End If

            mstrNotes = Value
        Catch exc As Exception
            mobjBusErr.Add("Notes", exc.Message)
        End Try
    End Set
End Property

Public Property ReportsTo() As Integer
    Get
        Return mintReportsTo
    End Get
    Set(ByVal Value As Integer)
        Try
            'Test for null value
            If Value = 0 Then
                mintReportsTo = Nothing
                Exit Property
            End If

            mintReportsTo = Value
        Catch exc As Exception
            mobjBusErr.Add("Reports To", exc.Message)
        End Try
    End Set
End Property
```

```
Public Property PhotoPath() As String
    Get
        Return mstrPhotoPath
    End Get
    Set(ByVal Value As String)
        Try
            'Test for null value
            If Value Is Nothing Then Exit Property

            'Test for empty string
            If Value.Length = 0 Then
                mstrPhotoPath = Nothing
                Exit Property
            End If

            'Test for max length
            If Value.Length > 255 Then
                Throw New MaximumLengthException(255)
            End If

            If FileSystem.FileLen(Value) > 0 Then
            'do nothing, if the file is not found, a
            'FileNotFoundException will be thrown automatically
            End If

            mstrPhotoPath = Value
        Catch exc As Exception
            mobjBusErr.Add("Photo Path", exc.Message)
        End Try
    End Set
End Property
```

```
        Public Property Territories() As String()
            Get
                Return mstrTerritory
            End Get
            Set(ByVal Value As String())
                Try
                    If Value Is Nothing Then
                        Throw New Exception("An employee must be " _
                        & "assigned to at least one territory.")
                    Else
                        If Value.Length = 0 Then
                            Throw New Exception("An employee must " _
                            & "be assigned to at least one territory.")
                        End If
                    End If
                    mstrTerritory = Value
                Catch exc As Exception
                    mobjBusErr.Add("Territories", exc.Message)
                End Try
            End Set
        End Property
    #End Region
    End Class
```

NOTE   For the purpose of the Windows interface you are creating, the photopath property is unnecessary and you will not be using it.

Now that you have entered (or at least reviewed) that incredibly long listing, let's review specific parts of the code to help clarify certain things you have not seen before.

This first section of code from the TitleOfCourtesy property demonstrates how to check for and allow only specific values to be assigned to the property. I have chosen to use a Select Case statement here for consistency and because it is usually far cleaner than using If..Then statements. It also gives you the opportunity to handle different values differently if you choose to do so. Using a Select Case statement does require one piece of code that I generally find sloppy—having a Case to which you do not respond. In this situation, it is necessary; otherwise the Case Else statement would trap everything:

```
'Test for specific values
Select Case Value
    Case "Mr.", "Ms.", "Dr.", "Mrs."
        'Do nothing
    Case Else
        Throw New AllowedValuesException("Mr., Ms., Dr., Mrs.")
End Select
```

Handling a date is always a tricky task. The next new piece of code is for handling the BirthDate property. The first check is to see if the employee is younger than 18. Notice that the check is by days and not by years. This is because of how the year check is made.

 CAUTION It is a simple method for checking the number of days that occur between the employee's date of birth and the current day. But this does not take into account leap years and other considerations, so this can spawn a whole other discussion on how to handle dates. One way is to perform a year difference calculation, then a month difference calculation, and then a day difference calculation. The choice is up to you. Your choice should generally be made based on the accuracy required of the calculation.

The next check is to see if the employee is older than 67. This check is not as precise as the underage check because I am making an assumption (a lousy assumption as it turns out) that you are not going to have employees nearly that old. As with the previous date check, there are many ways to make this check more accurate. These date checks are for demonstration purposes only:

```
'Check for under 18
If DateDiff(DateInterval.Day, Value, Now) < (18 * 365) Then
    Throw New UnderAgeException(18)
End If
```

```
'Check for over 67
If DateDiff(DateInterval.Year, Value, Now) > 67 Then
    Throw New OverAgeException(67)
End If
```

The hire date property is checking to see how far in the future a person is listed as being hired. It might be standard practice for a company to list a person as hired and wait for them to complete a security check or undergo some other type of waiting period. For this you throw a SpecificFutureDateException, passing in the value of two weeks for an allowable period. The company creation date is fairly simple—you cannot hire anybody before the company was created:

```
'Check for a future date
If Value > DateAdd(DateInterval.Day, 14, Now) Then
    Throw New SpecificFutureDateException(2, _
        SpecificFutureDateException.Unit.Weeks)
End If


'Check for before company creation date
If Value < #1/1/1976# Then
    Throw New BeforeCompanyCreatedException()
End If
```

The extension property allows a value that can be null—that is, a value that is not required. If the value is nothing, you simply exit the property and leave the module-level variable unset. If the property was passed an empty string, you set it equal to nothing. If the value was set, then you check any additional constraints. Being able to have a null value has additional consequences as you will see when you go to save the object:

```
'Test for null value
If Value Is Nothing Then Exit Property


'Test for empty string
If Value.Length = 0 Then
    mstrExtension = Nothing
    Exit Property
End If


'Test for max length
If Value.Length > 4 Then
    Throw New MaximumLengthException(4)
End If
```

Next, you move on to your five, now-standard methods in the data-centric class. First is the LoadProxy method (shown in Listing 9-10). This is the same as the previous classes (and it will always be identical) except for the name of the stored procedure you are calling.

Listing 9-10. The Employee LoadProxy Method

```
Public Function LoadProxy() As DataSet Implements IEmployee.LoadProxy
    Dim strCN As String = _
        ConfigurationSettings.AppSettings("Northwind_DSN")
    Dim cn As New SqlConnection(strCN)
    Dim cmd As New SqlCommand()
    Dim da As New SqlDataAdapter(cmd)
    Dim ds As New DataSet()

    cn.Open()

    With cmd
        .Connection = cn
        .CommandType = CommandType.StoredProcedure
        .CommandText = "usp_employee_getall"
    End With

    da.Fill(ds)

    cmd = Nothing
    cn.Close()

    Return ds
End Function
```

Second is the LoadRecord routine. There are several variations in this object from what you have seen before, so you will see those differences after you enter the LoadRecord method in Listing 9-11.

Listing 9-11. The Employee LoadRecord Method

```
Public Function LoadRecord(ByVal intID As Integer) As structEmployee _
Implements IEmployee.LoadRecord
    Dim strCN As String = ConfigurationSettings.AppSettings("Northwind_DSN")
    Dim cn As New SqlConnection(strCN)
    Dim cmd As New SqlCommand()
    Dim da As New SqlDataAdapter(cmd)
    Dim ds As New DataSet()
    Dim dRow As DataRow
    Dim i As Integer
    Dim sEmployee As structEmployee
```

```vb
        cn.Open()

With cmd
    .Connection = cn
    .CommandType = CommandType.StoredProcedure
    .CommandText = "usp_employee_getone"
    .Parameters.Add("@id", intID)
End With

da.Fill(ds)

cmd = Nothing
cn.Close()

With ds.Tables(0).Rows(0)
    sEmployee.EmployeeID = Convert.ToInt32(.Item("EmployeeID"))
    sEmployee.LastName = Convert.ToString(.Item("LastName"))
    sEmployee.FirstName = Convert.ToString(.Item("FirstName"))
    sEmployee.Title = Convert.ToString(.Item("Title"))
    sEmployee.TitleOfCourtesy = _
        Convert.ToString(.Item("TitleOfCourtesy"))
    sEmployee.BirthDate = Convert.ToDateTime(.Item("BirthDate"))
    sEmployee.HireDate = Convert.ToDateTime(.Item("HireDate"))
    sEmployee.Address = Convert.ToString(.Item("Address"))
    sEmployee.City = Convert.ToString(.Item("City"))
    If Not IsDBNull(.Item("Region")) Then
        sEmployee.Region = Convert.ToString(.Item("Region"))
    End If
    sEmployee.PostalCode = Convert.ToString(.Item("PostalCode"))
    sEmployee.Country = Convert.ToString(.Item("Country"))
    sEmployee.HomePhone = Convert.ToString(.Item("HomePhone"))
    If Not IsDBNull(.Item("Extension")) Then
        sEmployee.Extension = Convert.ToString(.Item("Extension"))
    End If
    If Not IsDBNull(.Item("Photo")) Then
        sEmployee.Photo = CType(.Item("Photo"), Byte())
    End If
    If Not IsDBNull(.Item("Notes")) Then
        sEmployee.Notes = Convert.ToString(.Item("Notes"))
    End If
```

```
        If Not IsDBNull(.Item("ReportsTo")) Then
            sEmployee.ReportsTo = Convert.ToInt32(.Item("ReportsTo"))
              sEmployee.ReportsToLastName = _
                    Convert.ToString(.Item("ReportsToLastName"))
            sEmployee.ReportsToFirstName = _
                    Convert.ToString(.Item("ReportsToFirstName"))
        End If
        If Not IsDBNull(.Item("PhotoPath")) Then
              sEmployee.PhotoPath = Convert.ToString(.Item("PhotoPath"))
        End If
    End With

    ReDim sEmployee.Territories(ds.Tables(1).Rows.Count - 1)

    For Each dRow In ds.Tables(1).Rows
        sEmployee.Territories(i) = _
              Convert.ToString(dRow.Item("TerritoryID"))
        i += 1
    Next

    ds = Nothing

    Return sEmployee
End Function
```

The major difference here is that you now have the possibility of null values being returned from the database. For every value that can be null in the database, you need to check to see if the value is null. Instead of the IsNothing method in VB 6, you now have the IsDBNull method, which accepts an object as its parameter. The check is simple: If it is nothing, you skip it; otherwise you assign the property.

Another difference is the block of code to grab the TerritoryIDs. Notice that you are pulling the rows from table 1 in the dataset's table collection. For every Select statement in the stored procedure, a table is added to the dataset to contain the results of that Select statement. Here you simply loop through the table and add the values to the Territory array. This ensures that you are opening the connection to the database for the shortest possible time, which gives your application maximum efficiency and scalability.

The Delete method (shown in Listing 9-12) is the same as in the previous objects except for the stored procedure that you call.

Listing 9-12. The Employee Delete Method

```
Public Sub Delete(ByVal intID As Integer) Implements IEmployee.Delete
    Dim strCN As String = ConfigurationSettings.AppSettings("Northwind_DSN")
    Dim cn As New SqlConnection(strCN)
    Dim cmd As New SqlCommand()

    cn.Open()

    With cmd
        .Connection = cn
        .CommandType = CommandType.StoredProcedure
        .CommandText = "usp_employee_delete"
        .Parameters.Add("@id", intID)
        .ExecuteNonQuery()
    End With

    cmd = Nothing
    cn.Close()
End Sub
```

The GetBusinessRules method is identical to the previous classes, but as you can see (in Listing 9-13), it is a bit more extensive.

Listing 9-13. The Employee GetBusinessRules Method

```
Public Function GetBusinessRules() As BusinessErrors _
Implements IEmployee.GetBusinessRules
    Dim objBusRules As New BusinessErrors()
    With objBusRules
        .Add("Last Name", "The value cannot be null.")
        .Add("Last Name", "The value cannot be more than 20 characters " _
        & "in length.")
        .Add("First Name", "The value cannot be null.")
        .Add("First Name", "The value cannot be more than 10 characters " _
        & "in length.")
        .Add("Title", "The value cannot be null.")
        .Add("Title", "The value cannot be more than 30 characters " _
        & "in length.")
        .Add("Title Of Courtesy", "The value cannot be more than 25 " _
        & "characters in length.")
        .Add("Title Of Courtesy", "The value must one of the " _
```

```
            & "following: Mr., Ms., Dr. or Mrs.")
            .Add("Birth Date", "The value cannot be a date in the future.")
            .Add("Birth Date", "The employee must be 18 years of age or " _
            & "older.")
            .Add("Birth Date", "The employee must be younger than 60 years " _
            & "of age.")
            .Add("Hire Date", "The value may not be more than two weeks in " _
            & "the future.")
            .Add("Hire Date", "The value may not be before the company " _
            & "was created.")
            .Add("Address", "The value cannot be null.")
            .Add("Address", "The value cannot be more than 60 characters " _
            & "in length.")
            .Add("City", "The value cannot be null.")
            .Add("City", "The value cannot be more than 15 characters in " _
            & "length.")
            .Add("Region", "The value cannot be more than 15 characters in " _
            & "length.")
            .Add("Postal Code", "The value cannot be more than 10 " _
            & "characters in length.")
            .Add("Country", "The value cannot be more than 15 characters " _
            & "in length.")
            .Add("Home Phone", "The value cannot be null.")
            .Add("Home Phone", "The value cannot be more than 24 characters " _
            & "in length.")
            .Add("Extension", "The value cannot be more than 4 characters " _
            & "in length.")
            .Add("Photo Path", "The value cannot be more than 255 " _
            & "characters in length.")
        End With

        Return objBusRules
End Function
```

NOTE This is a small number of business rules. I have worked on projects where objects have had hundreds of business rules each (fortunately those objects are few and far between). The choice to display the business rules to the users is a personal one (or maybe a mandatory one), but in general it saves a lot of calls to technical support.

In the next chapter, you will see how to report an object's business rules with only one line of code (at least, one line of code in this particular method)!

The last method to add is the Save method. This method is a little longer than you have seen before because there are more properties in the object. Also, this is the first time that you are using an ADO.NET transaction, which works slightly differently than in VB 6. You will work through the Save method a little at a time. Listing 9-14 shows the first part of the Save method.

Listing 9-14. The Employee Save Method (Part 1)

```
Public Function Save(ByVal sEmployee As structEmployee, ByRef intID As _
Integer) As BusinessErrors Implements IEmployee.Save
    Dim strCN As String = ConfigurationSettings.AppSettings("Northwind_DSN")
    Dim cn As New SqlConnection(strCN)
    Dim cmd As New SqlCommand()
    Dim trans As SqlTransaction
    Dim i As Integer
    Dim intTempID As Integer

    intTempID = sEmployee.EmployeeID

    mobjBusErr = New BusinessErrors()

    With sEmployee
        Me.mintEmployeeID = .EmployeeID
        Me.LastName = .LastName
        Me.FirstName = .FirstName
        Me.Title = .Title
        Me.TitleOfCourtesy = .TitleOfCourtesy
        Me.BirthDate = .BirthDate
        Me.HireDate = .HireDate
        Me.Address = .Address
        Me.City = .City
        Me.Region = .Region
        Me.PostalCode = .PostalCode
        Me.Country = .Country
        Me.HomePhone = .HomePhone
        Me.Extension = .Extension
        Me.Photo = .Photo
        Me.Notes = .Notes
        Me.ReportsTo = .ReportsTo
        Me.PhotoPath = .PhotoPath
        Me.Territories = .Territories
    End With
```

There are two differences between this Save method and the previous Save methods. The first is the inclusion of the following declaration:

```
Dim trans As SqlTransaction
```

In .NET, a transaction is a separate object. However, there are some rules regarding transactions. You will learn about these after you see how the transaction is started, committed, and rolled back, as shown in Listing 9-15.

Listing 9-15. The Employee Save Method (Part 2)

```
If mobjBusErr.Count = 0 Then

        Try
            Dim prm As SqlParameter
            cn.Open()
            trans = cn.BeginTransaction()

            With cmd
                .Connection = cn
                .Transaction = trans
                .CommandType = CommandType.StoredProcedure
                .CommandText = "usp_employee_save"
                .Parameters.Add("@id", mintEmployeeID)
                .Parameters.Add("@lname", mstrLastName)
                .Parameters.Add("@fname", mstrFirstName)
                .Parameters.Add("@title", mstrTitle)
                .Parameters.Add("@courtesy", mstrTitleOfCourtesy)
                .Parameters.Add("@birth", mdteBirthDate)
                .Parameters.Add("@hire", mdteHireDate)
                .Parameters.Add("@address", mstrAddress)
                .Parameters.Add("@city", mstrCity)
                .Parameters.Add("@region", mstrRegion)
                .Parameters.Add("@postal", mstrPostalCode)
                .Parameters.Add("@country", mstrCountry)
                .Parameters.Add("@phone", mstrHomePhone)
                If mstrExtension = "" Then
                    .Parameters.Add("@extension", DBNull.Value)
                Else
                    .Parameters.Add("@extension", mstrExtension)
                End If
```

```
                    If mbytPhoto Is Nothing Then
                        .Parameters.Add("@photo", DBNull.Value)
                    Else
                        prm = New SqlParameter("@photo", SqlDbType.Image, _
                        mbytPhoto.Length, ParameterDirection.Input, False, _
                        0, 0, Nothing, DataRowVersion.Current, _
                        mbytPhoto)
                        cmd.Parameters.Add(prm)
                    End If
                    If mstrNotes = "" Then
                        .Parameters.Add("@notes", DBNull.Value)
                    Else
                        .Parameters.Add("@notes", mstrNotes)
                    End If
                    If mintReportsTo = 0 Then
                        .Parameters.Add("@reports", DBNull.Value)
                    Else
                        .Parameters.Add("@reports", mintReportsTo)
                    End If
                    If mstrPhotoPath = "" Then
                        .Parameters.Add("@photopath", DBNull.Value)
                    Else
                        .Parameters.Add("@photopath", mstrPhotoPath)
                    End If
                    cmd.Parameters.Add("@new_id", intID).Direction = _
                    ParameterDirection.Output
                End With

                cmd.ExecuteNonQuery()
```

Because this is a lot of code and it is difficult to break up into smaller blocks of code, let's review some of the code that you entered previously (namely the code that you have not seen before). The first thing is this declaration:

```
Dim prm As SqlParameter
```

Although you have been adding parameters with the Parameter.Add method, you can also create a parameter object. In this case it is necessary because one of the constructors that is provided by the object offers you functionality that you cannot get any other way, as you will see when you get to the photo array. The next piece of new code is the following line:

```
trans = cn.BeginTransaction()
```

You begin the transaction on the connection object, but after that point, you can make any changes to the transaction state against the transaction object instead of the connection. Next is the following:

```
.Transaction = trans
```

You must assign the transaction to the command object explicitly. This is mandatory and is one of the rules for using a transaction. Every single command executed against the connection, once the transaction has been started, must be associated with the transaction. Failure to do so will cause a runtime error.

This block of code is a new one also:

```
If mstrExtension = "" Then
     .Parameters.Add("@extension", DBNull.Value)
Else
     .Parameters.Add("@extension", mstrExtension)
End If
```

You may ask the following questions: Why are you checking for an empty string if you never set the object equal to anything—wouldn't it be nothing? The answer is that because this is a string object, it is automatically initialized to an empty string so you can check for an empty string or nothing. Second, why do you have to pass the value of DBNull.Value if your object is equal to nothing? The answer is that failure to do this generates a rather unique error. Figure 9-1 shows the error that is generated.

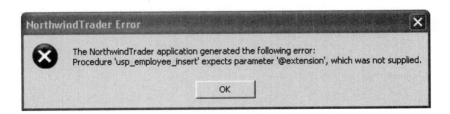

Figure 9-1. SQL Server null value error

Of course, you supplied a null value, but SQL Server will not see it. To pass a null value, you must pass DBNull.Value. So, every place where a null value can be inserted into the database, this check must be made.

TIP It may be helpful to create some type of method that can return either the value or DBNull.value and overload it for every type of data. This saves a great deal of If..Then statements and makes the code more readable.

The last block of code you have not seen so far is the following:

```
If mbytPhoto Is Nothing Then
     .Parameters.Add("@photo", DBNull.Value)
Else
     prm = New SqlParameter("@photo", SqlDbType.Image, _
     mbytPhoto.Length, ParameterDirection.Input, False, _
     0, 0, Nothing, DataRowVersion.Current, _
     mbytPhoto)
     cmd.Parameters.Add(prm)
End If
```

Because the photo parameter is of type image, you have to do a little bit more work. You need to identify to SQL Server that you are passing in an image to the parameter, and you need to specify the length of the value being passed in and the actual object you are passing in. Only the overloaded constructor allows you to specify all of the needed values. So, you create the parameter object first and then add it to the parameters collection of the command object.

Next, you need to add the records that associate the employee with the territory. To do this, enter the code in Listing 9-16 into the Save method of the Employee class.

Listing 9-16. The Employee Save Method (Part 3)

```
If intTempID > 0 Then
     cmd = New SqlCommand()
     With cmd
          .Connection = cn
          .Transaction = trans
          .CommandType = CommandType.StoredProcedure
          .CommandText = "usp_employee_territory_delete"
          .Parameters.Add("@employee_id", mintEmployeeID)
          .ExecuteNonQuery()
     End With
     cmd = Nothing
End If
```

First, you need to check to see if this is a new employee. If it is a new employee, you can skip this part. If it is not a new employee, you need to delete the employee/territory relationships. It is easier to simply rewrite the values than to try to figure out what changes were made, especially in a table comprised of only foreign keys.

NOTE An Identifying relationship is one in which the join table is comprised of two or more foreign keys, and these foreign keys make up the primary key of the join table. Updating the values in the table is much more difficult. You identify the row in the table with two or more columns and then you *change* one of the values in the same column you used to identify that row. That means you can no longer identify that row in the same way. Although you do have the new values in your object, you do not have the old values, so how do you find the record you need to update? That requires a lot more work.

After that, you assign the new employee ID to the module-level variable so that you can use it later. (You could use the value stored in intID, except it is more intuitive if you place that value in the mintEmployeeID variable.) This next block of code associates the employee with the territories. Add this code (in Listing 9-17) to the end of the Employee Save method. Notice that you need to loop through the Territory array and add each relationship one at a time. There is no really good way to do this, so simple is better and less likely to cause problems.

Listing 9-17. The Employee Save Method (Part 4)

```
If Not sEmployee.Territories Is Nothing Then
    For i = 0 To sEmployee.Territories.Length - 1
        cmd = New SqlCommand()
        With cmd
            .Connection = cn
            .Transaction = trans
            .CommandType = CommandType.StoredProcedure
            .CommandText = "usp_employee_territory_insert"
            .Parameters.Add("@employee_id", mintEmployeeID)
            .Parameters.Add("@territory_id", sEmployee.Territories(i))
            .ExecuteNonQuery()
        End With
        cmd = Nothing
    Next
End If
```

Finally, you need to close out the transaction and ensure the object is in a stable state. Listing 9-18 contains the remainder of the code needed for the Employee Save method.

Listing 9-18. The Employee Save Method (Part 5)

```
            intID = mintEmployeeID
            trans.Commit()
            trans = Nothing
            cn.Close()
    Catch exc As Exception
            trans.Rollback()
            trans = Nothing
            cn.Close()
            Throw exc
        End Try
    Else
        Return mobjBusErr
    End If
End Function
```

If everything goes as planned, you call the commit method of the transaction object and then close the database connection. If anything goes wrong, you roll back the transaction and close the connection. You also rethrow the exception so that it can be displayed to the user. If there were rule violations, you return those to the user-centric objects so they can be reported to the user.

NOTE   Remember that the error handling routine allows for a Finally block that always runs, even if an exception occurs. Although this is technically true, it does not happen if an exception is thrown in the Catch block because the code execution stops at that point because you do not have a Catch block that can handle this exception. This is why you do not close the connection in a Finally block.

TIP   One thing to note is that you are not displaying the contents of a sqlException; you are only using the methods and properties of a base exception. You can increase error reporting by checking the exception that was thrown to see if it is a type of sqlException. If it is, you can report the errors in more detail.

That is it for the data-centric class; you are finally done. Next you will move on to the user-centric objects.

Employee User-Centric Objects

As with the other user-centric classes you have created before, this is simply more of the same with some slight additions to take care of the object aggregation. Also, you will notice that you are not handling all of the business rules in this class that you handled in the data-centric class.

To start with, add a new class to the NorthwindUC project and call it *Employee.vb*. Add the standard heading and Import statements at the top of the code module:

```
Option Strict On
Option Explicit On

Imports NorthwindTraders.NorthwindShared.Structures
Imports NorthwindTraders.NorthwindShared.Interfaces
Imports NorthwindTraders.NorthwindShared.Errors
Imports NorthwindTraders.NorthwindShared
```

Next, make sure that the class inherits from the business base class, declares your remote object constant, and declares the Errs event as in the following:

```
Public Class Employee
    Inherits BusinessBase
    Private Const REMENTRY As String = "EmployeeDC.rem"
    Public Event Errs(ByVal obj As BusinessErrors)
    Private msEmployee As structEmployee
```

As before, the module-level structure holds the Employee object in case you need to roll back a change. Now add the private variable declarations (these can, with two exceptions, be copied from the data-centric Employee class) as shown in Listing 9-19.

Listing 9-19. The User-Centric Employee Private Attributes

```
#Region " Private Attributes"
    Private mintEmployeeID As Integer = 0
    Private mstrLastName As String
    Private mstrFirstName As String
    Private mstrTitle As String
    Private mstrTitleOfCourtesy As String
    Private mdteBirthDate As Date = Now
    Private mdteHireDate As Date = Now
    Private mstrAddress As String
    Private mstrCity As String
    Private mstrRegion As String
    Private mstrPostalCode As String
    Private mstrCountry As String
    Private mstrHomePhone As String
    Private mstrExtension As String
    Private mbytPhoto() As Byte
    Private mstrNotes As String
    Private mintReportsTo As Integer
    Private mstrPhotoPath As String
    Private mobjReportsTo As Employee
    Private mobjTerritoryMgr As TerritoryMgr
#End Region
```

The two exceptions are the mobjReportsTo variable and the mobjTerritoryMgr object. The mobjReportsTo variable holds an object of type Employee. This allows you to manipulate the employee's manager as a separate object and to retrieve all of the information about this individual by way of the LoadRecord method. Once you program the Employee object, you can use it however you see fit. The mobjTerritoryMgr object is only one solution to the issue of maintaining the territories with which an employee is associated. Remember that you chose not to use the Singleton pattern when you created the TerritoryMgr object so that you can use the manager to maintain the collection of territories specific to this one employee. Another solution would be to use the territory manager as a Singleton and just maintain an array of territory IDs that just reference the TerritoryMgr object when you need to retrieve territory information. The method you choose is up to you, and each has its pros and cons.

NOTE These are only two possible solutions, but there are others as well. As a developer, you know that there is no one single solution to any given problem. You also know that there are, in some cases, as many solutions to a problem as there are developers who have had to face that problem. By using the ideas in this chapter as guides, you will be able to develop your own solutions that may work better for your particular situation.

You should also note that you have assigned default values of Now to the date variables. This is necessary so that when you create the user dates, you can set the DateTimePicker control to a default value based on what is in the object.

Now you will add the public member variables. These are checking a subset of the business rules in the data-centric objects. Listing 9-20 shows these properties (if you have not yet downloaded the code for this chapter, you may want to do so now—this is an extremely long listing).

Listing 9-20. The User-Centric Employee Public Properties

```
#Region " Public Attributes"

    Public ReadOnly Property EmployeeID() As Integer
        Get
            Return mintEmployeeID
        End Get
    End Property


    Public Property LastName() As String
        Get
            Return mstrLastName
        End Get
        Set(ByVal Value As String)
            Try
                'Test for null value
                If Value Is Nothing Then
                    Throw New ArgumentNullException("Last Name")
                End If
```

```
                        'Test for empty string
                        If Value.Length = 0 Then
                            Throw New ZeroLengthException()
                        End If

                        'Test for max length
                        If Value.Length > 20 Then
                            Throw New MaximumLengthException(20)
                        End If

                        If mstrLastName <> Value Then
                            mstrLastName = Value
                            If Not Loading Then
                                mobjRules.BrokenRule("Last Name", False)
                                mblnDirty = True
                            End If
                        End If
                    Catch exc As Exception
                        mobjRules.BrokenRule("Last Name", True)
                        mstrLastName = Value
                        mblnDirty = True
                        Throw exc
                    End Try
                End Set
            End Property

            Public Property FirstName() As String
                Get
                    Return mstrFirstName
                End Get
                Set(ByVal Value As String)
                    Try
                        'Test for null value
                        If Value Is Nothing Then
                            Throw New ArgumentNullException("First Name")
                        End If

                        'Test for empty string
                        If Value.Length = 0 Then
                            Throw New ZeroLengthException()
                        End If
```

```
            'Test for max length
            If Value.Length > 10 Then
                Throw New MaximumLengthException(10)
            End If

            If mstrFirstName <> Value Then
                mstrFirstName = Value
                If Not Loading Then
                    mobjRules.BrokenRule("First Name", False)
                    mblnDirty = True
                End If
            End If
        Catch exc As Exception
            mobjRules.BrokenRule("First Name", True)
            mstrFirstName = Value
            mblnDirty = True
            Throw exc
        End Try
    End Set
End Property

Public Property Title() As String
    Get
        Return mstrTitle
    End Get
    Set(ByVal Value As String)
        Try
            'Test for null value
            If Value Is Nothing Then
                Throw New ArgumentNullException("Title")
            End If

            'Test for empty string
            If Value.Length = 0 Then
                Throw New ZeroLengthException()
            End If

            'Test for max length
            If Value.Length > 30 Then
                Throw New MaximumLengthException(30)
            End If
```

```
                        If mstrTitle <> Value Then
                            mstrTitle = Value
                            If Not Loading Then
                                mobjRules.BrokenRule("Title", False)
                                mblnDirty = True
                            End If
                        End If
                    Catch exc As Exception
                        mobjRules.BrokenRule("Title", True)
                        mstrTitle = Value
                        mblnDirty = True
                        Throw exc
                    End Try
                End Set
            End Property

            Public Property TitleOfCourtesy() As String
                Get
                    Return mstrTitleOfCourtesy
                End Get
                Set(ByVal Value As String)
                    Try
                        'Test for null value
                        If Value Is Nothing Then
                            Exit Property
                        End If

                        'Test for empty string
                        If Value.Length = 0 Then
                            mstrTitleOfCourtesy = Nothing
                            Exit Property
                        End If

                        'Test for max length
                        If Value.Length > 25 Then
                            Throw New MaximumLengthException(25)
                        End If
```

```
                'Test for specific values
                Select Case Value
                    Case "Mr.", "Ms.", "Dr.", "Mrs."
                        'Do nothing
                    Case Else
                        Throw New AllowedValuesException("Mr., Ms., " _
                        & "Dr., Mrs.")
                End Select

                If mstrTitleOfCourtesy <> Value Then
                    mstrTitleOfCourtesy = Value
                    If Not Loading Then
                        mobjRules.BrokenRule("Title Of Courtesy", False)
                        mblnDirty = True
                    End If
                End If
            Catch exc As Exception
                mobjRules.BrokenRule("Title Of Courtesy", True)
                mstrTitleOfCourtesy = Value
                mblnDirty = True
                Throw exc
            End Try
        End Set
    End Property

    Public Property BirthDate() As Date
        Get
            Return mdteBirthDate
        End Get
        Set(ByVal Value As Date)
            Try
                If mdteBirthDate <> Value Then
                    mdteBirthDate = Value
                    If Not Loading Then
                        mobjRules.BrokenRule("Birth Date", False)
                        mblnDirty = True
                    End If
                End If
```

```
                        Catch exc As Exception
                            mobjRules.BrokenRule("Birth Date", True)
                            mdteBirthDate = Value
                            mblnDirty = True
                            Throw exc
                        End Try

            End Set
        End Property

        Public Property HireDate() As Date
            Get
                Return mdteHireDate
            End Get
            Set(ByVal Value As Date)
                Try
                    If mdteHireDate <> Value Then
                        mdteHireDate = Value
                        If Not Loading Then
                            mobjRules.BrokenRule("Hire Date", False)
                            mblnDirty = True
                        End If
                    End If
                Catch exc As Exception
                    mobjRules.BrokenRule("Hire Date", True)
                    mdteHireDate = Value
                    mblnDirty = True
                    Throw exc
                End Try
            End Set
        End Property

        Public Property Address() As String
            Get
                Return mstrAddress
            End Get
            Set(ByVal Value As String)
                Try
                    'Test for null value
                    If Value Is Nothing Then
                        Throw New ArgumentNullException("Address")
                    End If
```

```
                    'Test for empty string
                    If Value.Length = 0 Then
                        Throw New ZeroLengthException()
                    End If

                    'Test for max length
                    If Value.Length > 60 Then
                        Throw New MaximumLengthException(60)
                    End If

                    If mstrAddress <> Value Then
                        mstrAddress = Value
                        If Not Loading Then
                            mobjRules.BrokenRule("Address", False)
                            mblnDirty = True
                        End If
                    End If
                Catch exc As Exception
                    mobjRules.BrokenRule("Address", True)
                    mstrAddress = Value
                    mblnDirty = True
                    Throw exc
                End Try
            End Set
        End Property

        Public Property City() As String
            Get
                Return mstrCity
            End Get
            Set(ByVal Value As String)
                Try
                    'Test for null value
                    If Value Is Nothing Then
                        Throw New ArgumentNullException("City")
                    End If

                    'Test for empty string
                    If Value.Length = 0 Then
                        Throw New ZeroLengthException()
                    End If
```

```
                            'Test for max length
                            If Value.Length > 15 Then
                                Throw New MaximumLengthException(15)
                            End If

                            If mstrCity <> Value Then
                                mstrCity = Value
                                If Not Loading Then
                                    mobjRules.BrokenRule("City", False)
                                    mblnDirty = True
                                End If
                            End If
                        Catch exc As Exception
                            mobjRules.BrokenRule("City", True)
                            mstrCity = Value
                            mblnDirty = True
                            Throw exc
                        End Try
                    End Set
                End Property

                Public Property Region() As String
                    Get
                        Return mstrRegion
                    End Get
                    Set(ByVal Value As String)
                        Try
                            'Test for null value
                            If Value Is Nothing Then
                                Exit Property
                            End If

                            'Test for empty string
                            If Value.Length = 0 Then
                                mstrRegion = Nothing
                                Exit Property
                            End If

                            'Test for max length
                            If Value.Length > 15 Then
                                Throw New MaximumLengthException(15)
                            End If
```

```
            If mstrRegion <> Value Then
                mstrRegion = Value
                If Not Loading Then
                    mobjRules.BrokenRule("Region", False)
                    mblnDirty = True
                End If
            End If
        Catch exc As Exception
            mobjRules.BrokenRule("Region", True)
            mstrRegion = Value
            mblnDirty = True
            Throw exc
        End Try
    End Set
End Property

Public Property PostalCode() As String
    Get
        Return mstrPostalCode
    End Get
    Set(ByVal Value As String)
        Try
            'Test for null value
            If Value Is Nothing Then
                Throw New ArgumentNullException("Postal Code")
            End If

            'Test for empty string
            If Value.Length = 0 Then
                Throw New ZeroLengthException()
            End If

            'Test for max length
            If Value.Length > 10 Then
                Throw New MaximumLengthException(10)
            End If

            If mstrPostalCode <> Value Then
                mstrPostalCode = Value
                If Not Loading Then
                    mobjRules.BrokenRule("Postal Code", False)
                    mblnDirty = True
                End If
            End If
```

```
                Catch exc As Exception
                    mobjRules.BrokenRule("Postal Code", True)
                    mstrPostalCode = Value
                    mblnDirty = True
                    Throw exc
                End Try
            End Set
        End Property

        Public Property Country() As String
            Get
                Return mstrCountry
            End Get
            Set(ByVal Value As String)
                Try
                    'Test for null value
                    If Value Is Nothing Then
                        Throw New ArgumentNullException("Country")
                    End If

                    'Test for empty string
                    If Value.Length = 0 Then
                        Throw New ZeroLengthException()
                    End If

                    'Test for max length
                    If Value.Length > 15 Then
                        Throw New MaximumLengthException(15)
                    End If

                    If mstrCountry <> Value Then
                        mstrCountry = Value
                        If Not Loading Then
                            mobjRules.BrokenRule("Country", False)
                            mblnDirty = True
                        End If
                    End If
```

```
            Catch exc As Exception
                mobjRules.BrokenRule("Country", True)
                mstrCountry = Value
                mblnDirty = True
                Throw exc
            End Try
        End Set
    End Property

    Public Property HomePhone() As String
        Get
            Return mstrHomePhone
        End Get
        Set(ByVal Value As String)
            Try
                'Test for null value
                If Value Is Nothing Then
                    Throw New ArgumentNullException("Home Phone")
                End If

                'Test for empty string
                If Value.Length = 0 Then
                    Throw New ZeroLengthException()
                End If

                'Test for max length
                If Value.Length > 24 Then
                    Throw New MaximumLengthException(24)
                End If

                If mstrHomePhone <> Value Then
                    mstrHomePhone = Value
                    If Not Loading Then
                        mobjRules.BrokenRule("Home Phone", False)
                        mblnDirty = True
                    End If
                End If
```

```vb
            Catch exc As Exception
                mobjRules.BrokenRule("Home Phone", True)
                mstrHomePhone = Value
                mblnDirty = True
                Throw exc
            End Try
        End Set
End Property

Public Property Extension() As String
    Get
        Return mstrExtension
    End Get
    Set(ByVal Value As String)
        Try
            'Test for null value
            If Value Is Nothing Then
                Exit Property
            End If

            'Test for empty string
            If Value.Length = 0 Then
                mstrExtension = Nothing
                Exit Property
            End If

            'Test for max length
            If Value.Length > 4 Then
                Throw New MaximumLengthException(4)
            End If

            If mstrExtension <> Value Then
                mstrExtension = Value
                If Not Loading Then
                    mobjRules.BrokenRule("Extension", False)
                    mblnDirty = True
                End If
            End If
```

```
            Catch exc As Exception
                mobjRules.BrokenRule("Extension", True)
                mstrExtension = Value
                mblnDirty = True
                Throw exc
            End Try
        End Set
    End Property


    Public Property Photo() As Byte()
        Get
            Return mbytPhoto
        End Get
        Set(ByVal Value As Byte())
            If Not mbytPhoto Is Value Then
                mbytPhoto = Value
                If Not Loading Then
                    mblnDirty = True
                End If
            End If
        End Set
    End Property


    Public Property Notes() As String
        Get
            Return mstrNotes
        End Get
        Set(ByVal Value As String)
            If mstrNotes <> Value Then
                mstrNotes = Value
                If Not Loading Then
                    mblnDirty = True
                End If
            End If
        End Set
    End Property
```

```vbnet
Public Property PhotoPath() As String
    Get
        Return mstrPhotoPath
    End Get
    Set(ByVal Value As String)
        Try
            'Test for null value
            If Value Is Nothing Then
                Exit Property
            End If

            'Test for empty string
            If Value.Length = 0 Then
                mstrPhotoPath = Nothing
                Exit Property
            End If

            'Test for max length
            If Value.Length > 255 Then
                Throw New MaximumLengthException(255)
            End If

            If FileSystem.FileLen(Value) > 0 Then
                'do nothing, if the file is not found, a
                'FileNotFoundException will be thrown automatically
            End If

            If mstrPhotoPath <> Value Then
                mstrPhotoPath = Value
                If Not Loading Then
                    mobjRules.BrokenRule("Photo Path", False)
                    mblnDirty = True
                End If
            End If
        Catch exc As Exception
            mobjRules.BrokenRule("Photo Path", True)
            mstrPhotoPath = Value
            mblnDirty = True
            Throw exc
        End Try
    End Set
End Property
```

```
Public Property ReportsTo() As Employee
    Get
        Return mobjReportsTo
    End Get
    Set(ByVal Value As Employee)
        If Not mobjReportsTo Is Value Then
            mobjReportsTo = Value
            If Not Loading Then
                mblnDirty = True
            End If
        End If
    End Set
End Property
```

The only property you have left out so far is the property involving the territory manager. That is because it is just a bit different than a regular property. Add the following property for the territory manager object:

```
Public ReadOnly Property Territories() As TerritoryMgr
    Get
        Return mobjTerritoryMgr
    End Get
End Property
```

```
#End Region
```

This may seem kind of strange because this looks like you can only read the territory manager object. However, this is not the case—what this does is return the territory manager and allow you to manipulate it however you want. So although this is a read-only method, once you get the territory manager you can do whatever you want with the manager object. This presents you with an additional problem, though. How do you know when a territory associated with the employee changed? The answer is that you do not. So why is this a problem and how do you solve it? It is a problem because you control the enabling and disabling of buttons based on whether the object is dirty. If the user only changes a territory, the employee would never be marked as dirty and would never be saved! Listing 9-21 shows an additional method you need to add that requires some explanation.

Listing 9-21. The Shadowed IsDirty Method

```
Public Shadows Function IsDirty() As Boolean
    Dim i As Integer
    Dim dictEnt As DictionaryEntry
    Dim blnFound As Boolean

    If Not mblndirty Then
        If Not msEmployee.Territories Is Nothing Then
            If mobjTerritoryMgr.Count <> msEmployee.Territories.Length Then
                mblndirty = True
            Else
                For Each dictEnt In mobjTerritoryMgr
                    Dim objTerritory As Territory = _
                    CType(dictEnt.Value, Territory)
                    blnFound = False
                    For i = 0 To msEmployee.Territories.Length - 1
                        If objTerritory.TerritoryID = _
                        msEmployee.Territories(i) Then
                            blnFound = True
                            Exit For
                        End If
                    Next
                    If Not blnFound Then
                        mblndirty = True
                        Exit For
                    End If
                Next
            End If
        End If
    End If

    Return mblndirty
End Function
```

The first thing to note about this method is the signature—specifically the Shadows keyword. In this particular instance you could also use the overrides keyword, but you have not marked the IsDirty method as overridable in the BusinessBase class. You have avoided a full-blown discussion of the different methods for using objects because there is a great deal more to discuss than could be included in this book. However, because you are using the Shadows keyword,

I will briefly explain its use. You have a method called *IsDirty* in your BusinessBase class. But that method only returns the value of the mblnDirty variable. What the Shadow keyword does is that when you call the IsDirty method on an instance of the Employee class, you will be calling the method from the Employee class. But, if you call the IsDirty method on the Employee class if it has been instantiated as the BusinessBase class, then you will be calling the IsDirty method on the BusinessBase object. Although this may seem confusing, perhaps the following example code snippet will help:

```
Dim objEmployee as Employee
objEmployee = New Employee()
'This will call the isDirty method on the Employee object
Dim blnValue as Boolean = objEmployee.IsDirty

Dim objEmployee as Employee
objEmployee = New BusinessBase()
'This will call the IsDirty method on the BusinessBase object
Dim blnValue as Boolean = objEmployee.IsDirty
```

NOTE For more information on object-oriented design and keywords, refer to the list of references in Appendix B.

CAUTION You should shadow a method as a last resort. The reason for this is that unless the author of a class marks a method as overridable, it can be inferred that the author did not intend for the behavior of the method to change. By using the Shadows keyword, you are overriding the behavior anyway. This can lead to some unexpected side effects depending on how the objects are being used.

The rest of this method simply compares your array of IDs with your TerritoryMgr object to look for differences. If it finds differences, then you mark the object as dirty.

Next, add the two constructors that you need for the Employee class (see Listing 9-22).

Listing 9-22. Employee Class Constructors

```
Public Sub New()
      MyBase.New(REMENTRY)
      mobjRules = New BrokenRules()
      mobjTerritoryMgr = New TerritoryMgr(False)
      With mobjrules
          .BrokenRule("Last Name", True)
          .BrokenRule("First Name", True)
          .BrokenRule("Title", True)
          .BrokenRule("Address", True)
          .BrokenRule("City", True)
          .BrokenRule("Postal Code", True)
          .BrokenRule("Country", True)
          .BrokenRule("Home Phone", True)
      End With
   End Sub

   Public Sub New(ByVal intID As Integer)
      MyBase.New(REMENTRY)
      mobjRules = New BrokenRules()
      mintEmployeeID = intID
      mobjTerritoryMgr = New TerritoryMgr(False)
   End Sub
```

The only rules you break in the first constructor are for those properties that do not have default values (such as the BirthDate and HireDate properties) and those properties that cannot be null. You also instantiate any manager objects that the class will maintain. Now you have a small problem here—if you look at the TerritoryMgr class, you will notice that you have only one constructor and it calls the Load method. You do not want that to happen because you want an empty TerritoryMgr object! To alleviate this problem, modify the constructor in the TerritoryMgr object as shown in Listing 9-23.

Listing 9-23. The Modified TerritoryMgr Constructor

```
Public Sub New(Optional ByVal blnLoad As Boolean = True)
      If blnLoad Then
          Load()
      End If
End Sub
```

Now your original code can remain untouched, but you have the option of not loading up the TerritoryMgr object from the database.

As you did in previous classes, you will override the ToString method by adding the following code to the Employee class:

```
Public Overrides Function ToString() As String
    Return mstrLastName & ", " & mstrFirstName
End Function
```

In this case, your ToString method will return the whole name of the employee.

Now add the LoadRecord method and its associated methods as shown in Listing 9-24.

Listing 9-24. The Employee LoadRecord and Related Methods

```
Public Sub LoadRecord(ByRef objTerritoryMgr As TerritoryMgr)
    Dim objIEmp As IEmployee

    objIEmp = CType(Activator.GetObject(GetType(IEmployee), _
    AppConstants.REMOTEOBJECTS & REMENTRY), IEmployee)
    msEmployee = objIEmp.LoadRecord(mintEmployeeID)
    objIEmp = Nothing

    LoadObject(objTerritoryMgr)
End Sub

Private Sub LoadObject(ByRef objTerritoryMgr As TerritoryMgr)
    Dim i As Integer

    With msEmployee
        Me.mintEmployeeID = .EmployeeID
        Me.mstrLastName = .LastName
        Me.mstrFirstName = .FirstName
        Me.mstrTitle = .Title
        Me.mstrTitleOfCourtesy = .TitleOfCourtesy
        Me.mdteBirthDate = .BirthDate
        Me.mdteHireDate = .HireDate
        Me.mstrAddress = .Address
        Me.mstrCity = .City
        Me.mstrRegion = .Region
        Me.mstrPostalCode = .PostalCode
        Me.mstrCountry = .Country
        Me.mstrHomePhone = .HomePhone
        Me.mstrExtension = .Extension
        Me.mbytPhoto = .Photo
        Me.mstrNotes = .Notes
        Me.mstrPhotoPath = .PhotoPath
```

```
        If .ReportsTo > 0 Then
            mobjReportsTo = New Employee(.ReportsTo)
            mobjReportsTo.FirstName = .ReportsToFirstName
            mobjReportsTo.LastName = .ReportsToLastName
        End If

        mobjTerritoryMgr.Clear()
        If Not .Territories Is Nothing Then
            For i = 0 To .Territories.Length - 1
                mobjTerritoryMgr.Add((objTerritoryMgr.Item(.Territories(i))))
            Next
        End If
    End With
End Sub

Public Sub Rollback(ByRef objTerritoryMgr As TerritoryMgr)
    LoadObject(objTerritoryMgr)
End Sub
```

There are a couple of new items here and at least one warning note that you need to be aware of, so let's examine this code. As before, you have a LoadRecord method, but the LoadObject method does the real work. This method is also called by the rollback method (in case the user cancels an edit) as you have seen before.

You first instantiate the mobjReportsTo object (which is of type Employee) and assign the manager information to this class. One important thing to understand about the values that you are assigning to this class is that you have given it enough information to be able to load itself (the EmployeeID), and you have given it enough information so that the ToString method of the Employee Manager will return something. This is important if you want this object to be able to be placed in a listbox or combobox (as you will do when you build the user interface).

 CAUTION In a situation like this, do not fall into the trap of having one object load another object's state. This destroys the principle of encapsulation. The only time this rule should be broken is when one object is fully aggregated into another object. An example of this would be an Order Detail object. An Order Detail cannot stand on its own; it must be a part of an Order object. In this situation, it is perfectly acceptable to have the Order object instantiate the Order Detail object because the Order Detail object would not have enough information to instantiate itself.

The other item to note is how you get the TerritoryMgr object and assign values from this object to the territories collection object contained within the Employee object. You are now relying on an external object to give you some assistance in loading your Employee object. This breaks the "strict" object-oriented design principle of encapsulation, but on the other hand this is exactly what it means to have aggregated objects! Notice also that you have passed the manager ByRef because you need your Employee object's collection of territories to point to the same place as those territories currently in memory. The act of assigning territories to your internal manager in this particular way means that the objects are stored in the collection ByRef, so any changes to the territory object will be immediately visible in the Employee object.

 CAUTION This will propagate a problem mentioned earlier in this chapter concerning the use of identifying columns. The twist here is the following: The territory table uses a non-system-generated number, which means the user can change this number during the course of program execution. Because this field is the key that is used in the collections, this has the potential to be a huge problem because as soon as you change the Territory ID, you cannot reference that territory in the collection again! This is why I never use a non-system-generated key on any table in a real application.

Listing 9-25 shows the Delete method. This follows the same pattern as the earlier classes.

Listing 9-25. The Employee Object Delete Method

```
Public Sub Delete()
    Dim objIEmp As IEmployee

    objIEmp = CType(Activator.GetObject(GetType(IEmployee), _
    AppConstants.REMOTEOBJECTS & REMENTRY), IEmployee)
    objIEmp.Delete(mintEmployeeID)
    objIEmp = Nothing
End Sub
```

Last but certainly not least is the Save method, as shown in Listing 9-26. You will see the differences between this and previous Save methods next.

Listing 9-26. The Employee Class Save Method

```
Public Sub Save()
    Dim objBusErr As BusinessErrors

    If mobjRules.Count = 0 Then
        If IsDirty() = True Then
            Dim objIEmp As IEmployee
            Dim intID As Integer
            Dim sEmployee As structEmployee
            Dim i As Integer = 0
            Dim objTerritory As Territory
            Dim dictEnt As DictionaryEntry

            intID = mintEmployeeID

            With sEmployee
                .EmployeeID = mintEmployeeID
                .LastName = Me.mstrLastName
                .FirstName = Me.mstrFirstName
                .Title = Me.mstrTitle
                .TitleOfCourtesy = Me.mstrTitleOfCourtesy
                .BirthDate = Me.mdteBirthDate
                .HireDate = Me.mdteHireDate
                .Address = Me.mstrAddress
                .City = Me.mstrCity
                .Region = Me.mstrRegion
                .PostalCode = Me.mstrPostalCode
                .Country = Me.mstrCountry
                .HomePhone = Me.mstrHomePhone
                .Extension = Me.mstrExtension
                .Photo = Me.mbytPhoto
                .Notes = Me.mstrNotes
                .PhotoPath = Me.mstrPhotoPath
                If Not mobjReportsTo Is Nothing Then
                    .ReportsTo = mobjReportsTo.EmployeeID
                End If
```

```
            ReDim .Territories(mobjTerritoryMgr.Count - 1)
             i = 0
             For Each dictEnt In mobjTerritoryMgr
                 objTerritory = CType(dictEnt.Value, Territory)
                 .Territories(i) = objTerritory.TerritoryID
                 i += 1
             Next
         objIEmp = CType(Activator.GetObject(GetType(IEmployee), _
         AppConstants.REMOTEOBJECTS & REMENTRY), IEmployee)

         objBusErr = objIEmp.Save(sEmployee, mintEmployeeID)
         objIEmp = Nothing

         If Not objBusErr Is Nothing Then
             RaiseEvent Errs(objBusErr)
         Else
             mblndirty = False
             msEmployee = sEmployee
             If intID = 0 Then
                 CallChangedEvent(Me, New _
                 ChangedEventArgs(ChangedEventArgs.eChange.Added))
             Else
                 CallChangedEvent(Me, New _
                 ChangedEventArgs(ChangedEventArgs.eChange.Updated))
             End If
         End If
        End If
      End If
    End If
End Sub
```

There are only two things that differ in this method from the previous Save methods, and both of them deal with your aggregated objects. The first difference is the ReportsTo property. Instead of assigning the object to your structure, you assign the ID only because that is the only information about the manager that you need to save when you save the Employee object to the database. The second difference are the Territory objects. You store only the ID in the Territory array because you only need this information to be able to enter information into the join table. Any updates to the individual territory objects can be handled by the Territory objects.

Finally, you need to add an employee manager collection class, as shown in Listing 9-27. Add this class to the end of the Employee code module.

Listing 9-27. The EmployeeMgr Class

```
Public Class EmployeeMgr
    Inherits System.Collections.DictionaryBase

    Private Shared mobjEmployeeMgr As EmployeeMgr

    Public Shared Function GetInstance() As EmployeeMgr
        If mobjEmployeeMgr Is Nothing Then
            mobjEmployeeMgr = New EmployeeMgr()
        End If
        Return mobjEmployeeMgr
    End Function

    Protected Sub New()
        Load()
    End Sub

    Public Sub Add(ByVal obj As Employee)
        dictionary.Add(obj.EmployeeID, obj)
    End Sub

    Public Function Item(ByVal Key As Object) As Employee
        Return CType(dictionary.Item(Key), Employee)
    End Function

    Public Sub Remove(ByVal Key As Object)
        dictionary.Remove(Key)
    End Sub

    Private Sub Load()
        Dim objIEmployee As IEmployee
        Dim dRow As DataRow
        Dim ds As DataSet

        'Obtain a reference to the remote object
        objIEmployee = CType(Activator.GetObject(GetType(IEmployee), _
        AppConstants.REMOTEOBJECTS & "EmployeeDC.rem"), IEmployee)
        ds = objIEmployee.LoadProxy()
        objIEmployee = Nothing
```

```
    'Loop through the dataset adding region objects to the collection
    For Each dRow In ds.Tables(0).Rows
        'Assign the ID in the constructor since we can't assign it
        'afterwards
        Dim objEmployee As New _
        Employee(Convert.ToInt32(dRow.Item("EmployeeID")))
        With objEmployee
            'Set the loading flag so the object isn't marked as edited
            .Loading = True
            .LastName = Convert.ToString(dRow.Item("LastName"))
            .FirstName = Convert.ToString(dRow.Item("FirstName"))
            .Title = Convert.ToString(dRow.Item("Title"))
            .Loading = False
        End With
        'Add the object to the collection
        Me.Add(objEmployee)
    Next

    ds = Nothing
End Sub

Public Sub Refresh()
    dictionary.Clear()
    Load()
End Sub

End Class
```

There is no difference between this manager class and the Region manager class you created before. However, you will note that this time your LoadProxy method does generate a partial object, not a full object because you have a lot more information than you had before and you do not want to load it all up at once—especially if the user does not need or want to see that information. This is why it is called a *proxy*—it is not complete, but it represents the full object.

Employee User Interface

The Employee List form is almost identical to the previous list forms, but the edit form is much more complicated. You will not review the list form, but you will see the edit form in detail because you will be examining some new techniques for displaying data.

Employee List Form

Because this now-standard list form is no different from any of the previous list forms (except for the objects that it operates on), I simply present the code in Listing 9-28 without further explanation. Add a new form that inherits from your frmListBase form and call it *frmEmployeeList*. Add all of the code in Listing 9-28 to the list form.

Listing 9-28. Employee List Form

```
Option Explicit On
Option Strict On

Imports NorthwindTraders.NorthwindUC

Public Class frmEmployeeList
    Inherits UserInterface.frmListBase

    Private mobjEmployeeMgr As EmployeeMgr
    Private WithEvents mfrmEdit As frmEmployeeEdit
    Private WithEvents mobjEmployee As Employee
    Private mobjTerritoryMgr As TerritoryMgr

#Region " Windows Form Designer generated code "

    Public Sub New()
        MyBase.New("Employees")

        'This call is required by the Windows Form Designer.
        InitializeComponent()

        'Add any initialization after the InitializeComponent() call
        LoadList()
    End Sub

    'Form overrides dispose to clean up the component list.
    Protected Overloads Overrides Sub Dispose(ByVal disposing As _
    Boolean)
        If disposing Then
            If Not (components Is Nothing) Then
                components.Dispose()
            End If
        End If
        MyBase.Dispose(disposing)
    End Sub
```

```vb
    'Required by the Windows Form Designer
    Private components As System.ComponentModel.IContainer

    'NOTE: The following procedure is required by the Windows Form
    'Designer
    'It can be modified using the Windows Form Designer.
    'Do not modify it using the code editor.
    <System.Diagnostics.DebuggerStepThrough()> Private Sub _
InitializeComponent()
        components = New System.ComponentModel.Container()
    End Sub

#End Region

    Private Sub LoadList()
        Dim objEmployee As Employee
        Dim objDictEnt As DictionaryEntry

        Try
            mobjTerritoryMgr = New TerritoryMgr(True)

            lvwList.BeginUpdate()

            If lvwList.Columns.Count = 0 Then
                With lvwList
                    .Columns.Add("Last Name", CInt(.Size.Width / 3) - _
                    8, HorizontalAlignment.Left)
                    .Columns.Add("First Name", CInt(.Size.Width / 3) - _
                    8, HorizontalAlignment.Left)
                    .Columns.Add("Title", CInt(.Size.Width / 3) - 8, _
                    HorizontalAlignment.Left)
                End With
            End If

            lvwList.Items.Clear()

            mobjEmployeeMgr = mobjEmployeeMgr.GetInstance
```

```
                    For Each objDictEnt In mobjEmployeeMgr
                        objEmployee = CType(objDictEnt.Value, Employee)
                        Dim lst As New ListViewItem(objEmployee.LastName)
                        lst.Tag = objEmployee.EmployeeID
                        lst.SubItems.Add(objEmployee.FirstName)
                        lst.SubItems.Add(objEmployee.Title)
                        lvwList.Items.Add(lst)
                    Next

                    lvwList.EndUpdate()

                    lblRecordCount.Text = "Record Count: " & lvwList.Items.Count
                Catch exc As Exception
                    LogException(exc)
                End Try
            End Sub


            Protected Overrides Sub AddButton_Click(ByVal sender As Object, _
            ByVal e As System.EventArgs)
                Try
                    If mfrmEdit Is Nothing Then
                        mobjEmployee = New Employee()
                        mfrmEdit = New frmEmployeeEdit(mobjEmployee, _
                        mobjTerritoryMgr)
                        mfrmEdit.MdiParent = Me.MdiParent
                        mfrmEdit.Show()
                    End If
                Catch exc As Exception
                    LogException(exc)
                End Try
            End Sub


            Private Sub mfrmEdit_Closed(ByVal sender As Object, _
            ByVal e As System.EventArgs) Handles mfrmEdit.Closed
                mfrmEdit = Nothing
            End Sub


            Private Sub mobjEmployee_ObjectChanged(ByVal sender As Object, _
            ByVal e As ChangedEventArgs) _
            Handles mobjEmployee.ObjectChanged
                Try
                    Dim lst As ListViewItem
                    Dim objEmployee As Employee = CType(sender, Employee)
```

```vb
            Select Case e.Change
                Case ChangedEventArgs.eChange.Added
                    mobjEmployeeMgr.Add(objEmployee)

                    lst = New ListViewItem(objEmployee.LastName)
                    lst.Tag = objEmployee.EmployeeID
                    lst.SubItems.Add(objEmployee.FirstName)
                    lst.SubItems.Add(objEmployee.Title)
                    lvwList.Items.Add(lst)
                    lblRecordCount.Text = "Record Count: " & _
                    lvwList.Items.Count
                Case ChangedEventArgs.eChange.Updated
                    For Each lst In lvwList.Items
                        If Convert.ToInt32(lst.Tag) = _
                        objEmployee.EmployeeID Then
                            lst.Text = objEmployee.LastName
                            lst.SubItems(1).Text = objEmployee.FirstName
                            lst.SubItems(2).Text = objEmployee.Title
                            Exit For
                        End If
                    Next
            End Select

            lvwList.Sort()
        Catch exc As Exception
            LogException(exc)
        End Try
    End Sub

    Protected Overrides Sub EditButton_Click(ByVal sender As Object, _
    ByVal e As System.EventArgs)
        Try
            If mfrmEdit Is Nothing Then
                If lvwList.SelectedItems.Count > 0 Then
                    Cursor = Cursors.WaitCursor
                    mobjEmployee = _
                    mobjEmployeeMgr.Item(lvwList.SelectedItems(0).Tag)
                    mobjEmployee.LoadRecord(mobjTerritoryMgr)
                    mfrmEdit = New frmEmployeeEdit(mobjEmployee, _
                    mobjTerritoryMgr)
                    mfrmEdit.MdiParent = Me.MdiParent
                    mfrmEdit.Show()
                End If
            End If
```

```vbnet
        Catch exc As Exception
            LogException(exc)
        Finally
            Cursor = Cursors.Default
        End Try
    End Sub

    Protected Overrides Sub DeleteButton_Click(ByVal sender As Object, _
    ByVal e As System.EventArgs)
        Dim objEmployee As Employee
        Dim dlgResult As DialogResult

        Try
            If lvwList.SelectedItems.Count > 0 Then
                objEmployee = _
                mobjEmployeeMgr.Item(lvwList.SelectedItems(0).Tag)
                dlgResult = MessageBox.Show("Do you want to delete " _
                & "employee: " & objEmployee.ToString & "?", _
                "Confirm Delete", MessageBoxButtons.YesNo, _
                MessageBoxIcon.Question)
                If dlgResult = DialogResult.Yes Then
                    objEmployee.Delete()
                    mobjEmployeeMgr.Remove(objEmployee.EmployeeID)
                    lvwList.SelectedItems(0).Remove()
                    lblRecordCount.Text = "Record Count: " _
                    & lvwList.Items.Count
                End If
            End If
        Catch exc As Exception
            LogException(exc)
        End Try
    End Sub
End Class
```

The only difference I will mention is the creation of the TerritoryMgr object. This object must be passed to the edit form—you will see why momentarily. Do not forget to set the text property of the form to *Employee List*. Next you will create your Employee Edit form.

Employee Edit Form

The Employee Edit form is considerably more complicated than what you have
seen before. It also introduces some new concepts and techniques that you have
not covered yet. When you are done creating the Employee Edit form, it looks like
the form in Figure 9-2. To begin, add a new inherited form called *frmEmployeeEdit*.
This form inherits from the frmEditBase form.

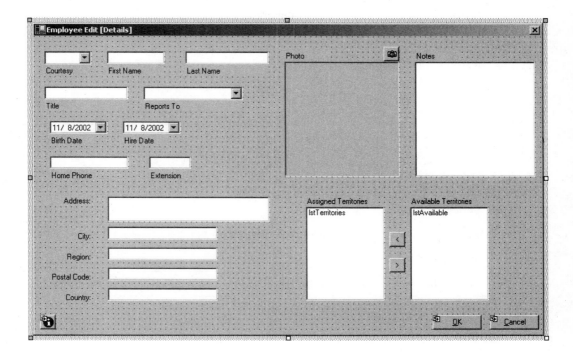

Figure 9-2. The Employee Edit form

To create the form, add the controls and set their properties as in Table 9-2.

Table 9-2. Employee Edit Form Controls

Control	Control Name	Control Text
TextBox	txtFirstName	
TextBox	txtLastName	
TextBox	txtTitle	
TextBox	txtExtension	
TextBox	txtHomePhone	
TextBox	txtAddress	
TextBox	txtCountry	
TextBox	txtPostalCode	
TextBox	txtRegion	
TextBox	txtCity	
ComboBox	cboCourtesy	
ComboBox	cboReportsTo	
PictureBox	picPhoto	
DateTimePicker	dtpBirthDate	
DateTimePicker	dtpHireDate	
RichTextBox	rtbNotes	
Listbox	lstTerritories	
Listbox	lstAvailable	
Button	btnAdd	<
Button	btnRemove	>
Button	btnPhoto	(Camera Image)

Table 9-2. Employee Edit Form Controls (Continued)

Control	Control Name	Control Text
Label	lblFirstName	First Name
Label	lblLastName	Last Name
Label	lblTitle	Title
Label	lblTitleOfCourtesy	Courtesy
Label	lblAddress	Address
Label	lblHireDate	Hire Date
Label	lblBirthDate	Birth Date
Label	lblExtension	Extension
Label	lblHomePhone	Home Phone
Label	lblReportsTo	Reports To
Label	lblRegion	Region
Label	lblPostalCode	Postal Code
Label	lblCountry	Country
Label	lblNotes	Notes
Label	lblPhoto	Photo
Label	lblTerritories	Assigned Territories
Label	lblCity	City
Label	lblAvailable	Available Territories
Form	frmEmployeeEdit	Employee Edit

Remember to set the Icon Alignment on erpMain property to the middle left for all of the controls that can be edited (even if they currently cannot have a business rule violation). Several controls have special properties that need to be set or overridden to work correctly (see Table 9-3).

Table 9-3. Special Properties of the Employee Edit Form Controls

Control	Property	Value	Explanation
cboCourtesy	DropDownStyle	DropDownList	You only want users picking values from the combo box.
cboReportsTo	DropDownStyle	DropDownList	You only want users picking values from the combo box.
txtAddress	Multiline	True	The database stores both lines of the address in one field with a CR/LF to get to the second line of the address.
txtAddress	Icon Alignment on erpMain	TopLeft	Because this is a multiline textbox, you want the icon to show up in the top left instead of the middle of a high text box.
rtbNotes	Icon Alignment on erpMain	TopLeft	Because this is a multiline textbox, you want the icon to show up in the top left instead of the middle of a high text box
cboCourtesy	Items Collection	"Mr.", "Mrs.", "Ms.", "Dr."	List of available values.
lstTerritories	Sorted	True	
lstAvailable	Sorted	True	

Table 9-3. Special Properties of the Employee Edit Form Controls (Continued)

Control	Property	Value	Explanation
frmEmployeeEdit	AcceptButton	None	Any form that contains a multiline textbox or richtextbox control can have the acceptbutton property set, but then the user will not be able to press the Enter key while they are in the textbox or richtextbox to go down to the next line—note that you can change this programmatically if needed.

Also, remember to set the tab order to a logical order. The Windows standard is left to right, top to bottom. The last thing you have to do in the designer is add an OpenFileDialog control to the form. To do this, select and drag the OpenFileDialog from the Toolbox to the form and it will be placed in the nonvisible controls section of the designer. It will be named OpenFileDialog1, and you will use it to select a photo for an employee.

To start off with, your form's code will look similar to what you have seen before. Listing 9-29 shows the header and constructor code.

Listing 9-29. Employee Edit Header and Constructor Code

```
Option Strict On
Option Explicit On

Imports NorthwindTraders.NorthwindUC

Public Class frmEmployeeEdit
    Inherits UserInterface.frmEditBase

    Private WithEvents mobjEmployee As Employee
    Private mblnErrors As Boolean = False
    Private mobjTerritoryMgr As TerritoryMgr
```

```
#Region " Windows Form Designer generated code "

    Public Sub New(ByRef objEmployee As Employee, _
    ByRef objTerritoryMgr As TerritoryMgr)
        MyBase.New()

        'This call is required by the Windows Form Designer.
        InitializeComponent()

        'Add any initialization after the InitializeComponent() call
        mobjEmployee = objEmployee
        mobjTerritoryMgr = objTerritoryMgr

        If Not mobjEmployee.IsValid Then
            btnOK.Enabled = False
        End If
    End Sub
```

There are two small differences in this listing. The first is the inclusion of the mblnErrors variable. You will see the purpose for this variable shortly. The second is the TerritoryMgr object, which is passed ByRef. Because you are not using a Singleton object for the TerritoryMgr, you need to pass this value in to the Employee Edit form. The reason for this is that you need a master list of territories to place in the available territory list. Otherwise, everything is as straightforward as it was before.

The first routine to add is the frmEmployeeEdit_Load method. This method is somewhat more complicated than you have seen before, so let's walk through it here:

```
Private Sub frmEmployeeEdit_Load(ByVal sender As Object, _
ByVal e As System.EventArgs) Handles MyBase.Load
    Dim i As Integer
    Dim strValue As String
    Dim DictEnt As DictionaryEntry
    Dim objEmployeeMgr As EmployeeMgr
        Try
            objEmployeeMgr = objEmployeeMgr.GetInstance
            For Each DictEnt In objEmployeeMgr
                Dim objEmployee As Employee = CType(DictEnt.Value, Employee)
                cboReportsTo.Items.Add(objEmployee)
            Next

            cboReportsTo.Items.Remove(mobjEmployee)
```

In this first section of code, the EmployeeMgr object fills the ReportsTo listbox. At the bottom of this block of code, you remove the employee that you are editing because they cannot report to themselves!

This block loads all of the territories into the available territories list box:

```
For Each DictEnt In mobjTerritoryMgr
    Dim objTerritory As Territory = CType(DictEnt.Value, _
    Territory)
    lstAvailable.Items.Add(objTerritory)
Next
```

Here you loop through the contents of the TitleOfCourtesy combo box and look for the courtesy that applies to this employee and then you select it:

```
With mobjEmployee
    For i = 0 To cboCourtesy.Items.Count - 1
        strValue = CType(cboCourtesy.Items(i), String)
        If strValue = .TitleOfCourtesy Then
            cboCourtesy.SelectedIndex = i
            Exit For
        End If
    Next
```

Here you set the person who the employee reports to, just as in the code to set the title of courtesy:

```
txtFirstName.Text = .FirstName
txtLastName.Text = .LastName
txtTitle.Text = .Title

If Not .ReportsTo Is Nothing Then
    For i = 0 To cboReportsTo.Items.Count - 1
        Dim objEmployee As Employee = _
        CType(cboReportsTo.Items(i), Employee)
        If objEmployee.EmployeeID = .ReportsTo.EmployeeID _
        Then
            cboReportsTo.SelectedIndex = i
            Exit For
        End If
    Next
End If
```

This next code assigns the object values to the controls. Note that for the DateTimePicker controls, you need to specify the Value property, not the text property:

```
dtpBirthDate.Value = .BirthDate
dtpHireDate.Value = .HireDate
txtHomePhone.Text = .HomePhone
txtExtension.Text = .Extension
txtAddress.Text = .Address
txtCity.Text = .City
txtRegion.Text = .Region
txtPostalCode.Text = .PostalCode
txtCountry.Text = .Country
rtbNotes.Text = .Notes
```

The following code loads a photograph if there is one, using the Image.FromStream method. This is a radical change from how images had to be loaded in VB 6 and earlier. You can now take streams of data (assuming they have the correct format), assign them to a picture box, and the control will draw the data. Here you are taking the information from the photo byte array and reading it into a stream format:

```
If Not .Photo Is Nothing Then
    Dim mStream As New IO.MemoryStream(.Photo)
    mStream.Write(.Photo, 0, .Photo.Length - 1)
    picPhoto.Image = Image.FromStream(mStream)
End If
```

This code loads each territory that the employee is associated with into the territories list box and then removes that territory from the list of available territories:

```
            For Each DictEnt In .Territories
                Dim objT As Territory = CType(DictEnt.Value, Territory)
                lstTerritories.Items.Add(objT)
                lstAvailable.Items.Remove(objT)
            Next

        End With
    Catch exc As Exception
        LogException(exc)
    End Try
End Sub
```

Now you need to add the code to take care of associating and removing an employee from an association with a territory (see Listing 9-30).

Listing 9-30. The btnAdd and btnRemove Methods

```
Private Sub btnAdd_Click(ByVal sender As System.Object, _
    ByVal e As System.EventArgs) Handles btnAdd.Click
        Try
            If Not lstAvailable.SelectedItem Is Nothing Then
                lstTerritories.Items.Add(lstAvailable.SelectedItem)
                mobjEmployee.Territories.Add(CType(lstAvailable.SelectedItem, _
                Territory))
                lstAvailable.Items.Remove(lstAvailable.SelectedItem)
            End If
        Catch exc As Exception
            LogException(exc)
        End Try
    End Sub

Private Sub btnRemove_Click(ByVal sender As System.Object, _
    ByVal e As System.EventArgs) Handles btnRemove.Click
        Try
            If Not lstTerritories.SelectedItem Is Nothing Then
                Dim objTerritory As Territory = _
                CType(lstTerritories.SelectedItem, Territory)
                lstAvailable.Items.Add(objTerritory)
                mobjEmployee.Territories.Remove(objTerritory.TerritoryID)
                lstTerritories.Items.Remove(lstTerritories.SelectedItem)
            End If
        Catch exc As Exception
            LogException(exc)
        End Try
    End Sub
```

Listing 9-31 shows the code to add a photograph to your employee.

Listing 9-31. Associating a Photograph with an Employee

```
Private Sub btnPhoto_Click(ByVal sender As System.Object, _
    ByVal e As System.EventArgs) Handles btnPhoto.Click
        Dim bytArray() As Byte
        Try
            With OpenFileDialog1
                .Title = "Select Employee Photo"
                .ShowDialog()
            End With

        If OpenFileDialog1.FileName <> "" Then
            Dim fs As New IO.FileStream(OpenFileDialog1.FileName, _
            IO.FileMode.Open)
            ReDim bytArray(Convert.ToInt32(fs.Length - 1))
            fs.Read(bytArray, 0, bytArray.Length - 1)
            mobjEmployee.Photo = bytArray
            fs.Close()

            picPhoto.Image = Image.FromFile(OpenFileDialog1.FileName)
        End If
        Catch exc As Exception
            LogException(exc)
        End Try
End Sub
```

The first part of the method simply displays an Open File dialog box so that the user can select a photograph. Next, you open the file using a filestream, then you initialize a byte array to the size of the file to hold the image, and then you read the contents of the filestream into the byte array. Finally, you assign the byte array to the photo property and load the picture from the file into the picturebox.

 CAUTION If you try to load the file into the picturebox first and then read it into a byte array, you will receive an error stating that the file is in use.

Listing 9-32 shows the code for the rules button and the broken rule event from your Employee object.

Listing 9-32. Displaying the Business Rules and Enabling/Disabling the OK Button

```
Private Sub btnRules_Click(ByVal sender As System.Object, _
    ByVal e As System.EventArgs) Handles btnRules.Click
        Dim frmRules As New frmBusinessRules(mobjEmployee.GetBusinessRules)
        frmRules.ShowDialog()
        frmRules = Nothing
    End Sub

    Private Sub mobjEmployee_BrokenRule(ByVal IsBroken As Boolean) _
    Handles mobjEmployee.BrokenRule
        If IsBroken Then
            btnOK.Enabled = False
        Else
            btnOK.Enabled = True
        End If
    End Sub
```

Listing 9-33 is the block of code for the validation events for your properties. It is just a lot of code, and it is nothing you have not seen before.

Listing 9-33. The Employee Validation Events

```
#Region " Validate Events"

    Private Sub txtFirstName_Validated(ByVal sender As Object, _
    ByVal e As System.EventArgs) Handles txtFirstName.Validated
        Dim txt As TextBox = CType(sender, TextBox)

        Try
            mobjEmployee.FirstName = txt.Text
            erpmain.SetError(txt, "")
        Catch exc As Exception
            erpmain.SetError(txt, "")
            erpmain.SetError(txt, exc.Message)
        End Try
    End Sub
```

```vb
Private Sub txtLastName_Validated(ByVal sender As Object, _
ByVal e As System.EventArgs) Handles txtLastName.Validated
    Dim txt As TextBox = CType(sender, TextBox)

    Try
        mobjEmployee.LastName = txt.Text
        erpmain.SetError(txt, "")
    Catch exc As Exception
        erpmain.SetError(txt, "")
        erpmain.SetError(txt, exc.Message)
    End Try
End Sub

Private Sub cboCourtesy_Click(ByVal sender As Object, _
ByVal e As System.EventArgs) Handles cboCourtesy.Validated
    Dim cbo As ComboBox = CType(sender, ComboBox)

    Try
        mobjEmployee.TitleOfCourtesy = cbo.Text
        erpmain.SetError(cbo, "")
    Catch exc As Exception
        erpmain.SetError(cbo, "")
        erpmain.SetError(cbo, exc.Message)
    End Try
End Sub

Private Sub txtTitle_TextChanged(ByVal sender As System.Object, _
ByVal e As System.EventArgs) Handles txtTitle.Validated
    Dim txt As TextBox = CType(sender, TextBox)

    Try
        mobjEmployee.Title = txt.Text
        erpmain.SetError(txt, "")
    Catch exc As Exception
        erpmain.SetError(txt, "")
        erpmain.SetError(txt, exc.Message)
    End Try
End Sub
```

```vb
Private Sub cboReportsTo_Click(ByVal sender As Object, _
ByVal e As System.EventArgs) Handles cboReportsTo.Validated
    Dim cbo As ComboBox = CType(sender, ComboBox)

    Try
        mobjEmployee.ReportsTo = CType(cbo.SelectedItem, Employee)
        erpmain.SetError(cbo, "")
    Catch exc As Exception
        erpmain.SetError(cbo, "")
        erpmain.SetError(cbo, exc.Message)
    End Try
End Sub


Private Sub dtpBirthDate_Validated(ByVal sender As Object, _
ByVal e As System.EventArgs) Handles dtpBirthDate.Validated
    Dim dtp As DateTimePicker = CType(sender, DateTimePicker)

    Try
        mobjEmployee.BirthDate = dtp.Value
        erpmain.SetError(dtp, "")
    Catch exc As Exception
        erpmain.SetError(dtp, "")
        erpmain.SetError(dtp, exc.Message)
    End Try
End Sub


Private Sub dtpHireDate_Validated(ByVal sender As Object, _
ByVal e As System.EventArgs) Handles dtpHireDate.Validated
    Dim dtp As DateTimePicker = CType(sender, DateTimePicker)

    Try
        mobjEmployee.HireDate = dtp.Value
        erpmain.SetError(dtp, "")
    Catch exc As Exception
        erpmain.SetError(dtp, "")
        erpmain.SetError(dtp, exc.Message)
    End Try
End Sub
```

```
Private Sub txtHomePhone_Validated(ByVal sender As Object, _
ByVal e As System.EventArgs) Handles txtHomePhone.Validated
    Dim txt As TextBox = CType(sender, TextBox)

    Try
        mobjEmployee.HomePhone = txt.Text
        erpmain.SetError(txt, "")
    Catch exc As Exception
        erpmain.SetError(txt, "")
        erpmain.SetError(txt, exc.Message)
    End Try
End Sub

Private Sub txtExtension_Validated(ByVal sender As Object, _
ByVal e As System.EventArgs) Handles txtExtension.Validated
    Dim txt As TextBox = CType(sender, TextBox)

    Try
        mobjEmployee.Extension = txt.Text
        erpmain.SetError(txt, "")
    Catch exc As Exception
        erpmain.SetError(txt, "")
        erpmain.SetError(txt, exc.Message)
    End Try
End Sub

Private Sub txtAddress_Validated(ByVal sender As Object, _
ByVal e As System.EventArgs) Handles txtAddress.Validated
    Dim txt As TextBox = CType(sender, TextBox)

    Try
        mobjEmployee.Address = txt.Text
        erpmain.SetError(txt, "")
    Catch exc As Exception
        erpmain.SetError(txt, "")
        erpmain.SetError(txt, exc.Message)
    End Try
End Sub
```

```vbnet
Private Sub txtCountry_Validated(ByVal sender As Object, _
ByVal e As System.EventArgs) Handles txtCountry.Validated
    Dim txt As TextBox = CType(sender, TextBox)

    Try
        mobjEmployee.Country = txt.Text
        erpmain.SetError(txt, "")
    Catch exc As Exception
        erpmain.SetError(txt, "")
        erpmain.SetError(txt, exc.Message)
    End Try
End Sub

Private Sub txtPostalCode_Validated(ByVal sender As Object, _
ByVal e As System.EventArgs) Handles txtPostalCode.Validated
    Dim txt As TextBox = CType(sender, TextBox)

    Try
        mobjEmployee.PostalCode = txt.Text
        erpmain.SetError(txt, "")
    Catch exc As Exception
        erpmain.SetError(txt, "")
        erpmain.SetError(txt, exc.Message)
    End Try
End Sub

Private Sub txtRegion_Validated(ByVal sender As Object, _
ByVal e As System.EventArgs) Handles txtRegion.Validated
    Dim txt As TextBox = CType(sender, TextBox)

    Try
        mobjEmployee.Region = txt.Text
        erpmain.SetError(txt, "")
    Catch exc As Exception
        erpmain.SetError(txt, "")
        erpmain.SetError(txt, exc.Message)
    End Try
End Sub
```

```
Private Sub txtCity_Validated(ByVal sender As Object, _
ByVal e As System.EventArgs) Handles txtCity.Validated
    Dim txt As TextBox = CType(sender, TextBox)

    Try
        mobjEmployee.City = txt.Text
        erpmain.SetError(txt, "")
    Catch exc As Exception
        erpmain.SetError(txt, "")
        erpmain.SetError(txt, exc.Message)
    End Try
End Sub

Private Sub rtbNotes_Validated(ByVal sender As Object, _
ByVal e As System.EventArgs) Handles rtbNotes.Validated
    Dim rtb As RichTextBox = CType(sender, RichTextBox)

    Try
        mobjEmployee.Notes = rtb.Text
        erpmain.SetError(rtb, "")
    Catch exc As Exception
        erpmain.SetError(rtb, "")
        erpmain.SetError(rtb, exc.Message)
    End Try
End Sub

#End Region
```

Finally, you get to the OK button click event, which is shown in Listing 9-34. There is one difference in this method that you have not seen before.

Listing 9-34. The OK Button Click Event

```
Private Sub btnOK_Click(ByVal sender As System.Object, _
    ByVal e As System.EventArgs) Handles btnOK.Click
    Try
        If mobjEmployee.IsDirty Then
            Cursor = Cursors.WaitCursor
            mblnErrors = False
            mobjEmployee.Save()
        End If
```

```
        If Not mblnErrors Then
            Close()
        End If
    Catch exc As Exception
        LogException(exc)
    Finally
        Cursor = Cursors.Default
    End Try
End Sub
```

This is the first time you are not just automatically closing the form, which you did on the two previous edit forms. This is because this is the first time that you can break a rule on the server that you cannot break on the workstation.

> **NOTE** This does not mean that the previous two edit forms should not be set up this way. In a real application, all edit forms, even the ones that share identical rules between the data-centric and user-centric classes, should be set up this way. What if you decide to add additional business logic later? Then you are in for a lot of rework.

So, where does the mblnErrors variable get set? The answer is in Listing 9-35, which you have also not implemented up to this point.

Listing 9-35. Trapping Employee Server-Side Errors

```
Private Sub mobjEmployee_Errs(ByVal obj As _
NorthwindTraders.NorthwindShared.Errors.BusinessErrors) Handles _
mobjEmployee.Errs
    Try
        Dim i As Integer
        Dim ctl As Control

        For Each ctl In Me.Controls
            If TypeOf ctl Is TextBox Or TypeOf ctl Is ComboBox _
            Or TypeOf ctl Is RichTextBox Then
                erpMain.SetError(ctl, "")
            End If
        Next
```

```
For i = 0 To obj.Count - 1
    Select Case obj.Item(i).errProperty
        Case "Last Name"
            erpMain.SetError(Me.txtLastName, _
            obj.Item(i).errMessage)
        Case "First Name"
            erpMain.SetError(Me.txtFirstName, _
            obj.Item(i).errMessage)
        Case "Title"
            erpMain.SetError(Me.txtTitle, _
            obj.Item(i).errMessage)
        Case "Title Of Courtesy"
            erpMain.SetError(Me.cboCourtesy, _
            obj.Item(i).errMessage)
        Case "Birth Date"
            erpMain.SetError(Me.dtpBirthDate, _
            obj.Item(i).errMessage)
        Case "Hire Date"
            erpMain.SetError(Me.dtpHireDate, _
            obj.Item(i).errMessage)
        Case "Address"
            erpMain.SetError(Me.txtAddress, _
            obj.Item(i).errMessage)
        Case "City"
            erpMain.SetError(Me.txtCity, _
            obj.Item(i).errMessage)
        Case "Region"
            erpMain.SetError(Me.txtRegion, _
            obj.Item(i).errMessage)
        Case "Postal Code"
            erpMain.SetError(Me.txtPostalCode, _
            obj.Item(i).errMessage)
        Case "Country"
            erpMain.SetError(Me.txtCountry, _
            obj.Item(i).errMessage)
        Case "Home Phone"
            erpMain.SetError(Me.txtHomePhone, _
            obj.Item(i).errMessage)
        Case "Extension"
            erpMain.SetError(Me.txtExtension, _
            obj.Item(i).errMessage)
```

```
                Case "Notes"
                        erpMain.SetError(Me.rtbNotes, _
                        obj.Item(i).errMessage)
                Case "Territories"
                        erpMain.SetError(Me.lstTerritories, _
                        obj.Item(i).errMessage)
            End Select
        Next
        mblnErrors = True
    Catch exc As Exception
        logexception(exc)
    End Try
End Sub
```

The For..Each block of code simply clears any existing errors from each of the controls. The Select..Case block of code is the one that some people may chastise me for because it sort of ties the data-centric objects to the user interface. The property name that the code is looking for is the property name that you gave to the attribute in the data-centric object, which means that the user interface needs to know what an object two layers away is doing with it. To create an efficient error handling routine that reports all of the errors at once, this is the only way to do it. Now, with .NET you can get really fancy and play some neat tricks with attributes on class members (which you will see in the next chapter), but you still need to know something about the class—period. The reason why I said this *sort of* ties the user interface to the data-centric objects is because your user interface does not have to do anything with this information.

Next you set the errors flag so that the form will not close. Listing 9-36 shows the code for the Closing event of the edit form.

Listing 9-36. Employee Edit Form Closing Event

```
Private Sub frmEmployeeEdit_Closing(ByVal sender As Object, ByVal e As _
System.ComponentModel.CancelEventArgs) Handles MyBase.Closing
    Dim dlgResult As DialogResult

    Try
        If mobjEmployee.IsDirty Then
            dlgResult = MessageBox.Show("The Employee information has " _
            & "changed, do you want to exit without saving your " _
            & "changes?", "Confirm Cancel", MessageBoxButtons.YesNo, _
            MessageBoxIcon.Question)
```

```
                    If dlgResult = DialogResult.No Then
                        e.Cancel = True
                    Else
                        mobjEmployee.Rollback(mobjTerritoryMgr)
                    End If
            End If
        Catch exc As Exception
            LogException(exc)
        End Try
End Sub
```

As with our other forms, you simply check the status of our object so that the form does not close prematurely.

Testing the Employee Maintenance Function

As before, you need to make an entry in the database and add some code to frmMain to be able to test your Employee objects. Take the following steps to test the Employee objects:

1. Rebuild the solution.

2. Copy the NorthwindDC and NorthwindShared objects to the \bin folder in IIS.

3. Edit the web.config file and add the following wellknown tag:

```
<wellknown mode="Singleton"
    type="NorthwindTraders.NorthwindDC.EmployeeDC, NorthwindDC"
    objectUri="EmployeeDC.rem"/>
```

4. Next, edit frmMain and add a new Case statement to the MainMenu_Click method as follows:

```
Case "&Employees"
    LoadEmployees()
```

5. Add a new module-level variable to frmMain for the frmEmployeeList form:

```
Private WithEvents mfrmEmployeeList As frmEmployeeList
```

6. Next, add a LoadEmployees method as shown in Listing 9-37.

Listing 9-37. The LoadEmployees Method

```
Private Sub LoadEmployees()
    Try
        If mfrmEmployeeList Is Nothing Then
            Cursor = Cursors.WaitCursor
            mfrmEmployeeList = New frmEmployeeList()
            mfrmEmployeeList.MdiParent = Me
            mfrmEmployeeList.Show()
        Else
            mfrmEmployeeList.Focus()
        End If
    Catch exc As Exception
        LogException(exc)
    Finally
        Cursor = Cursors.Default
    End Try
End Sub
```

The last thing you need to do is add a method that sets the mfrmEmployeeList equal to nothing when the Employee List form closes:

```
Private Sub mfrmEmployeeList_Closed(ByVal sender As Object, _
ByVal e As System.EventArgs) Handles mfrmEmployeeList.Closed
    mfrmEmployeeList = Nothing
End Sub
```

Now you can run the application and play with it a little. To see how the server-side errors are handled, change the birth date to the current day. No error will be generated until you click the OK button; then you will see the error returned by the server!

CAUTION   The beta version of .NET 1.1 this was tested against produced an interesting error. When you try to save an employee record with no photo, it fails. Trying this in version 1.0 worked fine, though. The reason it is failing is because even when you assign a value of DBNull.Value to a photo parameter, it actually assigns a value of " ." and there is no way to get rid of it.

Summary

This chapter has shown you different techniques for dealing with the differences between server-side and client-side business rules. Having looked at the amount of business rules for an object as simple as the Employee object, you have seen how important business rules are and that in the majority of applications, they are the application.

You have covered one way of performing object aggregation and you have examined some of the pros and cons of this method. You have also briefly touched on some other methods of aggregating objects. This gives you a solid point of reference on how to perform this task in your own applications.

You learned how to easily load and save image information to and from SQL Server and how to display that information in a picture box control.

At this point, you have built as much of the NorthwindTraders application as you will be building in this book. The rest of the book concentrates on streamlining code using reflection, creating and consuming a Web service, building a Web site using your already-built components, and localizing the application for use in Spanish and French.

In the next chapter, you will see how to use reflection to achieve a marked reduction in the number of lines of code that you write. You will actually be able to quantify the amount of lines of code saved and what you will see is an application that is maintained much more easily and efficiently.

CHAPTER 10

Using Reflection

REFLECTION IS THE ABILITY of code to examine itself. The fact that code has the ability to examine itself should come as no surprise because this ability is needed for even such mundane tasks as figuring out the particular address of a method that needs to be called. But Microsoft has taken the mundane and made it spectacular. Microsoft has given you the ability to examine code. The fact that code has knowledge of itself is nothing new, but just because the code knew about itself did not mean you could get that information. And then Microsoft introduced one more awesome ability: You can create custom attributes with which to tag your code, and you can read these attributes using reflection. This is something unique to the .NET Framework.

NOTE To be fair, Java has had reflection since its inception, but Java does not give the developer the ability to create custom attributes. So you can examine the code all you want to determine things about it, but you cannot say anything about it.

In this chapter you will examine reflection in the context of two practical examples. The first example demonstrates reading from attributes to determine how to load a listview without knowing anything about the object that you are taking data from and without knowing anything about the data itself. This project is a small, independent demonstration. For the second example you will incorporate attribute classes into your application in the RegionDescription class. This example shows you how to turn the business rules that you have created into custom attributes and make the class truly self-aware.

TIP After developing this method of implementing business rules, my team and I were able to save approximately 30,000 lines of code in a recent project. We were able to quantify this by extrapolating out the amount of code we saved after converting just a few classes to this method. This also made maintenance of the application much simpler!

Generating Code Dynamically

One other ability of reflection that I wanted to mention (but that I will not cover in this book) is the ability to dynamically create code. The namespace that contains the classes necessary to do this is the Reflection.Emit namespace. Dynamic generation of code can get very complicated, so you should be careful about using this ability, but you can do some incredible things with it. Imagine if you have an application that performs complex calculations, but you do not necessarily know what all of those calculations are beforehand. Say you have given the users the ability to create calculations later and specify how the application processes the calculation. To do this you might take a calculation and dynamically generate the code needed to process the calculation, and then you gain the ability for an application to be expanded without any additional coding by a developer!

I do not expect this ability to catch on overnight because it is a highly complex area of development. To develop code using Reflection.Emit, you need to know a great deal about the Microsoft Intermediate Language (MSIL). An excellent book on the subject is *Compiling for the .NET Common Language Runtime* by John Gough (Prentice Hall, 2001).

Understanding Attribute Classes

The root of all reflection is the System.Attribute class. An attribute class provides information about a coding construct. So what is an attribute class? An *attribute class* is a class you can create and, for lack of a better description, "attach" to anything. You could attach them to a class, property, method, structure, enum, and so on. You can designate properties that only allow an attribute class to be attached to certain types of code structures or to everything—it is completely up to you. And how does this help you? It allows you to describe, or give additional properties to, a specific piece of code. Using reflection, you can examine these classes to learn information about your code elements.

NOTE Attribute classes are passive. That is, they are compiled into the code, and they cannot *react* to changes in data—they can only examine the data after the fact. So, if you need to stop a property from being changed unless it follows certain rules (as opposed to changing the value and marking it as a broken rule), you need to use a combination of attribute classes and business rule checking as shown in earlier chapters.

Used properly, reflection can make classes more flexible and more reusable. It can also give you the ability to dynamically generate information based on your classes. The example you will see first demonstrates that ability. After you have worked through this example, you will probably find some creative ways to use this unique and awesome ability of the .NET Framework.

Setting Up the Scenario

Let's say, for the sake of argument, that you have a bunch of classes you want to display in forms that contain listviews. And let's say that you only want to write the load routine once so that it can be used on all of the list forms in such a way that each developer does not have to come up with their own code to create and fill that list form. Does this sound familiar? If you have worked through the first nine chapters of this book, you will understand this scenario. You had to code each of the load listview routines. Now, expand that out by 20 or 30 forms…. Extrapolating out what you have created so far, each load list routine minus comments and empty lines, is approximately 30 lines of code. If you have 20 forms in an application that do the same thing, that is 600 lines of code that can be removed from the application if you implement this using reflection! And let me say that this is only the tip of the iceberg.

 CAUTION   After seeing what you can do with this ability, you might be encouraged to start doing everything with reflection—do not. Reflection is great for certain tasks, but for other tasks it is a great deal more work than it is worth. Also, planning these types of classes correctly takes time. So, before you decide to start implementing attribute classes all over the place, think about the complexity and maintainability of the application. In general, reflection allows you to consume classes by using generic routines that do not have to be customized for each implementation.

The way this attribute class works is the following: You will attach an attribute class to each property you want to display in the listview. The listview load method looks in your class and determines which properties to add to the listview as columns. It creates those columns and then adds the values of the object to the listview. Once you have created this method the first time, it is a cinch to reuse it.

Setting Up the Project

Create a new Windows application and call it *ClassAttributeDemo*. Add a new class to the project and call it *ListAttributes*. On the default form that is created, add the controls and set the properties as shown in Table 10-1.

Table 10-1. Form Controls for the ClassAttributeDemo Application

Control	Name	Property	Value
Form1	frmList	Text	Class Attribute Demo
Listview	lvwList	View	Details
Button	btnComputers	Text	Computer List
Button	btnBooks	Text	Book List

When you are done, the form should look like Figure 10-1.

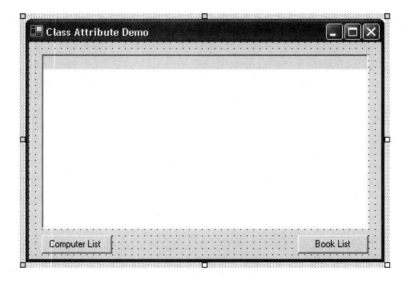

Figure 10-1. The ClassAttributeDemo application

Creating the Attribute Class

Open up the ListAttribute code module and alter the class signature so that it reads as follows:

```
<AttributeUsage(AttributeTargets.Property)> _
Public Class ListAttribute
     Inherits System.Attribute

End Class
```

The AttributeUsage tag turns a class into an attribute class. The enumerated value, AttributeTargets, allows you to specify what type of code block can be the target of this class. The valid values are as follows:

All	Interface
Assembly	Method
Class	Module
Constructor	Parameter
Delegate	Property
Enum	ReturnValue
Event	Struct
Field	

In this case, you are saying that this class can only be applied to a property. Notice also that your class inherits from the System.Attribute class. This marks your class as an attribute in .NET.

NOTE By convention, all attribute classes should have a suffix of *Attribute*, but when you associate them with a method, you do not have to specify the word *Attribute*. You will see an example of this in Listing 10-2.

So, what properties would you need to do what you want to do? Well, you really only need two properties: one to hold the header text and the other to hold the order in which the properties get added to the listview. So, to do this, let's add the following properties and constructor to the ListAttribute class:

```
Public Heading As String
Public Column As Integer

Public Sub New(ByVal Header As String, ByVal Col As Integer)
    Heading = Header
    Column = Col
End Sub
```

That was pretty easy—you are done with your ListAttribute class. You can see that these classes can be easy to create. Or, as with an attribute class that you have already seen—the SerializableAttribute class used for your BusinessErrors class—they can be very complex.

Creating the ComputerList Class

Add a new class to the project and call it *ComputerList*. To keep this simple, use the code in Listing 10-1 for the class.

Listing 10-1. The ComputerList Class

```
Public Class ComputerList
    Private mstrName As String
    Private mstrProc As String
    Private mdblSpeed As Double
    Private mdblPrice As Double
    Private mstrManuf As String

    Public ReadOnly Property Proc() As String
        Get
            Return mstrProc
        End Get
    End Property

    Public ReadOnly Property Speed() As Double
        Get
            Return mdblSpeed
        End Get
    End Property

    Public ReadOnly Property Cname() As String
        Get
            Return mstrName
        End Get
    End Property
```

```vbnet
    Public ReadOnly Property Price() As Double
        Get
            Return mdblPrice
        End Get
    End Property


    Public ReadOnly Property Manufacturer() As String
        Get
            Return mstrManuf
        End Get
    End Property


    Public Sub New(ByVal Name As String, ByVal Process As String, _
    ByVal Sp As Double, ByVal Pr As Double, ByVal Man As String)
        mstrName = Name
        mstrProc = Process
        mdblSpeed = Sp
        mdblPrice = Pr
        mstrManuf = Man
    End Sub
End Class
```

This simple class has five private variables and five public read-only variables. The variables all get set in the constructor. Next, you are going to tag three of the properties with your ListAttribute class so that only those three properties show up in the list. Add a List tag in front of the properties Cname, Process, and Speed so that each property looks like that in Listing 10-2.

Listing 10-2. Three Properties with the ListAttribute Applied

```vbnet
<List("Processor", 1)> Public ReadOnly Property Proc() As String
    Get
        Return mstrProc
    End Get
End Property


<List("Speed", 2)> Public ReadOnly Property Speed() As Double
    Get
        Return mdblSpeed
    End Get
End Property
```

```
<List("Computer Name", 0)> Public ReadOnly Property Cname() As String
    Get
            Return mstrName
    End Get
End Property
```

You will note that when you open the attribute tag (<) only the word *List* appears in the list of available attributes not the whole class name, *ListAttribute*. As mentioned previously, the word *Attribute* is dropped from the end of the attribute class. That is all you need to do to set up the ComputerList class. Now you need to create a collection class to hold a couple of values.

Create a class (in the same code module as the ComputerList class) called *ComputerListMgr* that inherits from the CollectionBase class. Use the code in Listing 10-3.

Listing 10-3. The ComputerListMgr Class

```
Public Class ComputerListMgr
    Inherits System.Collections.CollectionBase

    Public Sub Add(ByVal obj As ComputerList)
        list.Add(obj)
    End Sub

    Public Sub Remove(ByVal Index As Integer)
        list.RemoveAt(Index)
    End Sub

    Public Function Item(ByVal Index As Integer) As ComputerList
        Return CType(list.Item(Index), ComputerList)
    End Function
End Class
```

Examining Property Attributes in Code

Before getting into examining property attributes in code, you need to be aware that you cannot set Option Strict to On.

CAUTION To elaborate, you cannot set Option Strict to On in the code module where you process the property attributes. This is because the type of reflection you are performing requires late binding. In general, this is not a good practice, but it is acceptable in this situation.

Now, having said that, let's start coding. Go into the form code module and import the System.Reflection namespace. Next, add a module-level variable for the ComputerListMgr as follows:

```
Private mobjCLMgr As ComputerListMgr
```

Add the code in Listing 10-4 to the frmList class.

Listing 10-4. The btnComputers_Click Method

```
Private Sub btnComputers_Click(ByVal sender As Object, _
ByVal e As System.EventArgs) Handles btnComputers.Click
    Dim t As Type = GetType(ComputerList)
    mobjCLMgr = New ComputerListMgr()

    mobjCLMgr.Add(New ComputerList("Lightning", "P4", 1.4, 699.0, "Dell"))
    mobjCLMgr.Add(New ComputerList("Thunder", "P4", 1.7, 799.0, "Dell"))
    LoadList(t, CType(mobjCLMgr, CollectionBase))
End Sub
```

The first line of this code gets the type of the ComputerList class and stores it in a type variable. Next you instantiate the computer list manager and add two items to the collection. Finally you call the LoadList method (which you will code next) and pass in your object type and your collection. Notice, however, that you are passing your manager in as a CollectionBase object. In a real application, you would probably want to overload this method to accept virtually any type of collection. The reason why you are passing in generic values is so that the LoadList method remains as flexible as possible. Listing 10-5 contains the code for the LoadList method. Do not panic! You will get an explanation of everything line by line after the listing.

Listing 10-5. The LoadList Method

```
Private Sub LoadList(ByVal t As Type, ByRef col As CollectionBase)
    Dim p As PropertyInfo()
    Dim i, j As Integer
    Dim SortedL As New Collections.SortedList()

    lvwList.Clear

    p = t.GetProperties(BindingFlags.Public Or BindingFlags.Instance)

    For i = 0 To p.Length - 1
        Dim a As Object()
        a = p(i).GetCustomAttributes(False)
        If a.Length > 0 Then
            For j = 0 To a.Length - 1
                If a(j).GetType Is GetType(ListAttribute) Then
                    Dim la As ListAttribute = CType(a(j), ListAttribute)
                    SortedL.Add(la.Column, p(i))
                End If
            Next
        End If
    Next

    For i = 0 To SortedL.Count - 1
        Dim pi As PropertyInfo = CType(SortedL.Item(i), PropertyInfo)
        Dim a As Object = pi.GetCustomAttributes(False)
        For j = 0 To a.Length - 1
            If a(j).GetType Is GetType(ListAttribute) Then
                Dim la As ListAttribute = CType(a(j), ListAttribute)
                lvwList.Columns.Add(la.Heading, _
                lvwList.Width / SortedL.Count - 2, _
                HorizontalAlignment.Left)
                Exit For
            End If
        Next
    Next

    Dim obj As Object
    Dim myObject() As Object
```

```
    For Each obj In col
        Dim cl As Object = Convert.ChangeType(obj, t)
        Dim k As Integer
        Dim lst As New ListViewItem()
        For i = 0 To SortedL.Count - 1
            Dim pr As PropertyInfo = CType(SortedL.Item(i), PropertyInfo)
            Dim strValue As String = ""
            strValue = Convert.ToString(t.InvokeMember(pr.Name, _
            BindingFlags.GetProperty, Nothing, cl, myObject))
            If i = 0 Then
                lst.SubItems(i).Text = strValue
            Else
                lst.SubItems.Add(strValue)
            End If
        Next
        lvwList.Items.Add(lst)
    Next
End Sub
```

So now that you think you may be lost, let's try to straighten everything out and explain what is going on here. The first line declares an array of PropertyInfo variables. The PropertyInfo type holds information about—you guessed it—properties. The i and j variables are just counter variables. The SortedL variable stores the properties in the order you have specified they be displayed in (by way of your attribute settings in the ComputerList class). You will see this in action in a minute. Then you clear the listview of all of its current contents—headers and all:

```
Dim p As PropertyInfo()
Dim i, j As Integer
Dim SortedL As New Collections.SortedList()

lvwList.Clear
```

This next line calls the GetProperties method on your type variable. So this line reads, "Get all of the properties of the type (in this case, the ComputerList class) that are public or instance properties." This method returns an array of PropertyInfo types:

```
p = t.GetProperties(BindingFlags.Public Or BindingFlags.Instance)
```

The next block of code continues your process of discovering information about the properties. First, you start by looping through the array of PropertyInfo values:

```
For i = 0 To p.Length - 1
```

The variable a is an object array to hold all of the custom attributes on the specific property:

```
Dim a As Object()
```

The GetCustomAttributes returns an object array because there may be several types of attributes associated with the property you are examining. The False parameter indicates that you do not want to look at any other property values in the inheritance chain for this class:

```
a = p(i).GetCustomAttributes(False)
```

Now you check the length of the array to see if there were any custom attributes associated with the property. Remember, for your class there are only three: the Cname, Proc, and Speed properties:

```
If a.Length > 0 Then
```

If it does find at least one custom attribute, you loop through the array of custom attributes:

```
For j = 0 To a.Length - 1
```

Here you check the type of custom attribute. This is the only known type in the entire method:

```
If a(j).GetType Is GetType(ListAttribute) Then
```

If the custom attribute is of type ListAttribute, then you convert that custom attribute into a value that you can manipulate easily by performing a ctype on it:

```
Dim la As ListAttribute = CType(a(j), ListAttribute)
```

Finally, you add the column number as the key in the sorted list, and you add the PropertyInfo variable as the object in the sorted list so you can reference it later:

```
SortedL.Add(la.Column, p(i))
```

The next block of code adds the column headers to the listview. You start by looping through the sorted list collection and retrieving the PropertyInfo objects. Then you get the custom attributes of the property. Next, you again loop through the custom attributes looking for the ListAttribute. When you find it, you convert it into a ListAttribute variable and extract the heading name. When this block of code finishes executing, the column headers will have been added to the listview:

```
For i = 0 To SortedL.Count - 1
    Dim pi As PropertyInfo = CType(SortedL.Item(i), PropertyInfo)
    Dim a As Object = pi.GetCustomAttributes(False)
    For j = 0 To a.Length - 1
        If a(j).GetType Is GetType(ListAttribute) Then
            Dim la As ListAttribute = CType(a(j), ListAttribute)
            lvwList.Columns.Add(la.Heading, _
            lvwList.Width / SortedL.Count - 2, _
            HorizontalAlignment.Left)
            Exit For
        End If
    Next
Next
```

The obj variable helps you iterate through the ComputerListMgr collection. Because you only know that this is a collection, you cannot use a For Next loop to iterate through the collection. You can only use the For Each enumeration. And because you do not know what type of object is returned to you by the collection (remember, this is a wholly generic routine, so you cannot declare a variable of type ComputerList anywhere), you need to use an object variable. The myObject object array is used as a parameter to the InvokeMethod call. It is a throwaway variable:

```
Dim obj As Object
Dim myObject() As Object
```

Finally, you get to the block of code that adds the values from the collection into the listview. Before you start examining this block of code, think about what it is doing. You are taking a collection that you know nothing about, that stores objects you know nothing about, and that has properties you know nothing about and extracting that data and placing it in a listview! This block of code, in a nutshell, shows exactly how powerful the .NET Framework can be when used to its fullest potential.

Let's now look at what is happening here. The For Each statement, as mentioned earlier, is the only way to iterate through your collection object:

```
For Each obj In col
```

The cl variable is an object that you are converting to the type you have passed in to the method—in this case, the ComputerList type. You do this using the ChangeType method of the Convert class. This is an example of late binding and the chief reason you cannot use Option Strict On in this code module:

```
Dim cl As Object = Convert.ChangeType(obj, t)
```

The k variable is just a counter variable, and lst is the listviewitem you will be adding to the listview:

```
Dim k As Integer
Dim lst As New ListViewItem()
```

Next you loop through the sorted list collection (yet again) to get the properties for which you need to retrieve the values:

```
For i = 0 To SortedL.Count - 1
```

This line retrieves the PropertyInfo from the sorted list collection:

```
Dim pr As PropertyInfo = CType(SortedL.Item(i), PropertyInfo)
```

StrValue holds the value you retrieve from whatever property you are calling. It is initialized to an empty string because you may have a property that was not set and this would leave strValue with a value of nothing, which you absolutely do not want:

```
Dim strValue As String = ""
```

This next line is the workhorse of this method. This line says the following: "Call the method whose name is returned by PropertyInfo variable (pr). Look for this method in the class's collection of properties using the default binder (do not worry about what this is right now, for more information check the MSDN documentation). Call this method on the given object (cl) with the parameters given in myObject and store the return value in the string variable strValue." That was a handful to say the least. The myObject array would, if you were calling a method that required parameters to be passed to it, contain a list of values to pass in to the method:

```
strValue = Convert.ToString(t.InvokeMember(pr.Name, _
BindingFlags.GetProperty, Nothing, cl, myObject))
```

If this is the first time through the loop, assign the value to item 0 of the sub-items collection (because you already instantiated the lst variable previously); otherwise, add a new subitem to the listviewitem. Finally, add the listviewitem to the listview:

```
    If i = 0 Then
        lst.SubItems(i).Text = strValue
    Else
        lst.SubItems.Add(strValue)
    End If
Next
lvwList.Items.Add(lst)
```

Now, if you have not done so yet, run the application and click the Computer List button. The result should look something like Figure 10-2.

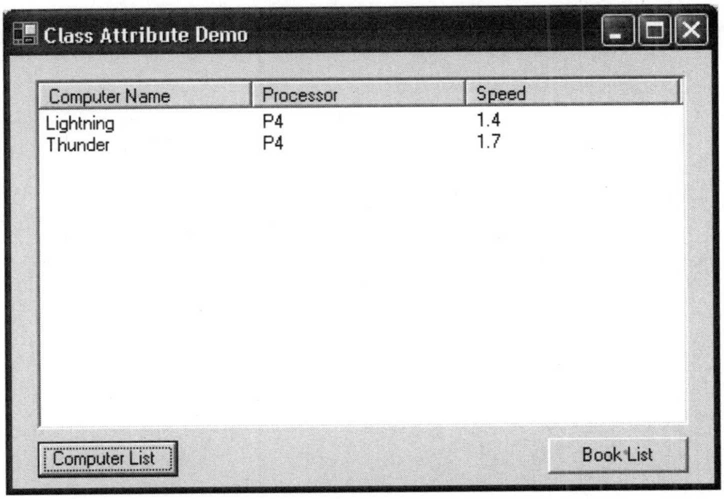

Figure 10-2. List of computers displayed by the LoadList method

Now, as a test, edit the ComputerList class and change the order you would like things to display on the screen (by changing the numeric value in the List Attribute tag) and run the application again. Pretty neat, huh?

Listing 10-6 contains the code for the BookList class and the BookListMgr class. They are the same as what you have just done, but they have different properties.

Listing 10-6. The BookList and BookListMgr Classes

```
Public Class BookList
    Private mstrTitle As String
    Private mstrAuthor As String
    Private mdblPrice As Double
    Private mstrPublisher As String

    Public ReadOnly Property Price() As Double
        Get
            Return mdblPrice
        End Get
    End Property

    Public ReadOnly Property Publisher() As String
        Get
            Return mstrPublisher
        End Get
    End Property

    <List("Author", 1)> Public ReadOnly Property Author() As String
        Get
            Return mstrAuthor
        End Get
    End Property

    <List("Book Title", 0)> Public ReadOnly Property Title() As String
        Get
            Return mstrTitle
        End Get
    End Property

    Public Sub New(ByVal sTitle As String, ByVal sAuthor As String, _
    ByVal dPrice As Double, ByVal sPub As String)
        mstrTitle = sTitle
        mstrAuthor = sAuthor
        mdblPrice = dPrice
        mstrPublisher = sPub
    End Sub

End Class
```

```
Public Class BookListMgr
    Inherits System.Collections.CollectionBase

    Public Sub Add(ByVal obj As BookList)
        list.Add(obj)
    End Sub

    Public Sub Remove(ByVal Index As Integer)
        list.RemoveAt(Index)
    End Sub

    Public Function Item(ByVal Index As Integer) As BookList
        Return CType(list.Item(Index), BookList)
    End Function
End Class
```

Next, add the following module-level declaration in frmList:

```
Private mobjBKMgr As BookListMgr
```

Finally, Listing 10-7 shows the code for the btnBooks_Click method.

Listing 10-7. The btnBooks_Click Method

```
Private Sub btnBooks_Click(ByVal sender As Object, _
ByVal e As System.EventArgs) Handles btnBooks.Click
    Dim t As Type = GetType(BookList)
    mobjBKMgr = New BookListMgr()

    mobjBKMgr.Add(New BookList("Life With .NET", "Anonymous", 49.95, _
    "Apress"))
    mobjBKMgr.Add(New BookList("Life With Java", "Unknown", 19.95, _
    "ABC Publishing"))
    LoadList(t, CType(mobjBKMgr, CollectionBase))
End Sub
```

Now try running the application and clicking either button. Try changing the methods with which the custom attributes are associated. No matter what you do, this code will work.

Implementing Business Rules Using Custom Attributes

To work through this example, you will need to complete the coding up through the first part of Chapter 8, "Reusing Code." When you are done with this example you will have created a set of classes that you can reuse in your own projects to implement business rules.

NOTE   I found the basis for this code online at the Newtelligence AG company (http://www.newtelligence.com), which built this code in C# as the basis for a Web security interface application. I converted this code to Visual Basic and enhanced it to fit within the framework of the application you have been creating in this book. The code from AG New Intelligencer was developed under a BSD-style license and is used here with the author's permission (Clemens F. Vasters, who can be reached at clemensv@newtelligence.com). Although the code presented here is different from the original code, the implementation of this idea came from the original code.

You can extend this small amount of code, which needs to be written only once, to fit virtually any type of business rule that you may need to create.

NOTE   When I originally came across this code, I was thinking of having a class of business rules usable by an entire organization. In this manner, no one in an organization would ever need to build the basic set of business rules ever again, and everyone would have access to these rules.

Creating the BusinessRules Project

You are going to create a separate project to hold all of the business rule attributes and the validation routines. In this way you can distribute the rules to other applications. This project will be another shared project that must exist on both the client and the server. The reason for this is that the class attributes you create will be used in both the data-centric and user-centric objects.

To begin, open the current Northwind solution, add a new Class Library project to the solution, and call it *BusinessRules*. Rename the Class1.vb file that is created by default to *Attributes.vb*. Then delete the default class definition that was created in this code module. You will create the business rule attributes and the necessary interface in this code module. You will eventually create another set of classes to check the business rules specified by the attributes.

Add the following code to the Attributes code module:

```
Option Explicit On
Option Strict On

Imports System.Reflection

Namespace Attributes

End Namespace
```

The interface and all of the classes you create will be created in the Attributes namespace. Before you begin adding classes, let's review the business rules in place in the RegionDC class:

- RegionDescription cannot be null.

- RegionDescription cannot be a zero-length string.

- RegionDescription cannot be more than 50 characters in length.

This gives you the basis for creating your first set of class attributes.

 NOTE   These are the only attributes you will be creating for this project; however, in the code available for download, there are a considerable number of additional business rule attribute classes.

Going by this list of rules, you need to create three attribute classes that check for the following: a null value, an empty length string, and a maximum number of characters.

Creating the ITest Interface

Before creating the classes, you need to create an interface that all of your classes will support.

NOTE You need the interface because these are all generic classes. When you code the routines that check the rules, you will see that you do not care what the attribute class is, only that it is a rule and that you need to check the rule. In this way, you can continue to add additional business rules without once having to change the way in which you check the rules.

Add the code for the ITest interface as shown in Listing 10-8 to the Attributes namespace in the Attributes code module.

Listing 10-8. The ITest Interface

```
Public Interface ITest
    Function TestCondition(ByVal Value As Object, ByRef cls As Object) As Boolean
    Function GetRule() As String
End Interface
```

The TestCondition method actually determines if the value has broken the specific business rule. It accepts the value stored in the field or property and the object in which the property resides. This is enough information for a method to determine everything about a given class. It returns a value of True if the rule has been broken and a value of False if the rule has not been broken. The GetRule method simply returns a string that describes the rule in plain English. This will be used (in conjunction with another method) to eliminate the need for all of the code in the GetBusinessRules method.

Creating the NotNullAttribute Class

Now you can create the first business rule attribute class: NotNullAttribute. Add the code for the NotNullAttribute class as shown in Listing 10-9.

Listing 10-9. The NotNullAttribute Class

```
<AttributeUsage(AttributeTargets.Field Or AttributeTargets.Property)> _
Public Class NotNullAttribute
    Inherits System.Attribute

    Implements ITest
```

```
    Public Function TestCondition(ByVal Value As Object, ByRef cls As Object) _
    As Boolean Implements ITest.TestCondition
        If Value Is Nothing Then
            Return True
        Else
            If IsNumeric(Value) Then
                If Convert.ToDecimal(Value) = 0 Then
                    Return True
                End If
            End If
            Return False
        End If
    End Function

    Public Function GetRule() As String Implements ITest.GetRule
        Return "Value cannot be null."
    End Function
End Class
```

Let's examine this code to determine exactly what is happening. The signature tells you that this class can only be applied to a field or property within a class.

```
<AttributeUsage(AttributeTargets.Field Or AttributeTargets.Property)> _
Public Class NotNullAttribute
```

As before, all classes that are attribute classes must inherit from the System.Attribute class. Next, your class implements the ITest interface as will all of your attribute classes. Now you come to the TestCondition method, which does the real work of the class. This first check just tests to see if the value is null; if it is, it returns True and the method ends:

```
If Value Is Nothing Then
    Return True
Else
```

The second part of this routine may or may not be controversial. Because numbers are not nullable, when they are instantiated they are initialized with a value of zero. If a numeric value can be a zero, you should not apply this attribute to it because this attribute is supposed to deal with nulls and is named accordingly, but for simplicity it is useful to keep it in this class. You can always create a separate class called *ValueNotZeroAttribute* and add this code into it—the choice is yours. This code checks to see if the value is numeric, and if it is, it checks to see if the value is equal to zero:

```
If IsNumeric(Value) Then
    If Convert.ToDecimal(Value) = 0 Then
        Return True
    End If
End If
Return False
```

The last method in the class, the GetRule method, simply returns what the rule for the property is.

Creating the DisplayNameAttribute Class

Now, you have one small problem here—how do you show the property to the user in a way that looks nice to the user? If you go by just the name of the property, it is going to look ugly because there are no spaces and sometimes property names do not reflect what the user sees on the screen. To overcome this you are going to add another class called *DisplayNameAttribute* that will store the name for the property you want to show the user.

Add the DisplayNameAttribute class as shown in Listing 10-10.

Listing 10-10. The DisplayNameAttribute Class

```
<AttributeUsage(AttributeTargets.Field Or AttributeTargets.Property)> _
Public Class DisplayNameAttribute
    Inherits System.Attribute

    Private _strValue As String

    Public Sub New(ByVal Value As String)
        _strValue = Value
    End Sub

    Public ReadOnly Property Name() As String
        Get
            Return _strValue
        End Get
    End Property
End Class
```

Creating the NotEmptyAttribute Class

Now you will create the rule that will check to make sure that a string value is not empty. Listing 10-11 shows the code for this class.

Listing 10-11. The NotEmptyAttribute Class

```
<AttributeUsage(AttributeTargets.Field Or AttributeTargets.Property)> _
Public Class NotEmptyAttribute
    Inherits System.Attribute

    Implements ITest

    Public Function TestCondition(ByVal Value As Object, ByRef cls As Object) _
    As Boolean Implements ITest.TestCondition
        If Value Is Nothing Then
            Return True
        Else
            Dim str As String = CType(Value, String)
            If str.Trim.Length = 0 Then
                Return True
            Else
                Return False
            End If
        End If
    End Function

    Public Function GetRule() As String Implements ITest.GetRule
        Return "Value cannot be a zero length string."
    End Function
End Class
```

Everything that is occurring in this class should be straightforward except for the check to see if the value is nothing. This check must be made in some form or another in every class that checks a property. After all, how can you check the value of something if the value is nothing? Notice also how similar this is to the first attribute class you created. The beauty of creating rules this way is that the code is compact, easy to understand, and even easier to debug. And once you get it right here, you never need to check it again or write code to perform the same type of validation.

Creating the MaxLengthAttribute Class

This last attribute class is substantially identical to the previous two business rule attributes that you created. Listing 10-12 presents the code for this class.

Listing 10-12. The MaxLengthAttribute Class

```
<AttributeUsage(AttributeTargets.Field Or AttributeTargets.Property)> _
Public Class MaxLengthAttribute
    Inherits System.Attribute

    Implements ITest

    Private _intValue As Integer

    Public Sub New(ByVal Value As Integer)
        _intValue = Value
    End Sub

    Public Function TestCondition(ByVal Value As Object, ByRef cls As Object) _
    As Boolean Implements ITest.TestCondition
        Dim strValue As String = Convert.ToString(Value)

        If strValue.Length > _intValue Then
            Return True
        Else
            Return False
        End If
    End Function

    Public Function GetRule() As String Implements ITest.GetRule
        Return "Value cannot be longer than " & _intValue & " characters."
    End Function
End Class
```

This class simply checks the length of a string value to determine if it has more characters than allowed. Notice that your GetRule method now incorporates the value that you set into the string that is returned. In this case, the RegionDescription property would return a rule that said, "Region Description cannot be longer than 50 characters."

Now that you have all of the business rules in place, you can apply them to your object.

Assigning Data-Centric Business Rule Attributes

To begin, right-click the NorthwindDC references node and select Add Reference. From the Projects tab, select the BusinessRules project by double-clicking it and then click OK. Next, switch to the RegionDC class, expand the Public Attributes region, and delete the public RegionDescription property. In a single move you have eliminated 19 lines of code from your project (yes, it is at the expense of adding all of the code for the business rule attributes, but think about it, you never need to add them again and this is not all of the code you will delete). Expand the Private Attributes region and change the mstrRegionDescription variable to the following:

```
Public RegionDescription As String
```

Next, go to the Save method and change the mstrRegionDescription variable to *RegionDescription*. Before you apply the attributes, you have to import the BusinessRules.Attributes namespace; once that is done you can start applying attributes. So, add the line to perform this to the top of the RegionDC module.

Now you need to apply the attributes. Change the RegionDescription declaration line so that it reads as follows:

```
<DisplayName("Region Description"), NotNull(), NotEmpty(), MaxLength(50)> _
Public RegionDescription As String
```

It may be anticlimactic, but in reality an easy-to-maintain system does not throw many complicated surprises at you! These three tags tell your class what the value cannot be. The DisplayName attribute tells you the human readable name you will display to the user.

Retrieving the List of Business Rules

Before you get into retrieving the business rules, you need to make one change to your application. You need to move your BusinessErrors class and your structErrors structure to the BusinessRules project. The reason you need to do this is so that your new attribute class is modular and can be used by other applications. Follow these steps to accomplish this:

1. Add a new class module to the BusinessRules project called *Errors.vb*.

2. Delete the default class that is created in this code module.

3. Add a namespace in the Errors code module called *Errors* (this will now be referenced by using BusinessRules.Errors).

4. Cut the BusinessErrors class from the NorthwindShared Errors code module and paste it into the Errors namespace in the BusinessRules project.

5. Cut the structErrors structure from the NorthwindShared Structures code module and paste it into the Errors namespace in the BusinessRules project.

6. Add a reference to the BusinessRules project in the NorthwindUC, NorthwindShared, and NorthwindTraders projects.

7. In each edit form code module, all the data-centric and all the user-centric code modules, as well as the NorthwindShared Interfaces code module and the frmBusinessRules module, replace northwindshared.errors and northwindtraders.northwindshared.errors with businessrules.errors.

As you perform steps 4 and 5 of this list, you will see several errors in the Task List. Not to worry, though—once you are through with the last step, you will not have any errors. That was the hardest part. The next step is to add a new class code module to the BusinessRules project called *Validate*. Once you have done that, delete the default class and add the following code to the Validate class module:

```
Option Explicit On
Option Strict On

Imports BusinessRules.Attributes
Imports BusinessRules.Errors
Imports System.Reflection

Namespace Validate
    Public Class Validation

    End Class
End Namespace
```

The Validation class is the only class you are going to create in this namespace. Now, add the GetDisplayName method to the Validation class as shown in Listing 10-13.

Listing 10-13. The GetDisplayName Method

```
Private Shared Function GetDisplayName(ByVal member As MemberInfo) As String
    Dim obj() As Object = member.GetCustomAttributes(True)
    Dim i As Integer

    If obj.Length > 0 Then
        For i = 0 To obj.Length - 1
            If TypeOf (obj(i)) Is DisplayNameAttribute Then
                Dim objDisplayNameAttribute As DisplayNameAttribute = _
                CType(obj(i), DisplayNameAttribute)
                Return objDisplayNameAttribute.Name
            End If
        Next i
    End If
    Return member.Name
End Function
```

Let's examine what this code does, line by line. One important thing to note is the method signature. This is a shared method because it will be called by a shared method. In fact, all of the methods in this class will be shared methods so this class never has to be instantiated. This provides you with immense speed benefits (especially when you move to the user-centric classes), and because this class maintains no state at all, it is OK to do.

The first line retrieves a list of all of the custom attributes associated with the class member. The True parameter tells the code to retrieve all of the custom attributes along the entire inheritance chain:

```
Dim obj() As Object = member.GetCustomAttributes(True)
```

Next, you check to see if there are any custom attributes:

```
If obj.Length > 0 Then
```

If there are, you loop through them looking for an attribute that is a DisplayNameAttribute:

```
If TypeOf (obj(i)) Is DisplayNameAttribute Then
```

If we find one, you convert it to a true DisplayNameAttribute object and you return the value of the Name property:

```
Dim objDisplayNameAttribute As DisplayNameAttribute = CType(obj(i), _
DisplayNameAttribute)
Return objDisplayNameAttribute.Name
```

Finally, if there was no Display Name attribute found, you simply return the name of the property. Now that you can return the display name, it is time to be able to return the rules.

Add the code for the GetBusinessRules method to the Validate class as shown in Listing 10-14.

Listing 10-14. The GetBusinessRules Method

```
Public Shared Function GetBusinessRules(ByVal cls As Object) As BusinessErrors
    Dim t As Type = cls.GetType
    Dim m As MemberInfo() = t.GetMembers
    Dim i As Integer

    Dim objBusErr As New BusinessErrors

    For i = 0 To m.Length - 1
        Dim obj() As Object = m(i).GetCustomAttributes(True)
        If obj.Length > 0 Then
            Dim j As Integer
            For j = 0 To obj.Length - 1
                If TypeOf obj(j) Is ITest Then
                    Dim objI As ITest = CType(obj(j), ITest)
                    objBusErr.Add(GetDisplayName(m(i)), objI.GetRule)
                End If
            Next
        End If
    Next

    Return objBusErr
End Function
```

This is the first routine where you access the ITest interface, so you will see the workings of this method line by line. The method accepts an object, which is the class you want to get the business rules from, and it returns a BusinessErrors object. The first line retrieves all of the type information about the class. The second line retrieves all of the members of the class and stores them in an array of MemberInfo objects:

```
Public Shared Function GetBusinessRules(ByVal cls As Object) As BusinessErrors
    Dim t As Type = cls.GetType
    Dim m As MemberInfo() = t.GetMembers
```

Next you loop through all of the members of the class and you retrieve the custom attributes of each member (you retrieve all of the custom attributes along the inheritance chain). This allows your inherited classes to use the business rules of any base classes. There may be a point at which this is not desirable, though, so you may need to modify this code to suit your particular needs. Then you check to see if there were in fact any custom attributes retrieved from the member:

```
For i = 0 To m.Length - 1
    Dim obj() As Object = m(i).GetCustomAttributes(True)
    If obj.Length > 0 Then
```

Finally, you loop through all of the custom attributes associated with the member. You check to see if the custom attribute implements the ITest interface, and, if it does, you call the GetRule method on it to retrieve the rule. You also extract the Display Name from the member and add them both to the BusinessErrors object:

```
For j = 0 To obj.Length - 1
    If TypeOf obj(j) Is ITest Then
        Dim objI As ITest = CType(obj(j), ITest)
        objBusErr.Add(GetDisplayName(m(i)), objI.GetRule)
    End If
Next
```

Now that you have added this method, let's implement it. In the RegionDC class, add the following declaration:

```
Private mobjVal As BusinessRules.Validate.Validation
```

Alter the GetBusinessRules method so that it now reads as follows:

```
Public Function GetBusinessRules() As BusinessErrors _
Implements IRegion.GetBusinessRules
        Return mobjVal.GetBusinessRules(Me)
End Function
```

Now, build the application, but when you go to deploy the remote assemblies, be sure to deploy all three assemblies: NorthwindDC, NorthwindShared, and BusinessRules. Then run the application, go to Maintenance ➤ Regions, and select one of the existing regions to edit (or select the Add button). Then click the Rules button, and you should see the rules screen with your three business rules. Any changes you make to the business rules will be automatically reflected the next time the application is compiled and run, and you never need to change the GetBusinessRules method again.

Checking Business Rules with Custom Attributes

Now that you can retrieve the business rules, it is time to put them to their real use—constraining data. You will eventually end up writing two different methods to perform this task: one for the data-centric classes and one for the user-centric classes. They are different methods because they do the task in slightly different ways. However, you are only going to worry about the data-centric classes right now. You are going to add a new method to the Validation class (shown in Listing 10-15). This method is a little more involved than the GetBusinessRules method because you have to take into account the differences between fields and properties; but for the most part there are not a lot of differences between this method and the GetBusinessRules method.

Listing 10-15. The Validate Method

```
Public Shared Function Validate(ByVal cls As Object) As BusinessErrors
    Dim t As Type = cls.GetType
    Dim i, j As Integer
    Dim bln As Boolean

    Dim objBusErr As New BusinessErrors

    Dim m As MemberInfo() = t.GetMembers

    For i = 0 To m.Length - 1
        Dim objAttrib() As Object = m(i).GetCustomAttributes(True)
        For j = 0 To objAttrib.Length - 1
            If TypeOf objAttrib(j) Is ITest Then
                Dim objI As ITest = CType(objAttrib(j), ITest)

                If TypeOf m(i) Is FieldInfo Then
                    Dim fld As FieldInfo = CType(m(i), FieldInfo)
                    bln = objI.TestCondition(fld.GetValue(cls), cls)
                End If
```

```
            If TypeOf m(i) Is PropertyInfo Then
                Dim pro As PropertyInfo = CType(m(i), PropertyInfo)
                bln = objI.TestCondition(pro.GetValue(cls, Nothing), _
                cls)
            End If

            If bln Then
                objBusErr.Add(m(i).Name, objI.GetRule())
            End If
        End If
    Next
  Next

  Return objBusErr
End Function
```

The real difference in this listing is the test to determine if the member is a field or a property. The reason for this test is that the methods for retrieving the instance values are different for each type. This is because a property is a method, so it does not just retrieve a value; it actually invokes the method to return a value. You then call the TestCondition method, and if the value breaks the rule you add it to the BusinessError method.

One thing to note about this method of validating business rules is that *all* of the rules for each property will be checked as opposed to what you had before. Before only one rule at a time was being checked and thrown as an error. So this method provides you with a little more robust business rule handling and reporting.

Code Reduction Metrics

Many companies today are trying to take a cost-conscious approach to coding—so the first question asked when faced with a new technology is, "How much effort (read: money) will this save and how much easier is it to maintain?" If anyone was looking for a justification to use the .NET Framework, this is it.

On average, you can assume that you will save six lines of code for every business rule that is checked via a custom attribute as opposed to the previous method you were using. This should be able to help you extrapolate out the cost in savings by using custom attributes. In your RegionDC class, for example, you originally had 20 lines of code for the public RegionDescription property, one line for the private RegionDescription field, and nine lines of code for the GetBusinessRules. Now we have one line of code for the public RegionDescription field and three lines of code for the GetBusinessRules method. Thirty lines down to four is a big improvement.

A larger example is your EmployeeDC class. It has 18 properties, which have approximately 518 lines of code devoted to the public attributes plus another 26 lines of code devoted to the GetBusinessRules method. Using reflection, you can knock the number of lines of code down to 21—18 for the properties and three for the GetBusinessRules method. That is 544 lines of code knocked down to just 21 lines of code.

Furthermore, your objects are now truly self-describing. Any changes you make to your business rules are now instantly reflected when you retrieve the business rules from the class. The code reduction plus the self-describing class means that your maintenance costs will go through the floor. No longer do developers have to hunt through the code looking for the rule—they just have to check the attribute tag. Also, this reduces the number of code defects caused by bad business rule checks. Because your business rules are encapsulated, if they are wrong in one place, they are wrong in every place, and it will be much easier to capture these defects and correct them.

With all of the wonderful things that reflection provides, you may be asking yourself at this point why you saw the original method for handling business rules at all. After all, what is the point because this is so much easier and provides so many more advantages? The reason is that this is not a one-size-fits-all solution. On several occasions I have had to create systems that use a rules database because the business rules changed so quickly. In cases such as this, the objects generally need to open up a connection to a database to read the rule information. This is a lot of overhead and in the few tests that I have run is not well served by the reflection model. The reason for this is that the attributes cannot be dynamically changed at runtime by reading from a database. So, it is best to know both methods and apply them as necessary.

There is one last change you need to make to the RegionDC class—it is a change to the Save method. Currently, the first part of your Save method looks like the following:

```
mobjBusErr = New BusinessErrors

With sRegion
    Me.mintRegionID = .RegionID
    Me.RegionDescription = .RegionDescription
End With
```

The change you need to make is simple. Delete the first line from the previous code, and add the following line of code below the With block:

```
mobjBusErr = mobjVal.validate(Me)
```

Now, after all of your properties are assigned, you call the Validate method, retrieve the business errors, and continue as before.

Implement User-Centric Business Rule Attribute Classes

Checking business rules with custom attributes is a little different on the user-centric side. The reason for this is that you check the rules one property at a time. Not only do you still need to throw an exception when an error occurs, but you also need to add an entry to the BrokenRules object. That is a lot more work than you had to do in the data-centric class. Specifically, you cannot get rid of the public properties in the user-centric class like you did in the data-centric class. However, your job is made much easier by the presence of the BusinessBase class.

Before you modify your user-centric classes, let's add a new method to the Validation class. This method throws an exception on the first broken rule it encounters. Add the method shown in Listing 10-16 to the Validation class.

Listing 10-16. The ValidateAndThrow Method

```
Public Shared Sub ValidateAndThrow(ByVal cls As Object, ByVal field As String)
    Dim t As Type = cls.GetType
    Dim m As MemberInfo() = t.GetMember(field)
    Dim i As Integer
    Dim bln As Boolean
    Dim obj() As Object = m(0).GetCustomAttributes(True)

    If obj.Length > 0 Then
        For i = 0 To obj.Length - 1
            If TypeOf obj(i) Is ITest Then
                Dim objI As ITest = CType(obj(i), ITest)

                If TypeOf m(0) Is FieldInfo Then
                    Dim fld As FieldInfo = CType(m(0), FieldInfo)
                    bln = objI.TestCondition(fld.GetValue(cls), cls)
                End If

                If TypeOf m(0) Is PropertyInfo Then
                    Dim pro As PropertyInfo = CType(m(0), PropertyInfo)
                    bln = objI.TestCondition(pro.GetValue(cls, Nothing), cls)
                End If
```

```
                    If bln Then
                          Throw New Exception(objI.GetRule())
                    End If
              End If
        Next
    End If
End Sub
```

This code is similar to what you have seen before, with the exception that when a broken rule is encountered, an exception is thrown. Notice that it does not specify the property that the exception is thrown on—you know what it is because you had to pass the property into the method. Notice also at the top of the method that you are only retrieving the information for the one property or field that you specified, not for the whole class. That is the extent of this method; now you can implement it in the BusinessBase class.

To begin with, modify the BusinessBase class by adding the following declaration:

```
Protected mobjVal As BusinessRules.Validate.Validation
```

Next you need to add a method that will call the ValidateAndThrow method and will process the results appropriately. Listing 10-17 shows the method, which should be added to the BusinessBase class.

Listing 10-17. The Validate Method of the BusinessBase Class

```
Protected Sub Validate(ByVal strProperty As String)
    Try
        mblnDirty = True
        mobjVal.ValidateAndThrow(Me, strProperty)
        mobjRules.BrokenRule(strProperty, False)
    Catch exc As Exception
        mobjRules.BrokenRule(strProperty, True)
        Throw exc
    End Try
End Sub
```

This method is simple—it takes a property name and calls the ValidateAndThrow method. If no exceptions are thrown, the property is set to not broken; if there is an exception, the property is marked as broken and the exception is rethrown.

Next you need to modify the Region class; specifically, you need to modify the public RegionDescription property. Before you do anything else, you need to add the following Imports line to the Region.vb code module:

```
Imports BusinessRules.Attributes
```

Then you need to tag the RegionDescription property with your business rule attributes. Change the property signature to read as follows:

```
<DisplayName("Region Description"), NotNull(), NotEmpty(), MaxLength(50)> _
Public Property RegionDescription() As String
```

Note that technically you do not need the DisplayName tag here, but it cannot hurt to have it—the choice is yours. Now that you have modified the tag, you need to alter the Set part of the method to read as follows:

```
Set(ByVal Value As String)
    If mstrRegionDescription.Trim <> Value Then
        mstrRegionDescription = Value
        If Not Loading Then
            Me.Validate("RegionDescription")
        End If
    End If
End Set
```

All of the functionality that had been in this method is now encapsulated in either the ValidateAndThrow method or the Validate method of the BusinessBase class. In either case, this property was originally 28 lines of code and it is now 13 lines of code—and that is just for one property!

Summary

This chapter showed you one of the most powerful abilities of the .NET framework: reflection. This is the ability of the Framework to examine itself and invoke things it knows nothing about. There are virtually an unlimited number of things you can do with this ability. You created a sample application to dynamically load a listview from an unknown object with unknown column headers and unknown information. Most importantly, you created a reusable business rule project that will save you countless hours in development time, lines of code, and maintenance costs. You implemented these rules on both the data-centric and user-centric classes and you made a truly self-describing class.

In the next chapter you will move on to one of the hottest topics in Information Technology today: Web services. You will learn a little bit about what they are and you will turn part of your NorthwindTraders application into a Web service. Then you will see how to consume the Web service and publish it using Microsoft's .NET Server 2003 Universal Description, Discovery, and Integration (UDDI).

Implementing Web Services and the UDDI

THERE HAS BEEN a great deal of hype in the business world concerning Web services. You have probably heard all about them recently, you may have read an article about them. The truth is that I have heard as many different explanations for what a Web service is as people I have heard try to explain what it is. This chapter gives you a solid definition (at least, my version) of what a Web service is and a practical overview of how to implement one. This chapter covers how to create a Web service and how to incorporate the code that you already created for the rest of the NorthwindTraders application. It also covers how to access that Web service from another Windows forms application. You will also see you how to create classes based on a Web service using the Web Service Description Language (WSDL) utility that ships with .NET. This chapter does not cover Web service security, which is an extremely large topic, or the many competing standards and organizations pushing for those standards.

NOTE   You can find several resources in Appendix B that will point you in the direction of the different standards bodies working toward unified Web service standards.

The second half of this chapter looks at the UDDI that ships with .NET Enterprise Server 2003. It covers setting up the UDDI, adding Web services to the UDDI, and programmatically accessing the UDDI Server.

What Are Web Services?

In its simplest form, a *Web service* is a Remote Procedure Call (RPC). In other words, it is a method invocation across a process boundary. That is the extent of the similarities between a Web service and a standard RPC. What differentiates Web services is that the call is made using the Hypertext Transfer Protocol (HTTP) and the request is made and received using the Simple Object Access Protocol

(SOAP) format. This format is essentially an Extensible Markup Language (XML)–like document format, as shown in Listing 11-1.

Listing 11-1. A Web Service Request in SOAP Format

```
POST /webservice1/service1.asmx HTTP/1.1
Host: localhost
Content-Type: text/xml; charset=utf-8
Content-Length: length
SOAPAction: "http://tempuri.org/GetAllEmployees"

<?xml version="1.0" encoding="utf-8"?>
<soap:Envelope xmlns:xsi="http://www.w3.org/2001/XMLSchema-instance"
xmlns:xsd="http://www.w3.org/2001/XMLSchema"
xmlns:soap="http://schemas.xmlsoap.org/soap/envelope/">
  <soap:Body>
    <GetAllEmployees xmlns="http://tempuri.org/" />
  </soap:Body>
</soap:Envelope>
```

This is a sample of what the SOAP request would look like if you needed to create the SOAP data to send to the Web service yourself.

NOTE What makes XML Web services so powerful is that anybody who can write a properly formatted SOAP message can call a Web service. You do not need to use a powerful language such as C#, Visual Basic, or Java. This is what makes Web services a "universal" way of sending and receiving data. Anything that can process text can send and receive SOAP messages.

The part of the SOAP message to note in Listing 11-1 is the SOAP body tag, which contains the actual call to the GetAllEmployees method. You will walk through creating this Web service later in this chapter (in the "Creating the GetAllEmployees Web Service" section). Listing 11-2 shows an example of the SOAP response format that will be returned by the method call.

Listing 11-2. The SOAP Response Format

```
HTTP/1.1 200 OK
Content-Type: text/xml; charset=utf-8
Content-Length: length

<?xml version="1.0" encoding="utf-8"?>
<soap:Envelope xmlns:xsi=http://www.w3.org/2001/XMLSchema-instance
 xmlns:xsd="http://www.w3.org/2001/XMLSchema"
xmlns:soap="http://schemas.xmlsoap.org/soap/envelope/">
  <soap:Body>
    <GetAllEmployeesResponse xmlns="http://tempuri.org/">
      <GetAllEmployeesResult>
        <xsd:schema>schema</xsd:schema>xml</GetAllEmployeesResult>
    </GetAllEmployeesResponse>
  </soap:Body>
</soap:Envelope>
```

This shows the format in which the SOAP response will be encoded. Again, the important thing to note is the SOAP body tag. The GetAllEmployeeResult tag contains an XML Schema Definition (XSD) schema tag and the word *xml*. This denotes that the returned value will contain an XSD, followed by the XML that contains your employee data.

Setting Up a Web Service Project

Now that you have been introduced to Web services, let's dive in and actually create one. I find that most technical explanations of Web services are pointless until someone actually creates a Web service. So, to start with, open Visual Studio and select File ➤ New ➤ Project. From the Visual Basic Projects node, click the ASP.NET Web Service template, as shown in Figure 11-1. Click OK to create the Web service application with the default name of *WebService1*.

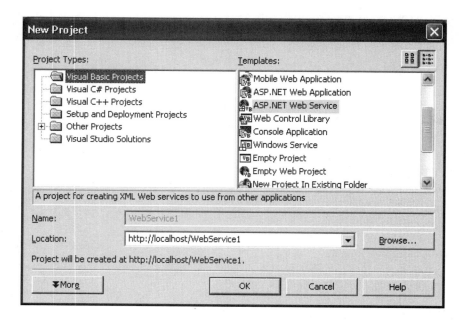

Figure 11-1. The New Project dialog box with an ASP.NET template selected

For your purposes, you want the Web service to be in the same virtual directory as your NorthwindTraders application.

NOTE   This is by no means a necessity. You could make the call to your objects from another Internet Information Server (IIS) virtual directory, but this approach simplifies things a great deal. Although Web services are quite simple to implement, there are many choices to make while securing and deploying the individual components.

To move the location, close Visual Studio and navigate to the \wwwroot\webservice1 folder. Copy all of the files in the folder *except* the web.config file (because you do not want to overwrite your web.config file) and the bin folder and then paste these files into the \wwwroot\northwind folder. Finally, in the northwind folder, edit the webservice1.vbproj.webinfo file with Notepad. Listing 11-3 shows the original file.

Listing 11-3. The Webservice1.vbproj.webinfo File

```
<VisualStudioUNCWeb>
    <Web URLPath = "http://localhost/webservice1/WebService1.vbproj" />
</VisualStudioUNCWeb>
```

Change the URLPath so that it reads as follows:

```
<Web URLPath = "http://localhost/northwind/WebService1.vbproj" />
```

Now you can close and save the file. Finally, navigate to the project folder (this is usually located in \My Documents\Visual Studio Projects\Webservice1) and edit the webservice1.sln file with Notepad (see Listing 11-4). Change the location from *http://localhost/Webservice1/WebService1.vbproj* to http://localhost/northwind/WebService1.vbproj.

Listing 11-4. The webservice1.sln File

```
Microsoft Visual Studio Solution File, Format Version 8.00
Project("{F184B08F-C81C-45F6-A57F-5ABD9991F28F}") = "WebService1",
    "http://localhost/Webservice1/WebService1.vbproj", "{E05A1271-91EB-4A84-8F7F-
    000A1065D7DE}"
    ProjectSection(ProjectDependencies) = postProject
EndProjectSection
EndProject
Global
    GlobalSection(SolutionConfiguration) = preSolution
        Debug = Debug
        Release = Release
    EndGlobalSection
    GlobalSection(ProjectConfiguration) = postSolution
        {E05A1271-91EB-4A84-8F7F-000A1065D7DE}.Debug.ActiveCfg =
        Debug|.NET
        {E05A1271-91EB-4A84-8F7F-000A1065D7DE}.Debug.Build.0 = Debug|.NET
        {E05A1271-91EB-4A84-8F7F-000A1065D7DE}.Release.ActiveCfg = Release|.NET
        {E05A1271-91EB-4A84-8F7F-000A1065D7DE}.Release.Build.0 = Release|.NET
    EndGlobalSection
    GlobalSection(ExtensibilityGlobals) = postSolution
    EndGlobalSection
    GlobalSection(ExtensibilityAddIns) = postSolution
    EndGlobalSection
EndGlobal
```

Next, double-click the webservice1.sln file to bring Visual Studio back up.

Creating the GetAllEmployees Web Service

The first thing you will see is the design view (see Figure 11-2). The view looks a little strange, but the reason is straightforward—there is no user interface in a Web service!

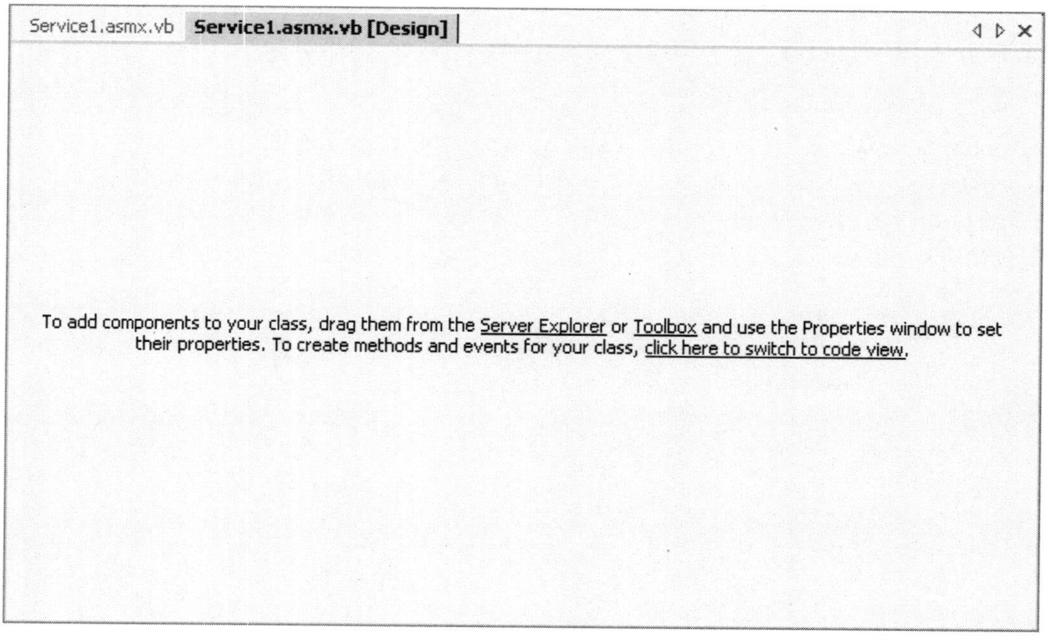

Figure 11-2. The Web service design interface

Switch to the code view so that you can really start working on your Web service. The first thing to note is the Imports line:

```
Imports System.Web.Services
```

All of the Web service functionality is contained in the System.Web.Services namespace. The second thing to note is the large block of text and code that has been commented out—the Hello World Web service:

```
' WEB SERVICE EXAMPLE
' The HelloWorld() example service returns the string Hello World.
' To build, uncomment the following lines then save and build the project.
' To test this web service, ensure that the .asmx file is the start page
' and press F5.
'
'<WebMethod()> Public Function HelloWorld() As String
'       HelloWorld = "Hello World"
' End Function
```

This is probably included to show people how easy it is to create a Web service. The only difference between this method and any other method you have seen is the inclusion of the <WebMethod()> attribute tag in front of the method signature. At this point I can move on to the UDDI portion of the chapter because you have now implemented a Web service. Placing this attribute in front of a method exposes it as a Web service. That is all that is needed. However, the reality is that it is all of the other little things that are required to fully understand, find, and use Web services that are the somewhat more difficult parts of developing Web services. And you thought this chapter would be that easy....

Before creating your Web service, you need to add a reference to the NorthwindDC and NorthwindShared components. To do this, right-click the References node and select Add Reference. Click Browse and browse to the \bin folder in the Northwind folder. Select both DLLs and click OK. Next, add the following two Imports statements at the top of the code module:

```
Imports NorthwindTraders.NorthwindShared.Structures
Imports NorthwindTraders.NorthwindDC
```

Then, delete the block of commented text and code and add the GetAllEmployees method shown in Listing 11-5.

Listing 11-5. The GetAllEmployees Method

```
<WebMethod()> Public Function GetAllEmployees() As DataSet
    Dim objEmployee As New EmployeeDC()
    Dim ds As DataSet

    ds = objEmployee.LoadProxy

    objEmployee = Nothing

    Return ds
End Function
```

This fairly straightforward method calls the LoadProxy method on your EmployeeDC object and returns the resulting dataset. In general, if you have built the components well enough, this is all that is required of a Web service—a set of interfaces available over the Web.

Invoking a Web Service with Internet Explorer

At this point, save the project and right-click service1.asmx in the Project Explorer. Then, select Set as Start Page and press F5. The page displayed in Internet Explorer looks like the page in Figure 11-3. Depending on the operating system, the information listed below the GetAllEmployees link may or may not be displayed.

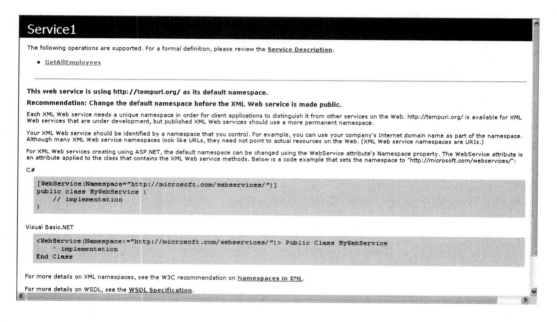

Figure 11-3. Your first Web service interface

.NET creates this page so people can gather information about the Web service. Notice that the GetAllEmployees method is listed here. Click the GetAllEmployees link. This presents you with another Web page that contains a SOAP request and response message as well as an HTTP GET request and response message. However, all you really care about is the top part of the Web page, as shown in Figure 11-4.

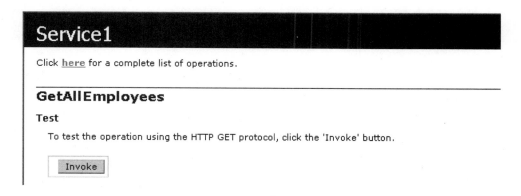

Figure 11-4. The GetAllEmployees test screen

Because this method takes no parameters, you are simply presented with an Invoke button. Click the button and take a look at the output, which is partially displayed in Listing 11-6.

Listing 11-6. Partial Output from the GetAllEmployees Method

```
<?xml version="1.0" encoding="utf-8" ?>
- <DataSet xmlns="http://tempuri.org/">
- <xs:schema id="NewDataSet" xmlns=""
xmlns:xs="http://www.w3.org/2001/XMLSchema"
xmlns:msdata="urn:schemas-microsoft-com:xml-msdata">
- <xs:element name="NewDataSet" msdata:IsDataSet="true">
- <xs:complexType>
- <xs:choice maxOccurs="unbounded">
- <xs:element name="Table">
- <xs:complexType>
- <xs:sequence>
  <xs:element name="EmployeeID" type="xs:int" minOccurs="0" />
  <xs:element name="LastName" type="xs:string" minOccurs="0" />
  <xs:element name="FirstName" type="xs:string" minOccurs="0" />
  <xs:element name="Title" type="xs:string" minOccurs="0" />
  </xs:sequence>
  </xs:complexType>
  </xs:element>
  </xs:choice>
  </xs:complexType>
  </xs:element>
  </xs:schema>
- <diffgr:diffgram xmlns:msdata="urn:schemas-microsoft-com:xml-msdata"
```

```
xmlns:diffgr="urn:schemas-microsoft-com:xml-diffgram-v1">
- <NewDataSet xmlns="">
- <Table diffgr:id="Table1" msdata:rowOrder="0">
  <EmployeeID>1</EmployeeID>
  <LastName>Davolio</LastName>
  <FirstName>Nancy</FirstName>
  <Title>Sales Representative</Title>
  </Table>
- <Table diffgr:id="Table2" msdata:rowOrder="1">
  <EmployeeID>2</EmployeeID>
  <LastName>Fuller</LastName>
  <FirstName>Andrew</FirstName>
  <Title>Vice President, Sales</Title>
  </Table>
```

Even if you have never seen an XSD document before, this should still be fairly easy to understand. Everything in the xs:schema tags describes the format of the data. Following this you can see the records from your employee table. Remember that your proxy method only returns a partial list of employee data.

 NOTE One thing to be aware of is the tag that reads *<XS:complexType>*. Any complex return type is not likely to be easily understood by any other language. In other words, something such as a dataset could be easily read and understood by a .NET language, but Java has no concept of a dataset. A Java application could read this because it is just plain text, but being able to do something useful with it (such as create a dataset out of the content) is far more difficult. This is important to remember when creating Web services that will be read by other applications within an enterprise.

You have just created your first Web service—and with no pain at all!

Creating the GetEmployeeDetails Web Service

The next step is to create the equivalent of the LoadRecord method as a Web service. As before, this is a simple call to your already built objects. Add the code for this method, as shown in Listing 11-7.

Listing 11-7. The GetEmployeeDetails Web Method

```
<WebMethod()> Public Function GetEmployeeDetails(ByVal EmployeeID _
As Integer) As structEmployee
    Dim objEmployee As New EmployeeDC()
    Dim sEmployee As structEmployee

    sEmployee = objEmployee.LoadRecord(EmployeeID)

    objEmployee = Nothing

    Return sEmployee
End Function
```

This method is different from your previous method in that it accepts a parameter and returns a structure instead of a dataset. Now run the application again. Figure 11-5 shows the Web interface to your Web services.

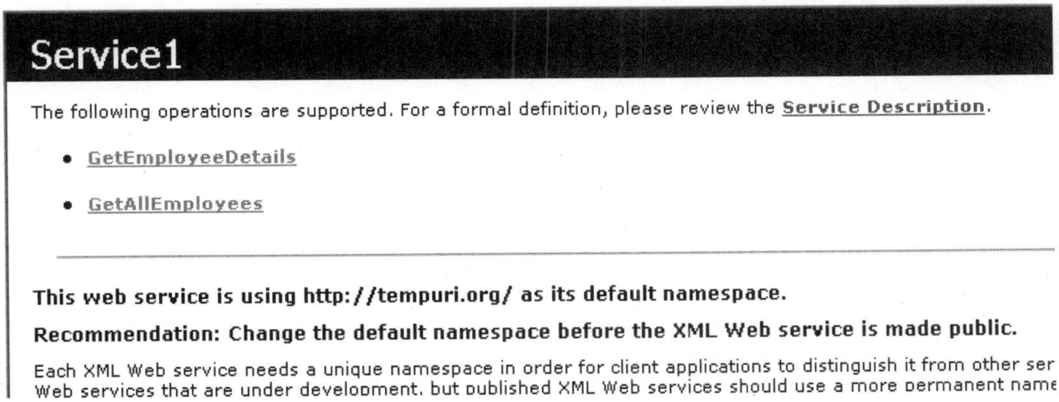

Service1

The following operations are supported. For a formal definition, please review the **Service Description**.

- **GetEmployeeDetails**
- **GetAllEmployees**

This web service is using http://tempuri.org/ as its default namespace.

Recommendation: Change the default namespace before the XML Web service is made public.

Each XML Web service needs a unique namespace in order for client applications to distinguish it from other ser Web services that are under development, but published XML Web services should use a more permanent name

Figure 11-5. The updated Web service Internet Explorer interface

Selecting the GetEmployeeDetails link takes you to a Web page that looks like Figure 11-6.

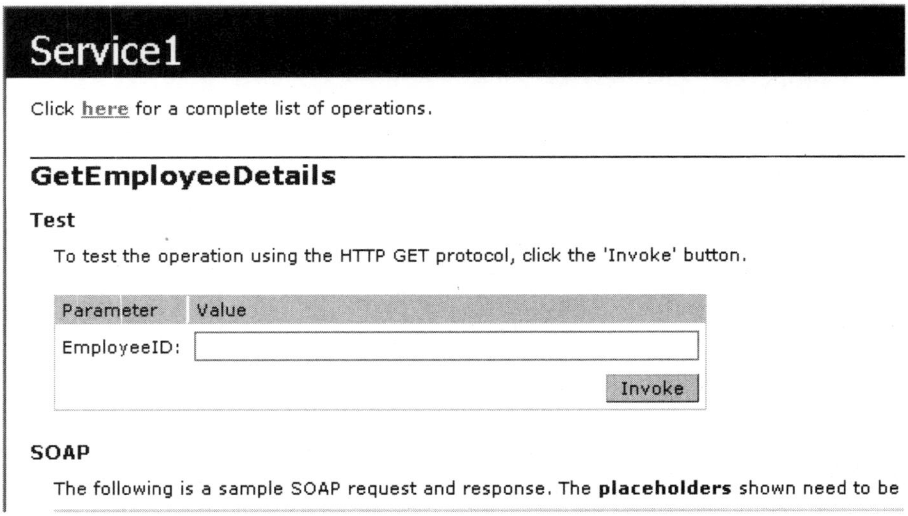

Figure 11-6. The GetEmployeeDetails test screen

Notice that there is now a parameter list that accepts a value for the EmployeeID parameter. Enter the value 1 and click the Invoke button. Listing 11-8 shows the results.

Listing 11-8. The GetEmployeeDetails Results

```
<?xml version="1.0" encoding="utf-8" ?>
- <structEmployee xmlns:xsd="http://www.w3.org/2001/XMLSchema"
xmlns:xsi="http://www.w3.org/2001/XMLSchema-instance"
xmlns="http://tempuri.org/">
  <EmployeeID>1</EmployeeID>
  <LastName>Davolio</LastName>
  <FirstName>Nancy</FirstName>
  <Title>Sales Representative</Title>
  <TitleOfCourtesy>Ms.</TitleOfCourtesy>
  <BirthDate>1948-12-08T00:00:00.0000000-08:00</BirthDate>
  <HireDate>1992-05-01T00:00:00.0000000-07:00</HireDate>
  <Address>507 - 20th Ave. E. Apt. 2A</Address>
  <City>Seattle</City>
  <Region>WA</Region>
  <PostalCode>98122</PostalCode>
  <Country>USA</Country>
  <HomePhone>(206) 555-9857</HomePhone>
  <Extension>5467</Extension>
```

```
<Photo><Photo>
<Notes>Education includes a BA in psychology from Colorado State
University in 1970. She also completed "The Art of the Cold Call." Nancy is a
member of Toastmasters International.</Notes>
  <ReportsTo>2</ReportsTo>
  <ReportsToFirstName>Andrew</ReportsToFirstName>
  <ReportsToLastName>Fuller</ReportsToLastName>
  <PhotoPath>http://accweb/emmployees/davolio.bmp</PhotoPath>
- <Territories>
  <string>06897</string>
  <string>19713</string>
  </Territories>
  </structEmployee>
```

Note that I purposely omitted the values in the Photo tag because it takes up a
large amount of space. An important thing to note is that there is no XSD schema
with this SOAP response. Go back and look at the original Web page and take a look
below at the SOAP response (shown in Listing 11-9).

Listing 11-9. The SOAP Response for the GetEmployeeDetails Method

```
HTTP/1.1 200 OK
Content-Type: text/xml; charset=utf-8
Content-Length: length

<?xml version="1.0" encoding="utf-8"?>
<soap:Envelope xmlns:xsi="http://www.w3.org/2001/XMLSchema-instance"
xmlns:xsd="http://www.w3.org/2001/XMLSchema"
xmlns:soap="http://schemas.xmlsoap.org/soap/envelope/">
  <soap:Body>
    <GetEmployeeDetailsResponse xmlns="http://tempuri.org/">
      <GetEmployeeDetailsResult>
        <EmployeeID>int</EmployeeID>
        <LastName>string</LastName>
        <FirstName>string</FirstName>
        <Title>string</Title>
        <TitleOfCourtesy>string</TitleOfCourtesy>
        <BirthDate>dateTime</BirthDate>
        <HireDate>dateTime</HireDate>
        <Address>string</Address>
        <City>string</City>
        <Region>string</Region>
        <PostalCode>string</PostalCode>
        <Country>string</Country>
```

```
            <HomePhone>string</HomePhone>
            <Extension>string</Extension>
            <Photo>base64Binary</Photo>
            <Notes>string</Notes>
            <ReportsTo>int</ReportsTo>
            <ReportsToFirstName>string</ReportsToFirstName>
            <ReportsToLastName>string</ReportsToLastName>
            <PhotoPath>string</PhotoPath>
            <Territories>
               <string>string</string>
               <string>string</string>
            </Territories>
         </GetEmployeeDetailsResult>
      </GetEmployeeDetailsResponse>
   </soap:Body>
</soap:Envelope>
```

It should be fairly clear from this code that the data type of each value is placed between the tags for the value. Also note that this return value is not denoted as a complex type.

Consuming a Web Service

Now that you have seen how to create two small Web services, it is time to figure out how to invoke and display the return value from an application. A Web service is, after all, designed to be called from any type of application that chooses to call it (or pays for the service). The first question that should come to mind is this: How do I figure out what Web services are out there? Good question.

Introducing the UDDI

Universal Description, Discovery, and Integration (UDDI) is the standard created by IBM, Microsoft, and Ariba. You can learn more about this standard by visiting the http://www.uddi.org Web site. Basically, the UDDI specification allows companies to publish information about their Web services, and it allows companies to manually, or *programmatically*, look through, or *walk*, the UDDI registry for specific types of businesses. Figure 11-7 shows the Microsoft UDDI Business Registry.

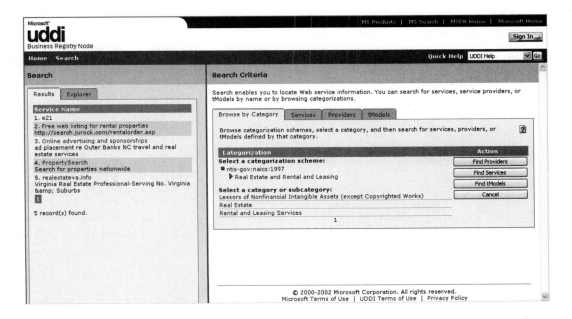

Figure 11-7. The Microsoft UDDI Business Registry

As you can see in the figure, I have browsed into the Real Estate and Rental and Leasing category. By selecting Find Services, I receive five services. The major Web service players would like to see this list in the thousands. This registry is available through Visual Studio .NET, as you will see shortly. Later on in this chapter you will set up the UDDI Server that comes with .NET Server 2003.

Building the Consumer Application

You are going to build a small Windows application to consume your two Web services. An ASP.NET application, which you will create in the next chapter, can also consume the Web services. To begin, create a new Windows application and call it *NwindConsumer*. For the purposes of this application, the interface will be simple.

Creating the List Form

Add a DataGrid control and three buttons to the Form1 form. Set the properties according to Table 11-1.

Table 11-1. Form1 Properties

Control	Name	Text
Form	frmMain	Employee Web Service Consumer
DataGrid	grdEmployees	--
Button	btnLoad	Load Employees
Button	btnEdit	Edit Employee
Button	btnClose	Close

When you are done, the form should like Figure 11-8.

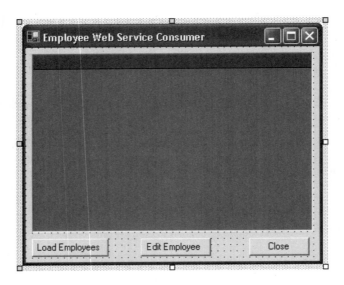

Figure 11-8. The Employee Web Service Consumer form

NOTE   Before you do anything else, make sure to set the startup object in the project's Properties dialog box to *frmMain*.

Next, you need to add a reference to your Web services. To do this, right-click the References node in the Solution Explorer and select Add Web Reference. The Add Web Reference dialog box displays, as shown in Figure 11-9.

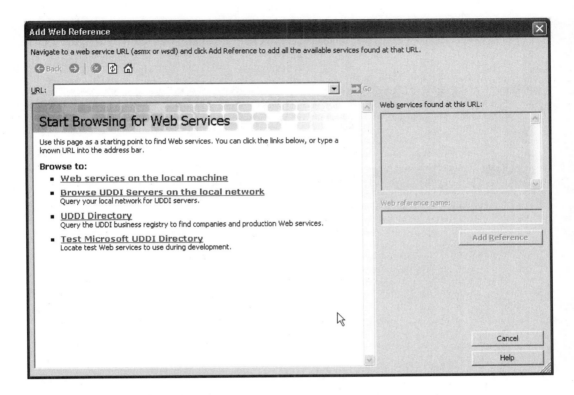

Figure 11-9. The Add Web Reference dialog box

NOTE Microsoft has changed the Web services dialog boxes between version 1.0 and 1.1 of Visual Studio .NET. Figure 11-9 shows version 1.1. However, because version 1.1 includes everything 1.0 did and more, I assume you are using version 1.0. Where there are significant differences, I explicitly note them.

The UDDI Directory link and the Test Microsoft UDDI Directory link take you to the Microsoft UDDI Business Directory that you have already seen. You will come back to this later when adding a Web service to a UDDI. For right now, enter the Uniform Resource Locator (URL) of your local Web service into the URL drop-down box. If you have done everything by using the default location, the URL should be *http://localhost/northwind/service1.asmx*. Once you enter this URL and click Go, the dialog box changes to look like the dialog box shown in Figure 11-10.

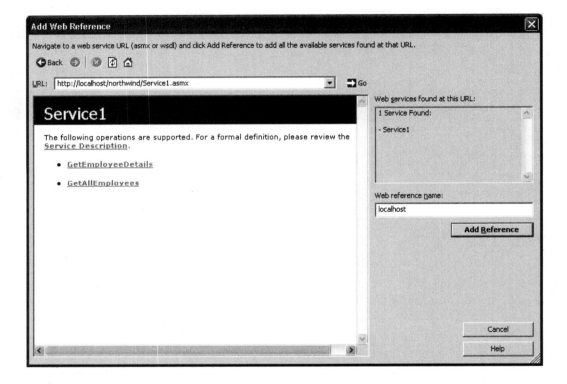

Figure 11-10. The Add Web Reference dialog box with your Web services

Notice that this is identical to the Web page you receive when you go directly to the URL in Internet Explorer.

NOTE If you are using Visual Studio .NET version 1.0, you will note that the Web service description displays below the Web services listed here. This information is not displayed in Visual Studio .NET version1.1.

Click the Add Reference button to add your Web services. The Solution Explorer for your project will now have some additional nodes, as shown in Figure 11-11.

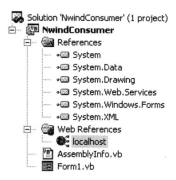

Figure 11-11. Solution Explorer for NwindConsumer

Localhost becomes another namespace in the application through which you can call the Web service. If this had been a different Web site, that Web site name would have become the namespace.

NOTE In Visual Studio .NET version 1.1, you can change the name of this Web service before you add a reference to it.

NOTE Visual Studio .NET version 1.0 listed several other files below the localhost node that contained the discovery map and Web service methods. In version 1.1, you need to double-click the localhost node to bring up the object browser. Viewing the Web service in the object browser, you will see the screen in Figure 11-12.

Now, add some code to retrieve the data. Add a module-level variable to frmMain to hold the dataset:

```
Private mds As DataSet
```

Next, enter the code from Listing 11-10 in frmMain to retrieve the data.

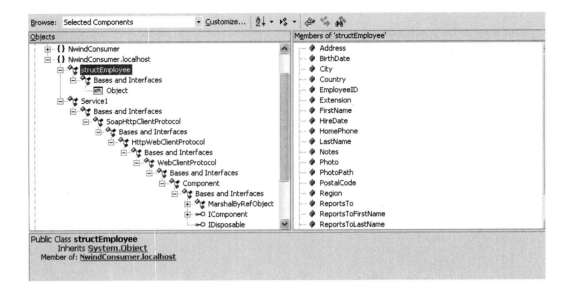

Figure 11-12. The Web services as displayed in the object browser

Listing 11-10. The btnLoad Method

```
Private Sub btnLoad_Click(ByVal sender As System.Object, _
ByVal e As System.EventArgs) Handles btnLoad.Click
    Dim objWS As localhost.Service1

    Try
        Cursor = Cursors.WaitCursor
        objWS = New localhost.Service1()
        mds = objWS.GetAllEmployees
        grdEmployees.DataSource = mds.tables(0)
    Catch exc As Exception
        MessageBox.Show(exc.Message)
    Finally
        objWS = Nothing
        Cursor = Cursors.Default
    End Try
End Sub
```

That is all you need to call your Web service—but it will not work. If you try running the application, you will receive the error shown in Figure 11-13.

Figure 11-13. IIS "Access Denied" message

So why did you get the message? The reason is because your Web service is running under Windows Integrated Authentication only and you did not pass your client credentials. But how do you pass those credentials? It is not like a remoting application where you can control the channel—but you can specify that your credentials get passed to IIS. This is not the only way to solve your security problem. There are five or six different ways plus a number of ways currently being developed by third parties (see the sidebar "Web Service Security").

Web Service Security

Although I do not fully discuss the available security options for a Web service, I'll present a brief overview here. When you accessed the Web service from Internet Explorer, the browser was passing your identity to IIS (as it always tries to do by default). Therefore, your identity was known to IIS and, because you have impersonation turned on, everything works fine. However, when you make a call to a Web service from an application, you are doing so through an HTTP channel, just as you do with your remoting calls. But, the major difference is that your network credentials are not passed unless you specifically request that they are passed. In an enterprise environment, you can pass your Windows Token, but what about users of your service that are external to your enterprise? This is the quandary you face: How do you authenticate and authorize a user of a Web service, and how can you access resources on behalf of that user calling that Web service?

Web services are the latest in distributed applications and easy to use, but security will likely be a stumbling block for a while. With this in mind, and the fact that the Windows .NET family of servers will incorporate a UDDI directory, internal Web services will probably be the norm for the first year or so. So, right now, this discussion is largely theoretical. There are some approved Web service security standards and many more in the works, but until they are approved and implemented companies will still shy away from Web services to a certain degree.

A standard Web application usually uses Forms security. There is a logon page that a user can go to, and once they have entered a user ID and password, they are allowed access to the site. There is no user interface with a Web service, so that option is not available to you either. But, with Forms security, to verify a user's security information, a connection must be made to a database to validate the information.

So how is that connection made when there is no real way to set up a SQL Server Logon for every user of a Web service? The answer is that the connection is made under a specific account to SQL Server using the appSettings section of the web.config file. Another solution is to add the IUSR account to the list of valid SQL Server logons. That way, you can still use integrated security. Still, that is hardly the best solution because anyone who gains control of the IIS session can access your database!

Another way to control security is to request that a user pass a logon and password just as they would for a regular Web application before they call the real Web service. This information can be encrypted and decrypted using custom methods or over a Secure Sockets Layer (SSL) connection. A Web service in IIS has the cool ability to maintain session state, just as in a regular Web application. Or, the logon information can be passed as part of every call.

All of these options have pros and cons, and as mentioned earlier, this is a topic for a book that specializes in Web services and Web service security. Because this is a book about enterprise application development, it demonstrates how to continue using Windows Integrated Authentication. To pass your Windows Token, add the following line of code immediately after the Service1 instantiation line:

```
objWS.Credentials = System.Net.CredentialCache.DefaultCredentials
```

That is all it takes to get you authenticated on the IIS server. This is identical to setting the defaultCredentials attribute of the HTTP channel.

NOTE   Remember, you can do this only when both IIS and the client system run under the same network domain.

If you run the application and click the Load Employees button, your form should look like Figure 11-14.

Figure 11-14. Consumer implementation of the GetAllEmployees Web service

Creating the Details Form

Just to keep things easy, you are going to create a form that displays the details of
the employee but does nothing else. You have already seen how to handle everything involved with editing an employee's data, and none of that code would have
to change here. All you will examine is how to get the data from your Web service
and how to display it.

> **TIP**   This is why business logic should always be encapsulated in sepa-
> rate DLLs. Imagine if you had coded your initial application with all of
> the logic in the forms? You would have had to completely rewrite that
> logic for use in your Web service. This is a trap into which I have seen
> too many projects fall.

What you need to do now is add another form to your project and call it *frmDetails*. Open your original NorthwindTraders project (in a separate instance of the development environment) and display the frmEmployeeEdit form in the designer. Then, select all of the controls on the form except for the inherited controls (the business rules, the OK and Cancel buttons, and FileOpenDialog and ErrorProvider) and copy those controls. Then go to the frmDetails form, resize it large enough to hold the copied controls, and paste those controls.

 NOTE If you select the inherited controls, you will not be able to copy anything at all.

This places all of the controls you need onto the frmDetails form. Next, add a private module-level variable to frmDetails as follows:

```
Private msEmployee As localhost.structEmployee
```

This holds your employee structure so it can be used in the form_load method. Next, create a second constructor in frmDetails, as shown in Listing 11-11.

Listing 11-11. Second frmDetails Constructor

```
Public Sub New(ByVal sEmployee As localhost.structEmployee)
    MyBase.New()

    'This call is required by the Windows Form Designer.
    InitializeComponent()

    'Add any initialization after the InitializeComponent() call
    msEmployee = sEmployee
End Sub
```

Finally, add the Form_Load method as shown in Listing 11-12.

Listing 11-12. The frmDetails_Load Method

```
Private Sub frmDetails_Load(ByVal sender As Object, _
ByVal e As System.EventArgs) Handles MyBase.Load
    Dim i As Integer
    Dim strValue As String

    Try
        With msEmployee
            cboCourtesy.Text = .TitleOfCourtesy
            txtFirstName.Text = .FirstName
            txtLastName.Text = .LastName
            txtTitle.Text = .Title
            dtpBirthDate.Value = .BirthDate
            dtpHireDate.Value = .HireDate
            txtHomePhone.Text = .HomePhone
            txtExtension.Text = .Extension
            txtAddress.Text = .Address
            txtCity.Text = .City
            txtRegion.Text = .Region
            txtPostalCode.Text = .PostalCode
            txtCountry.Text = .Country
            rtbNotes.Text = .Notes

            If Not .Photo Is Nothing Then
                Dim mStream As New IO.MemoryStream(.Photo)
                mStream.Write(.Photo, 0, .Photo.Length - 1)
                picPhoto.Image = Image.FromStream(mStream)
            End If

        End With
    Catch exc As Exception
        MessageBox.Show(exc.Message)
    End Try
End Sub
```

You will notice right off that this is a slightly abbreviated version of the load method in your NorthwindTraders application. That is because you no longer have your collections of objects to load the combo boxes and listboxes. But that is OK because now you have the ability to add the methods necessary to call those methods and return that data yourself.

The last thing you need to do for this step is to add the edit employee method in the frmMain form, as shown in Listing 11-13.

Listing 11-13. The btnEdit_Click Method

```
Private Sub btnEdit_Click(ByVal sender As System.Object, _
ByVal e As System.EventArgs) Handles btnEdit.Click
    Dim objWS As localhost.Service1
    Dim frm As frmDetails
    Dim sEmployee As localhost.structEmployee

    Try
        Cursor = Cursors.WaitCursor
        objWS = New localhost.Service1()
        objWS.Credentials = System.Net.CredentialCache.DefaultCredentials
        With grdEmployees
            sEmployee = _
        objWS.GetEmployeeDetails(Convert.ToInt32(.Item(.CurrentRowIndex, _
        0)))
        End With
        objWS = Nothing
        frm = New frmDetails(sEmployee)
        frm.ShowDialog()
    Catch exc As Exception
        MessageBox.Show(exc.Message)
    Finally
        Cursor = Cursors.Default
    End Try
End Sub
```

As you can see, you are simply passing the ID of the employee to the GetEmployeeDetails method. You then pass the resulting structure to your form. Try the application out now to see how it works. You will notice that the response time is fairly fast considering the overhead of the call. You cannot actually edit the code at this point, but you should be able to create the Web service necessary to do this.

CAUTION   You must take into account the resulting network load when implementing a Web service. In the original NorthwindTraders application, you will recall that you used a binary formatter to compress the data as much as possible. A Web service can *only* pass data in a SOAP format, which creates a much larger amount of network traffic.

Using the WSDL Utility

The Web Services Description Language (WSDL) utility that comes with Visual Studio .NET is designed to reverse engineer a SOAP message into a class that can hold the information. For example, in the employee details case, you have a structure called *structEmployee*. And you can access the methods of this structure, but you do not have the structure. What if you want to use this in another part of your application? When the Web service reference is added to your application, the Integrated Development Environment (IDE) must somehow retrieve information about the objects that you will be passing to the Web service to create the proxy objects (the object definitions displayed in the object browser). For these and other reasons, you can turn to the WSDL utility.

Wsdl.exe is located in the \Microsoft Visual Studio .NET\FrameworkSDK\Bin folder (for version 1.0) or the \Microsoft Visual Studio .NET\SDK\v1.1\bin\ folder (for version 1.1). You need to run it from the command line or set it up as an external tool within the .NET Framework. For this example, add it as an external tool because you probably will not use it frequently, and if you have not set up an external tool before, now is a great time to learn. Select Tools ➤ External Tools from the VS IDE main menu. That brings up the External Tools dialog box, as shown in Figure 11-15.

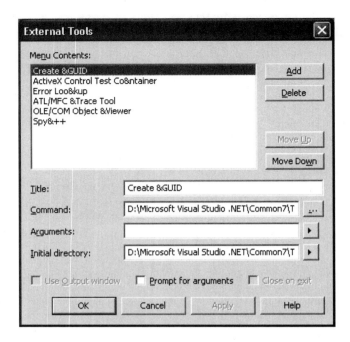

Figure 11-15. The External Tools dialog box

Click the Add button and enter information as shown in Table 11-2.

Table 11-2. The Wsdl External Tools Properties

Property	Value
Title	Wsdl
Command	(Path to the wsdl.exe file)
Arguments	/l:VB
Initial Directory	$(SolutionDir)
Prompt For Arguments	Checked

Once you have entered these values, click the OK button. The /l:VB entry for the argument specifies that the output should be formatted as a Visual Basic code file; the default is C#. You need to prompt for the arguments because you need to specify the location of the .wsdl file. If you look at the Tools menu again, you should see an entry for the Wsdl application. Clicking the Wsdl entry causes the dialog box in Figure 11-16 to appear.

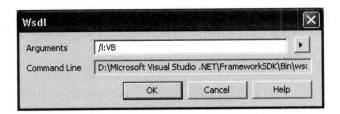

Figure 11-16. The Wsdl dialog box

At the end of the Arguments parameter, add *http://localhost/northwind/ service1.asmx?wsdl* and then click the OK button. You will then see a command window appear briefly as the Service1.vb file is being written. Next, navigate to your solution folder and you will see this file. Double-click it to open it in the VS IDE. Take some time to examine it. The class created is all you need to call the service (as opposed to adding a Web reference as you did earlier). It creates a class called *structEmployee* (not a structure) and all of the methods to call both of your Web services—synchronously and asynchronously.

TIP   It does not matter if you use a structure or a class when you are dealing with XML serialization. As long as the class (or structure) name is the same as the original class or structure, and all of the public properties are identically named, you can deserialize a class object to a structure object and vice versa.

The real strength of this utility, combined with the awesome features of the .NET Framework, allows you to dynamically generate and compile code to call these Web services even if you know absolutely nothing about them!

Now that you have examined how to create and consume Web services, let's look at how you actually go about publishing them and finding other published Web services.

Using .NET Server 2003 UDDI

The .NET servers come in several flavors. Currently, these include the Standard version, Web version, and Enterprise version. They all contain a variety of programs for use within the enterprise. All three versions come with the .NET Framework installed. By default, UDDI Server is not installed when the server is installed; you must install it afterward (as a note, IIS is not installed either).

NOTE All information in this section was gathered using Release Candidate 2 (RC2) of .NET Enterprise Server 2003.

Installing UDDI Server

Before installing UDDI Server, you should install SQL Server. UDDI Server uses the SQL Server engine to store Web service information, but if SQL Server is not installed, the Microsoft Data Engine (MSDE) is installed. This gives you far less control over the data in the backend because you need a third-party tool to view the database (such as Access).

TIP You can also use the Microsoft Management Console (MMC) to control SQL Server. To do this, open Administrative Tools and drill down into the Services and Applications node. You will notice that the interface is almost identical to that of the SQL Server Enterprise Manager.

CAUTION At the time of this writing, VS .NET 1.1 could not be installed on the same machine as .NET Server 2003 RC2. In the following examples I have placed *localhost* in the URL to make the code and reference paths generic.

To install the server, go to the Control Panel ➤ Add or Remove Programs ➤ Add/Remove Windows Components and select UDDI Services, as shown in Figure 11-17.

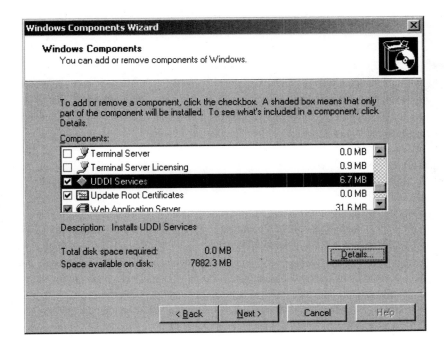

Figure 11-17. Adding UDDI Services

This installs three tools required to use the UDDI Services: the administration console, database components, and Web server components. You administer UDDI Services through a simple (but pretty slick) Web interface. If IIS has not already been installed, it will be installed now.

NOTE There are several questions you will need to answer as you move through the different dialog boxes for installing UDDI Server. Most of the configuration choices you make will be based on the setup of your system and network. The only choice you should make for this example is to not use SSL encryption unless you happen to have a Certificate Authority Server installed and running.

After you have installed UDDI Services, you can access them by opening Internet Explorer and navigating to http://localhost/uddi, as shown in Figure 11-18.

Microsoft has included a fairly nice guide to publishing Web services, and the links to UDDI resources on the Web are extremely helpful. The UDDI resources on the Web take you to http://uddi.microsoft.com/netserverinfo, which in turn takes you to all sorts of different information.

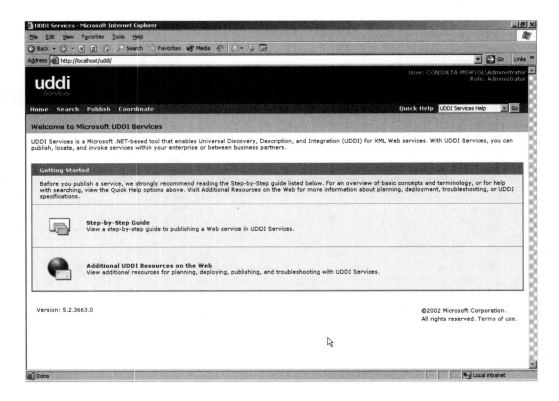

Figure 11-18. The UDDI Services administration console

Publishing a Web Service

Select the Publish link from the main administration page, and you will see the
screen shown in Figure 11-19.

NOTE   You will not see the Northwind nodes (on the left side of the screen)
until you have added the Web services you created into the UDDI.

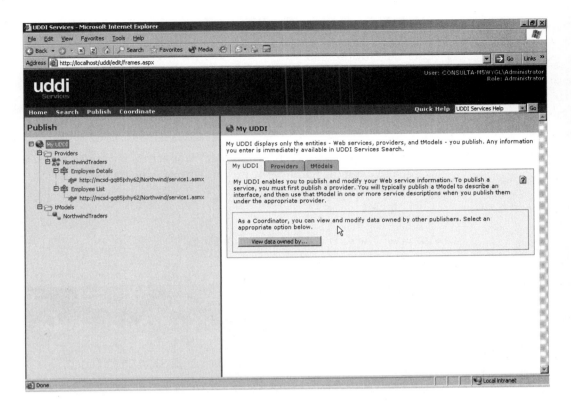

Figure 11-19. The UDDI Web service publishing interface

This is the main screen for publishing a Web service. In Figure 11-19 you can see the NorthwindTraders Web services created earlier (you will walk through publishing these Web services here). As mentioned earlier, Microsoft has included an excellent guide, so I just touch on the highlights and show how to publish your Web services specifically.

Providers are the companies that provide Web services. tModels are service definitions. There has been a great deal of confusion over what a tModel is, and the documentation and publishing mechanism do not make this a whole lot more clear. A *tModel* is a service description—that is all. It can be anything from a Word document that explains the service to a published WSDL schema. It is anything you want it to be or nothing at all, although it is recommended you provide a tModel. In the left pane of the Web page is the published provider and a tree of the services provided. On the right is the list of providers and tModels displayed so that they can be drilled down into.

To publish the NorthwindTraders Web services, do the following:

1. Click the Providers tab.

2. Click the Add Provider button from the next screen.

3. Click the Edit button from the next screen.

4. Select the language (you can have as many languages for a provider as you want) and enter the name of the provider (NorthwindTraders).

5. Click Update.

This gives you the screen shown in Figure 11-20.

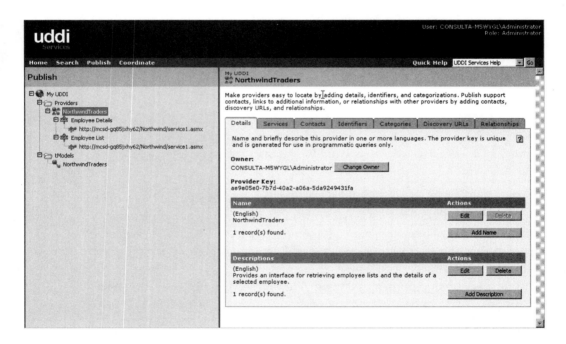

Figure 11-20. The NorthwindTraders provider screen

Next, click the Services tab and do the following to add your two services:

1. Click the Add Service button.

2. Click the Edit button.

3. Select the service language and enter the name of the service (Employee List).

4. Click the Update button.

5. Click the Bindings tab.

6. Click the Add Binding button.

7. Click the Edit button.

8. Enter the URL of the Web service (if everything is on the same machine then the URL is *http://localhost/Northwind/service1.asmx*).

9. Click the Update button.

10. Click the NorthwindTraders link at the top of the dialog box.

11. Repeat these steps for the Employee Details Web service.

When you are finished, the Services tab of the Northwind Provider looks similar to the screen in Figure 11-21. Note that both services have the same URL, which will be typical for a group of services.

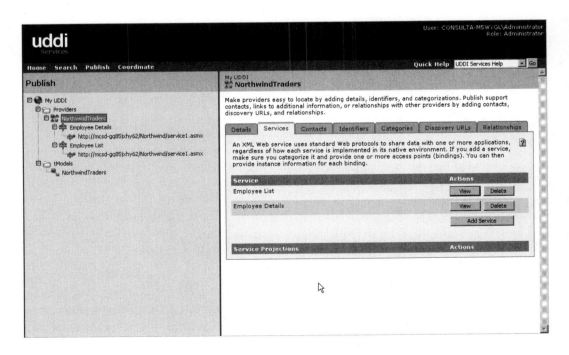

Figure 11-21. The Services tab of the Northwind provider

As far as setting up a Web service, that is as much work as you need to do. However, look at the Discovery URLs tab (shown in Figure 11-22).

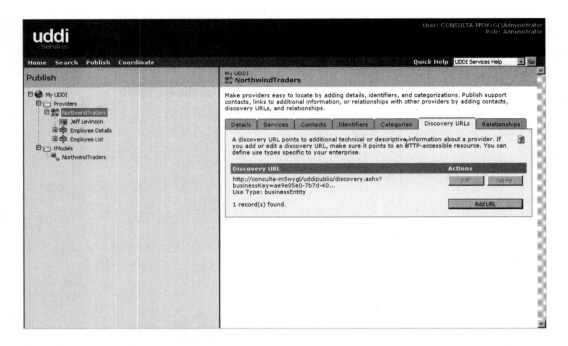

Figure 11-22. The Discovery URLs tab

The URL listed here is the URL that a user would need to navigate to in order to gather information about this Web service.

Notice also in Figure 11-22 that my name now appears under the NorthwindTrader provider. I clicked the Contacts tab and added myself in as a contact for the Web service, which in an enterprise is going to be an absolute necessity.

Accessing the UDDI Programmatically

If you are accessing the UDDI from another system, or you would like to access it as a user would access it, you need to use the URL http://[machine name]/uddipublic. This is the public URL that people coming into your UDDI will use to determine information about the available services. In this section you will put together a small application to read the information about Web services programmatically. There can be many reasons why you might want to do this. These reasons include being able to check new additions and changes to UDDI services, and to incorporate Web services programmatically. There will undoubtedly be many other reasons to do so as Web services expand and are used by more enterprises.

Web Services in the Enterprise

There has been a lot of talk lately about Web services and their possibilities, but at the time of this writing there are few companies putting Web services to use in a public (external of the enterprise) manner. As I write this chapter, the two major players are Microsoft (with its MapPoint Web service and the new .NET Alerts Web service) and Amazon.com. I suspect that the majority of enterprises will hold off on implementing any type of public Web service for at least the next six months until enterprises can get a good grasp of what a Web service is and how to use it.

Currently enterprises should be putting together a list of standards for use within the organization for creating and organizing the services that they have available. At the beginning these will probably be simple internal Web services for things such as a customer database or an employee database—information that is typically spread out or duplicated all over an enterprise. By coming up with uniform standards, the task of searching for Web services becomes much easier. But beware—all UDDIs are not created equal. Even though there is a UDDI standard/ specification, each UDDI works a little differently unfortunately. Much of what you can do as developers will fail if the major players cannot agree to a true common standard; and in the long run, the businesses that want to use UDDI will be the ones that suffer.

To be able to access the UDDI programmatically, you need to download and install the UDDI Software Development Kit (SDK) version 2.0 from http:// www.microsoft.com/downloads/release.asp?releaseid=35940.

 NOTE   At the time this writing, only the UDDI SDK version 2.0 Beta is available. It is not backward compatible with the UDDI 1.0 specification. This URL may become out-of-date, in which case you can check http://msdn.microsoft.com/uddi.

NOTE   As of this writing, the UDDI version 3.0 specification is current. There is no SDK for this at this time.

Introducing the UDDI Object Model

You will build a small application that will programmatically retrieve entries from the UDDI. Regardless of how many providers or services there are, the code to retrieve that information remains the same. To that end, this application will give you a good start toward building a full-fledged system to handle UDDI tasks through code.

Although the code to get the data can be fairly long winded, it is pretty straightforward once you understand the basic structure of the UDDI objects; see the UDDI object maps shown on the inside front and back covers of this book. The current documentation is pretty scant as of this writing because this is only a beta SDK. Many of the namespaces and objects will look familiar to you if you spend some time looking at a UDDI directory. The Uddi namespace contains the bulk of the objects that you will be working with, and it provides an entry to most of the other objects available to you in the other namespaces. For example, under the Business namespace you will see the BusinessEntity object, and under the Uddi namespace you will see a method called GetBusinessDetail that returns the BusinessEntityCollection. This illustrates how you can drill down into the UDDI starting at the top, which is what you will do in your little application.

Building the UDDI Explorer

Start by creating a new Windows project called *UddiExplorer*, and then add a reference to the Microsoft.Uddi.Sdk assembly—this will be in the list of .NET Framework components because it is installed in the Global Access Cache (GAC). When you are done building the form, it will look like the form shown in Figure 11-23.

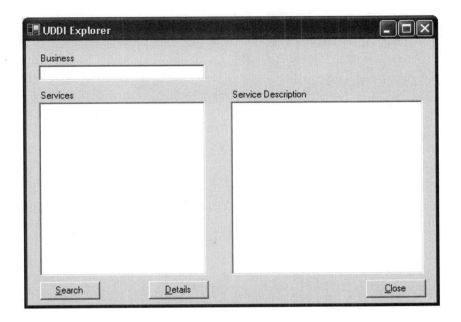

Figure 11-23. The UDDI Explorer interface

Add the controls to the form and name them according to Table 11-3.

Table 11-3. The UDDI Explorer Controls

Control	Name	Text
Label		Business
Textbox	txtBusiness	
Label		Services
Treeview	tvwServices	
Label		Service Description
Textbox	txtServiceDescription	
Button	btnSearch	&Search
Button	btnDetails	&Details
Button	btnClose	&Close

The only property you need to alter is the Multiline property of the txtDetails textbox; set it to *true*. Now that you have your form, switch over to the code view and add the following header information:

```
Option Explicit On
Option Strict On

Imports Microsoft
Imports Microsoft.Uddi
Imports Microsoft.Uddi.Api
```

Next, add the code for the btnSearch_Click method to the form as shown in Listing 11-14.

Listing 11-14. The btnSearch_Click Method

```
Private Sub btnSearch_Click(ByVal sender As System.Object, _
ByVal e As System.EventArgs)
Handles btnSearch.Click
    Try
        Cursor = Cursors.WaitCursor
        Inquire.Url = "http://localhost/uddipublic/inquire.asmx"

        Dim fb As New FindBusiness
        Dim bList As BusinessList
        Dim bus As Business.BusinessInfo

        fb.Names.Add(Me.txtBusiness.Text)
        bList = fb.Send

        For Each bus In bList.BusinessInfos
            Dim ndeBus As New TreeNode(bus.Name)
            ndeBus.Tag = bus.BusinessKey

            Dim gBusinessDetail As New GetBusinessDetail
            Dim bDetail As BusinessDetail

            gBusinessDetail.BusinessKeys.Add(bus.BusinessKey)
            bDetail = gBusinessDetail.Send
```

```
            Dim i As Integer
            Dim gServices As New GetServiceDetail
            Dim bService As ServiceDetail
            Dim bEntity As Business.BusinessEntity

            For Each bEntity In bDetail.BusinessEntities
                  For i = 0 To bEntity.BusinessServices.Count - 1
                        Dim nde As New _
                        TreeNode(bEntity.BusinessServices(i).Names(0).Text)
                        nde.Tag = bEntity.BusinessServices(i).ServiceKey
                        ndeBus.Nodes.Add(nde)
                  Next
            Next

            tvwServices.Nodes.Add(ndeBus)
      Next

   Catch ex As Exception
         MessageBox.Show(ex.Message)
   Finally
         Cursor = Cursors.Default
   End Try
End Sub
```

Let's examine this code in detail so that you can figure out what is happening. To begin with, you need to know where the UDDI is located and where you can inquire about the services it contains. You accomplish this by setting the inquiry URL with the following line:

```
Inquire.Url = "http://localhost/uddipublic/inquire.asmx"
```

Next you need to find the business for which you are looking. Every item in a UDDI that can be searched has a Find object (FindBusiness, FindService, FindTModel, and so on). In this case you are going to be looking for the business.

 NOTE In a practical situation, you will probably want to search for a service that falls within a specific category such as Financial, Customer Information, and so on. You are performing your search this way because of the limited amount of information in your UDDI. The process is the same no matter what you are searching for, so extending this application is simple.

The BusinessInfo object enumerates through the collection of businesses that are returned to you. You can search for as many businesses at a time as you want by adding business names to the FindBusiness object. Finally, to actually go find the businesses, you call the Send method of the FindBusiness object. This call to FindBusiness returns a BusinessList object, which contains all of the businesses that matched your search. Each object that can perform a find in the UDDI has a method called Send:

```
Dim fb As New FindBusiness
Dim bList As BusinessList
Dim bus As Business.BusinessInfo

fb.Names.Add(Me.txtBusiness.Text)
bList = fb.Send
```

Next, you loop through the businesses that were returned to you and store the business name in a tree node. You also store the business key in the node in case you want to drill down into the business (covered next):

```
For Each bus In bList.BusinessInfos
    Dim ndeBus As New TreeNode(bus.Name)
    ndeBus.Tag = bus.BusinessKey
```

Now you need to get information about your business to figure out what services the business provides. To do this you declare a GetBusinessDetail object, which performs basically the same function as the FindBusiness object—it searches the UDDI for businesses that match a list of BusinessKeys. As with the FindBusiness object, to perform the search, you call the Send method, which returns a collection of business details:

```
Dim gBusinessDetail As New GetBusinessDetail
Dim bDetail As BusinessDetail

gBusinessDetail.BusinessKeys.Add(bus.BusinessKey)
bDetail = gBusinessDetail.Send
```

Next you have to dive into finding out what services your business provides. The GetServiceDetail and ServiceDetail perform the same functions as the GetBusinessDetail and BusinessDetail previously mentioned, except at the service level:

```
Dim i As Integer
Dim gServices As New GetServiceDetail
Dim bService As ServiceDetail
Dim bEntity As Business.BusinessEntity
```

You start off by looping through the business entities returned to you by the call to the GetBusinessDetail object. Within each business, you loop through all of the services provided by that business. For each service you create a new node and set the text property equal to the service name. Each service can have multiple names for various reasons (such as for different languages), but you are only going to take the first one because you have given your services only one name each. Then you set the tag property equal to the service key so you can easily get information about this service later. Finally, you add the node to your root node and you add the root node to the treeview:

```
For Each bEntity In bDetail.BusinessEntities
    For i = 0 To bEntity.BusinessServices.Count - 1
        Dim nde As New TreeNode(bEntity.BusinessServices(i).Names(0).Text)
        nde.Tag = bEntity.BusinessServices(i).ServiceKey
        ndeBus.Nodes.Add(nde)
    Next
Next

    tvwServices.Nodes.Add(ndeBus)
Next
```

You now have enough code to run the application, so run that application and enter the name *NorthwindTraders* in the Business name textbox (or enter only the first part of the name because a partial search is performed). The form should look like Figure 11-24 after you click the Search button.

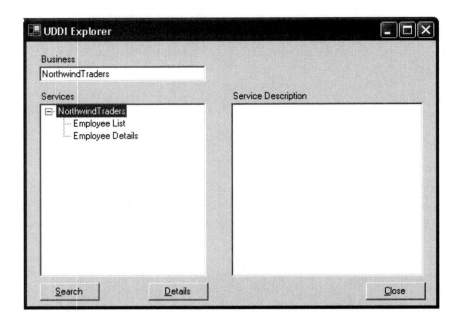

Figure 11-24. The search results in the UDDI Explorer application

Now you will add the ability to get the details of a particular service. Add the code in Listing 11-15 to Form1. This code allows you to retrieve the details for a given service.

Listing 11-15. The btnDetails_Click Method

```
Private Sub btnDetails_Click(ByVal sender As System.Object, _
ByVal e As System.EventArgs) Handles btnDetails.Click
    Dim gServiceDetail As New GetServiceDetail
    Dim bService As ServiceDetail
    Dim i, j As Integer

    gServiceDetail.ServiceKeys.Add(tvwServices.SelectedNode.Tag.ToString)
    bService = gServiceDetail.Send

    txtDetails.Text = ""

    For i = 0 To bService.BusinessServices.Count - 1
        txtServiceDescription.Text = "Service Name: " & _
        bService.BusinessServices(i).Names(0).Text
        txtServiceDescription.Text += ControlChars.CrLf
```

```
        txtServiceDescription.Text += "Descriptions: " & ControlChars.CrLf
        For j = 0 To bService.BusinessServices(i).Descriptions.Count - 1
            txtServiceDescription.Text += _
            bService.BusinessServices(i).Descriptions(j).Text
            txtServiceDescription.Text += ControlChars.CrLf
        Next

        txtServiceDescription.Text += "Category Bag: " & ControlChars.CrLf
        For j = 0 To bService.BusinessServices(i).CategoryBag.Count - 1
            txtServiceDescription.Text += "Key Name: " & _
            bService.BusinessServices(i).CategoryBag(j).KeyName & _
            ControlChars.CrLf
            txtServiceDescription.Text += "Key Value: " & _
            bService.BusinessServices(i).CategoryBag(j).KeyValue & _
            ControlChars.CrLf
            txtServiceDescription.Text += "tModel Key: " & _
            bService.BusinessServices(i).CategoryBag(j).TModelKey & _
            ControlChars.CrLf
            txtServiceDescription.Text += ControlChars.CrLf
        Next

        txtServiceDescription.Text += "Business Key: " & _
        bService.BusinessServices(i).BusinessKey
        txtServiceDescription.Text += ControlChars.CrLf
        txtServiceDescription.Text += "Service Key: " & _
        bService.BusinessServices(i).ServiceKey
        txtServiceDescription.Text += "Access Point: " & _
        bService.BusinessServices(i).BindingTemplates(0).AccessPoint.Text _
        & ControlChars.CrLf
    Next
End Sub
```

The code starts out similar to your Search method, except that you are looking to find a service with a key you already know, so you can skip a lot of the extraneous work. Once you get a reference to the service you are looking for, you just pull out all of the information about that service. The most important piece of information is in the last line of this procedure, the BindingTemplate AccessPoint, which provides the URL of the service. By appending *?wsdl* to the end of the AccessPoint, you will have the URL needed to use the WSDL utility. When you run the application, click a service node and then click the Details button. The results should look something like Figure 11-25.

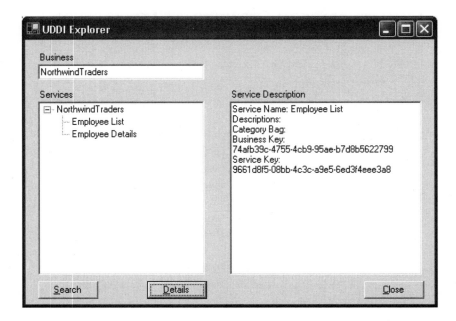

Figure 11-25. Service details

This small application gives you an overall understanding of the organization of UDDI Server and how to retrieve the information you need, when you need it.

Summary

You saw how to create a Web service based on existing components, and you looked at a couple of the security mechanisms available to developers. You added a Web reference to a Windows application to call the Web service while maintaining security. And you displayed that information in forms that you built just for that purpose. You also learned to use the WSDL utility to gather technical information about the structures, classes, and methods needed to call a Web service with little effort.

Through this chapter you also gained the experience of setting up UDDI Server and adding Web services to it. You should now have an appreciation for the structural organization of UDDI Server and the ability to search through it programmatically.

In the next chapter you will create an ASP.NET application that serves as an interface for the components you created for your NorthwindTraders application. You will also hook up your Web service to this application so that you gain the experience of calling a Web service from both a Windows and a Web application.

CHAPTER 12

Creating a
Web Forms Interface

IN THIS CHAPTER you will add a Web interface to your application. You will approach it from two ways: the first as a frontend to the Web service you created in the previous chapter and the second as a frontend that hooks directly to the components you created in Chapters 3 to 10.

First, you will examine the different methods of securing an application that does not use Windows Integrated Authentication and you will implement one of these methods for handling security. After you create your new security mechanism, you will hook up your Web user interface to see how everything works.

Targeting Corporate Intranets

Building a Web forms application for an intranet is a whole lot easier than building a Web forms application for an extranet or the World Wide Web. The reason, in a word, is security. Using Windows Integrated Authentication is more than enough security for your application right now. When possible, Windows authentication is always the way to go. It is simple, it is external to the code, and it is strongly encrypted. Also, by using Windows authentication, impersonation, and delegation, the user's identity is authenticated at Internet Information Server (IIS) and at SQL Server. No one can go "around" your security setting. In many Internet applications, a user is authenticated once and given a tag that says they were authenticated successfully. At that point someone can "hijack" a session and continue working as that user. This is not the case with a Windows Authentication security scheme—the user is always revalidated every time they try to connect to a resource.

Targeting Corporate Extranets

Extranets generally cause a developer the most headaches. Figure 12-1 compares an intranet to an extranet.

Machines linked in an intranet can use the same Windows Integrated security, but on the extranet that is rarely a desirable situation. Notice in Figure 12-1 that an external corporation is hitting IIS, which is external to the company from which

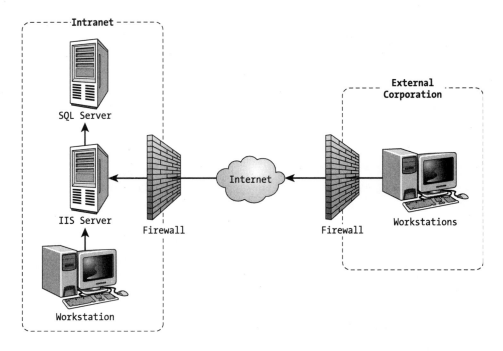

Figure 12-1. A corporate intranet/extranet

they want information. Usually IIS sits on the boundary of the corporate intranet. Whatever the exact setup is, unless there is a Virtual Personal Network (VPN) that goes directly into your company intranet, the external customer is not going to be able to log on using Windows Authentication. So, you need to come up with another scheme to authenticate the users. You really only have two choices: Forms Authentication and Passport Authentication. This chapter covers setting up Forms Authentication.

NOTE You can practice setting up a Passport Authentication scheme by applying for a development and testing Passport account. You can get more information about this at http://www.microsoft.com/myservices/passport. You will also need to install the Passport Software Development Kit (SDK), which you can find at http://msdn.microsoft.com/downloads.

There are many more detailed scenarios than the one you will be creating here. This is designed to be an overview of how to secure an ASP.NET application, but it does not cover all of the details.

Setting Up the Application

To begin with, you are going to place a Web frontend onto your Web service. Figure 12-2 shows a basic deployment diagram.

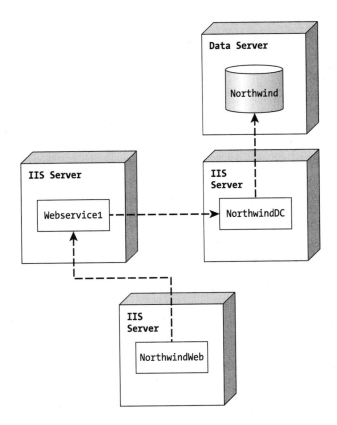

Figure 12-2. The Web interface deployment diagram

As you can see from Figure 12-2, this is a rather roundabout way to get to your data, but it does show you how easy it is to allow additional points of entry to your components. When you get to the "Referencing Your Objects Directly" section, you will go directly to the original components to access the database.

Setting Up SQL Server

Before beginning, you need to add a new table to your Northwind database. The new table stores your usernames and passwords (well, sort of). Execute the SQL in Listing 12-1 to create the new table and associated stored procedures.

Listing 12-1. The UserList Table

```
USE Northwind
GO
CREATE TABLE UserList
(username VARCHAR(20) PRIMARY KEY,
 userpass VARCHAR(100) NOT NULL)
GO
CREATE PROCEDURE usp_AddNewUser
@uid varchar(20),
@pwd varchar(100)
AS
INSERT INTO UserList (username, userpass)
  VALUES (@uid, @pwd)
GO
CREATE PROCEDURE usp_ValidateUser
@uid varchar(20),
@pwd varchar(100),
@valid int OUTPUT
AS
DECLARE
@count int

SET @count = (SELECT count(*)
    FROM    UserList
    WHERE    username = @uid
    AND    userpass = @pwd)

IF @count = 1
   SET @valid = 1
ELSE
   SET @valid = 0
```

As you can see, this table is very simple. The username column stores a unique username (this is the reason it is a primary key—so usernames cannot be duplicated), and the userpass column stores a hash of the user password. The AddNewUser stored procedure inserts new users into your UserList table, and the ValidateUser stored procedure verifies that the user has presented valid credentials to be logged on to the system.

Setting Up Security

The logon page is always the first entry into your private data. There can be other pages on the Web site with nonprivate data that do not need to be protected, but you are only concerned with the pages that need protection. After the user is authenticated against the Web site, you then need to figure out how to allow them access to the data. Right now you have SQL Server and IIS set up to allow only Windows Authentication—so you need to make some hard decisions when you determine if you want to continue using this scheme.

CAUTION You must set the Directory Security on the Northwind virtual folder and Webservice1 virtual folder in IIS so that it allows Anonymous access. If you do not, this will not work! You can do this from the Directory Security tab in the Properties dialog box for the Northwind virtual directory in IIS.

Any discussion of setting up a database for possible external (to the company) access must include a discussion on security and best practices. So, you are going to take a little time out to discuss some of the security issues and how to best set up your database for your Web application.

Storing Passwords

I have seen several different schemes for storing passwords in a database. One is to store the username and password in clear text and then retrieve the password based on the username and compare them. Another method is to encrypt the password and store the encrypted password in the database and then decrypt it to authenticate the user (or encrypt the password the user gave and match it to the encrypted password in the system).

However, Microsoft recommends that a hash be made of the password and that only the hash gets stored in the system. When dealing with a hash, it is almost impossible to get the original value back out of the hash, and it is case sensitive. Using this method, no one, not even the Database Administrator (DBA) can get your password. It is easy to figure out if a system is configured this way because if you lose your password, the only solution is for a system administrator to reset your password to something such as "password" and require that you change it on your next logon. Note, though, that if you use this scheme, you need to make sure you supply the DBA with a hash of the word *password* and not the word itself!

Because Microsoft considers this a best practice approach, this is what this chapter demonstrates.

Now you need some way to log on to the database to verify a user's credentials. This becomes the second issue that you have to deal with when determining how to secure your application. If you continue to use the current setup (Windows Integrated Authentication), you need to grant access to SQL Server to a specific user account and use that for all of your connections to the database. That is not a bad idea, but not every Web site is using a database that allows Windows Integrated Authentication for the backend, and it could possibly introduce security holes.

TIP   You can use Windows Integrated Authentication to connect to the database instead of using a SQL Server account, but you must do this with caution. For an example of this type of successful setup, see the eWeek Web site (http://www.eweek.com) and search for *OpenHack IV*. Microsoft successfully used this setup to create a Web site that withstood more than 80,000 attempted hacks!

So, what is the first line of defense? Always use components to connect to the database and make sure the components are independent of the user interface. But is that all you can do to make this more hacker proof?

TIP   One advantage of using individual user accounts is that you can control strict access to specific stored procedures, views, tables, and functions. Using a single account to connect to the database, you lose this ability. Also, you can update tables with the identity of the user who updated the record without having to pass the user's name in every time they call a stored procedure.

After all, if the connection is made entirely from within the firewall, why not use Windows Integrated Authentication there? The answer is that you can, except that as mentioned earlier, not everyone is using SQL Server as the backend. Also, numerous other security considerations have nothing to do with how you program your application, but with how the network administrators have configured your network.

You can take additional steps to secure yourself. The first, and easiest, way to do this is to place the SQL connection string in the web.config file on your component server (behind the firewall) and include the username and password there. Then, grant access to the SQL Server for that username/password combination. Now you have the problem of storing a username and password in clear text on a machine that can be reached by people internal to the company—and that is another bad idea. To mitigate the risk, you can take a slightly different step to store and retrieve the username and password for the database—use the registry. You can store the information in a key specifically created for this purpose. The information can be encrypted (if needed) and the appropriate Access Control List (ACL) placed on this key. This is probably the best solution because it keeps people both internal and external to the company from getting this information easily. Is it 100-percent hacker proof? Well, you cannot ever make that assumption because the first time you do, you will get burned, but it is better than storing database logon information in an easily accessible text file.

TIP   Generally, it is also a good idea to place the entire connection string in the registry because it protects the location of the database from a hacker. This can help protect against "man in the middle" attacks.

Because this is the best way to do this, you are going to create a registry key specifically for this purpose and place your logon information in it.

To start with, you need to change SQL Server from Windows authentication mode to Mixed Mode authentication (if it is not already set that way). To do this, take the following steps:

1. Open SQL Server Enterprise Manager.

2. Right-click the database instance that needs to be changed and select Properties.

3. Select the Security tab (as shown in Figure 12-3).

4. Ensure that the SQL Server and Windows option button is selected.

5. Click OK.

When asked if you want to restart the server, select Yes.

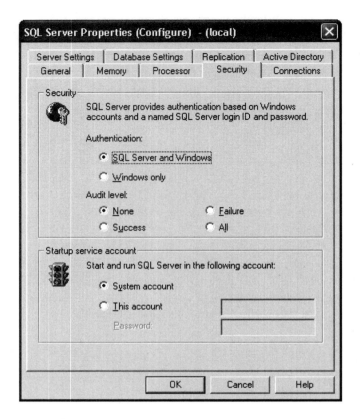

Figure 12-3. The SQL Server Properties dialog box's Security tab

Creating the User Account

Next you need to create a user account for accessing the Northwind database. To do this, execute the following SQL in SQL Query Analyzer:

```
Use Northwind
exec sp_addlogin N'nwAccount', 'password', 'Northwind'
go
sp_grantdbaccess N'nwAccount', 'nwAccount'
```

This creates a new account called *nwAccount* with the password *password* and sets the default database to Northwind. Then you give permissions for this account to actually access the Northwind database. Execute the following SQL to give your nwAccount permissions to execute all of the stored procedures you have created up to this point:

```
Use Northwind
GO
GRANT  EXECUTE  ON [dbo].[usp_AddNewUser]  TO [nwAccount]
GO
GRANT  EXECUTE  ON [dbo].[usp_ValidateUser]  TO [nwAccount]
GO
GRANT  EXECUTE  ON [dbo].[usp_application_errors_save]  TO [nwAccount]
GO
GRANT  EXECUTE  ON [dbo].[usp_employee_delete]  TO [nwAccount]
GO
GRANT  EXECUTE  ON [dbo].[usp_employee_getall]  TO [nwAccount]
GO
GRANT  EXECUTE  ON [dbo].[usp_employee_getone]  TO [nwAccount]
GO
GRANT  EXECUTE  ON [dbo].[usp_employee_save]  TO [nwAccount]
GO
GRANT  EXECUTE  ON [dbo].[usp_employee_territory_delete]  TO [nwAccount]
GO
GRANT  EXECUTE  ON [dbo].[usp_employee_territory_insert]  TO [nwAccount]
GO
GRANT  EXECUTE  ON [dbo].[usp_region_delete]  TO [nwAccount]
GO
GRANT  EXECUTE  ON [dbo].[usp_region_getall]  TO [nwAccount]
GO
GRANT  EXECUTE  ON [dbo].[usp_region_getone]  TO [nwAccount]
GO
GRANT  EXECUTE  ON [dbo].[usp_region_save]  TO [nwAccount]
GO
GRANT  EXECUTE  ON [dbo].[get_menu_structure]  TO [nwAccount]
GO
GRANT  EXECUTE  ON [dbo].[usp_territory_delete]  TO [nwAccount]
GO
GRANT  EXECUTE  ON [dbo].[usp_territory_getall]  TO [nwAccount]
GO
GRANT  EXECUTE  ON [dbo].[usp_territory_getone]  TO [nwAccount]
GO
GRANT  EXECUTE  ON [dbo].[usp_territory_save]  TO [nwAccount]
GO
```

Now that you have set up SQL Server, it is time to add a registry entry to hold your username and password information.

Setting Up the Registry

To begin, select the Start menu ➤ Run and type *regedit32* and click OK. This brings up the Registry Editor, as shown in Figure 12-4.

Figure 12-4. The Windows Registry Editor

To create the appropriate registry keys, take the following steps:

1. Expand the HKEY_LOCAL_MACHINE node.

2. Expand the SOFTWARE node.

3. Right-click the SOFTWARE node and select New ➤ Key.

4. When the new node is created, enter the name *NorthwindTraders* and press Enter.

5. Right-click the NorthwindTraders key that you just created and select New ➤ Key.

6. When the new node is created, enter the name *dbLogon* and press Enter.

7. Right-click the dbLogon node and select New ➤ String Value and enter the text *username*.

8. Right-click the dbLogon node and select New ➤ String Value and enter the text *password*.

9. Right-click the username entry and select Modify. Enter the username *nwAccount*.

10. Right-click the password entry and select Modify. Enter the password *password*.

NOTE As mentioned earlier, this information can be encrypted, but that requires writing a separate program to store the information in an encrypted state. For your purposes you will not be doing this, but it is a simple matter to write information to the registry.

You have now created the registry keys and you are done with the registry. Later in the "Accessing the Registry" section, you will look at how to retrieve and use these pieces of information.

Setting Up the Web Site

To begin with, let's create the Web site using Visual Studio, which will serve as your "external" Web site. Start Visual Studio and select File ➤ New ➤ Project and select the ASP.NET Web Application template. Change the location name to read *http:// localhost/NorthwindWeb* and click OK. Before you start building any pages, let's set up a secure folder and an empty form in that folder so that you have some place to redirect the user when they log on successfully. You will also set up an access denied page to redirect the user to when they fail a logon attempt.

Rename WebForm1.aspx to *Logon.aspx* (remember to switch to the code view afterward and rename the class from *WebForm1* to *Logon*). Next, add a new WebForm and call it *AccessDenied.aspx*. Then create a new folder for the application and call it *secure*. Under this folder add one more WebForm called *employees.aspx*. When you are done, the Solution Explorer should look like Figure 12-5.

Figure 12-5. The NorthwindWeb Solution Explorer

The last thing you need to do to set up the Web site is to alter the web.config file so that you can use Forms Authentication. First, change the authentication section of the web.config file from `<authentication mode = "Windows" />` to the following:

```
<authentication mode="Forms">
    <forms loginUrl="Logon.aspx" />
</authentication>
```

This specifies that you will be using Forms Authentication and that any unauthenticated users will be redirected to the Logon.aspx page. Next, you need to mark your secure folder as secure so that only authenticated users can get to that page. To do this you need to add a location tag to the web.config file. Add the code in Listing 12-2 to the third line of the web.config file (below the <configuration> tag and above the <system.web> tag).

Listing 12-2. The Location Tag

```
<location path="secure">
  <system.web>
    <authorization>
      <deny users="?" />
    </authorization>
  </system.web>
</location>
```

This says that any unknown users will not be given access to the secure folder.

> **TIP** You can also accomplish this by placing another web.config file in the secure folder and setting the authorization to deny users="?".

Finally, go to the IIS Console and open the properties for the NorthwindWeb folder. Go to the Directory Security tab and edit the security settings by unchecking the Integrated Windows authentication. This sets up your Web site as though you would set up a Web site that allowed access to external users.

Accessing the Database

Now that you have set up everything you need for the Web site, you need to code some functionality for accessing not only the registry, but the database as well. To do this, you need to do four things:

1. Create a class to access the registry and retrieve your database settings.

2. Create a class to verify a user's identity.

3. Deploy the component to your "internal" web server (in other words, a server that doesn't sit right on the firewall).

4. Connect to this component.

Accessing the Registry

Open the NorthwindTraders project (from Chapter 10, "Using Reflection," because you need to edit the data-centric objects) and add a new class to the NorthwindDC project called *RegReader*. This class is going to be simple—it creates the connection string that will be used by each of the classes that currently reads the appSettings section of the configuration file.

NOTE   You could create this as a separate, reusable object, but you are not going to in the interests of simplicity. You are just going to add the functionality to validate a username/password combination in your already existing objects.

To do this you will create a simple shared object that reads the information from the registry key and stores it in two variables. It will then be the responsibility of this class to create the connection string to pass to the different classes.

NOTE   This change of course requires you to perform a search and replace on your code that is not perfect in an ideal world. One method around this would be to create a class that actually opens up a connection and returns a connection to the calling code. The only problem with this solution is that every class has to instantiate this object and destroy it every time—on top of declaring and destroying the connection object. This was a design choice on my part, but if you know that you will be changing the application to allow access to users who are not trusted, then you can make this decision up front.

Before you write the code for this, let's change the Northwind_DSN key in the configuration file by removing the `Trusted_Connection=Yes;` part of the string so that it looks like the following:

```
value="server=localhost;Initial Catalog=Northwind"
```

Add the code for the RegReader class (shown in Listing 12-3) to the RegReader code module (after deleting the existing class code).

Listing 12-3. The RegReader Class

```
Option Explicit On
Option Strict On

Imports Microsoft.Win32
Imports System.Configuration

Public Class RegReader
    Private Shared UserName As String
    Private Shared Password As String

    Shared Sub New()
        Dim regKey As RegistryKey

        regKey = _
        Registry.LocalMachine.OpenSubKey("SOFTWARE\\NorthwindTraders\\dbLogon", _
        False)
        UserName = CType(regKey.GetValue("username"), String)
        Password = CType(regKey.GetValue("password"), String)
    End Sub

    Public Shared Function getConnString() As String
        Dim strCN As String = ConfigurationSettings.AppSettings("Northwind_DSN")
        Dim strID As String = "uid=" & UserName & ";pwd=" & Password & ";"

        Return strID & strCN
    End Function
End Class
```

This code is fairly straightforward. It is shared, so it is only instantiated once. The read from the registry is performed on instantiation (and it is very fast), and the values are stored in two shared variables. Finally, the getConnString returns the connection string based partially on the values in the registry and partially on the string in the configuration setting. That way it is still easy to change the database location/catalog, but it is more difficult to get at the username and password values.

The last thing you need to do is replace the calls to the AppSettings method with a call to the getConnString method. To do this, go to Edit ➤ Find and Replace ➤ Replace in Files. You will need to find the following code:

```
ConfigurationSettings.AppSettings("Northwind_DSN")
```

and replace it with *RegReader.getConnString*. The only problem you will encounter is that the find and replace also replaces the configuration statement in the RegReader class, so you will have to put it back in after the find and replace.

At this point you can rebuild the application and re-deploy the data-centric objects, and the application should work as advertised. However, you still have one more little thing you need to take care of...adding and validating users.

Adding and Validating Users

You need to build the code to access the specific stored procedures that you need to call in your data-centric objects. Add a new class to the NorthwindDC project called *WebUserDC*. You are going to create two simple methods to add and validate users to your Web site. Set up the code module by importing the System.Data.sqlClient namespace and then add the code for the ValidateUser method as shown in Listing 12-4.

Listing 12-4. The ValidateUser Method

```
Public Function ValidateUser(ByVal strUser As String, _
ByVal strPass As String) As Boolean
    Dim strCN As String = RegReader.getConnString
    Dim cn As New SqlConnection(strCN)
    Dim cmd As New SqlCommand
    Dim intValid As Integer

    cn.Open()

    With cmd
        .Connection = cn
        .CommandType = CommandType.StoredProcedure
        .CommandText = "usp_ValidateUser"
        .Parameters.Add("@uid", strUser)
        .Parameters.Add("@pwd", strPass)
        .Parameters.Add("@valid", Nothing).Direction = ParameterDirection.Output
        .ExecuteNonQuery()
        intValid = Convert.ToInt32(.Parameters("@valid").Value)
    End With

    cmd = Nothing
    cn.Close()
```

```
        If intValid = 1 Then
            Return True
        Else
            Return False
        End If
End Function
```

The ValidateUser method is simple in that it takes a username and a password hash, compares them against a value in the database, and returns a 1 if the values matched a record and 0 if they did not. You are simply returning a boolean indicating whether they were validated.

The AddUser method is also simple in that it takes a username and password hash and stores it in the database. Add this method to the WebUserDC class as shown in Listing 12-5.

Listing 12-5. The AddUser Method

```
Public Function AddUser(ByVal strUser As String, _
ByVal strPass As String) As Boolean
        Dim strCN As String = RegReader.getConnString
        Dim cn As New SqlConnection(strCN)
        Dim cmd As New SqlCommand
        Dim intValid As Integer

        Try
            cn.Open()

            With cmd
                .Connection = cn
                .CommandType = CommandType.StoredProcedure
                .CommandText = "usp_AddNewUser"
                .Parameters.Add("@uid", strUser)
                .Parameters.Add("@pwd", strPass)
                .ExecuteNonQuery()
            End With

            cmd = Nothing
            cn.Close()

            Return True
            Catch
                Return False
            End Try
End Function
```

Now that you have set up your application to validate a user, you need to modify your Web service so that it can make these calls against your objects. Before you do that, rebuild and re-deploy the NorthwindDC assembly to the bin folder so that your Web service can reference your new methods.

 CAUTION   I have shown you a way to secure the credentials to access the database and you have already seen that ASP.NET will write out an authentication cookie to the user's machine. But there is one thing I have not discussed—the "replay" attack. This is when a hacker basically "records" your session (including the authentication cookie) and then replays it back to the server, giving them access to everything to which you have access. Secure Sockets Layer (SSL) is an excellent means of defending against this type of attack. For more information on setting up a secure Web site and links to other information, visit http://www.msdn.microsoft.com/library/default.asp?url=/library/en-us/dnnetsec/html/openhack.asp.

Updating the Web Service

This is a fairly simple process, so the code will not be explained. Open the Web service project you created in the previous chapter and add the two methods shown in Listing 12-6.

Listing 12-6. The Web Service Implementation of the Security Functions

```
<WebMethod()> Public Function ValidateUser(ByVal strUser As String, _
ByVal strPass As String) As Boolean
        Dim objWebUser As New NorthwindTraders.NorthwindDC.WebUserDC
        Dim blnValid As Boolean = objWebUser.ValidateUser(strUser, strPass)
        objWebUser = Nothing
        Return blnValid
End Function

<WebMethod()> Public Function AddUser(ByVal strUser As String, _
ByVal strPass As String) As Boolean
        Dim objWebUser As New NorthwindTraders.NorthwindDC.WebUserDC
        Dim blnValid As Boolean = objWebUser.AddUser(strUser, strPass)
        objWebUser = Nothing
        Return blnValid
End Function
```

Remember to rebuild the project! Once you are done with this, you are ready to build your Web interface.

Building the Logon Page

Open the NorthwindWeb project that you created at the beginning of the chapter to create the Web pages. Now you need to create the logon page. When you are done, the page will look similar to that in Figure 12-6. Add the controls and set the properties of the controls as indicated in Table 12-1 to the Logon.aspx page.

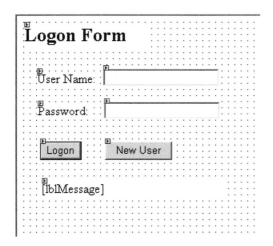

Figure 12-6. The NorthwindWeb logon page

Table 12-1. The Logon Page Controls and Properties

Control	Property	Value
Label	Text	Logon Form
	Font	Large
Label	Text	User Name
Textbox	ID	txtUserName
Label	Text	Password
Textbox	ID	txtPassword
	TextMode	Password

Table 12-1. The Logon Page Controls and Properties (Continued)

Control	Property	Value
Label	ID	lblMessage
Button	Name	btnLogon
	Text	Logon
Button	Name	btnNewUser
	Text	New User

Because you just created this little application, there are no users in the system. You will code the New User functionality first.

 NOTE   As you go through these exercises, you will probably think of many more things that you can do. This is not intended to be a complete text on the subject of Web security; it is intended as an overview to give you some experience with creating a secure Web site structure using .NET.

Before you start coding, you need to add a reference to your Web service so that you can call the validate and add routines. To do this, right-click the References node in the Solution Explorer and select Add Web Reference. Enter the Uniform Resource Locator (URL) for the Web service you created (http://localhost/ Northwind/service1.asmx) or select the link for Web Services on the Local Machine. Select localhost/Northwind/Service1 and click Add Reference.

Return to your Logon.aspx form and double-click the btnNewUser button to go to its code page and create the click event for this method. Add the following lines to the top of the code module (above the class):

```
Option Explicit On
Option Strict On

Imports System.Web
Imports System.Web.Security
Imports System.Security.Cryptography
Imports NorthwindWeb.Localhost
Imports System.Configuration
```

Implementing the Add New User Functionality

Next, add the code from Listing 12-7 to the btnNewUser_Click method.

Listing 12-7. The Add New User Functionality

```
Dim objSecurity As Service1
Dim blnValid As Boolean
Dim bytPassword(), bytEncrypted() As Byte
Dim strEncryptedPassword As String
Dim i As Integer
Dim sec As New SHA1Managed
Dim ue As New System.Text.UnicodeEncoding

Try
     bytPassword = ue.GetBytes(txtPassword.Text)
     bytEncrypted = sec.ComputeHash(bytPassword)

     For i = 0 To bytEncrypted.Length - 1
     strEncryptedPassword += bytEncrypted(i).ToString
     Next

     objSecurity = New Service1
     blnValid = objSecurity.AddUser(txtUserName.Text, strEncryptedPassword)
     If blnValid = False Then
          Throw New Exception("Failed to add user.")
     End If

     FormsAuthentication.SetAuthCookie(txtUserName.Text, False)
     Response.Redirect("secure/Employees.aspx")
Catch exc As Exception
     lblMessage.Text = "An error occurred while adding user " & txtUserName.Text
End Try
```

The first line converts the password string into a series of bytes for use in the creation of the hash:

```
bytPassword = ue.GetBytes(txtPassword.Text)
```

The next line actually creates the hash and returns the result as a byte array:

```
bytEncrypted = sec.ComputeHash(bytPassword)
```

This loop extracts all of the values from the hashed array and stores them in one string variable so that you can easily store the value in the database:

```
For i = 0 To bytEncrypted.Length - 1
    strEncryptedPassword += bytEncrypted(i).ToString
Next
```

Next you call the Web service to add the values to the UserList table. After that, you set the authentication cookie using this line:

```
FormsAuthentication.SetAuthCookie(txtUserName.Text, False)
```

The False argument just states that you do not want to persist this cookie after the session ends. And finally, once you have indicated that the user has been authenticated, you direct them to the secure section of the application using the following line:

```
Response.Redirect("secure/Employees.aspx")
```

If you tried to redirect the user without setting the authentication cookie first, you would be returned to this logon page because ASP.NET would not recognize that the user had been authenticated.

TIP Another method you can use to redirect users is the FormsAuthentication.RedirectFromLoginPage method. Say, for example, that a user has bookmarked a secured page in your application and they use this link to go directly to the page. If the user has not been authenticated, they will be redirected to the login page. After they have successfully logged on, then the application will automatically redirect them to the page they were trying to reach originally. You will not be using this method on this small application because you are not creating a "default" page that the user would go to first.

Lastly, note that when an error occurs you only tell the user of the application that an error occurred while adding the user—you do not tell them what the error was.

NOTE Way too many Web sites fail to authenticate a user and then give a hacker a helpful message along the lines of "Login for user X failed because the password was invalid." Well, now the hacker knows that they have a valid username, so it will not be long before they get the password right.

You should now be able to run the Web application, supply a username and password, click the New User button, and be redirected to your empty employee.aspx page.

Implementing the Validate User Functionality

Now you will implement the logon (Validate User) functionality that is almost identical to the previous method. Enter the code in Listing 12-8 to validate the user.

Listing 12-8. Validating the User

```
Private Sub btnLogon_Click(ByVal sender As System.Object, _
ByVal e As System.EventArgs) Handles btnLogon.Click
    Dim objSecurity As Service1
    Dim blnValid As Boolean
    Dim bytPassword(), bytEncrypted() As Byte
    Dim strEncryptedPassword As String
    Dim i As Integer
    Dim sec As New SHA1Managed
    Dim ue As New System.Text.UnicodeEncoding

    bytPassword = ue.GetBytes(txtPassword.Text)
    bytEncrypted = sec.ComputeHash(bytPassword)

    For i = 0 To bytEncrypted.Length - 1
        strEncryptedPassword += bytEncrypted(i).ToString
    Next

    objSecurity = New Service1
    blnValid = objSecurity.ValidateUser(txtUserName.Text, _
    strEncryptedPassword)
    If blnValid = False Then
        Response.Redirect("AccessDenied.aspx")
    Else
        FormsAuthentication.SetAuthCookie(txtUserName.Text, False)
        Response.Redirect("secure/Employees.aspx")
    End If
End Sub
```

This method creates a hash out of the password and sends the username and hashed password to the database for verification. If there is an entry with that username/password combination, then the user is authenticated; otherwise they are redirected to your access denied page (which you have not coded).

CAUTION I had to code this form in this manner because otherwise an error was thrown during the Response.Redirect to the Employees.aspx page. The exception received was a "Thread was being aborted" error. This is possibly because I was working with two betas at the same time (.NET 1.1 beta and Release Candidate 2 of .NET Web Server 2003).

Creating the Employee List Page

You will be using all of the functionality of your existing application for the employee pages that you are going to create, but you are going to modify how the data displays just a little.

NOTE The reason for using classes and class managers in a Windows forms application is because you maintain the state of the data and it makes it easier for you to keep track of your objects' state. When writing a Web application, there is no (or very little) state persistence that you can directly manage. To that extent, Microsoft has done an excellent job of encapsulating state management within the dataset.

Using Dataset Objects

I have had several people ask me, during the course of writing this book, why I do not use datasets more extensively. After all, they have a pretty incredible form of state management built into them, you can constrain values entered into the fields, and you can display errors in a datagrid just as you did with the ErrorProvider on the forms. You can also bind certain controls for editing specific types of data to a grid and get the same functionality you would on a form (for example, you can set the date/time combo box so that you can use it from within a grid to edit date fields).

There is one reason why I do not use datasets extensively: They do not offer enough control over the data, and I am a data control freak. For many people, the dataset functionality works great, and Microsoft has done an excellent job of creating the dataset to be everything that developers who used Visual Basic 6 and earlier wanted. But there are a couple of things you cannot do with it and a couple of workarounds you need to put in place to make these things work.

As an example of what you cannot do with them, consider business rules. You cannot check values in the dataset granularly against a business rule—for every record you update, you need to extract the information from the dataset, pass it to an object that can check the rules, and return the information to the dataset. In essence you can use the dataset, but you still need to have the classes and all of the business rules written in almost the same way. It also ties the database to each of the other layers much more tightly than a distributed application should be tied. For a two-tier application this is probably perfectly acceptable, but for a distributed application, it is not.

Also, the prepared commands using the CommandBuilder object are extremely bulky, time consuming, and difficult to code.

Add a datagrid to the employees.aspx Web page (do not do anything but drop it on the form). Switch to the code view and edit the Page_Load method so that it is identical to the code in Listing 12-9.

Listing 12-9. The Employees.aspx Page_Load Method

```
Private Sub Page_Load(ByVal sender As System.Object, _
ByVal e As System.EventArgs) Handles MyBase.Load
    Dim objService As New localhost.Service1()
    DataGrid1.DataSource = objService.GetAllEmployees
    DataGrid1.DataBind()
    objService = Nothing
End Sub
```

Updating the Employee List Web Page

After making the previous change, running the application, and following the same steps to add a new user (or using the user you created earlier) as you did in the previous section, you should see the Employees.aspx page (see Figure 12-7).

EmployeeID	LastName	FirstName	Title
1	Davolio	Nancy	Sales Representative
2	Fuller	Andrew	Vice President, Sales
3	Leverling	Janet	Sales Representative
4	Peacock	Margaret	Sales Representative
5	Buchanan	Steven	Sales Manager
6	Suyama	Michael	Sales Representative
7	King	Robert	Sales Representative
8	Callahan	Laura	Inside Sales Coordinator
9	Dodsworth	Anne	Sales Representative

Figure 12-7. The Employees.aspx Web page

Now, this is a pretty weak page, so you need to make some changes to it—not only to make it look nicer, but you need a way to see the details for an individual employee. When you're done updating the page it will look like the page in Figure 12-8.

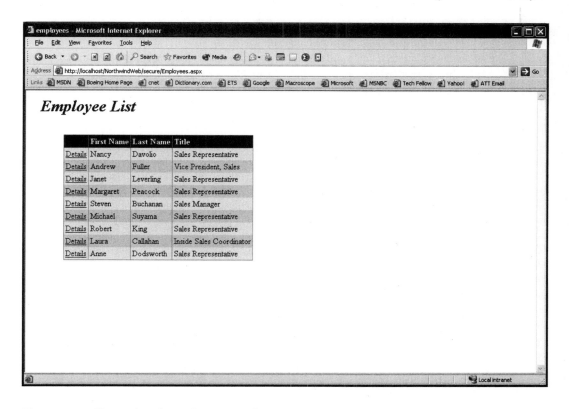

The browser window shows:

Employee List

	First Name	Last Name	Title
Details	Nancy	Davolio	Sales Representative
Details	Andrew	Fuller	Vice President, Sales
Details	Janet	Leverling	Sales Representative
Details	Margaret	Peacock	Sales Representative
Details	Steven	Buchanan	Sales Manager
Details	Michael	Suyama	Sales Representative
Details	Robert	King	Sales Representative
Details	Laura	Callahan	Inside Sales Coordinator
Details	Anne	Dodsworth	Sales Representative

Figure 12-8. The updated Employee Details page

One of the advantages of .NET is that you can make these changes without adding a single line of code to the application. To set up the page to look like the one in Figure 12-8, take the following steps:

1. Add a label above the grid and set the caption to *Employee List*.

2. Set the font for this label to X-Large, Bold, and Italic.

3. Right-click the datagrid in design mode and select Auto Format.

4. Select Professional 1 for the format (or you can select one of your own choice).

5. Then, right-click the datagrid again and select Property Builder.

6. Select the Columns item from the list on the left (see Figure 12-9).

7. Click the HyperLink Column item from the Available Columns list and add it to the Selected Columns column.

8. Set the properties for the Hyperlink column according to Table 12-2.

9. Next, add a bound column for the FirstName, LastName, and Title columns (click bound column from the list of available columns and click the right-arrow button three times).

10. For each of these fields, enter the column name in the Data Field box and enter a formatted name in the header box.

11. Lastly, make sure to uncheck the Create Columns Automatically at Runtime box and click OK.

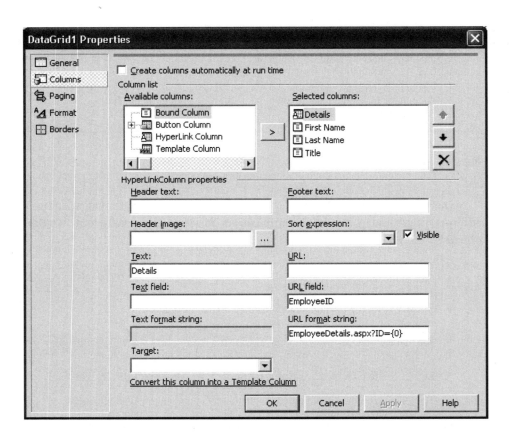

Figure 12-9. DataGrid Property Builder dialog box

Table 12-2. The HyperLink Column Properties

Property	Value	Purpose
Text	Details	Text displayed in the grid
URL field	EmployeeID	Value to be used for the URL
URL format string	EmployeeDetails.aspx?ID={0}	A .NET string expression where the token ({0}) is replaced by the value in the URL Field

Now, run the application and visit this page again. It should look identical to Figure 12-8 now. Notice when you hold your cursor over a Details hyperlink that the ID value corresponds to the ID of the employee that the cursor is over.

Creating the Employee Details Page

Now you need to create the page to display the employee details to the user. Add a new Web form to the project in the secure folder and call it *EmployeeDetails.aspx*. When you are done creating this page, it will look like the page in Figure 12-10.

NOTE   You will not be displaying the employee photo for a simple reason—you would have to have a method to synchronize the image in the database with the image located on the Web site. Although this is obviously doable, you will not take the time to do it here.

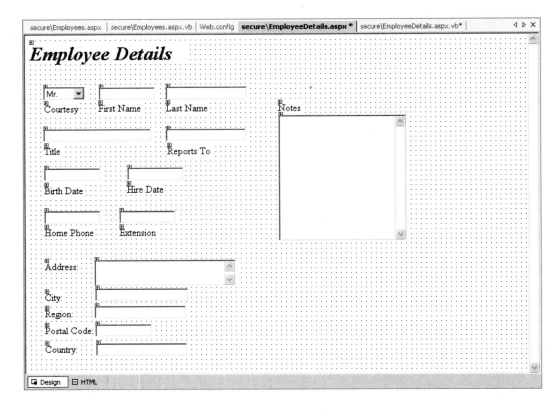

Figure 12-10. The completed Employee Details page

Add the controls and set the names of the controls according to Table 12-3.

NOTE   You might be tempted to not change the label names, but in
Chapter 13, "Globalizing and Localizing Your Application," you will
need to be able to access these labels by name, so now is as good a time
as any to set the right names.

Table 12-3. The Employee Details Controls and Names

Control	ID	Label ID
DropDownList	ddlCourtesy	lblCourtesy
Textbox	txtFirstName	lblFirstName
Textbox	txtLastName	lblLastName
Textbox	txtTitle	lblTitle
Textbox	txtReportsTo	lblReportsTo
Textbox	txtBirthDate	lblBirthDate
Textbox	txtHireDate	lblHireDate
Textbox	txtHomePhone	lblHomePhone
Textbox	txtExtension	lblExtension
Textbox	txtAddress	lblAddress
Textbox	txtCity	lblCity
Textbox	txtRegion	lblRegion
Textbox	txtPostal	lblPostal
Textbox	txtCountry	lblCountry
Textbox	txtNotes	lblNotes

A few of the controls require some additional properties to be set (see Table 12-4).

Table 12-4. Additional Control Property Settings

Control	Property	Value
ddlCourtesy	Items	Add "Mr.", "Ms.", "Mrs.", "Dr." and use these values as the text and value
txtAddress	TextMode	MultiLine
txtNotes	TextMode	MultiLine

OK, that is enough to get your page built. Let's hook up some data and then you will come back and update the page. As mentioned, when you hold the cursor over the Details hyperlink, it displays the URL as *EmployeeDetails.aspx?ID=x* where *x* is the ID of the employee. This is called the *query string*. I will not go into a lot of detail about it, but I will show you how to pull the value out of it so that you can load the complete employee record. Let's add the code in Listing 12-10 to the Page_Load event of the Employee Details page.

Listing 12-10. Employee Details Page_Load Method

```
Dim objService As New localhost.Service1()
Dim sEmp As localhost.structEmployee
Dim i As Integer
Dim intID As Integer

intID = Convert.ToInt32(Page.Request.QueryString.Item("ID"))
objService.Credentials = System.Net.CredentialCache.DefaultCredentials
sEmp = objService.GetEmployeeDetails(intID)
objService = Nothing

With sEmp
    For i = 0 To ddlCourtesy.Items.Count - 1
        If ddlCourtesy.Items(i).Text = .TitleOfCourtesy Then
            ddlCourtesy.SelectedIndex = i
            Exit For
        End If
    Next

    txtFirstName.Text = .FirstName
    txtLastName.Text = .LastName
    txtTitle.Text = .Title
    txtReportsTo.Text = .ReportsToFirstName & " " & .ReportsToLastName
    txtBirthDate.Text = .BirthDate.ToShortDateString
    txtHireDate.Text = .HireDate.ToShortDateString
    txtHomePhone.Text = .HomePhone
    txtExtension.Text = .Extension
    txtAddress.Text = .Address
    txtCity.Text = .City
    txtRegion.Text = .Region
    txtPostal.Text = .PostalCode
    txtCountry.Text = .Country
    txtNotes.Text = .Notes
End With
```

The only part of this code that is new to you is this line:

```
intID = Convert.ToInt32(Page.Request.QueryString.Item("ID"))
```

To get at the contents of the QueryString, you have to access the Page Request object. Each item in the QueryString becomes an item in the QueryString collection that can be accessed by name or index. In this case, you only have one item that you are passing, the employee ID that you can access by "ID". At this point, you can run the application and when you click an employee's Details hyperlink, that employee's details come up in the Employee Details page.

Referencing Your Objects Directly

Up to this point you have been referencing the Web Services that you created to display this information. But how different is it to hook up to the assemblies that you originally created? And what about editing and adding new employees? Because you have not created methods in your Web service to handle this, you will see how easy it is to reference your original objects and perform add and updates in this section. You will also look at displaying errors to the users on the client side and see how to treat the errors that come from the data-centric objects.

The first question you need to ask is this: How do you best reference these objects? Because you have not placed them in the Global Assembly Cache (GAC), the best solution is to use remoting to access them. But to do that you have to make some slight changes to the WebUserDC class and the NorthwindShared assembly.

NOTE Remember that your remote objects are called by using interfaces that you have not set up on your WebUserDC class and that you need to be able to validate a user. This method also keeps your application distributed in that you only need to create a reference to the shared objects. After you are done with this, you would still be able to place the user interface on a different machine than the data-centric assemblies, which is always the goal of a distributed application.

To begin, open the NorthwindTraders solution so that you can edit the WebUserDC and the shared objects. Open the Interfaces.vb code module in the NorthwindShared project and add the following interface:

```
Public Interface IWebUser
    Function ValidateUser(ByVal strUser As String, ByVal strPass As String) _
As Boolean
    Function AddUser(ByVal strUser As String, ByVal strPass As String) _
As Boolean
End Interface
```

Next, edit the WebUserDC class and add the following Imports statement to the top of the code module:

```
Imports NorthwindTraders.NorthwindShared.Interfaces
```

Next, set the class so that it inherits from the MarshalByRefObject by adding the following line after the class declaration:

```
Inherits MarshalByRefObject
```

Finally, implement the IWebUser interface that you just created by adding the following line:

```
Implements IWebUser
```

 NOTE If you are using Visual Studio .NET 1.1, the Integrated Development Environment (IDE) automatically creates two new methods—AddUser1 and ValidateUser1—that implement the two methods of the interface. You need to delete these methods before this works correctly.

Modify the ValidateUser and AddUser methods so that they implement the appropriate interface functions. For example, add the following to the end of the signature for the AddUser method:

```
Implements NorthwindShared.Interfaces.IWebUser.AddUser
```

Add the similar clause to the signature for the ValidateUser method. Before you re-deploy the data-centric assemblies, add a new entry in the web.config file for the WebUserDC class, as shown here:

```
<wellknown mode="Singleton"
    type="NorthwindTraders.NorthwindDC.WebUserDC, NorthwindDC"
    objectUri="WebUserDC.rem"/>
```

Now, rebuild the project and re-deploy the NorthwindDC and NorthwindShared assemblies to the northwind\bin folder.

Switch to the NorthwindWeb solution, right-click the References node, and select Add Reference. Then, browse to the northwind\bin folder and add a reference to the NorthwindShared and BusinessRules assemblies. Before you click OK, add another reference to the System.Runtime.Remoting assembly so that you can communicate with your remote objects. Finally, remove the reference to the Web service by right-clicking the Web reference in the Solution Explorer and choosing Exclude from Project. This throws up a lot of errors, but the fixes are fairly easy.

In your Windows forms application you opened the remoting channel in the Form.Load method of your Multiple Document Interface (MDI) form and you closed the channel in the Form.Unload method. A Web forms application works much the same way, except that the starting and ending of an application triggers events in the Global class, which is located in the Global.asax code module. Switch to the Global.asax code module and add the following two Imports lines to the top of the code module:

```
Imports System.Runtime.Remoting.Channels
Imports System.Runtime.Remoting.Channels.Http
```

Next, add a private module-level variable for the channel object to the Global class as follows:

```
Private chan As HttpChannel
```

Then add the following two lines of code to the Application_Start method:

```
chan = New HttpChannel(Nothing, New BinaryClientFormatterSinkProvider, New _
    BinaryServerFormatterSinkProvider)
ChannelServices.RegisterChannel(chan)
```

This is almost an exact duplicate of your Windows forms application except that you are no longer passing your credentials to the remote components because you have set the Northwind application to allow Anonymous access. Finally, add the following line of code to the Application_End method:

```
ChannelServices.UnregisterChannel(chan)
```

This simply closes the channel when the application stops running.

NOTE Although I avoid a complete discussion of Web applications and their lifecycles, if you are working toward becoming a Web developer, you should look at some other texts that go into more detail. An excellent book on the subject is *Developing Web Applications with Microsoft Visual Basic .NET and Microsoft Visual C# .NET* (Microsoft Press, 2002), which is part of Microsoft's MCAD/MCSD Self-Paced Training Kit.

Now that you have set your channel, let's fix each of the three forms that have errors. In the Logon.aspx page, add the following Imports line:

```
Imports NorthwindTraders.NorthwindShared.Interfaces
```

Modify the btnNewUser_Click method so that it looks like the method in Listing 12-11. The changes here are pretty simple—the objSecurity object is now an IWebUser object and you are now making a call on the interface over a remoting channel just as you did in your Windows forms application. Aside from that, everything is identical.

Listing 12-11. The Modified btnNewUser_Click Method

```
Private Sub btnNewUser_Click(ByVal sender As System.Object, _
ByVal e As System.EventArgs) Handles btnNewUser.Click
    Dim objSecurity As IWebUser
    Dim blnValid As Boolean
    Dim bytPassword(), bytEncrypted() As Byte
    Dim strEncryptedPassword As String
    Dim i As Integer
    Dim sec As New SHA1Managed
    Dim ue As New System.Text.UnicodeEncoding

    Try
        bytPassword = ue.GetBytes(txtPassword.Text)
        bytEncrypted = sec.ComputeHash(bytPassword)

        For i = 0 To bytEncrypted.Length - 1
        strEncryptedPassword += bytEncrypted(i).ToString
        Next
```

```
        objSecurity = CType(Activator.GetObject(GetType(IWebUser), _
        "http://localhost:80/northwind/WebUserDC.rem"), IWebUser)
        blnValid = objSecurity.AddUser(txtUserName.Text, strEncryptedPassword)
        objSecurity = Nothing
        If blnValid = False Then
            Throw New Exception("Failed to add user.")
        End If

        FormsAuthentication.SetAuthCookie(txtUserName.Text, False)
        Response.Redirect("secure/Employees.aspx")
    Catch exc As Exception
        lblMessage.Text = "An error occurred while adding user " _
        & txtUserName.Text
    End Try
End Sub
```

Make this same change to the btnLogon_Click method. Listing 12-12 shows the changes. Everything else remains the same in the method.

Listing 12-12. Modifications to the btnLogon_Click Method

```
Dim objSecurity As IWebUser
.
.
objSecurity = CType(Activator.GetObject(GetType(IWebUser), _
"http://localhost:80/northwind/WebUserDC.rem"), IWebUser)
```

Next, switch to the employees.aspx page and add the following Imports statement to the top of the code module:

```
Imports NorthwindTraders.NorthwindShared.Interfaces
```

Edit the Page_Load method so that it looks like the method in Listing 12-13.

Listing 12-13. The Page_Load Method of the employee.aspx Page

```
Private Sub Page_Load(ByVal sender As System.Object, _
ByVal e As System.EventArgs) Handles MyBase.Load
        Dim objIEmployee As IEmployee
        Dim ds As DataSet
```

```
'Obtain a reference to the remote object
objIEmployee = CType(Activator.GetObject(GetType(IEmployee), _
    "http://localhost:80/northwind/EmployeeDC.rem"), IEmployee)
ds = objIEmployee.LoadProxy()
objIEmployee = Nothing

DataGrid1.DataSource = ds
DataGrid1.DataBind()
End Sub
```

Next, switch to the EmployeeDetails.aspx page and add the following two Imports statements to the top of the code module:

```
Imports NorthwindTraders.NorthwindShared.Interfaces
Imports NorthwindTraders.NorthwindShared.Structures
```

Then modify the top half of the Page_Load method so that it looks like the method in Listing 12-14.

Listing 12-14. The Page_Load Method of the EmployeeDetails.aspx Page

```
Private Sub Page_Load(ByVal sender As System.Object, _
ByVal e As System.EventArgs) Handles MyBase.Load
    Dim objService As IEmployee
    Dim sEmp As structEmployee
    Dim i As Integer
    Dim intID As Integer

    objService = CType(Activator.GetObject(GetType(IEmployee), _
        "http://localhost:80/northwind/EmployeeDC.rem"), IEmployee)
    intID = Convert.ToInt32(Page.Request.QueryString.Item("ID"))
    sEmp = objService.LoadRecord(intID)
    objService = Nothing
        .
        .
```

Finally, remove the NorthwindWeb.Localhost Imports statement and you are done with the changes. The application should run as before.

As you have seen here, you have completely changed the underlying technology that you use to make your application work quickly and easily.

Implementing Editing Capabilities

Now that you are hooked up to your original objects, you have full access to all of the methods contained within them. That means you can implement the add and edit functionality in your details form. It also means that you can examine how to display client-side errors to the user. To start, add a hyperlink to the Employees.aspx page so that you can add a new employee and set the properties according to Table 12-5.

Table 12-5. Add Employee Hyperlink Properties

Property	Value
ID	hypAdd
Text	Add Employee
NavigateUrl	EmployeeDetails.aspx?ID=0

Make sure to place this new hyperlink above the employee grid, not below it. The reason is that the datagrid will expand and become written underneath the link, making it sloppy. Next, you need to edit the Employee Details page so that it recognizes the fact that an ID of zero is a new employee. To do this, you just add a simple If..Then statement to enclose the body of the Page_Load method:

```
If Page.Request.QueryString.Item("ID") <> "0" Then

    .

    .

    .

End If
```

You should move the code you have previously written to the body of the If..Then statement. Now you can bring up the Employee Details page and actually add information to it. But you have a couple of things that you need to address first. One is adding a method to save the newly added employee and returning you back to the employee list page and the other is a way to trap user-centric errors.

To handle user-centric errors in an ASP.NET application (and also to reduce the server load), you are going to use some of the validators that Microsoft provides (see Table 12-6).

Table 12-6. Available ASP.NET Field Validator Controls

Validator	Purpose
RequiredFieldValidator	This control requires that something be entered in the associated control. It does not check the value for any type of conformity.
CompareValidator	This control compares the entered value with the value of another field on the form.
RangeValidator	This control ensures that a given value falls within a specific range.
RegularExpressionValidator	This is probably the most powerful validation control in that it can ensure that a given value matches a particular pattern. This is important for fields such as phone number, e-mail address, or social security number.
CustomValidator	This control validates a given value against a custom expression. The expression takes the form of a method in the client-side code.
ValidationSummary	This is not really a validation control, but it does display a list of all of the error messages for all of the controls that failed validation.

Using the Required Field Validator

This section starts with a couple of simple examples to illustrate the major points and then it explains how you should apply all of the validations. When you are done, the screen will look like Figure 12-10. First, add a Save button to the Employee Details page and change the name to *btnSave* and set the caption to *Save*. Then, add a Validation Summary control to the Employee Details page and place it at the bottom of the page (below the Country textbox). Next, add a RequiredFieldValidator control to the form and set the properties for it according to Table 12-7.

Position the control to the right of the txtFirstName control as shown in Figure 12-11.

Table 12-7. First RequiredFieldValidator Control Properties

Property	Value
ID	rfvFirstName
ControlToValidate	txtFirstName
ErrorMessage	First name cannot be null
Text	*

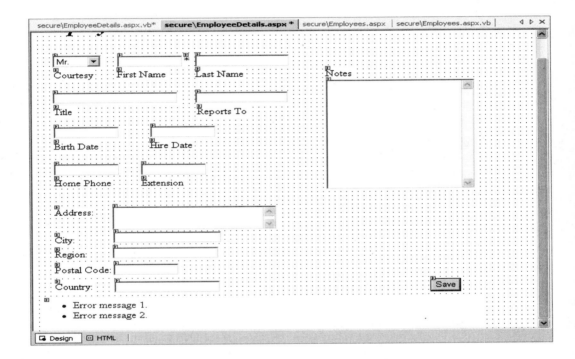

Figure 12-11. The RequiredFieldValidator and ValidatorSummary controls

Now, run the application and click Add Employee. When the Employee Details screen comes up, click the Save button. The results should look like those in Figure 12-12.

Add another RequiredFieldValidator for the Last Name field and set the properties as you did for the First Name field (but link them to the Last Name field, of course). These are the only two required fields.

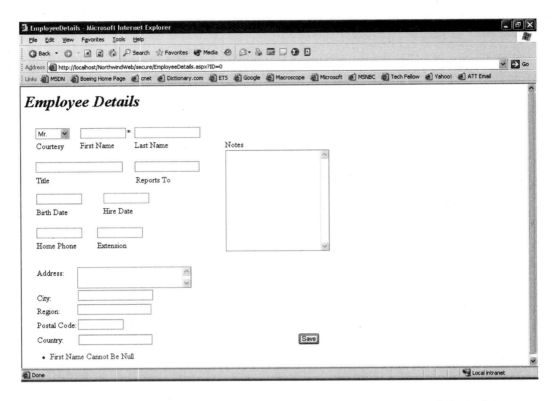

Figure 12-12. The RequiredFieldValidator and ValidationSummary Controls In Action

TIP The ValidatorSummary control only displays when the form is submitted. In this example, if the user makes an error and tabs out of the field, the value will be checked by the field validator. However, because the ValidatorSummary control does not display until the user clicks the Save button, the only indication of an error that the user sees is the red asterisk next to the field.

Using the Regular Expression Validator

For the Birth Date and Hire Date fields, though, you have no intrinsic Date dropdown control available, so you need to have another way to validate the date. For this you will use the RegularExpressionValidator control.

NOTE Microsoft does not include a Date/Calendar drop-down Web control, but this is not too much of a problem. Many third-party vendors already have these controls available for .NET. My favorite .NET vendor is Infragistics (which was Sheridan Software and ProtoView Development, two of the top ActiveX control creators). Its selection of .NET controls is top of the line and easy to use once you understand the framework.

Using Regular Expressions

Regular expressions have been around for a long time, having come from the Unix world. If you have programmed in Perl or any similar language, you have probably used regular expressions. But what is this great and powerful tool? In its simplest form the regular expression engine matches patterns in text. You specify the pattern with a series of rather cryptic text, and the engine goes and searches for the pattern. The pattern can be almost anything and is not limited to matching only one part of the string like you can do with the substring or instring functions. If you wanted, you could match only the third character of every word in a 10,000-page document (I do not know why you would, but you could). Expanding on this concept, the regular expression engine can also perform replacements on text. If you look at the Replace dialog box in VS .NET, the last option on the left allows you to use regular expressions in a Find or Find and Replace operation. On top of all that, you can use regular expressions to parse an entire document so that you only remove the things that you want to remove. All of these capabilities make regular expressions a powerful tool.

This is a pretty simple explanation of a regular expression. For more information, refer to the e-book *Regular Expressions with .NET* by Dan Appleman. It is available from his Web site at `http://www.desaware.com`. Read this book if you want to learn more about regular expressions; it is one of the few references that I cannot do without.

Add a new RegularExpressionValidator control to the page and set the properties according to Table 12-8.

Table 12-8. RegularExpressionValidator Property Settings

Property	Value
ID	revBirthDate
ControlToValidate	txtBirthDate
ErrorMessage	Birth Date must be in the format xx/xx/xxxx
Text	*
ValidationExpression	\d{1,2}/\d{1,2}/\d{4}

So what does this validation expression mean? This regular expression breaks down into the meaning shown in Table 12-9.

Table 12-9. Validation Expression for RegularExpressionValidator

Expression	Meaning
\d{1,2}	A minimum of 1 digit up to a maximum of 2 digits (\d stands for a number)
/	A forward slash
\d{1,2}	A minimum of 1 digit up to a maximum of 2 digits (\d stands for a number)
/	A forward slash
\d{4}	Four digits

This translates into you allowing a date in any of the following formats: xx/xx/xxxx, x/xx/xxxx, x/x/xxxx, or xx/x/xxxx. Pretty nifty, huh? Try to write code to parse out the value to ensure that it is correct.

If you run the application, you do not have to enter anything in the Birth Date field, but if you do, it is checked against the regular expression.

Next, let's add a validator to ensure that the first name is not longer than 10 characters. To do this you have two choices: using a CustomValidator and writing some code, or using a RegularExpressionValidator and typing in seven characters. Which do you think is going to be easier? I will save you the suspense: The Regular-ExpressionValidator is easier.

CAUTION When you use a custom validation, you must write a script that runs on both the client and server side. The reason for this is that all rules checked on the client side are rechecked on the server side. This prevents a malicious user from bypassing the validation checks.

Add a new RegularExpressionValidator and set the properties for it according to Table 12-10.

Table 12-10. RegularExpressionValidator Property Settings for FirstName

Property	Value
ID	revFirstNameLength
ControlToValidate	txtFirstName
ErrorMessage	First Name cannot be more than 10 characters in length
Text	*
ValidationExpression	.{1,10}

This regular expression breaks down into what is shown in Table 12-11.

Table 12-11. Validation Expression for RegularExpressionValidator

Expression	Meaning
.	Match any character but a newline
{1,10}	Match at least one time, but no more than 10 times

Because entering 11 or more characters causes a match to be made more than 10 times, it fails the regular expression check. Wasn't that much easier than entering code? Table 12-12 summarizes all of the validators that need to be added to check all of the database constraint rules.

Table 12-12. Validators for the Employee Details Page

Control	Validator	Expression (If Needed)	Error Message	Text
txtFirstName	RequiredFieldValidator		First Name cannot be null	*
txtFirstName	RegularExpressionValidator	.{1,10}	First Name cannot be more than 10 characters in length	*
txtLastName	RequiredFieldValidator		Last Name cannot be null	*
txtLastName	RegularExpressionValidator	.{1,20}	Last Name cannot be more than 20 characters in length	*
txtTitle	RegularExpressionValidator	.{1,30}	Title cannot be more than 30 characters in length	*
txtBirthDate	RegularExpressionValidator	\d{1,2}/\d{1,2}/\d{4}	Birth Date must be in the format: xx/xx/xxxx	*
txtHireDate	RegularExpressionValidator	\d{1,2}/\d{1,2}/\d{4}	Hire Date must be in the format: xx/xx/xxxx	*
txtHomePhone	RegularExpressionValidator*	.{1,24}	Home Phone cannot be more than 24 characters in length	*
txtExtension	RegularExpressionValidator*	.{1,4}	Extension cannot be more than 4 characters in length	*
txtAddress	RegularExpressionValidator	.{1,60}	Address cannot be more than 60 characters in length	*

Table 12-12. Validators for the Employee Details Page (Continued)

Control	Validator	Expression (If Needed)	Error Message	Text
txtCity	RegularExpressionValidator	.{1,15}	City cannot be more than 15 characters in length	*
txtRegion	RegularExpressionValidator	.{1,15}	Region cannot be more than 15 characters in length	*
txtPostal	RegularExpressionValidator	.{1,10}	Postal Code cannot be more than 10 characters in length	*
txtCountry	RegularExpressionValidator	.{1,15}	Country cannot be more than 15 characters in length	*

* The HomePhone and Extension fields are both varchar fields in the database, which is why you are only checking for length and not format or digits only.

Once you have added all of the field validators, it is time to write the code to save the object. The code do to this is fairly simple—you just load a structure and call the Save method when the user clicks the Save button (as shown in Listing 12-15). Also, I have added the Imports statements at the top of code module, which is displayed in Listing 12-15 as well.

Listing 12-15. The Save Method, Employee Details

```
Imports NorthwindTraders.NorthwindShared.Errors
Imports NorthwindTraders.NorthwindShared.Structures
Imports NorthwindTraders.NorthwindShared.Interfaces
Imports BusinessRules.Errors

Private Sub btnSave_Click(ByVal sender As System.Object, _
ByVal e As System.EventArgs) Handles btnSave.Click
    Dim s As structEmployee
    Dim objEmployee As IEmployee
    Dim intID As Integer
    Dim objBusErr As BusinessErrors
```

```
With s
    .EmployeeID = Convert.ToInt32(Page.Request.QueryString.Item("ID"))
    .TitleOfCourtesy = ddlCourtesy.SelectedItem.Text
    .FirstName = txtFirstName.Text
    .LastName = txtLastName.Text
    .Title = txtTitle.Text
    If txtBirthDate.Text.Length > 0 Then
        .BirthDate = Convert.ToDateTime(txtBirthDate.Text)
    End If
    If txtHireDate.Text.Length > 0 Then
        .HireDate = Convert.ToDateTime(txtHireDate.Text)
    End If
    .HomePhone = txtHomePhone.Text
    .Extension = txtExtension.Text
    .Address = txtAddress.Text
    .City = txtCity.Text
    .Region = txtRegion.Text
    .PostalCode = txtPostal.Text
    .Country = txtCountry.Text
    .Notes = txtNotes.Text
End With

objEmployee = CType(Activator.GetObject(GetType(IEmployee), _
        "http://localhost:80/northwind/EmployeeDC.rem"), IEmployee)
objBusErr = objEmployee.Save(s, intID)
objEmployee = Nothing

If objBusErr Is Nothing Then
    Response.Redirect("Employees.aspx")
Else
    ShowErrors(objBusErr)
End If
End Sub
```

This method simply gathers all of the values into an Employee structure, calls the Save method, and then checks to see if there were any data-centric errors. You have not written the ShowErrors method yet (see Listing 12-16). But how do you show data-centric errors to the user? There is not any way to add a validator for the errors that might occur on the data-centric side of the process because you do not know what types of errors they are. You cannot add red asterisks to the form and place them beside the controls because there are no position values in the text boxes that you can check to position the asterisks! This is indeed a puzzle—and not one that is so simple to solve. There are a couple of choices, but these may affect the layout of the form and not give you the freedom you would like to have as Web page designers.

The first option is to put all of your controls into a Table control and leave an empty column at the end so that you can match errors up with the controls. This of course requires that the entire form go from top to bottom. Another option is to turn the background color of the control to a different color and display a tooltip message describing the error. You could also pop up another window with a list of errors, but then the user has to tile the windows to see the entry form and the list of errors. Because your previous error-displaying scheme involved showing the errors in tooltips, you will continue with that method in this section.

NOTE There are several other ways of displaying error information to the user. Mostly it is a matter of choice and organization standards. Whatever your decision, you should make it uniformly across the organization and in line with the basic Windows and Web application standards.

Add the code for the ShowErrors method as shown in Listing 12-16.

Listing 12-16. The ShowErrors Method

```
Private Sub ShowErrors(ByVal objBE As BusinessErrors)
    Dim i As Integer

    For i = 0 To objBE.Count - 1
        Select Case objBE.Item(i).errProperty
            Case "Last Name"
                txtLastName.BackColor = Color.LightPink
                txtLastName.ToolTip = objBE.Item(i).errMessage
            Case "First Name"
                txtFirstName.BackColor = Color.LightPink
                txtFirstName.ToolTip = objBE.Item(i).errMessage
            Case "Title"
                txtTitle.BackColor = Color.LightPink
                txtTitle.ToolTip = objBE.Item(i).errMessage
            Case "Title Of Courtesy"
                ddlCourtesy.BackColor = Color.LightPink
                ddlCourtesy.ToolTip = objBE.Item(i).errMessage
            Case "Birth Date"
                txtBirthDate.BackColor = Color.LightPink
                txtBirthDate.ToolTip = objBE.Item(i).errMessage
```

```
                        Case "Hire Date"
                            txtHireDate.BackColor = Color.LightPink
                            txtHireDate.ToolTip = objBE.Item(i).errMessage
                        Case "Address"
                            txtAddress.BackColor = Color.LightPink
                            txtAddress.ToolTip = objBE.Item(i).errMessage
                        Case "City"
                            txtCity.BackColor = Color.LightPink
                            txtCity.ToolTip = objBE.Item(i).errMessage
                        Case "Region"
                            txtRegion.BackColor = Color.LightPink
                            txtRegion.ToolTip = objBE.Item(i).errMessage
                        Case "Postal Code"
                            txtPostal.BackColor = Color.LightPink
                            txtPostal.ToolTip = objBE.Item(i).errMessage
                        Case "Country"
                            txtCountry.BackColor = Color.LightPink
                            txtCountry.ToolTip = objBE.Item(i).errMessage
                        Case "Home Phone"
                            txtHomePhone.BackColor = Color.LightPink
                            txtHomePhone.ToolTip = objBE.Item(i).errMessage
                        Case "Extension"
                            txtExtension.BackColor = Color.LightPink
                            txtExtension.ToolTip = objBE.Item(i).errMessage
                        Case "Notes"
                            txtNotes.BackColor = Color.LightPink
                            txtNotes.ToolTip = objBE.Item(i).errMessage
                        Case "Territories"
                            'Nothing yet
                End Select
        Next
    End Sub
```

As you can see, this is a fairly simple and straightforward way of handling errors. At this point, your save will still not work. The reason for this is that you have not added the territories into your form to be able to select any territories. The rule that this violates is that each employee must be assigned to at least one territory. So now you have to display the territories and allow the user to assign the employee to one or more territories. Again you have a decision to make: How do you best show the list of territories and allow the user to make a selection? In this case, you will use the same method that you did in the Windows forms application. You will have two listboxes and two buttons to move items back and forth between the listboxes. Now, that brings up another question: Do you use client-side scripting or server-side code? In this case, because this is a book about .NET in particular and not Web page scripting, you will use server-side code.

Let's add two listboxes and two buttons to the form in the lower-right corner. When you are finished, the form should look like Figure 12-13.

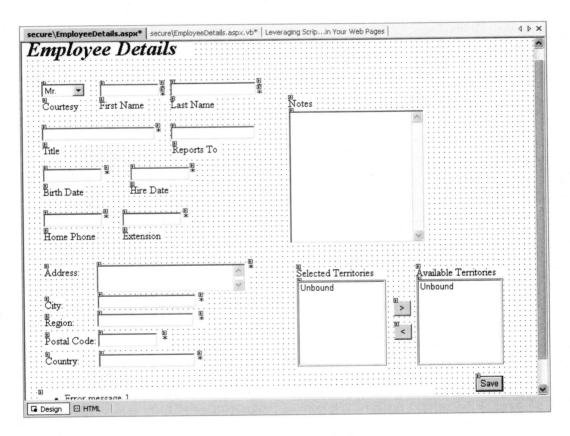

Figure 12-13. The Employee Details page with territory listboxes

Add the controls and set the properties according to Table 12-13.

Table 12-13. The Territory Controls

Control	Property	Value	Label Name
Listbox	ID	lstSelected	
Listbox	ID	lstAvailable	
Button	ID	btnRemove	
Button	ID	btnSelect	
Label	Text	Selected Territories	lblSelectedTerritories
Label	Text	Available Territories	lblAvailableTerritories
btnRemove	Text	>	
btnSelect	Text	<	

Next, you need to go back and modify the Page_Load method of the EmployeeDetails.aspx page. Add the code in Listing 12-17 to the beginning of the Page_Load method (above the QueryString check). Make sure you enclose the remaining code in the Page_Load method within the If..Then statement that you are adding here.

Listing 12-17. Modified Page_Load Method

```
Dim dsTerritories As DataSet
Dim dRow As DataRow

If Not Page.IsPostBack Then
    Dim objTerritories As ITerritory

    objTerritories = CType(Activator.GetObject(GetType(ITerritory), _
    "http://localhost:80/northwind/TerritoryDC.rem"), ITerritory)

    dsTerritories = objTerritories.LoadProxy
    objTerritories = Nothing
```

```
For Each dRow In dsTerritories.Tables(0).Rows
    Dim strDesc As String = _
    Convert.ToString(dRow.Item("TerritoryDescription"))
    Dim strID As String = Convert.ToString(dRow.Item("TerritoryID"))
    Dim lst As New ListItem(strDesc)
    lst.Value = strID
    lstAvailable.Items.Add(lst)
Next
```

The only thing you haven't seen at one point or another is the Page.IsPostBack statement. This merely instructs the application not to run this routine when a postback event occurs. Otherwise, every time you clicked a button that caused a trip to the server (which you will see in a moment), this code would run all over again. This minimizes the number of trips to the database and saves you a lot of headaches later. After you get the territory dataset, you simply loop through it and add everything to the available listbox. When you run the application now, you will see that the available territories are displayed in the available listbox. Now you need to add another block of code to display the territories that an employee is already associated with (if it is an existing employee). To do this, add the code in Listing 12-18 to the bottom of the With statement in the Page_Load method.

Listing 12-18. Assigning Associated Territories

```
For i = 0 To .Territories.Length - 1
    For Each dRow In dsTerritories.Tables(0).Rows
        Dim strDesc As String = _
        Convert.ToString(dRow.Item("TerritoryDescription"))
        Dim strID As String = Convert.ToString(dRow.Item("TerritoryID"))

        If strID = .Territories(i) Then
            Dim lst As New ListItem(strDesc)
            lst.Value = strID
            lstSelected.Items.Add(lst)
            lstAvailable.Items.Remove(lst)
            Exit For
        End If
    Next
Next
```

Now you should be able to select an existing employee, and their associated territories should be populated in the Selected Territories listbox. The last thing you need to do is to be able to move the territories from selected to available and vice versa, as you did with the Windows forms application.

Add the code in Listing 12-19 to the Employee Details form. This code moves an available territory to the selected territory listbox and removes it from the available territory listbox.

Listing 12-19. btnSelect Method

```
Private Sub btnSelect_Click(ByVal sender As System.Object, _
ByVal e As System.EventArgs) Handles btnSelect.Click
    Dim lst As ListItem = lstAvailable.SelectedItem
    lstAvailable.Items.Remove(lst)
    lstSelected.Items.Add(lst)
    lstSelected.SelectedIndex = lstSelected.Items.Count - 1
End Sub
```

When you run the application after adding this code, you will find one thing that is somewhat problematic—you cannot select a territory until you have entered enough information in the other controls to avoid causing any client-side errors. This is because clicking the btnSelect button causes a postback event and triggers the client-side validators to be checked. There is really no way around this, but it is a minor price to pay.

NOTE This is a situation where client-side scripting of this type of method is really useful.

Next, add the method in Listing 12-20 to the EmployeeDetails.aspx page.

Listing 12-20. The btnRemove_Click Method

```
Private Sub btnRemove_Click(ByVal sender As System.Object, _
ByVal e As System.EventArgs) Handles btnRemove.Click
    Dim lst As ListItem = lstSelected.SelectedItem
    lstSelected.Items.Remove(lst)
    lstAvailable.Items.Add(lst)
    lstAvailable.SelectedIndex = 0
End Sub
```

And finally, you need to assign your list of territories back to the territory array so that they can be saved with the employee. To do this add the code in Listing 12-21 to the end of the With statement in the btnSave_Click method of the Employee Details page.

Listing 12-21. The Modified btnSave_Click method

```
Dim i As Integer
ReDim .Territories(lstSelected.Items.Count - 1)

For i = 0 To lstSelected.Items.Count - 1
    .Territories(i) = lstSelected.Items(i).Value
Next
```

That is it. You should now be able to save information back to the database. Be careful when editing an existing employee record, because on an update you will delete the photo information. Adding a new employee immediately causes the new employee to be visible when the Employees.aspx page reloads.

 CAUTION   During the development of this code on the Beta 2 build I was getting an error message indicating that nvarchar was incompatible with type image. The error is caused because an image is not saved with the employee. For some reason .NET is converting the dbNull.value to a period (.). I have yet to see a workaround for this. The good news is that it only affects image data stored in SQL Server.

Summary

This chapter covered a lot. You saw how to consume a Web service from a Web application and how to hook that same application up to your original components. You examined how to handle client-side rules without code and received a little lesson on regular expressions. You gained some insight on what Web page developers must go through as opposed to what a Windows forms developer must go through. But mostly you have gained the insight that a well-coded data-centric component can save you a lot of headaches and that displaying business errors is pretty easy once you figure out how to report the errors to the user.

In addition, you learned how to store database credentials in the registry and how to retrieve those credentials in a secure manner. You examined a host of security issues that allow you to determine what possible security issues you might face on a particular project and how to get around some of them.

In the next chapter you will globalize and localize both your Windows forms application and your Web forms application so that you will have hands-on experience with how to modify an application to accommodate different languages.

CHAPTER 13

Globalizing and Localizing Your Application

CHAPTER 1, "Understanding Application Architecture: An Overview," mentioned that the business world is becoming global. Boundaries are being blurred every day, especially in the business world. More businesses are based in multiple countries now than any time in the past, and those businesses are putting out their messages to people all over the world via the Internet. This means that many programs may need to have built-in support for multiple languages.

This chapter introduces some of the ideas and best practices you will need to know to globalize applications. In addition, you will globalize the Employee Edit forms for both your Windows application and your Web application and go over some of the techniques used in globalization.

NOTE This chapter is not an in-depth chapter on globalization and localization. If you are interested in an excellent book on all of the different aspects of these techniques, refer to *Internationalization and Localization Using Microsoft .NET* by Nick Symmonds (Apress, 2002). This book goes into much greater detail and provides you with a wealth of information if you need it.

Globalization is the process of preparing an application to be localized. *Localization* is the process of taking an application and adding in the resources used to display the interface in a user's native language. This chapter examines both aspects.

NOTE I am one of those language-inept people. To quote Bruce Willis in *The Fifth Element*, "I speak two languages, English and Bad English." Because of this slight limitation on my part, the translations may not be entirely accurate, but I have tried my best to give them justice.

Introducing Globalization

You need to perform a couple of steps to globalize an application (most of which you have not done up to this point):

- Ensure there is enough space in labels to hold the maximum size strings.

- Store all strings (and images) if they are to be localized, externally of the executable.

- Store all data in the database using Unicode encoding.

- Do not concatenate strings at runtime for display.

NOTE   There is a much longer list of best practices in the MSDN help documentation under "Globalization, Best Practices" and "Localization, Best Practices."

These are the only areas covered in this chapter because each requires some technical insight. Most of the other globalization issues revolve around the do's and don'ts of different political systems, cultures, and so on. You do have one advantage using the .NET Framework: All controls that display text are Unicode enabled, so character sets are no longer an issue.

NOTE   This chapter is about converting an application to a different language, Appendix A contains a small example of adding special characters (including foreign language characters) in an application designed to support only one language.

So, let's examine each of the four requirements listed previously.

Ensure there is enough space in labels to hold the maximum size string: When you create labels to hold text that describes information in a textbox or listbox, you generally size the label just large enough to hold the text so you can have a nice, neat form. However, look at the following word in English, then in French and Spanish:

- Birth Date (English)

- Date de naissance (French)

- La Fecha del nacimiento (Spanish)

As you can see, it will not do to size labels to their minimum size when writing an application that eventually needs to be localized.

Store all strings (and images) if they are to be localized, externally of the executable: When you place a label on a form, you should store the text of that label in a place other than the text property of that label. In this case, I am specifically talking about a satellite assembly that contains resources. A *satellite assembly,* by definition, is an assembly that contains only resources. There is no application code in a satellite assembly. You should insert all text that is displayed in labels (and images that have local significance, such as flags, leaders, maps, and so on) into these labels at runtime.

Store all data in the database using Unicode encoding: Ensure that all character fields are created using the Unicode version (noted in SQL Server as *n* plus the datatype; for example, *varchar* would be *nvarchar*). This also covers the fact that monetary values should be stored in money fields and not decimal or float fields because these will not automatically be converted and formatted according to the region. You should also store dates in date columns, not as text columns formatted as dates.

Do not concatenate strings at runtime for display: This is a big no-no when dealing with foreign languages. Take the following example:[1]

- English: Release the hold and start the second by one press on S1 at the appropriate time.

- French translation: Publiez l'influence et commencez la seconde par une presse sur S1 au temps de l'appropriate.

- English translation from French: Publish the influence and start the second by pressing S1 at the time of the appropriate.

So, if you were to create a string by inserting variables into the string at the same locations in English and French, the results would be incomprehensible to anyone in the foreign language.

---

1. This was inspired by an example of "bad translation" at http://www.fortunecity.com/business/reception/19/mtex.htm.

You are going to create your own satellite assembly, read values from the assembly into your application dynamically, and resize labels where necessary. But before doing that, let's look at some of the tools available to you.

Exploring Resource Creation Tools

The following sections briefly discuss the tools you can use to create resources. For your purposes, you only need a text file, ResGen, and Assembly Linker, but I provide you with enough information to find out about the other tools available to you.

Using ResGen

ResGen is probably the most useful tool for creating .resources files. A file with the extension of *.resources* is the file that contains the binary information for displaying localized resources. ResGen can take a .txt file and convert it to a .resx, which is an Extensible Markup Language (XML) Resource File, or a .resources file. It can convert a .resx file to a .resources file or a .txt file, and it can convert a .resources file into a .resx or .txt file.

 CAUTION If you use ResGen to reverse a .resources file to a .txt file, any image or audio data will be lost. An entry describing the resource will display in the text file, but there will be no associated data.

So, how do you create the text file that will be used as an input to ResGen, and what format does it take? Well, hopefully you do not need help creating a text file. There are only two formats that can be used in the file: the first is a comment, and the second is the resource information. The following are examples of both:

```
Comment:        ;This is a comment and MUST come at the beginning of a line
; comments start with a semi-colon.
Resource:       COURTESY = Hello Mr. Smith
```

Again, the comment must come at the beginning of a line. If you put it at the end of the line, it will be included as part of the resource string. The format for a resource string is pretty straightforward as it is a name-value pair. You must separate the name and value with an equals (=) sign. The capitalization of the name is a naming convention and makes it easier to see what you are retrieving in your code.

NOTE   Comments are for your use only. They are not compiled into the resource and therefore are not decompiled if you use ResGen to convert a .resources file to a .txt file.

Some people may find creating a .resx file a little easier because it is created through an editor. To demonstrate this, start a new Visual Basic .NET (VB .NET) console application (the name of the project is unimportant). Select Project ➤ Add New Item and select the Assembly Resource File template. Call the file *MyResourceTest.resx*. You will see the screen shown in Figure 13-1, which is a grid for entering resource information.

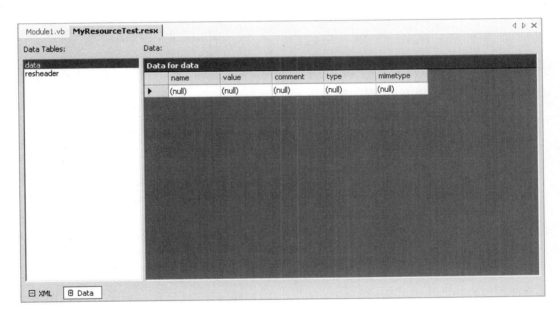

Figure 13-1. MyResourceTest resource editor

To demonstrate how ResGen works, enter the name *FIRST_NAME* and the value *First Name*. The data is stored in XML format, which you can see if you switch to the XML view. Save the file and exit the project.

TIP The easiest way to perform this next step is to copy the ResGen.exe file to the local directory or set the path environment variable so that it points to the folder that contains the ResGen.exe application. If you are using .NET 1.1 it will be located in the folder \Microsoft Visual Studio .NET 2003\SDK\v1.1\Bin. If you are using .NET 1.0, it will be located in the folder \Microsoft Visual Studio .NET\FrameworkSDK\bin.

Switch to the command line and type in the following command:

```
Resgen.exe MyResourceTest.resx MyResourceTest.resources
```

You should receive output identical to this:

```
Read in 1 resources from 'MyResourceTest.resx'
Writing resource file...  Done.
```

To reverse engineer it into a text file, simply set the input file as the resource file and the output file as a .txt file.

Using Assembly Linker

Assembly Linker creates a satellite assembly from a .resources file. This application can also generate multifile assemblies. It has considerably more power than the assembly capabilities of the Visual Studio .NET Integrated Development Environment (IDE), and a detailed explanation is beyond the scope of this chapter. You will use this utility to turn your .resources file into an assembly that can be consumed by your application.

Using the IDE Forms Designer

The IDE Forms Designer allows you to create one form per language. This gives you the advantage of not having to create labels, command buttons, and other controls that are larger than necessary. Each of the forms is packaged into its own assembly with other forms of the same language. The disadvantage to this of course is that depending on the number and complexity of the forms, your application, with all of its assemblies, may become much larger in size.

NOTE For additional information on this, see the MSDN help topic "Walkthrough: Localizing Windows Forms."

Using WinRes

The WinRes editor is a tool that is external to the .NET IDE (it is a subset of the .NET IDE) that is designed to edit form resources (.resx files that contain physical information about a form). You cannot write code within WinRes or do anything else except modify physical properties of the form. Most importantly, you can modify the text in controls. To use the WinRes editor, you must set the Localizable property of the form to *True*. Figure 13-2 shows the WinRes editor. You can see from the list of available properties for the selected button that you only have access to a subset of the properties.

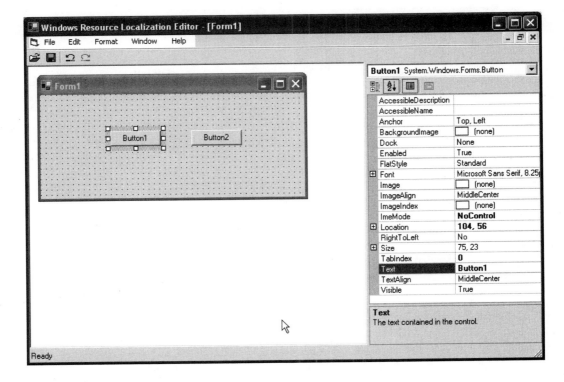

Figure 13-2. The WinRes editor

You can find the WinRes editor in the same folder as ResGen.

Exploring Languages Supported by the .NET Framework

Microsoft .NET supports 201 languages broken into 66 major languages. Table 13-1 shows the major languages.

Table 13-1. Major Languages Supported by .NET

Culture Name	Culture Identifier	Language-Country
"" (empty string)	0x007F	Invariant culture
af	0x0036	Afrikaans
sq	0x001C	Albanian
ar	0x0001	Arabic
hy	0x002B	Armenian
az	0x002C	Azeri
eu	0x002D	Basque
be	0x0023	Belarusian
bg	0x0002	Bulgarian
ca	0x0003	Catalan
hr	0x001A	Croatian
cs	0x0005	Czech
da	0x0006	Danish
div	0x0065	Dhivehi
nl	0x0013	Dutch
en	0x0009	English
et	0x0025	Estonian
fo	0x0038	Faroese
fa	0x0029	Farsi
fi	0x000B	Finnish
fr	0x000C	French
gl	0x0056	Galician
ka	0x0037	Georgian
de	0x0007	German

Table 13-1. Major Languages Supported by .NET (Continued)

Culture Name	Culture Identifier	Language-Country
el	0x0008	Greek
gu	0x0047	Gujarati
he	0x000D	Hebrew
hi	0x0039	Hindi
hu	0x000E	Hungarian
is	0x000F	Icelandic
id	0x0021	Indonesian
it	0x0010	Italian
ja	0x0011	Japanese
kn	0x004B	Kannada
kk	0x003F	Kazakh
kok	0x0057	Konkani
ko	0x0012	Korean
ky	0x0040	Kyrgyz
lv	0x0026	Latvian
lt	0x0027	Lithuanian
mk	0x002F	Macedonian
ms	0x003E	Malay
mr	0x004E	Marathi
mn	0x0050	Mongolian
no	0x0014	Norwegian
pl	0x0015	Polish
pt	0x0016	Portuguese
pa	0x0046	Punjabi
ro	0x0018	Romanian
ru	0x0019	Russian
sa	0x004F	Sanskrit
sk	0x001B	Slovak

Table 13-1. Major Languages Supported by .NET (Continued)

Culture Name	Culture Identifier	Language-Country
sl	0x0024	Slovenian
es	0x000A	Spanish
sw	0x0041	Swahili
sv	0x001D	Swedish
syr	0x005A	Syriac
ta	0x0049	Tamil
tt	0x0044	Tatar
te	0x004A	Telugu
th	0x001E	Thai
tr	0x001F	Turkish
uk	0x0022	Ukrainian
ur	0x0020	Urdu
uz	0x0043	Uzbek
vi	0x002A	Vietnamese

Dashes and a second set of letters indicate specific cultures. For example, you will notice that *en* is the code for English. Some specific cultural versions of the English language are en-AU (English spoken in Australia), en-US (English spoken in the United States), and en-CA (English spoken in Canada). In the section "Accessing Cultural Information in Code" you will see how to use this information to get access to specific language information.

Building the NorthwindTraders Resource Files

You now have enough information to be able to create your resource files for use with the Employee Edit form. Open the NorthwindTraders Windows application and add a new folder to the NorthwindTraders solution called *en-US*. Then add an Assembly Resource File to the folder by right-clicking the folder and selecting Add Existing Item; call it *NorthwindTraders.en-US.resx* (note that you must type in this entire name; if you leave off the .resx extension, the file will not be created properly in the designer). Add the entries to it as shown in Table 13-2 and make sure that the name entry is in all caps (this is a case-sensitive value).

Table 13-2. English Employee Resource List

Name	Value
COURTESY	Courtesy
FIRST_NAME	First Name
LAST_NAME	Last name
TITLE	Title
REPORTS_TO	Reports To
BIRTH_DATE	Birth Date
HIRE_DATE	Hire Date
HOME_PHONE	Home Phone
EXTENSION	Extension
ADDRESS	Address
CITY	City
REGION	Region
POSTAL_CODE	Postal Code
COUNTRY	Country
PHOTO	Photo
NOTES	Notes
SELECTED_TER	Selected Territories
AVAILABLE_TER	Available Territories
OK	OK
CANCEL	Cancel

Save this file and add another folder to the NorthwindTraders project called *fr-FR*. Then add another Assembly Resource File to the folder and call it *NorthwindTraders.fr-FR.resx* (note that you must type in this entire name; if you leave off the .resx extension, the file will not be created properly in the designer).

TIP You can copy the NorthwindTraders.en-US.resx file to the fr-FR folder and then rename it to *NorthwindTraders.fr-FR.resx*. Then you can just add it to the solution and you only need to enter the French translation.

Add the entries to it as shown in Table 13-3.

Table 13-3. French Employee Resource List

Name	Value	Literal Translation
COURTESY	Courtoisie	
FIRST_NAME	Premier Nom	
LAST_NAME	Dernier Nom	
TITLE	Titre	
REPORTS_TO	Est sous l'autorité de	Is under the authority of
BIRTH_DATE	Date de naissance	
HIRE_DATE	Engager la Date	
HOME_PHONE	Téléphone particulier	
EXTENSION	Téléphoner l'Extension	
ADDRESS	Adresse	
CITY	Ville	
REGION	Région	
POSTAL_CODE	Code postal	
COUNTRY	Pays	
PHOTO	Photo	
NOTES	Notes	
SELECTED_TER	Territoires choisis	
AVAILABLE_TER	Territoires disponibles	
OK	D'ACCORD	
CANCEL	Annuler	

Save this file and add another folder to the NorthwindTraders project called *es-ES*. Then add another Assembly Resource File to the folder and call it *NorthwindTraders.es-ES.resx* (note that you must type in this entire name; if you leave off the .resx extension, the file will not be created properly in the designer). Add the entries to it as shown in Table 13-4.

Table 13-4. Spanish Employee Resource List

Name	Value	Literal Translation
COURTESY	La cortesía	
FIRST_NAME	Primero Nombre	
LAST_NAME	El apellido	The surname
TITLE	El título	
REPORTS_TO	Los informes a	The reports to
BIRTH_DATE	La Fecha del nacimiento	
HIRE_DATE	Emplee la Fecha	
HOME_PHONE	El Teléfono buscador	
EXTENSION	La extensión	
ADDRESS	La dirección	
CITY	La ciudad	
REGION	La región	
POSTAL_CODE	El Código postal	
COUNTRY	El país	
PHOTO	La foto	
NOTES	Las notas	
SELECTED_TER	Los Territorios escogidos	
AVAILABLE_TER	Los Territorios disponibles	
OK	BUENO	
CANCEL	Cancele	

When you have finished, save this file as well.

CAUTION Be sure to set the Build Action property for each of the .resx files to *None*. This prevents the file from being built into the application and deployed in an invalid form by accident. The .NET IDE cannot create satellite assemblies. You have placed the resources files in the project because it is easier to keep everything together.

Creating the Satellite Assemblies

This next step converts the .resx files to .resources files and the .resources files to satellite assemblies. To start, you will use ResGen as you did earlier (this assumes that the path to the ResGen.exe application is in your environment path). In each of the three folders, run the following at the command line:

```
ResGen NorthwindTraders.[culture].resx NorthwindTraders.[culture].resources
```

Replace *[culture]* with the cultural designator (en-US, es-ES, or fr-FR). Each folder should now have two files: a .resx file and a .resources file.

 CAUTION You must do this in separate directories because the next step causes each .resources file to be created with the same name. Needless to say, if everything is in the same folder you will only end up with one DLL.

Next, you will use Assembly Linker to create the actual satellite assemblies for use by your application. You can find Assembly Linker in the C:\%windows%\ Microsoft .NET\Framework\[framework version number]. It is a good idea to put this folder into your environment path. Run the following at the command line in each of the three folders (line breaks are for formatting only; this should all be one line):

```
al /out:NorthwindTraders.Resources.dll /c:[culture]
/embed:NorthwindTraders.[culture].resources,
NorthwindTraders.[culture].resources
```

Again, replace *[culture]* with the correct cultural designator.

 CAUTION Do not leave a space in the embed tag after the comma or you will receive an unknown error and the file will not compile.

As mentioned earlier, Assembly Linker is beyond the scope of this book, but it is important to note that the /c switch determines which culture this assembly is referenced for. Because the filename has no indicator, nor do your resources, this is the only way for the Common Language Runtime (CLR) to determine whether to access the resources from this particular satellite assembly.

CAUTION   The MSDN documentation recommends using a *Hub and Spoke* model for packaging and deploying your application and dealing with satellite assemblies that contain resources. There is one small problem with this, though: You may not use the VS .NET IDE to compile your main executable. The only way to embed a resource (or link a resource) to an EXE is to compile the application with Assembly Linker.

Each language folder should now have a third file in it: the NorthwindTraders.Resources.dll. This is all you need to do to create the satellite assemblies. To actually use the resource information in your code, you need to do one more thing. Because your resources will not get deployed automatically when you build the application, you need to do it yourself. So, in Windows Explorer, copy the en-US, es-ES, and fr-FR folders from the NorthwindTraders folder to the NorthwindTraders\bin folder. You should delete the .resx and .resources files from the copied folders. When you are finished, the project directory structure should look like that in Figure 13-3.

Figure 13-3. The NorthwindTraders directory structure

Now you can access the resources from code.

Accessing Cultural Information in Code

Open the code module for the frmEmployeeEdit form and go to the frmEmployeeEdit_Load method. Add the following declaration to this method:

```
Dim locRes As New ResourceManager("NorthwindTraders", _
Me.GetType().Assembly)
```

The ResourceManager class is responsible for accessing all culture resources in an application. It can access either satellite assemblies or the .resources file directly (if you choose to deploy these files, but that is not recommended). This line creates a new instance of the resource manager and tells it to look for resource files for the NorthwindTraders application. Next, you add the code in Listing 13-1 to the frmEmployeeEdit_Load method just before the Try..Catch block.

Listing 13-1. Loading the Resource Strings

```
Me.lblCourtesy.Text = locRes.GetString("COURTESY")
Me.lblFirstName.Text = locRes.GetString("FIRST_NAME")
Me.lblLastName.Text = locRes.GetString("LAST_NAME")
Me.lblTitle.Text = locRes.GetString("TITLE")
Me.lblReportsTo.Text = locRes.GetString("REPORTS_TO")
Me.lblBirthDate.Text = locRes.GetString("BIRTH_DATE")
Me.lblHireDate.Text = locRes.GetString("HIRE_DATE")
Me.lblHomePhone.Text = locRes.GetString("HOME_PHONE")
Me.lblExtension.Text = locRes.GetString("EXTENSION")
Me.lblAddress.Text = locRes.GetString("ADDRESS")
Me.lblCity.Text = locRes.GetString("CITY")
Me.lblRegion.Text = locRes.GetString("REGION")
Me.lblPostalCode.Text = locRes.GetString("POSTAL_CODE")
Me.lblCountry.Text = locRes.GetString("COUNTRY")
Me.lblPhoto.Text = locRes.GetString("PHOTO")
Me.lblNotes.Text = locRes.GetString("NOTES")
Me.lblAssigned.Text = locRes.GetString("SELECTED_TER")
Me.lblAvailable.Text = locRes.GetString("AVAILABLE_TER")
Me.btnOK.Text = locRes.GetString("OK")
Me.btnCancel.Text = locRes.GetString("CANCEL")
```

NOTE If you develop like I do, you will probably have those moments of laziness where you do not want to give a label a proper name. Even when I teach classes, I teach that you generally do not ever need to give a label a specific name—except in one circumstance. Whenever you are going to access a label from code, you must give it a proper name. Initially this adds some development time because you have to make the necessary adjustments even though it is a tedious process. If you have not given these labels proper names, now is the time to do so. I have used a fairly logical scheme to name these.

You can use two methods to access resources: GetString() and GetObject(). You use GetObject for images and audio, so you will be using the GetString method in this example.

At this point, if you run the application and open the Employee Edit form, you should see all of your labels in English, exactly as you would expect. But, you want to test what it will look like in Spanish and French. To do this, you set the CurrentUICulture property of the CurrentThread using the CultureInfo class. This sounds complicated but it is as simple as this next line, which you should add to the frmEmployeeEdit constructor:

```
Thread.CurrentThread.CurrentUICulture = New CultureInfo("fr-FR")
```

After adding this line of code, run the application again. You should get a screen that looks something like Figure 13-4.

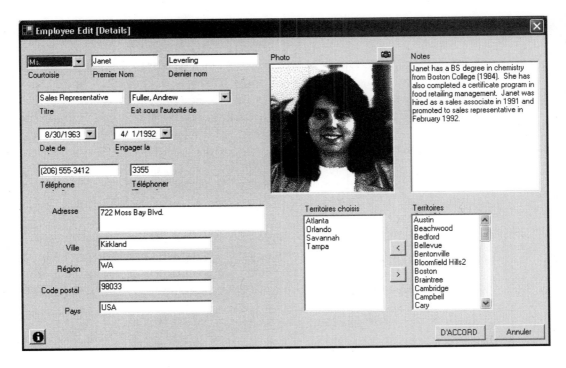

Figure 13-4. The Employee Edit form, localized in French

Pretty cool, huh? The only problem you will note is that some of the labels are not large enough to contain the text. Remember the rules: This is an easy fix at this point, but you would not want to have to go back and retrofit the entire application!

Localizing ASP.NET Applications

Up to this point you have see the process for localizing a Windows application, so now you will learn about localizing your Northwind Web application. There are several ways to localize a Web application. For the purpose of this chapter, though, you will concentrate on using your satellite assemblies and controlling localization through the web.config file.

First, you can use satellite assemblies just as you did with the Windows application. This solution is best when the same information is being presented in different languages. Alternatively, you can direct users to different Web sites depending on their language. This is usually the best situation when there is a lot of content that needs to be localized. By directing users to the specific pages based on their culture, the formatting looks good, and the pages are easier to maintain in the different languages.

What Culture Is the User Using?

The culture of a user's machine that is requesting a Web page is contained in the Request object in the UserLanguages property. This is an array, and element zero will always be the primary culture of the user. To demonstrate this, let's open the NorthwindWeb application and modify the Employee List page. Add a label to the page and call it *lblCulture*, then switch to the code view and enter the following at the end of the Page_Load method:

```
Dim c As New Globalization.CultureInfo(Request.UserLanguages(0))
lblCulture.Text = c.DisplayName
```

Run the application and you should get a value in the label that describes both the language and the localized version of the language in that language. In my case, the label text is *English (United States)*. As you can see, detecting the user's language is pretty easy. But how do you change this culture for the application?

Setting Globalization in the Web.Config

To change the language for an entire Web application, you will use the globalization tag of the web.config file. The globalization tag has the attributes shown in Table 13-5.

Table 13-5. Globalization Attribute Settings

Attribute	Purpose
requestEncoding	Character set used to read Request information
responseEncoding	Character set used to encode Response information
fileEncoding	Specifies the character set used to encode the application's Web pages
culture	The default culture for incoming requests
uiCulture	Specifies the culture to be used when rendering Web pages

Let's modify your globalization tag in the web.config file. Currently, the tag reads as follows:

```
<globalization requestEncoding="utf-8" responseEncoding="utf-8" />
```

Modify this tag so that it reads as follows:

```
<globalization requestEncoding="utf-8" responseEncoding="utf-8"
uiCulture="ru-RU" culture="ru-RU" />
```

Now, before you run the application again, go back and modify the code that you put in the Page_Load event so it reads as follows:

```
lblCulture.Text = _
Threading.Thread.CurrentThread.CurrentCulture.NativeName
```

Run the application again and the screen should look like Figure 13-5.

Employee List

русский (Россия)

Add Employee

	First Name	Last Name	Title
Details	Nancy	Davolio	Sales Representative
Details	Andrew	Fuller	Vice President, Sales
Details	Janet	Leverling	Sales Representative
Details	Margaret	Peacock	Sales Representative
Details	Steven	Buchanan	Sales Manager
Details	Michael	Suyama	Sales Representative
Details	Robert	King	Sales Representative
Details	Laura	Callahan	Inside Sales Coordinator
Details	Anne	Dodsworth	Sales Representative
Details	a	a	a

Figure 13-5. The Employee List screen, showing the web.config language

I just picked Russian because it has some cool characters, but you can do this with any language. The NativeName property specified in the previous code returns the localized name of the language. Notice also that you accessed the CurrentThread to determine the language. Using this method allows you to ignore the user's language and just set one language for the entire application. This is what you need to do to test your application with foreign languages. Now you will implement the satellite assemblies.

Implementing the Satellite Assemblies

This requires a little bit of work, but not too much. First, copy the en-US, es-ES, and fr-FR folders from the NorthwindTraders project (the folders that contain the .resx files) to the \bin folder of the NorthwindWeb project (if you installed it in the default location, this will be c:\inetpub\wwwroot\northwindweb\bin). After you have copied these folders, the directory structure should look like that in Figure 13-6.

Figure 13-6. The NorthwindWeb folder structure

Go into each of these three folders (once you have copied them) and delete the
.dll file and .resources file. Rename the .resx files to *NorthwindWeb.[culture].resx*
where *[culture]* is the culture-specific information. Run ResGen on each of the
.resx files so that you have one .resources file per .resx file in each folder. Next, run
Assembly Linker on each of the .resources files. This will be the same command as
you ran before, but the output file name will be *NorthwindWeb.Resources.dll*. Use
the following AL command to do this:

```
Al /out:NorthwindWeb.Resources.dll /c: [culture]
/embed:NorthwindWeb.[culture].resources,NorthwindWeb.[culture].resources
```

Once you are done with this step, each folder should have three files: a .resx,
.resources, and .dll file (again, you can delete the .resx and .resources files from
these folders). Next, let's alter the web.config globalization tag so the culture and
uiCulture attributes read *es-ES*. Lastly, you need to edit the code. Add the code in
Listing 13-2 to the Page_Load method of the EmployeeDetails.aspx page after the
IsPostBack check.

Listing 13-2. EmployeeDetails Page_Load Method Additions

```
Dim locRes As New Resources.ResourceManager("NorthwindWeb", _
GetType(NorthwindWeb.EmployeeDetails).Module.Assembly)

Me.lblCourtesy.Text = locRes.GetString("COURTESY")
Me.lblFirstName.Text = locRes.GetString("FIRST_NAME")
Me.lblLastName.Text = locRes.GetString("LAST_NAME")
Me.lblTitle.Text = locRes.GetString("TITLE")
Me.lblReportsTo.Text = locRes.GetString("REPORTS_TO")
Me.lblBirthDate.Text = locRes.GetString("BIRTH_DATE")
Me.lblHireDate.Text = locRes.GetString("HIRE_DATE")
Me.lblHomePhone.Text = locRes.GetString("HOME_PHONE")
Me.lblExtension.Text = locRes.GetString("EXTENSION")
Me.lblAddress.Text = locRes.GetString("ADDRESS")
Me.lblCity.Text = locRes.GetString("CITY")
Me.lblRegion.Text = locRes.GetString("REGION")
Me.lblPostal.Text = locRes.GetString("POSTAL_CODE")
Me.lblCountry.Text = locRes.GetString("COUNTRY")
Me.lblNotes.Text = locRes.GetString("NOTES")
Me.lblSelectedTerritories.Text = locRes.GetString("SELECTED_TER")
Me.lblAvailableTerritories.Text = locRes.GetString("AVAILABLE_TER")
Me.btnSave.Text = locRes.GetString("OK")
```

There is one last change that you will make, and this is mostly to demonstrate date formats. Change the code that sets the dates in the txtBirthDate and txtHireDate textboxes so that it reads as follows:

```
txtBirthDate.Text = .BirthDate.ToString("D")
txtHireDate.Text = .HireDate.ToString("D")
```

You will probably need to widen the textboxes that hold the dates. When you run the application and navigate to the Employee Details page, you should see a screen similar to Figure 13-7.

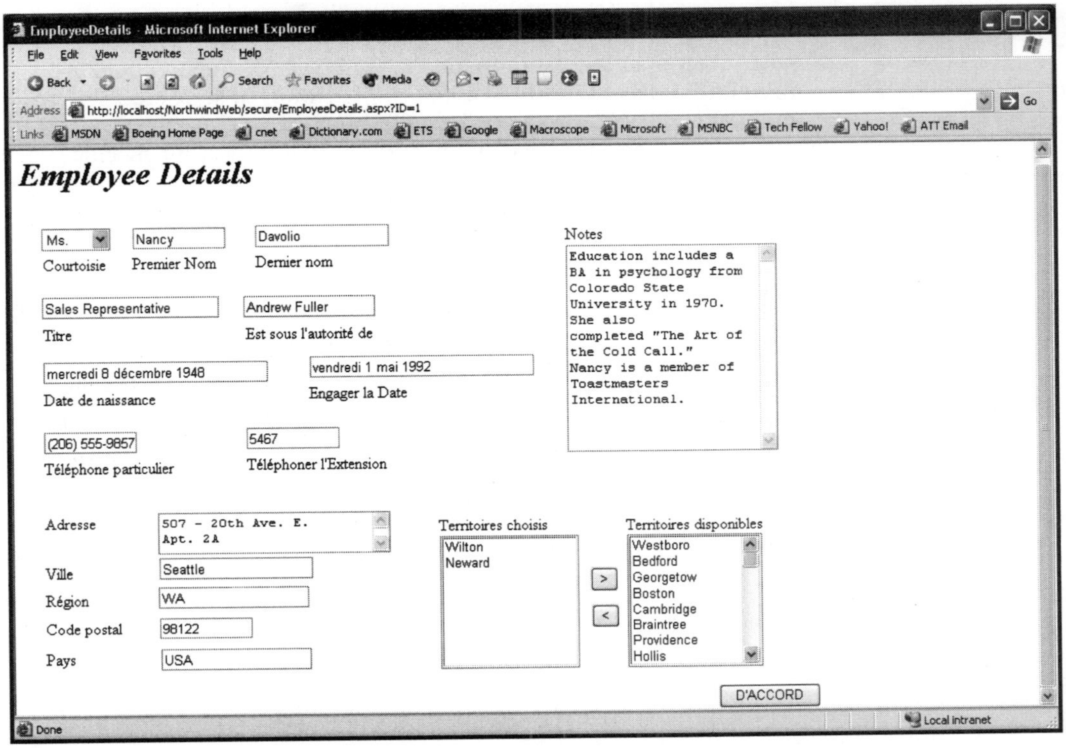

Figure 13-7. The Employee Details form localized in Spanish

I have taken the liberty of expanding the labels to be able to contain all of the necessary information. You can also change the web.config file to work with French or English now. Notice the dates also—they will be in the format of the local language thanks to the date format.

Summary

This has been sort of a whirlwind chapter on globalization and localization. You saw how to create satellite assemblies and associate them with both Windows and Web applications.

NOTE There is a lot of information in the MSDN documentation on installing and using localized applications. However, there are a certain number of inaccuracies in the help file. I suggest you take the time to perform your own research on the best way to localize your specific application.

This gives you the ability to create an application that can be used anywhere in the world with little extra work. Although the work may be more difficult at first because of having to name every label and write code to add text to every label, in the long run it will save you a lot of time and effort. This chapter should serve as a solid introduction to what you can do to create internationally enabled applications.

Adding Support for Unicode Characters

MANY COMPANIES THESE DAYS are global. Business is global. This means an application must support Unicode characters. By default, all of the controls provided with .NET can display Unicode characters, but that is not what I am talking about. Try typing the following character in a word document: ç. You cannot do it. The only way to do it is to select Insert ➤ Symbol from the menu and select the special character you want to add. This letter is part of the extended Latin character set and is common in the French language. What if this character is in someone's name? What if, as a business, you send a letter asking that person to buy something from your company? Will that person look favorably if you cannot even spell their name right? Probably not.

This appendix is certainly not meant to be a complete discussion of Unicode characters or the namespace that contains the classes for Unicode encoding/ decoding in .NET (the System.Text namespace). It demonstrates how you can incorporate unicode characters in your applications in a manner similiar to that used in Microsoft Word. For more information on the Unicode standard, you can visit the official Unicode Web site at http://www.unicode.org. This site contains all of the different character sets and associated codes. The example presented in this appendix is a simple but flexible means of displaying those characters to the user so that they can select and use one of them.

Start a new Windows Application project and call it *UnicodeSupport*. Rename *Form1.vb* to *frmUnicode.vb*. Then, switch to the Code View tab and rename the class *frmUnicode*. Next, set the following properties on the form as shown in Table A-1.

Table A-1. frmUnicode Properties

Property	Value
Text	Special Characters
Height	215
Width	451
FormBorderStyle	FixedDialogSingle
MaximizeBox	False

After you have set these properties, add a button and name it *btnCopy*. Set the text property to read *Special Characters* and position it in the lower-left corner of the form. When you are finished, your form should look identical to Figure A-1.

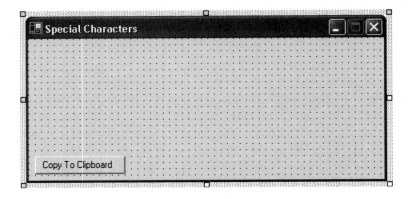

Figure A-1. Unicode support form

Now you can add some code. Add the standard Option Standard and Option Explicit statements at the top of the code module. Then, create the form load event by adding the code shown in Listing A-1.

Listing A-1. The frmUnicode_Load Method

```
Private Sub frmUnicode_Load(ByVal sender As Object, _
ByVal e As System.EventArgs) Handles MyBase.Load
    Dim i As Integer = &HFF
    Dim j, k As Integer
    Const BoxSize As Integer = 20
    Const RowSize As Integer = 20
    Dim CurrentX As Integer = 15
    Dim CurrentY As Integer = 15

    For j = 1 To 120
        Dim lbl As New Label()
        lbl.Size = New Drawing.Size(BoxSize, BoxSize)
        lbl.Location = New Drawing.Point(CurrentX, CurrentY)
        lbl.TextAlign = ContentAlignment.BottomCenter
        CurrentX += BoxSize
        lbl.Text = Convert.ToChar(i + j)
        lbl.BorderStyle = BorderStyle.FixedSingle
        lbl.BackColor = Color.White
```

```
        lbl.Visible = True
        Me.Controls.Add(lbl)
        AddHandler lbl.Click, AddressOf Label_Click
        If j Mod RowSize = 0 Then
            CurrentY += BoxSize
            CurrentX = 15
        End If
    Next
End Sub
```

This code requires a bit of explanation. This code adds labels to the form and loads a single character in the label. It places 20 labels on a row for as many characters as you decide to load. The specific characters you are loading are the characters that make up the Latin Extended-A character set. In hexadecimal, the character set starts at 0100 and ends at 017F. This turns out to be 120 characters if you subtract 0100 from 017F. The value of i is &HFF, which is hexadecimal for 100. The loop loads a new label and sets the size, location, and text alignment. It then adds a character to the label with the following line:

```
lbl.Text = Convert.ToChar(i + j)
```

Because Unicode support is already built in to .NET, all you have to do is convert the character code to a character and assign it to the label. After that, you set a few more properties, add the control to the forms' controls collection, and hook up the click event to the Label_Click method (which you will code next). Finally, if you have added 20 labels to the current row, move down to the next row and reset horizontal position. When you have added this code, you should be able to comment out the AddHandler line and run it. You will see the form in Figure A-2.

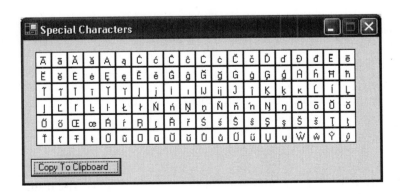

Figure A-2. The Latin Extended-A character set

After you have run the application and stopped it, you can uncomment the AddHandler line. Next you will add the Label_Click method. The Label_Click method highlights a character and enlarges it so that the user can see it better. It also clears this formatting for all of the other labels so that only one label at a time is highlighted and enlarged. Before you add this method, add the following module-level variable declaration:

```
Dim mstrValue As String
```

This variable stores the currently selected character so you can access the value more easily.

The code for the Label_Click method is as follows:

```
Private Sub Label_Click(ByVal sender As System.Object, _
ByVal e As System.EventArgs)
    Dim lbl As Label = CType(sender, Label)
    Dim sz As Size = lbl.Size
    Dim loc As Point = lbl.Location
    Dim ctl As Control
    Dim lblTemp As Label

    If lbl.Width <> 20 Then Exit Sub

    For Each ctl In Me.Controls
        If ctl.GetType Is GetType(Label) Then
            lblTemp = CType(ctl, Label)
            If lblTemp.Width <> 20 Then
                lblTemp.Size = sz
                lblTemp.BackColor = Color.White
                lblTemp.Font = New Font(lbl.Font.FontFamily, 10)
            End If
        End If
    Next

    lbl.BackColor = Color.Aquamarine
    lbl.Size = New Drawing.Size(lbl.Width + 10, lbl.Height + 10)
    lbl.Font = New Font(lbl.Font.FontFamily, 16)
    mstrValue = lbl.Text
End Sub
```

After adding this method, run the code again and click a character. The result should look something like Figure A-3.

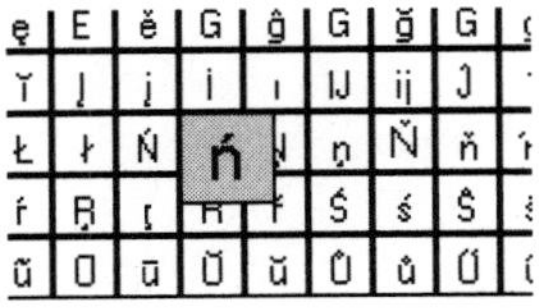

Figure A-3. Highlighted Unicode character

The last step is to enable the user to copy the value to the Clipboard. To do this, add the following code to handle the click event of the btnCopy button:

```
Private Sub btnCopy_Click(ByVal sender As Object, _
ByVal e As System.EventArgs) Handles btnCopy.Click
    Clipboard.SetDataObject(mstrValue)
End Sub
```

Now you can run the code, select a character, and copy it to the Clipboard. Then the user can paste it into any control that will accept a character. Add another form with a textbox to give it a try.

This has been a fairly simple demonstration of how to add Unicode support. The following are some suggestions for improving this code if you need additional support:

- Change the button to read *Insert* and insert a character directly into the active control.

- Use a picture box on the form, add a scrollbar, and fill the picture box with all of the Unicode characters.

- Add a drop-down box that lets the user select the Unicode character set that they want to choose from and load that character set dynamically.

These are just some suggestions. You will probably think of more. But always remember that in today's business world, international business is a way of life.

APPENDIX B
Recommended Reading

I RECOMMEND THE FOLLOWING books and online resources, categorized by topic and relevance.

Remoting

Rammer, Ingo. *Advanced .NET Remoting*. Apress, 2002.

Rammer, Ingo. *Advanced .NET Remoting in VB .NET*. Apress, 2002.

Object-Oriented Design/UML

Lau, Yun-Tung. *The Art of Objects: Object-Oriented Design and Architecture*. Addison-Wesley, 2000.

Fowler, Martin, and Kendall Scott. *UML Distilled: A Brief Guide to the Standard Object Modeling Language*, Second Edition. Addison-Wesley, 1999.

Security

Howard, Michael, and David C. LeBlanc. *Writing Secure Code*, Second Edition. Microsoft Press, 2002.

LaMacchia, Brian A., Sebastian Lange, Matthew Lyons, Rudi Martin, and Kevin T. Price. *.NET Framework Security*. Addison-Wesley Professional, 2002.

Bock, Jason, Pete Stromquist, Tom Fischer, and Nathan Smith. *.NET Security*. Apress, 2002.

 NOTE The Computer Emergency Response Team Coordination Center Web site (http://www.cert.org) contains information about current viruses and other security alerts. Additionally, you can subscribe to numerous security mailing lists on the SecurityFocus Web site (http://www.securityfocus.com).

ADO.NET/Databases

Thomsen, Carsten. *Database Programming with Visual Basic .NET.* Apress, 2001.

Design Patterns

Gamma, Erich, Richard Helm, Ralph Johnson, and John Vlissides. *Design Patterns: Elements of Reusable Object-Oriented Software.* Addison-Wesley, 1995.

Shalloway, Alan, and James R. Trott. *Design Patterns Explained: A New Perspective on Object-Oriented Design.* Addison-Wesley, 2001.

Fischer, Tom, John Slater, Peter Stromquist, and Cha-Ur Wu. *Professional Design Patterns in VB.NET: Building Adaptable Applications.* Wrox Press, 2002.

Regular Expressions

Appleman, Dan. *Regular Expressions with .NET.* Daniel Appleman, 2002.

Globalization and Localization

Symmonds, Nick. *Internationalization and Localization Using Microsoft .NET.* Apress, 2002.

Business Rules

Lhotka, Rockford. *Visual Basic 6.0 Business Objects.* Wrox Press, 1998.

.NET Framework (Intermediate Language)

Gough, John. *Compiling for the .NET Common Language Runtime.* Prentice Hall, 2001.

Visual Basic .NET Primer

Moore, Karl. *Karl Moore's Visual Basic .NET: The Tutorials.* Apress, 2002.

Web Services and UDDI

`http://www.uddi.org`: The home page of the UDDI Technical Committee in charge of the UDDI specification

`http://uddi.microsoft.com`: Microsoft's UDDI Business Registry and information Web site

`http://uddi.ibm.com`: IBM's UDDI Business Registry and information Web site

`http://www.w3c.org`: World Wide Web Consortium, responsible for almost all standards that govern the Internet, including SOAP and XML

General .NET Web Sites

`http://www.microsoft.com/net`: Microsoft's .NET Framework home page

`http://www.microsoft.com/vstudio`: Microsoft's Visual Studio home page

`http://www.gotdotnet.com`: A host of links, sample code, and helpful tips and news from the .NET product teams

`http://www.dotnet247.com`: Independent .NET Web site that is well organized and contains hundreds of code samples and explanations

`http://www.devx.com`: Good general Web site covering multiple languages

Index

HKEY_LOCAL_MACHINE node, 495

Howard, Michael, 58

HTML, translation of code to, 16

HTTP GET request, 446

HTTP (Hypertext Transfer Protocol), 24, 439

HttpChannel, 32, 94

Hub and Spoke model, 555

HyperLink Column, 511, *513*

HyperText Markup Language (HTML),
    translation of code to, 16

Hypertext Transfer Protocol (HTTP), 24, 439

I

IBaseInterface, 280

ICollection interface, 196

IComparer interface, 97

Icon Alignment property, *384*

Icon property, *182, 188*

IconAlignment On erpMain property, 189

IconAlignment property, 264

IconPadding on erpMain property, 189

icons, dynamically adding and removing,
    231–235

ICutCopyPaste interface, 212

ID property, *536*
    of Add Employee Hyperlink, *523*
    of First RequiredFieldValidator, *525*
    of Logon Page, *503, 504*
    of RegularExpressionValidator, *528, 529*

IDE Forms Designer, 546

Identity Impersonate flag, 133

IEmployee interface, 319

IEnumerable interface, 196

IFind interface, 218–219, 221

IIS (Internet Information Server), 16, 485
    advantages of, 24
    and CDO objects, 144
    scaling of applications via, 20
    setting up, 25–35
        creating web.config file, 27–29
        remoting configuration information,
            32–35

setting up authentication and
    authorization, 29–31
using appsettings section, 31–32

IList interface, 79, 196

ILogError class, 132

Image property, *184*

Image.FromStream method, 388

ImageList control, 222

ImageList Image Collection Editor, 223

Impersonation, 28

Imports keyword, 38

includeVersions property, 48

index number, 96

indexOf method, 225

Infragistics (.NET vendor), 527

Infragistics UltraWinToolbars, 196

Inheritance Picker form, 258

Inheritance Picker window, *90*

inheritance, visual, 259

inherited forms, 90–91

Initial Directory property, *466*

InitializeComponent call, 100

InnerException property, *126*

installing applications, benefits of using
    ASP.NET for, 16

integer value, converting to BitArray, 230

interface, user. *See* user interface

Interfaces Code Module, 56

*Internationalization and Localization Using
    Microsoft .NET* (Symmonds), 541

Internet Information Server. *See* IIS

intranets, 485

invariant culture, *548*

InvokeMethod call, 415

IRegion interface, 62–63, 169, 280

IsDBNull method, 339

IsDirty method, *274*, 366, 367

IsDirty property, 71, 252–253

ISerializable interface, 48, 132

IsMdiContainer, 85

IsNew property, 241

IsValid method, *274*

V

W

About Apress

Apress, located in Berkeley, CA, is a fast-growing, innovative publishing company devoted to meeting the needs of existing and potential programming professionals. Simply put, the "A" in Apress stands for *The Author's Press™*. Apress' unique approach to publishing grew out of conversations between its founders, Gary Cornell and Dan Appleman, authors of numerous best-selling, highly regarded books for programming professionals. In 1998 they set out to create a publishing company that emphasized quality above all else. Gary and Dan's vision has resulted in the publication of over 70 titles by leading software professionals, all of which have *The Expert's Voice™*.

Do You Have What It Takes to Write for Apress?

Apress is rapidly expanding its publishing program. If you can write and you refuse to compromise on the quality of your work, if you believe in doing more than rehashing existing documentation, and if you're looking for opportunities and rewards that go far beyond those offered by traditional publishing houses, we want to hear from you!

Consider these innovations that we offer all of our authors:

- **Top royalties with *no* hidden switch statements**
  Authors typically receive only half of their normal royalty rate on foreign sales. In contrast, Apress' royalty rate remains the same for both foreign and domestic sales.

- **Sharing the wealth**
  Most publishers keep authors on the same pay scale even after costs have been met. At Apress author royalties dramatically increase the more books are sold.

- **Serious treatment of the technical review process**
  Each Apress book is reviewed by a technical expert(s) whose remuneration depends in part on the success of the book since he or she too receives royalties.

Moreover, through a partnership with Springer-Verlag, New York, Inc., one of the world's major publishing houses, Apress has significant venture capital and distribution power behind it. Thus, we have the resources to produce the highest quality books *and* market them aggressively.

If you fit the model of the Apress author who can write a book that provides *What The Professional Needs To Know™*, then please contact us for more information:

editorial@apress.com